MW01405822

His Life and Music,
from The Hawks and
Bob Dylan to The Band

Richard
Manuel

STEPHEN T. LEWIS

SCHIFFER
PUBLISHING

Other Schiffer books on related subjects

Fleetwood Mac in Chicago: The Legendary Chess Blues Session, January 4, 1969
Jeff Lowenthal and Robert Schaffner
978-0-7643-6495-2

The Atlanta Rhythm Section: The Authorized History
Willie G. Moseley
978-0-7643-5564-6

Copyright © 2025 by Stephen T. Lewis

Library of Congress Control Number: 2024941513

All rights reserved. No part of this work may be reproduced or used in any form or by any means—graphic, electronic, or mechanical, including photocopying or information storage and retrieval systems—without written permission from the publisher.

The scanning, uploading, and distribution of this book or any part thereof via the Internet or any other means without the permission of the publisher is illegal and punishable by law. Please purchase only authorized editions and do not participate in or encourage the electronic piracy of copyrighted materials.

"Schiffer," "Schiffer Publishing, Ltd.," and the pen and inkwell logo are registered trademarks of Schiffer Publishing, Ltd.

Cover & design by Danielle D. Farmer
Type set in Job Clarendon/Gibson/Mrs Eaves OT

ISBN: 978-0-7643-6924-7
ePub: 978-1-5073-0532-4
Printed in China
10 9 8 7 6 5 4 3 2

Published by Schiffer Publishing, Ltd.
4880 Lower Valley Road
Atglen, PA 19310
Phone: (610) 593-1777; Fax: (610) 593-2002
Email: info@schifferbooks.com
Web: www.schifferbooks.com

For our complete selection of fine books on this and related subjects, please visit our website at www.schifferbooks.com. You may also write for a free catalog.

Schiffer Publishing's titles are available at special discounts for bulk purchases for sales promotions or premiums. Special editions, including personalized covers, corporate imprints, and excerpts, can be created in large quantities for special needs. For more information, contact the publisher.

We are always looking for people to write books on new and related subjects. If you have an idea for a book, please contact us at proposals@schifferbooks.com.

For Richard

Contents

Introduction		7
Acknowledgments		9
Prologue	One Way Home That's Guaranteed	11
Chapter 1	In a Station (1943–1958)	13
Chapter 2	Revol-ution! (1959–1961)	25
Chapter 3	Little Boy Blue (1960–1962)	43
Chapter 4	Keep the Engine Churning (1962–1964)	71
Chapter 5	Ghost of Electricity (1965)	95
Chapter 6	Gallant Knights (1965–1966)	119
Chapter 7	Open the Door, Richard (1966–1967)	147
Chapter 8	Beautiful Thing (1968)	171
Chapter 9	Rising of the Tide (1968–1969)	193
Chapter 10	Odd Man (1970–1971)	233
Chapter 11	The Great Pretender (1972–1976)	271
Chapter 12	Sleeping (1976–1986)	321
Postscript		369
Bibliography		373
Interviews		381
Richard Manuel Discography		385
Index		391

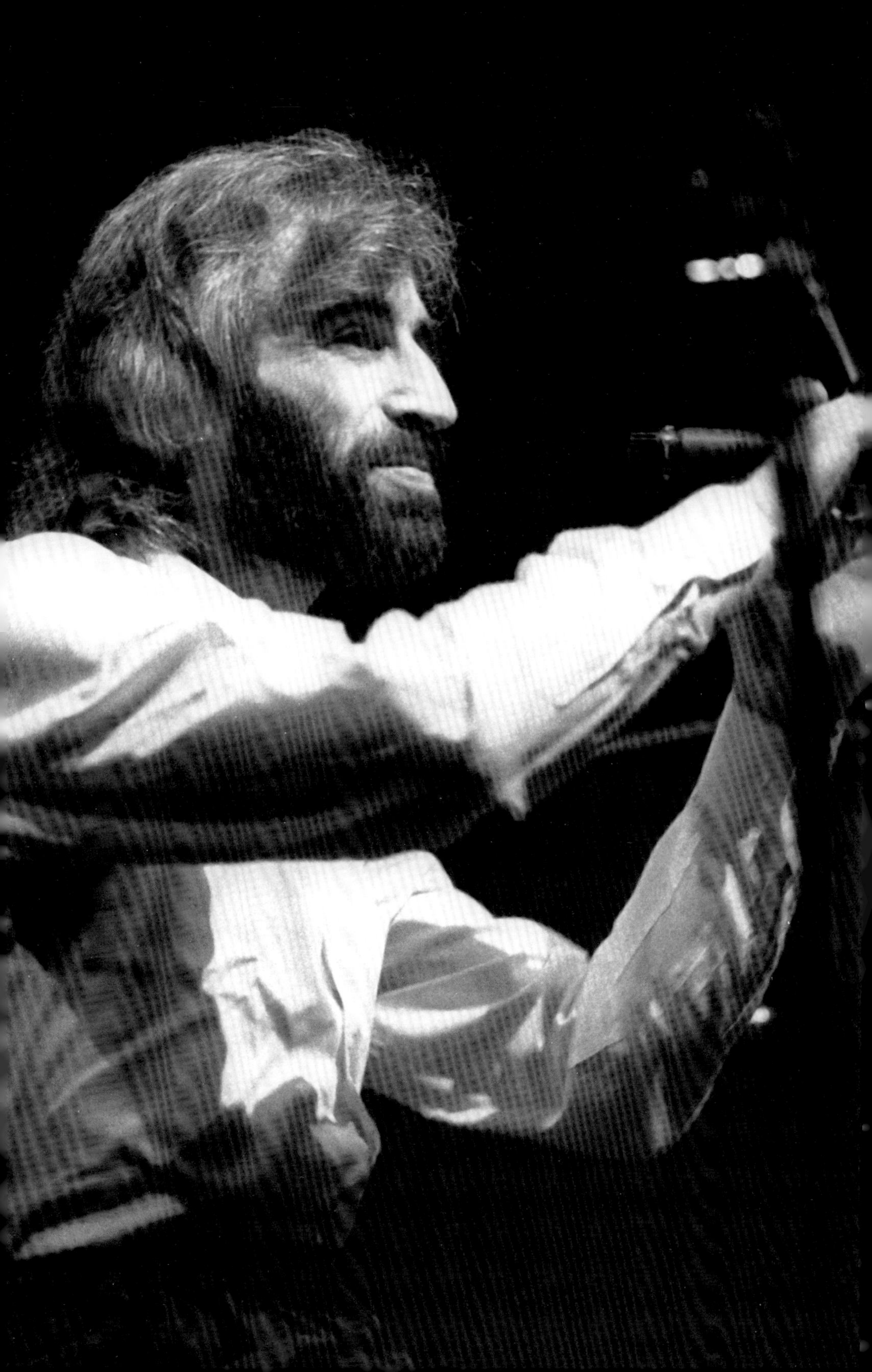

INTRODUCTION

My first impression of Richard Manuel was surely the same as that of many other rock music fans. I was watching *The Last Waltz* for the first—or was it the fiftieth?—time. The pulsing introduction of "The Shape I'm In" thumped out of the speakers and then there he was. Weighty eyes, dark beard, and loud plaid suit emerging from the ink of the stage shadows. Illuminated by the spotlight, he pulled back his shoulder, leaned into the microphone, and fired his vocals off into the arena.

The difference in this viewing of *The Last Waltz* was that I suddenly realized something that had previously passed through my mind unnoticed. Someone needed to tell his story. There was so much more to Richard than the screen allowed. I already sensed the indescribable spirit, the gravitational pull, to his existence. I wanted to know more. I wanted to know *why*.

I found that my research had already begun without my even realizing it. As a writer and self-proclaimed rock geek, I had cataloged quotes, analyzed melodies, and filed away stories for years. I had read every book imaginable about the Hawks and the Band, including Robbie Robertson's and Levon Helm's memoirs. I had brought up the idea of exploring the Hawks era to Garth Hudson while carrying his gear into the Colony Cafe on a brisk winter night in Woodstock, New York.

Thus began an almost predetermined series of coincidences, connections, and conversations that instilled in me the belief that I had to tell Richard Manuel's story. There had been other noble attempts, by other people, but nothing ever materialized. If I took this on, it was going to be done right and done through to its finish.

I was introduced to the great John Till, whose first words to me were "I don't have the time or inclination to write a biography on Richard Manuel." I was scared. Richard's story was tragic, and it had come to define him over the years. The wounds were still fresh, almost forty years after his death. A lot of time had gone by, memories were disappearing, and people had passed away.

Richard had two children whom I had to speak to before taking on his story. I wanted their blessing. I needed it.

John softened his stance with me, and we had a wonderful discussion. At that time, I didn't realize that he was sick and that his time was short. I will forever be indebted to him for his time and his help.

Visiting Stratford, Ontario, felt like returning to a version of the town where I grew up. I instantly felt a kinship with the area and its deep artistic roots. Signs of Richard sprouted from the town's concrete like hardy flowers. Going to Woodstock brought out ghosts and myths of a grander scale. Stratford fell into the rearview mirror in smoky Kodachrome, and Woodstock approached in a vibrant Technicolor.

Richard's talent was immense and his soul so complex that to capture his essence was like shoveling smoke. He was everything that had already been written, but so much more. Over the years that had passed since the demise of the Band and Richard's death, a singular narrative developed around him. Perhaps because he was so self-effacing, even in death his musical contributions became a footnote to more-salacious tales. My goal had become to diffuse the myths and uncover the true talents of the man.

Writing this book, I traversed my own peaks and pits. Over the four years I worked on Richard's story, I lost a job and a computer, fought against discouragement, and sometimes felt underqualified for the task.

The encouragement of those closest to Richard, conveying to me that I was on the right path, strengthened my confidence. Richard's family and friends needed this. My book started as a goal, became a reality, and concluded with what I hope is an honest and loving biography in the tradition of the hero's journey.

I know Richard would have been embarrassed that someone was ruminating about his musical accomplishments. I also know that it would have made his day to know that someone cared enough to do it.

ACKNOWLEDGMENTS

The writing of this book has been a true collaborative experience. It's a testament to Richard's legacy that so many people were willing to share and donate their time, memories, and art to tell his story. The collective selflessness illustrates the enduring effect that Richard had on both music and people. My goal was to receive these stories from the past and transmit them to paper to be immortalized in tribute for the future.

I'd like to thank the following people for their belief in me in telling Richard's story.

First and foremost, my friend and editor Jann Nyffeler for her patience, knowledge, and encouragement, and, most importantly, her belief in me and the book. This project would not have happened if not for Jann and her hard work in making sure that Richard's story was told in the clearest and most honest way possible. She is a legend.

My wife, Amiee, for her love and her understanding of my journey and selflessly allowing me to follow the path. She is my best friend and wing woman from Stratford to Woodstock.

My parents, George and Pam, for instilling in me the importance of hard work and taking no shit. My mom for always making sure that I could get to where I needed to be.

Josh Manuel, who not only supported me in searching for his father's essence but became a true friend in the process.

Paula Manuel for understanding.

Jane Manuel for her trust, her laughter, and allowing me into her home.

Arlie Manuel for her conversations, honesty, and encouragement.

Kathryn Manuel for her trust and belief in the book.

The entire Manuel family in Canada, New York, and California for their patience and positivity, and for welcoming me into their family.

Bub; Jeff Hochberg of the David Gahr Estate for his direction, knowledge, phone calls, and willingness to share all of it; Hank; Stephen Wilt for his unselfish vibe and his deep love of music and people; Dean Robinson, for his knowledge and direction; Vince Gratton; Watt Casey Jr., for the selfless contribution of several photographs; the Kid; Toots; Joe Forno, for always taking my calls, allowing me into his home, and trusting my vision; John Scheele and Elliott Landy, who expressed their love for Richard by allowing me to include their art in my book; Jake Jamison at the Barry Feinstein Estate; Caitlin Allyson at Landyvision; Alex Hime; Atlantic County Historical Society; Ellen Thomas at the Stratford-Perth Archives; Christine Schindler at the Stratford Festival Archives; Micaela Fitzsimmons at the Stratford Perth Museum; the estate of Jane Edmunds; Mark McKenna; Tim Gladwin, producer of *The Music of Richard Manuel*; Bob Kalmusky; Jeff Rosen; Parker Fishel; Mike Wiseman; Sick Dude Brad; Don and Nancy; Jack; Zac Dadic; Olivier Chastan; Dag Brethren, for his in-depth Band research and willingness to make it available; Anthony Millington; Dennis McNally; Greg Marra; Chris Bradford; Michael Eaton; Tom Kohn; Amy Collins, for her encouragement and honesty; Cheryl Pawelski, for the cool conversations; Schiffer Publishing; and Jan Hoiberg, for his priceless trove of information at the Band website, https://theband.hiof.no/.

Every single person who took the time and effort to patiently answer my inquiries and direct my search for things that were sometimes not there. The names of these fine folks can be found at the back of this book. I will forever be indebted to all of them for sharing memories and feelings with me.

If I have neglected to mention anyone, please know that I thank you from the bottom of my heart.

Prologue:
ONE WAY HOME THAT'S GUARANTEED

Richard Manuel's hand trembled as he reached to plug the RCA cable into the back of his electric piano. Pieces of music gear were scattered across the stage while the equipment load-in began. Richard absentmindedly scuffed his boot heel at a bird's nest of cables tangled at his feet. He caught the eye of a local crew member, grinned, and offered him a smoke.

As far back as 1969 when he was recording the Band's second LP, Richard always had a drink nearby to steady his hands before laying down his part. Now, sixteen years later, he was in a familiar situation. Only this time, the soundstage wasn't in Woodstock or Malibu—it was a stone's throw from his childhood home in Stratford, Ontario. Richard had paid his musical dues for the past twenty-five years. He had performed in halls and arenas all over the world, earned the respect of his peers, composed timeless music . . . and in the process had become an alcoholic and addict.

But Richard wouldn't have a drink that night, not for this gig. In fact, he had told a few friends that if he *ever* took another drink, he'd take his own life.

Richard and the Band visited his hometown in the fall of 1985 to perform a set of benefit performances at the ornate Stratford Festival Theatre, an intimate 1,800-seat venue usually reserved for stage plays during the town's annual Shakespeare Festival. But this was a special occasion in more ways than one. The theater had recently fallen on hard times, and the Band had been invited to headline this concert, appropriately named "Not the Last Waltz." For this particular show, Richard would not only get to play in front of his hometown crowd with the Band, but he would also be reuniting with his first group, the Revols. It had been twenty-five years since they'd played together.

The day before the concerts, Richard told Stratford news outlets that the shows "were a return to his roots. We'll try to mix it up, old favorites and maybe a little jazz. Not anything heavy metal," he said with his trademark wisecracking.

Truth be told, Richard hadn't felt this nervous since his 1962 debut with Ronnie Hawkins and the Hawks, when he was pushed out on the stage at nineteen—boozy, woozy, and with no safety net. Since those days, he had encountered a rolling series of peaks and pits, a daily pendulum of being wasted and even more wasted. He was finally pulling himself out of it. His people were rooting for him . . . and he was rooting for himself.

Richard's family and close friends were scattered throughout the audience, and teachers, schoolmates, and town officials filled the arena for both shows. The venue reflected the community's close-knit nature, with no seat more than 65 feet from the stage. The Revols minus Richard started the proceedings with an opening set that brought a cresting wave of rock nostalgia over the crowd.

Halfway through their performance, Richard stepped into the spotlight and walked to the grand piano at stage right. Cries of "Beak! Beak!" poured over the stage. Richard was beaming and looked spectacularly buttoned up in black pants and a white dress shirt. He was primed and polished . . . yet visibly shaken by the reception he received. Years later, Richard's brother Donald said, "Coming home after all those years was really exciting for him. I've never seen him so excited and nervous." Richard was dizzy with what he called "middle-aged teenage magic."

The performances were a resounding success. The Revols were anything but a flashback, and the Band played with a fire that reflected Richard's deep emotional state. Diamond eyed and flashing a toothy smile, he led the Revols through a memorable set that included Bobby Charles's "Before I Grow Too Old," Freddy King's "Hideaway," and Bobby Bland's "Share Your Love with Me."

For Richard, this was the final corner he needed to round to reach a straightaway in his life and career. He remembered why he started playing music and why he loved it. The adulation from his hometown people and support from his friends and family solidified it for him.

The Festival Theatre performances on November 2, 1985, were the closing of a circle and the culmination of a career musical arc. Revols guitarist Garth Picot attended the joyous after-show celebrations. Richard spotted him, smiled, and said, "We'll have to do this again sometime."

Chapter 1
IN A STATION
(1943-1958)

Richard had a lot of nerve. I remember there were these two old silos, and they were high . . . they were big silos; I guess they were used for coal for the railroad or something. They were side by side, and up at the top there was just like a plank that was about a two-by-six. He actually walked across it, you know. . . . He had as much nerve as Dick Tracy. Crazy—if he had a fall, that would've been it. . . . He was a daring person, for sure. That kind of enhanced his career. You've got to be a little bit that way to be successful in the music business.

—Chuck Kelly, Richard's childhood friend

When it came to nerve, Richard had about as much of it as anyone I've ever known.

—Levon Helm, Richard's friend and bandmate

Richard throttles the gas and cuts the corner with the precision of a protractor, swinging the 1955 Plymouth into a rutted grassy field at full speed. Always preferring the shortest route between two points, he giggles to himself, "Fuck intersections." He thumps the car back onto the highway, cranking the steering wheel as hard as he can. Spent beer cans rattle in the back seat, joining the chorus of radio static and the screaming of the engine. The car's interior is a tornado of cigarette smoke and the exhilaration of a late-summer night, as the wind sucks sparking streamers of loose ashes out of the side windows and into the slipstream.

Seventeen-year-old Richard "Beak" Manuel is hauling ass home from a rock concert in Port Dover, an hour south of Stratford, Ontario, well past his curfew. In defiance of his dad's orders to be home by 8:00 p.m. after that evening's Ronnie Hawkins and the Hawks performance, Beak got involved in an unplanned rendezvous with an attendee of the female persuasion. Now, he's speeding to make it home by first light because he has no choice: his father, James, nicknamed "Pierre," a lead mechanic at Kalbfleisch Bros. auto shop, needs the car to get to work.

Richard almost puts the car on two wheels and squeals into the driveway at 138 Well Street. The upstairs bathroom light is on; Pierre is up. Richard tosses his empties in the bushes, to be retrieved later, and creeps up the front steps. He sees his mother's silhouette drift past the front window, heading for the kitchen.

A train from the nearby Grand Trunk rail station bangs down the tracks as Richard cautiously opens the moaning door. Pierre immediately intercepts Richard in the doorway and shouts, "Dick, get upstairs and think about what you just did!" Richard, wincing, stands like a slackline, nervously chewing on the end of his thumb. He turns to speak, does not, and heads up the stairs to his room. Sitting down on the edge of his bed, Richard sighs. "What exactly is it I am supposed to think about?" He hears his youngest brother, Donald, giggle in the next room.

Stratford

Richard George Manuel was born the third of four boys on April 3, 1943, at Stratford General Hospital to James Edwin and Gladys (Haviland) Manuel. The Manuel family was blue collar, with a solid home and a strong faith. They were a gentle and funny family. Though the home was often chaotic, had dishes in the sink, and usually needed a good dusting, the boys were well loved and provided for.

Everyone, including Richard, referred to his mother as Kiddo. She was a simple woman, kind, down to earth, and fully invested in her family. She was strong and silent and ran the house as best as she could. Her stoicism would be passed along to Richard. His father, "Pierre," who got that nickname because of the stylish way he wore his beret, was the breadwinner. He was a hard worker and a funny man. Kiddo tried in vain to keep the house in some semblance of order. She had retired from teaching to devote her time to a house full of rambunctious boys.

Richard was raised in a modest, mustard-colored, three-bedroom, two-story home just a block from the railroad in a row of tightly placed houses. He could feel the vibrations of the tracks from his front steps, with the icehouse and the station just a few blocks away. The heavy drone of an approaching engine and the percussive rattling of the rails were sounds so imprinted on his psyche they became part of his internal rhythms.

Richard and his brothers found an endless world of exploration in Stratford's industrial railroad buildings and abandoned equipment. Bikes were king, and unencumbered riding along the banks of the Avon River and surrounding pastoral landscape offered the kids blissful days. Richard eventually picked up a paper route, delivering the *London Free Press* before school, but found it to be well before his desired wake-up time. He also was offered a job at the local salvage yard because of his mechanical curiosity. Richard was always disassembling and reassembling something.

138 Well Street as it looked when Richard was growing up. *Courtesy of the Richard Manuel family*

The Manuel brothers in the kitchen at Well Street, 1950. *Courtesy of the Richard Manuel family*

Richard and classmates at Anne Hathaway School. *Courtesy of the Stratford Perth Museum*

Young Richard, who along the way acquired the nickname "Beak," for his obvious and pronounced nose, attended the Anne Hathaway Stratford School until grade six, then the local Romeo School. He was also an active member of the 19 Stratford Royal Canadian Air Cadet Squadron and attended summer camps through his teenage years.

Chapter 1 | In a Station (1943–1958)

Richard's 19 Stratford Royal Canadian Air Cadet Squadron class, July 1957. *Courtesy of John Till*

Richard as a cadet, July 1957. *Courtesy of John Till*

At these camps, he wore short pants and a pressed uniform and made lifelong friendships with Chuck Kelly and Jimmy Winkler. The close-knit group of friends would embark on a number of crazy youthful adventures. Richard was renowned for his ample farting ability, and the talent to set said gas on fire. One legendary example of their juvenile hell-raising included Chuck and Richard liberating two bottles of gin from an abandoned house.

A favorite pastime of Beak and his pals was crawling up the steep, rocky slope of Stratford's Snake Hill to the underside of the railroad overpass. They sneaked beers and smoked cigarettes while the trains screamed by just above their heads. The gang would pedal down to the grassy shore of Lake Victoria to skinny-dip and would come out covered in freshwater leeches. Richard gave the swimming spot the name "Bare-Ass Beach."

The fact that Richard's birth, childhood, and coming of age ran concurrently with the artistic blooming of his hometown is no coincidence. Stratford is situated midway between Toronto and Detroit, due north of Cleveland. From a hawk's-eye view, Stratford is the connecting point between two artistic worlds and countries. Just as Richard would become a conduit for musical influence, the town straddled the fence between outside inspiration and internal artistic aspiration. Southern Ontario was also a melting pot of local and international personalities beamed in via Toronto's airwaves and far-flung AM radio stations.

A rattling railway industry supported the early years of the one-horse town. It was responsible for the municipality's growth and brought a diverse blend of people through the area. The railroad influenced the building of music venues and sports fields and encouraged a close-knit and artistically relevant community that appreciated hard work as well as leisure time.

Jimmy Winkler and Richard, 1957

Chuck Kelly, who grew up on Front Street within shouting distance of Richard's house, remembered the early years of their friendship. "He definitely knew what he wanted and knew where he was going to end up. He was just the same as I was. We had the same values, and we all grew up on the wrong side of the river, too close to the railway tracks."

Richard and friends in front of the cadet building, July 1957. *From left*: Jim Winkler, Billy Reinhart, PeeWee Brenner, Tom Hunter, Richard.

Chapter 1 | In a Station (1943–1958)

On October 31, 1952, when Richard was nine years old, the Stratford Festival was born. The town became home to an annual arts event celebrating the works of William Shakespeare. Growing up, Richard couldn't help but be affected in some way by the festival's dramatic presence, which brought an additional layer of influence to the town's artistic foundation and to Richard's formative years.

The Manuel family's faith was solid as stone, as illustrated by oldest brother Jim's leaving home to become a Baptist minister. Clearly, Richard had a different path. He was a demure soul prone to deep introspection. He would sometimes look like a kid misplaced. While often content to quietly observe, he would flash a crooked smile and a slyly raised eyebrow that revealed a mischievous side just beneath the surface. Richard spoke in a patient, measured way that conveyed he was a thoughtful conversationalist.

Kiddo, Donald, Pierre, Jim with wife (Sandra), and Richard after church. *Courtesy of the Richard Manuel family*

On pale Sunday mornings, Pierre, Kiddo, Richard, and his brothers Jim, Alan, and Donald would file into the kitchen to the sunlit scent of coffee and breakfast before church. They would then head over to Ontario Street Baptist for services.

Something stirred within Richard when the congregation rose up and a chorus of diverse voices swelled in joyous collaboration. When his own voice was added to the celebratory harmonies from the hymnal, young Beak surely felt the magic of music. As glorious songs reverberated throughout the sanctuary, Richard could hear his singular voice among the many, creating a beautiful whole of sound. Singing at church is what gave him an appreciation for harmonies. Stacked voices, transcendent chord changes, and gospel sensibilities filled his impressionable mind.

As he moved into his teen years, he began to tap into an endless well of hell-raising. He also had a dry wit and was always up for some sort of craziness. Beak often took the lead, always trying to make his pals laugh. Close friends recall that he fell victim to peer pressure and would act out to fit in. He wore the suit of the jester well and was more than willing to play the clown. But he also took on dares to feel part of the group. Richard didn't like to say no.

The living room of the Manuel home held a dusty upright piano. In the 1950s it was a usual occurrence in Canada, as well as the United States, for the children of the home to embark on some sort of creative, usually musical, pursuit, which often came in the form of piano lessons. Kiddo was the impetus for Richard's gently enforced musical excursions. She witnessed how much he enjoyed singing in church and watched him lean his head back, eyes pressed tight, singing songs of praise.

The official beginning of Richard's musical career can be traced to his first piano lessons. Mrs. Conroy, a local teacher, came to the house every week to teach piano to the Manuel boys. Richard reflected on the results of these lessons in a 1984 interview with Ruth Albert Spencer of the *Woodstock Times*:

> I quit piano lessons when my teacher literally slammed the lid on my fingers because I played a note that wasn't on the paper. It wasn't wrong; it was a different voicing; same chord, different voicing, like I put the E in a C chord on the top instead of in the middle. She slammed the lid on my fingers because she'd been at me to learn theory and I wasn't paying attention. I could play it, if I could get it in my head, I didn't see any reason to dwell on it. So that was the end of my formal piano lessons.

In what would become a trait typical for the antiauthoritarian Richard, he was going to do things his way. Somewhat discouraged, he quit playing piano for a little while, but the magnetism of music kept pulling him back. Luckily, the negative interaction with his teacher didn't deter him from exploring the instrument in greater detail.

While Richard's music teacher didn't last, his mother's musical influence cannot be overstated. Visitors to the Manuel home remember Kiddo's joyful laughter, patience, and unwavering support of the chaotic musical escapades taking place in the living room. Kiddo encouraged Richard to direct his focus on learning the instrument. She *made* him do it. He sat at the piano and, like all good musicians, would practice, practice, practice. This discipline that Kiddo instilled would form the way that Richard worked best and most creatively throughout his life.

Inspired by his burgeoning musical interest and abilities, Richard tapped his Ontario Street Baptist mate David Priest for lessons in the church basement. He knew it would be much easier to learn from a friend than a teacher. This way, he could process the things he felt best suited him, and move on. After Sunday services were over and the congregation spilled out onto the street, Richard and David scurried down to the basement piano. It was here that David gave Richard quick lessons before they heard the shouts from their parents upstairs to get going home.

While Richard's smoldering musical awareness had its genesis in church, his immersion in late-night radio at Well Street drove his increasing interest in playing music. The terrestrial radio waves from WLAC in Nashville, Tennessee, beamed in a powerful influence and organic musical training. WLAC's legendary reach influenced scores of aspiring rock 'n' roll musicians.

The station provided kids of Richard's age a deep well of inside jokes, sexual innuendo, and hip DJs—and most importantly, rhythm and blues. From eight at night until two in the morning, hosts Gene Nobles, John Richbourg, and Bill "Hossman" Allen would spin blues and gospel discs for an audience made up of eager ears like Richard's.

The radio shows were like an underground club for renegade youth. It was no coincidence that Richard's future bandmates were all doing the exact same thing, staying up late and tuning in to the secret airwaves from Marvel, Arkansas, to Toronto, Ontario. They were jamming to the R&B and rock they couldn't get anywhere else.

While listening, Richard began to mentally catalog chord progressions and thought about how to thump a boogie-woogie bass line with his left hand. He was an adept listener who never learned to read music and played completely by ear.

Kiddo continued to encourage Richard's musical interests. He had friends like Jimmy Winkler, who often stopped by the house and played impromptu drums using brushes on a tin table. Richard's mother would sit at the kitchen table and play solitaire for hours. But, beginning at dusk, they'd all migrate to the kitchen with Kiddo for radio-listening sessions.

Beak, his brother Donald (everybody called him Filbert), Chuck Kelly, and a couple of their mutual pals would brew some coffee and tune into the music shows. Sometimes if the boys got too loud, Pierre would yell down through a vent in the bathroom floor for them to quiet down. But like Kiddo, he was very understanding of his boys and their excitement about music. Chuck remembers Richard tuning in WCFL Chicago for *The Real McCoy* jazz show, where they would play Frank Sinatra singing Cole Porter's "At Long Last Love."

When the house grew dark, after his friends went home and his parents went to bed, Beak would tune in to WLAC's *John R. Rhythm and Blues Show*. He had devised an elaborate way of capturing the invisible signal. With a squinty-eyed focus, he fiddled with the amber Bakelite dial like a secret decoder ring, a rock 'n' roll robber cracking a safe, until finally focusing the frequency. It was as if he had a sense of his own future when he heard the sneaky minor key drag of Otis Rush's "Double Trouble" playing through the static.

Once he was properly tuned in, Richard would hotbox a cigarette out his cracked window or pound a can of beer he had slyly absconded with. It was time for Beak's type of school, where he studied every nuance and tribal rhythm cutting through the blue evening airwaves. He pulled out the detailed verbalizations of Ray Charles and Bobby "Blue" Bland like a blood draw. In his own late-night world, Richard would duet with Howlin' Wolf, Jimmy Reed, and Etta James while playing air piano on his wooden floor.

Into the midnight hour, Richard learned to hone his natural gifts through immersion and repetition. He listened intently, waiting for favorite songs to come on, and then was inspired to track down the singles. He focused on the strong woody thump of the heavy left hand of blues players such as Otis Spann and deft vocal and piano work of Fats Domino. Richard emulated it all in his own late-night R&B piano training. During commercial breaks, he excitedly scribbled down the addresses for mail-order singles and patiently waited until daybreak to ask Kiddo for some money to place an order.

When it came time to head to school, Richard strutted along with his hair swept into a makeshift duckbill and a cache of brand-new records tucked under his arm. He was blessed with a big mop of hair, so his "DA" was the best. Unlike most kids of the era, Richard didn't collect sports cards or comic books; he collected licks and melodies. He cradled 7-inch records of cuts such as "Ain't That a Shame" by Fats Domino or "A Fool for You" by Ray Charles. Richard liked being the inside man at an exclusive club. He was hooked on rock and blues and loved sharing his discoveries with his mates. His classmate John Till witnessed his evolution from shy choirboy to rock 'n' roll party star: "There was no blues around except for a few small circles, and he was the center of one of them."

Beak sat in the back of the classroom and played a pantomime of percussive piano on his wooden desk. His jerky movements and melodic hums often drew the attention of the girls in his class. They naturally gravitated toward the handsome musician in their midst. Richard loved girls, no doubt about it, and they loved him too. His honeyed voice and measured tone made them feel at ease. He was dark and handsome with sturdy French Canadian features, a wide-legged gait, and an earnestness that made classmates want to know more about what was going on with him.

Additional late-night listening sessions soon became the norm, with Richard and his like-minded pals gathering at their schoolmates' houses for hard-core sessions around the radio. Frank and Kenny Smith (nicknamed Cough and Drop for Smith Brothers' Cough Drops) had parents who often left town to visit their cottage, providing a house where the boys could conduct experiments with music listening, cigarettes, and beer.

Rumor had it that Richard had an inside connection that fed his quickly growing collection of vinyl records. Friends remember a relative who may have worked at a radio station who would send Richard rare promo lacquers. Many of the songs Richard played were often deep cuts that his pals were hearing for the first time.

Richard worked hard to convincingly interpret the music he loved. Becoming a specific character and, in turn, a melodic narrator is how he discovered his singing strengths. In addition to his deep affinity for Ray Charles, Richard lived every inflection and breath he heard in Bobby "Blue" Bland's singles. He was a great admirer of "Little Boy Blue," where he found inspiration for his own developing vocal approach. Richard's future bandmate Levon Helm said, "You had to imitate before you could possibly originate." He could have been speaking about Beak, who was emulating every nuance of the musical heroes he had never met.

Richard sang without any formal training. Later he told the *Woodstock Times*:

> I learned from Ray Charles and Bobby Bland, and Ricky Nelson probably influenced me too. Let's see . . . Howlin' Wolf, Muddy Waters, Jimmy Reed. Nearly all the singing influence is Black. People think I sound just like Ray Charles, but I don't sound like Ray Charles. I imply, I make the same implications, I infer the same things.

Richard's piano playing began rooted in the style of Ray Charles. Hard chording, a strong groove, and melodic single-note self-accompaniment were his focus. While he was blessed with a plethora of musical gifts, rhythm was the most important. Richard had yet to discover he was a drummer, but the natural beat in his soul gravitated to his left hand. He had a grandfather-clock rhythm, something that can't be taught.

Richard learned that his musical ability not only could get him attention from chicks but could also get him out of trouble. His pal Chuck Kelly, who lived at home with his grandmother, explained, "I was really proud of my grandma, because she smoked a pipe. I thought that was the coolest thing. I'd bring people home to show them and she'd get mad." The time he brought Richard home, Chuck's grandmother was not impressed with another intrusion of her privacy and ended up chasing the boys around the dining-room table in a great tizzy. Richard brought the chase to a close when he sat at the parlor piano for a mournful solo rendition of the standard "Cherry Pink and Apple Blossom White," which made Chuck's grandmother cry. She thought Richard was all right after that.

Party Star

Rock 'n' roll, cruisin', and girls were, for many kids Richard's age, a way out of a square world and into a new way of life. Greasy hair, hip clothes, and the sexually charged rhythms emanating from the radio were part of an invitation-only after-hours club. In Stratford, Richard was more than happy to be the founding member, as he told *Record Mirror* magazine in 1968: "I took piano lessons at nine but didn't see eye-to-eye with the teacher. She didn't want me to play by ear, and I knew I had a shortcut. I got back to it when I was twelve. Then I became a party star. In fact, I became a party!"

Richard's close pals remember seeing him hanging loose at the Saturday night Teen Twenty Dances at the Stratford YMCA, where he would post up in the smoking lounge and show off his piano skills by playing boogie-woogie. Beak loved to pull birds, and the teenage girls couldn't care less about a record-spinning DJ when there was a genuine rocker in their midst. Richard plowed through a Mose Allison cut or took a shot at singing Ray Charles when he wanted to up the charm, but no matter the song, everyone dug it. Beak was a natural. He was born to entertain.

This was an era when promoters put together big-package, multiple-act rock 'n' roll shows. *The Big Beat Show 1958*, emceed by famed Cleveland DJ and rock 'n' roll advocate Alan Freed, took a swing through Kitchener, forty minutes east of Stratford, in April 1958. A little over a week past Richard's fifteenth birthday, he and his pal Chuck went to the show at the Kitchener Memorial Auditorium with 5,200 other excitable teens. The evening's performance featured Buddy Holly and the Crickets, along with Jerry Lee Lewis, and was headlined by Mr. Riff himself, Chuck Berry. After an inspired evening of music, rebellion, and girls, the boys moved outside the venue to see their heroes off.

Shivering in the brisk evening air of an early Canadian spring, Richard watched Berry get into his pearly-white Cadillac and speed away from the venue. In that very instant, he took off in a dead sprint in what was an obviously fruitless chase. Silhouetted in exhaust and the icy mist of dusk, Richard stopped in the road, hands on knees and breathless, hearing the screams of fans around him. The propulsive lick of Berry's "You Can't Catch Me" spun in his consciousness. And gazing after Berry's taillights, he saw his own rock 'n' roll future come into focus.

Dave Michie
(The Manager)

is wearing the latest multi-coloured striped sport shirt. This shirt is styled by FORSYTH. It is available in Olive, Mauve, or Orange tones.

6.95

Doug Rhodes
(Vocal)

is wearing a smartly tailored sportshirt styled with both the Harry Belafonte neckline and the stitched double front. Available in several shades and sizes.

7.95

Richard Manuel
(Piano)

is modelling a well tailored and smartly styled, well tailored dark paisley patterned sportshirt by Lancer. Colours to suit and sizes to fit.

6.95

Jim Winkler
(Drums)

is wearing the newest in light tone sportshirts with a stitched double front, smartly styled dark paisley patterned LANCER. Available in several colours.

5.95

Ken Kalmusky
(Bass)

is wearing a sportshirt by Lancer in which light shades are interwoven with dark shades to give it that different look. Available in several shades and all sizes.

7.95

Garth Picot
(Head Guitar)

is modelling the latest style in dark toned sportshirts. Well tailored var- a large assortment of colours.

7.95

OTHER SPORTSHIRTS PRICED FROM **2.98** to **7.95**

THE REVOLS
Will Be Appearing At Queen's Park, Stratford

SAT. NIGHT

Chapter 2
REVOL-UTION!
(1959-1961)

If you walked by 138 Well Street on a Saturday afternoon in the late 1950s, you'd have heard the buzz of loud amplifiers and the clamoring of strange rhythms, the muffled chaotic sounds of a band in action. Just as with many early rock 'n' roll bands, friendships were the foundation of the music making. A standard of the early Well Street get-togethers was Beak's version of Franz Liszt's "Liebestraum" No. 3—the first piece that he learned to play, mostly by watching over his brother's shoulder. Richard turned the mellifluous classical piece on its ear, in the style of Jerry Lee Lewis.

By 1959, sixteen-year-old Richard Manuel had become infected with the "Rockin' Pneumonia and the Boogie Woogie Flu," and it was contagious! His perfectly poofted hair and growing record collection reflected his deep enthusiasm for the form. The next obvious move was to start a rock 'n' roll band.

James Dean's 1955 film *Rebel without a Cause* incited a revolution in middle-class homes across the United States and Canada for the way it expressed youthful freedom. In September 1956, Elvis Presley performed (from the waist up) for the first time on *The Ed Sullivan Show*, and an entire nation of kids were exposed to the primal urges of rock 'n' roll. It wasn't until 1957 that Presley's influence began to be felt in Canada, where popular rock 'n' roll music was still a novelty.

Richard was at the forefront of the rock movement in Stratford, a purist and a straight rhythm-and-blues head. At school, he daydreamed about meeting a like-minded group of local lads who could play instruments, cut loose, and maybe score some chicks. Richard may have been a quiet kid in school, but he had a party in his heart, and rock 'n' roll music allowed him to express it.

Robbie Robertson remembered the rock 'n' roll detonation in a 1995 video interview with WGBH's David Ables: "It seemed like on Monday there was no rock 'n' roll. There was Perry Como and Patty Page, the Four Lads, and whoever all these people were. Then on Tuesday it was like all of these people had been waiting in the chutes ready to come charging out. It didn't happen over a period of many years, like in 1955 or in 1956. All of a sudden, BAM! All of these people came at you, like, where were they on Monday? On Tuesday they're all here."

Avoiding the constraints of a workingman's life, like that of his father, was a priority for Richard. His piano playing was one way he could ensure that. Impromptu sessions for what would become his first rock 'n' roll band took place organically at Well Street around the Manuels' well-loved family piano. Casual connections among schoolmates, neighbors, and family friends resulted in spontaneous sing-alongs.

"Liebestraum" was the lodestone of Richard's musical development. Piano instrumentals were extremely popular, and he was inspired to try his hand at something new and original. It is in the work's A flat major construction and modulated melody that Richard discovered the power of thoughtful musical structure. Stratford friends and neighbors alike remember Beak playing his juiced-up arrangement for anyone willing to listen.

Stratford singer Doug Rhodes was present for these early jams, which also had appearances by local musicians Donald Hyde and Chick Chalmers, members of a local Stratford group named the Rebels. Some if not most of the members of the Rebels had stopped by the Manuel home's open jam sessions. Over time, the Rebels' members started to fall off and were slowly replaced by other musicians who were frequenting Beak's piano parties. This gradual change continued through 1959, when the Rebels started to become something different.

Jimmy Winkler, Richard's best friend, told him that if Richard ever played piano in a band, Jimmy would have to be his drummer. They'd been friends since the beginning, and Jimmy had graduated from brushes on the Manuels' tin-topped table to drumsticks. He soon procured a set of drums and started to bang along in real time. They made a pact that if either of them was to leave their band, the other one had to go too.

One day, Richard's younger brother Filbert brought his friend and young guitarist John Till over to their house on Well Street. When John heard raucous piano chords coming from the living room, he peeked around the corner and saw a skinny kid sitting at the piano, pounding out what sounded like a Jerry Lee Lewis song.

John turned to Filbert and said, "I'm a guitar player; I have a guitar." Richard overheard him and replied excitedly, "Bring it over!" Thus began the relationship between Richard Manuel and John Till and the start of a lifelong musical journey that would intersect multiple times throughout their lives. Till said, "You could feel even back then that he was cut from a special mold."

Till's musical development was intertwined with Richard's: "I was hearing things on the radio: Buddy Holly, Chuck Berry, that sort of thing, Everly Brothers, Fats Domino. But Richard opened the door to a lot of other music that I never knew about, the R&B stuff. Richard loved the blues." Richard recommended Southern artists such as Roscoe Gordon and Little Walter to Till, and though both could appreciate the mainstream, they shared an attraction to exclusive songs imbued with mystery and feeling.

Richard lived for showing Till the flip sides of Muddy Waters, Bobby "Blue" Bland, and of course Ray Charles's early Atlantic recordings. Beak and Till dug deep into Mose Allison, and Richard had an affinity for Nat King Cole's 1948 single "Nature Boy." These listening sessions led to an especially creative time for the two, and they easily started to write songs together. The collaborations came naturally. Till told the *Stratford Beacon Herald* in 2015, "What I really admired was his piano playing and singing. I'd never heard anybody do that. . . . He really loved music. He really loved to play."

Bassist Ken Kalmusky came into the fold through a well-timed meeting with Till on Stratford's Queen Street. Both lived close by, loved music, and just happened to be only a short walk from the Manuels' home. Once they all got together, the idea sprung of starting a band. All three family homes had a piano, but eventually rehearsals settled at Richard's house. Kalmusky's brother Bob said, "The Manuel house was always a great home, but it was a great home because of the family. They were a very kind, very loving family. There was always lots of music."

Richard's folks were very supportive of his enthusiastic musical direction and the yet-to-be-named band that congregated at their home. The house became a jam room full of loud instruments featuring Till playing guitar, Kalmusky playing bass, Winkler on the drum stool, and Richard playing the parlor piano. Doug Rhodes took on the lead vocals, since he had already been the front man for the Rebels.

The group got to work honing their craft. Rowdy rehearsals continued to take place at the Manuel home, with Kiddo and Pierre's patience the deciding factor in allowing the living room to become a rehearsal space. The Manuels let the boys come and go at their leisure and play to their hearts' content. Not only did the band play, but friends stopped by to listen. Not long after getting a few songs together, the guys started to gain an audience for their music.

The Evolution of the Rebels

The Rebels' debut took place at St. Joseph's Catholic Church in Stratford, playing to the Sunday night youth group. Performing onstage gave Richard a charge like the one he first got singing harmony in church. The band jammed through its limited repertoire, which included a gritty reading of Ray Charles's 1956 single "Hallelujah, I Love Her So," featuring Beak on lead vocals—his first foray into being a rock singer.

Richard had been working hard on emulating his favorite singers after hours in his bedroom. He also began the unique approach of getting his throat warmed and roughed up by burying his head into his pillow and screaming as loud as he could. After a few proper attempts, a sweaty-faced Beak would drop the needle on his next record, ready to tackle some Howlin' Wolf.

The group's first paying gig was on the barren stage of the Blue Water Lounge on Highway 21 outside Goderich, where the band made a cool $60 for the evening's performance. Still booked as the Rebels, the group played on a Friday night in minimalist fashion with their antiquated equipment. The group used two PA horns for their sound, and Richard's piano wasn't amplified yet.

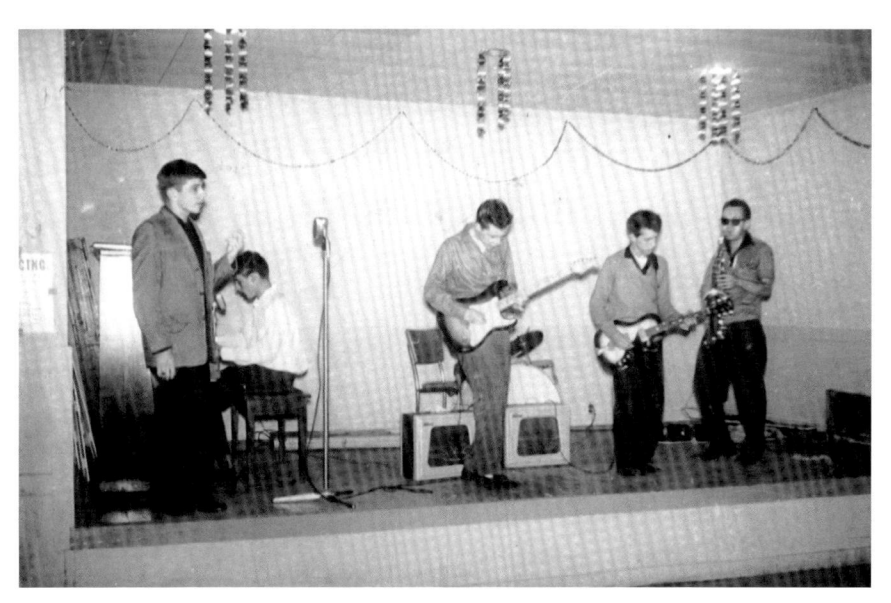

The Revols performing at the Blue Water Lounge, Goderich, Ontario, 1960. *From left*: Doug Rhodes, Richard Manuel, John Till, Ken Kalmusky, unnamed saxophone player. *Courtesy of the Stratford-Perth Archives*

Once the group began to receive a small amount of local popularity, the boys decided to move on from the Rebels tag in late 1958. The group was aware of Duane Eddy and the Rebels and felt inspired to come up with something hip and original. The new band name, inspired by Richard, was a twist on the old. The Rebels became the Revols.

The Revols name, short for revolutions, came from Richard's prowess at getting cars spinning in circles. This often occurred on the slick William Street ice right in front of the school, to ensure an audience. A second meaning, of course, referenced the speed at which records spun on a platter. Till told the *London Free Press*, "I remember the night Richard came up with it. He sprung that on us and that was great." The final and best-regarded element, as well as a constant source of amusement for the band members, was that Revol spelled backward was lover. Beak was working at becoming a professional in that field too.

Between 1959 and 1960, the Revols played multiple gigs every week and of every variety around southern Ontario. The group took every gig they could, and played as much as their school-age lives allowed. They started to sharpen their skills not only at arranging stage-worthy deep cuts, but also at composing original music. Till recalled that Richard instigated most of the songwriting for the Revols: "He'd just sit down and throw some chords down, then he would throw some lyrics out. There were one or two we worked on together, and the rest he wrote himself. It was an interesting eclectic sort of approach to

The Revols performing at the Blue Water Lounge, Goderich, Ontario, 1960. *From left*: Richard Manuel, Doug Rhodes, Jimmy Winkler, John Till, Ken Kalmusky. *Stratford-Perth Archives Image, #2001.76, Photos-Stratford-Music-The Revols*

music." Till and Richard wrote a number of good songs that were lost, since there was no way to document their creations. Richard could just "pull chords out of the air," he said. "He had a real nice way of fitting together original and different-sounding chord progressions."

Another of Richard's musical excursions came courtesy of the Western Ontario Conservatory of Music. The school had instituted a series of residential branches in London, St. Mary's, and Stratford that offered willing youth a number of classes for certification. Richard took full advantage of this opportunity and quickly earned his certificate in Hawaiian slide guitar.

He acquired a small Supro lap steel guitar and practiced until he could play tunes from his radio-listening sessions by memory. Santo and Johnny's drowsy 1959 single "Sleep Walk" was a favorite that Richard liked to perform for his friends and onstage with the Revols. He also embraced the slippery melodies of Muddy Waters's famed slide guitar in his own rapidly developing fashion. He was collecting musical clues like an eager crow from a fertile landscape and storing them away for his own use.

Stratford friend and city councilor George Brown remembered Richard's talents in 2015: "He could play almost any instrument that you put in front of him. . . . He was a natural talent: a good drummer, great on piano, organ, whatever. . . . He'd bring out a guitar and start playing or get on the drums, or piano."

The band and their mates hung out constantly and embarked on epic adolescent adventures. The search for girls and beer defined many of their nonmusical exploits. By all accounts from his friends and bandmates, Richard always had a smile for you and was game for anything that had the remote possibility of being a good time.

He would laugh until it hurt, revealing big pearly whites and a grin as bright as a set of high beams. The most legendary of the teenage tales usually spotlighted Beak's driving skills. Everyone who knew Richard had a story of white-knuckle heroism or sphincter-clenching regret when he got behind the wheel.

The Revols and their schoolmates often piled into Pierre's 1956 Plymouth four-door to go cruisin', some evenings traveling as far as Buffalo, New York, for some underaged troublemaking. One fateful evening after practice, a few of Beak's pals piled in to see if they could score a case of beer. Speeding along the flats of Harmony's back roads, just south of Stratford, Richard had the car slicing through what had become a thick fog.

When implored to slow down because of the poor visibility, Beak replied, "I couldn't see any better if I was going slower." Suddenly out of the milky air, a stop sign flashed in the periphery like a ghostly warning at sea—just before Pierre's ship slammed head on onto the rocks. Three hydro poles, a fence, and a cornfield landing later, Richard got out of the car to assess the damage. Shook up, sobered up, and stuck in a field, the guys took stock of their bits and pieces as a passing truck clipped the loose wires on the highway, sending blue arcs of flame into the dark night.

Richard and his friends gathered their wits and procured a nearby cow from the field to carry one of their crew (who had banged his knee in the crash) back to town. After the inevitable meeting with Pierre, Richard made his way downtown to the police station to confess his crimes.

Walking along the way, he was stopped by an officer on duty who inquired, "You wouldn't know anything about the car that was left on the outskirts of town, would you?" Richard replied that he did and was on his way to let the police know. The officer replied, "What took you so long to report the accident?" Richard said, "If you crashed your father's car, you wouldn't be in a hurry to let him know either!" Pierre let Richard spend the night in jail to teach him a lesson. It didn't work.

The Revols Get a Manager

Through all their gigging, rehearsing, and partying, Beak and his bandmates decided that it would be a good idea to get someone who could help them get their shit together. Richard was so laid back that he could be counted on for only so much. It wasn't neglect on his part; it was just so much easier to have a good time. The Revols first and only manager, the famed Canadian DJ David Marsden, who went by David Mickie at the time, explained how it all went down:

> When I was about fourteen, I started putting on dances at the local YMCA (in Stratford). I would rent the hall and then I'd put on a little dance to records. DJs would come in and play. This guy comes up to me one evening and says, "Hey, can we play for your next dance?" This was the 1950s, and there wasn't a lot of live music in the rock world, the Top 40 world or whatever it was called then. So, I said, "Tell me what you got." We were all probably fourteen, fifteen years old at the most. I said, "OK, I'm doing one in two weeks. Why don't you guys play? By the way, what's your name?" He says to me, "My name is Richard Manuel." And that is how it all started.

After a few of these gigs playing Marsden's dances, Richard got up the gumption to ask him to be their manager: "Would you like to help us or guide us or something?" Marsden was up for the same kind of fun and adventure as the band and immediately started attending Well Street rehearsals.

Marsden's arrival on the scene was pivotal in the band's ascending development. He had a car, got them gigs, acted as hip emcee, and helped carry the band's gear. "All successful groups need that guy, the problem solver, and David was that guy," Till said.

Richard knew what he wanted to do and was taking an active role in shaping it. Having an advocate in Marsden to handle the issues that didn't involve music was exactly what the Revols needed. All Richard wanted to do was play and have sex. Richard said in 1984 that he often felt sensitive to chains of events and had a second sense of where those events would lead. His instant connection with Marsden and that effect on the Revols made him contemplate the direction his life was taking and where his band could go.

Soon after, the band permanently moved rehearsals from the Manuels' home to bass player Ken Kalmusky's house at 127 Queen Street on the corner of Cobourg. Just as this change took place, the Revols came into a free piano, courtesy of the Black Swan coffee club around the corner on Ontario Street.

The Black Swan was a sinister-sounding place in a series of three look-alike brick houses lined up on Ontario Street. When word got around that the club had closed its doors, the guys in the Revols happily offered to move the piano. A Stratford schoolmate remembered, "I do have a clear memory of Beak playing 'Liebestraum' on an old piano that the boys had pushed along Ontario Street from the first Black Swan location, [first] to the Kalmusky sunporch and later to the basement." The piano was the final piece of the puzzle in the Kalmusky basement that gave the Revols a new home base and created a semiprivate retreat for Stratford's percolating rock 'n' roll scene.

When the Canadian winter settled on Stratford, the piano was forced from the sunporch. In a legendary move, the basement stairs had to be dismantled for the piano's journey to the weather-protected confines of the lower level. The steps were subsequently returned to their rightful location.

The Revols were poised to soar on the first breezes of what would become a Canadian gust of rock 'n' roll. Kalmusky's younger brother, Bob, recalled the early basement sessions at his home:

The Kalmusky basement, 127 Queen Street, Stratford, Ontario. *Courtesy of John Till*

When they were at our house, the basement was the clubhouse. At first, they used to rehearse a lot, but they got so busy they didn't have a lot of time for rehearsing because they were always playing. So then they would get together in our basement for parties and get-togethers. But when they did play . . . I remember being upstairs looking out the window, and there's always two or three girls outside kind of listening to the music and, you know, wanting to be *friends* with the band.

The electric vibrations of eager Revols music wafted from the charged room. Down the steep rebuilt steps into the subterranean music space, the basement aroma of stale beers and preserved smoke hung like an imaginary horizon in the air. The space was decorated with well-placed cutout photos and funnies plastered across the whitewashed paneling. Strands of faux ivy had been twisted around the basement supports and across the low ceiling, giving the jam room the funky essence of an attempt at a decorative touch.

An array of makeshift seating was nestled among a muddled mess of cords, guitars, wires, empty bottles, drum pieces, the Black Swan piano, John Till's National amp, and Kenny Kalmusky's Fender stack. It was in this windowless workshop that the Revols became a real band.

An exciting creative environment was being fostered in the Kalmuskys' basement. The loose musicality developing there was a precursor to Beak's musical trailblazing that would take place a decade down the line. Kenny and Bob's parents were hip, encouraging, and musical, with the elder Kalmusky sometimes blowing sax with the guys. The family was laid back and happy to have visitors, which was a helpful boost to the boys' ascending confidence by providing them with an intimate and friendly audience.

When rehearsing in the basement, the band could easily pull a case of beer and no one would be the wiser. Add in a few aspiring female fans and some dim lights, thick smoke, and loud music, and it was a ready-made party. Once he tipped a few back, Richard surprised those who were accustomed to the quiet kid in school by singing with a hell of a voice.

When Richard eased a bench up to the Black Swan piano to sing a Ray Charles number, a new man was revealed. One of his bandmates later told the Stratford newspaper, "He could get really crazy. He was a quiet guy a lot of the time; he had no problem with the girls. But every so often—wow!" Richard was side-splittingly funny, drunk or sober. His comedic timing was that of a practiced stand-up, with his deadpan drawl accentuating one-liners, punch lines, and snarky asides.

While Beak was often the apex of comedic shenanigans at Revols rehearsals, he was also central to any sort of technical tinkering in the basement. He and both Kalmusky and Till were often found soldering, running wires, and disassembling found instruments and speakers.

In one of their inspired moments of technological experimentation, the guys rigged hidden microphones throughout the basement, so that all private conversations and couch make-out sessions could be eavesdropped on via electronic trickery. The Revols took great joy in calling out their friends when conversations revealed sappy details that they could make public knowledge.

Musically, the group was bank-vault tight: they played constantly and worked hard at arranging a set list that expressed their likes and diverse layers of influence. The band's common goal was to get the crowd dancing and the girls swooning, and to have a good time doing it.

John Till at house party, December 1960. *Courtesy of John Till*

Richard playing piano at a house party, December 1960. *Courtesy of John Till*

The group was youthfully oblivious to the exclusiveness of their experimental approaches to music. The band was constantly striving for new sounds and ways to improve their own evolving identity. A high school friend would later find rogue 7-inch singles left behind in a Fender amplifier he loaned to both Till and Richard. Cuts like "Thunder" by Jody Reynolds & the Storms and Owen Bradley's "Big Guitar" are examples of the cupboards the Revols were pulling their influence from.

Listening to these cuts with the knowledge of hindsight, you can discern the abundant musical ground that Richard and Till were mining for their gold. They were discovering the importance of arrangements and ambiance. They were also experimenting with how certain chords, bass lines, and rhythms would give them control over shifts in dynamics.

Richard and his bandmates' collaborative enthusiasm for musical discovery didn't stop with 7-inch singles. The Revols were personalizing their sonic spread and updating their sound. One afternoon, Bob Kalmusky heard his brother Ken and Richard giggling away in the basement during an afternoon practice session. The pair was usually up to some sort of shenanigans down there, so Bob went down to investigate.

There, Bob found a mischievous Kenny and Beak, an open box of silvery tacks, and a dismantled piano. What the guys were doing was strategically placing tacks into the hammers of the old Black Swan piano in order to alter the sound. Soon after, the new honky-tonk strains of Richard playing "Liebestraum" emanated from the basement piano.

Young Kenny and Beak had created a tack piano, also referred to as a jangle piano. Essentially it's a modified version of a standard upright. By placing tacks on the felt-covered hammers where they strike the string, Kenny and Richard gave the piano a more ragtime or saloon-style percussive feel. This kind of piano personality was found mostly in westerns of the time, which the guys surely would have been into. This basement discovery is also worthy of note because the approach ultimately led to the slightly off-kilter and roly-poly style of Richard's playing.

Shortly after the tack piano event, Richard stopped by his friend Sam Wyatt's house. When he came into the home, Beak threw a keen raised eyebrow toward Sam's family piano and said, "You know what you need to do, lad, is take the front off and add some thumbtacks." This popular Richard directive was later confirmed by another schoolmate, who recalled that whenever he was going to play a new piano, he immediately attempted to dismantle it so he could get the sound he wanted.

One particular bugaboo facing the band was archaic amplification. There was the nagging problem of not hearing Richard's piano over the din of the guitars and drums. Sometimes in concert the group would mic the piano, but it still wasn't coming through the PA with any clarity. In another case of using musical ingenuity to remedy an issue, the guys sought out ceramic phonograph cartridges from varying turntables, removed them, and affixed them to the soundboard inside the piano.

The band eventually upgraded from this lo-fi fix to pickups from a guitar to enhance the clarity of their sound. Once these adjustments were made, the piano could be fed through an onstage amp directly, just like the guitar and bass.

David Marsden remembered that when the Revols would arrive at a venue for a show, Richard would immediately pop the lid on the piano, stick his head underneath, and place his pickups in the perfect spot. He would then trace the cord, hook it up to his amplifier, add electricity, and serve!

With their constant search for the perfect sound, the Revols unintentionally placed themselves on the cutting edge. Richard was becoming quite the perfectionist. He knew what he wanted, how he was going to play it, and how he wanted it to sound.

Bob Kalmusky recalled, "It was all experimental. Because in those days, there weren't a lot of groups around them, especially around Stratford. There were a few in London. But really, the Revols were the first."

Placing Richard and the Revols in a historical context, it must be noted that even ten years down the road, when rock 'n' roll concerts had become the norm, live sound simply hadn't evolved to a place where groups could be heard clearly. The Beatles stopped touring in 1966 because live sound hadn't progressed to a level that could match their studio experimentation.

The Revols initiated these elemental sonic experiments in the late 1950s with a youthful enthusiasm and without pretense. With Richard and two of his Revols bandmates later making music a career, it's obvious that the members were blessed with a knack for musical innovation and the foresight to keep on improving. Till modestly remembered that there was "some experimenting our way, but there was no particularly driven force to work that way. Everything just happened."

The famous proverb "Necessity is the mother of invention" could not have been truer for the band of Revols. Playing shows through primordial rock 'n' roll gear, at underequipped venues, the band faced several technological and logistical challenges. They moved their own rickety Bogen PA system, with its single microphone, from show to show. Humorously, while playing the YMCA in Stratford, Doug Rhodes had to sing from the running track that circumnavigated the band 20 feet above the floor, because the cable from the PA was too short to reach the band on the stage below.

The Revols flourished because of their struggles; they didn't know any better. Momentum was building locally, and a following was taking root in Stratford and the surrounding towns. The band was now referred to by fans as the Rockin' Revols. They were gigging fast and hard and got proficient seemingly overnight.

The group played anywhere and everywhere around Stratford, Goderich, and London, at basement parties, school functions, YMCA dances, garages, baseball fields, and train stations. The Revols even played on the back of a flatbed truck. One local, Dean Robinson, remembered that it was a sunstroked summer outfield where Beak stood, Jerry Lee Lewis style, at his precariously balanced piano while banging away a bit too close to the precipice. One more duck step and he might have flown off the edge. When Richard stood up from his piano stool and hammered out rock 'n' roll chord changes, it always charged up the crowd and quickly became a highlight of Revols performances.

Another early Revols gig was in Turkey Point, Ontario, where Richard dressed in memorable orange pants and played both "Great Balls of Fire" and "Whole Lotta Shakin'" for an assembled crowd of rockers.

The Revols' other singer, Doug Rhodes, remembered Richard becoming the star of the show quickly because "he sang and played so well." In the Revols stage show, Rhodes sang the hit parade, the Elvis numbers, and the ballads, with Beak taking on the down-and-dirty bluesy numbers.

As rock 'n' roll's popularity ascended, so did the opportunities for the Revols. Cool cars, full dance floors, and the pulsating beat of tribal rock 'n' roll brought in eager crowds. The Revols were experiencing, and in turn disseminating, the same cultural and musical reverberations as the Teddy

Boys in England and rockers in the States. Music making was fast becoming an alternative lifestyle and a way for the party to never stop. Girls, music, and cars were the order of the day—and not always necessarily in that order.

Friends and classmates remember the Revols being worshiped by the locals and being considered gods by attendees of the Stratford Central Secondary School. By the end of 1959, Richard was sixteen years old and hot shit, born to entertain, a big fish in a small pond. He was often seen walking the Stratford neighborhoods with his slow gait, on the prowl for someone to jam with. If there was music to be had, Richard was there, enthusiastically showing off his most recent discovery or lick and, of course, ready to cause some trouble. He taught his bandmates John Till and Ken Kalmusky how to play the piano. He was constantly finding and learning new songs and looking for ways to improve his band's presentation. Everybody loved Beak; you'd be hard pressed to find anyone who'd whisper a bad word about him.

One schoolmate recalled Richard playing piano at his house for a group of friends and their parents. In the midst of a heated jam, Richard exclaimed to the assembled crowd, "I'm so horny!" When he turned to the gal on the piano stool next to him, he realized it was a friend's mother!

By the end of the decade, the group had developed a strong set of songs from a diverse pool of artists. Most of the group's song choices delved into the catalogs of Jerry Lee Lewis, Buddy Holly and the Crickets, Bobby "Blue" Bland, Ray Charles, Elvis Presley, and Ricky Nelson. Beak was the headliner on cuts such as Jerry Lee's "Great Balls of Fire" and Bobby Bland's "Little Boy Blue." Till remembered, "The strongest stuff was when Manuel sang Bobby Bland." Performances were also peppered with Chuck Berry, Mose Allison, and Richard's already show-stopping Ray Charles numbers.

Ken Kalmusky and Richard dressed up for a special occasion. Stratford, Ontario, date unknown. *Photo courtesy of Bob Kalmusky*

Returning home after an evening of performing or shenanigans, Richard queued up whatever song the group wanted to learn next on his turntable. When it was time for him to turn in for the night, he would drop the needle on the record and let it auto-return all night long. By the time he woke up the next morning, the words and melody were firmly lodged in his subconscious.

In true rock 'n' roll fashion, the group was causing disturbances at school functions. One of their schoolmates remembered when Till and Beak played at a high school assembly: "They wowed all us kids when they played Duane Eddy's 'Three-30 Blues.' We were shouting and standing on the chairs when the principal came into the auditorium and shut it down and banned them from playing again."

Chapter 2 | Revol-ution! (1959–1961)

The Revols played at the YMCA, YWCA, and both Stratford and Mitchell high schools. They took the stage at local venues like the St. Joseph's Parish Hall and St. Paul's and St. James's churches. Richard got the band shows at the Masonic Temple, and eventually the band got a nightly gig at the Wagon Wheel.

In addition to local rock spots, the band started to carve out a solid reputation performing at venues outside Stratford. They played up and down the southern Ontario coast in Port Dover, Port Elgin, Bayfield, Seaforth, and London, and up north to Grand Bend. The band was all quite underage, especially John Till, who was now fifteen and looked the part. That didn't stop them from playing in local watering holes, pounding beers, and jamming up a storm.

In contrast to the authoritarian attitude of the schools and the illegality of the bars, the perfect musical venue for the Revols ended up being one that was right in front of them: the Pavilion band shell. The multipurpose Stratford venue sat on a high, lush plateau on the south side of the Avon River. Nestled in the trees adjacent to the Stratford Theatre, it offered location, good acoustics, and a ready-made crowd.

During the summer performing season at the Stratford Festival, there was ample opportunity to provide a musical interlude for folks young and old. Employed by the City of Stratford, the band was provided a venue along a park thoroughfare, perfectly positioned to receive students and to entertain both patrons of the theater and locals who frequented the beautiful area.

The backside of the venue was enclosed and could hold dances and other local events in inclement weather or for special occasions. The Revols took full advantage of the facilities. After a hot afternoon of playing for anyone who cared to listen, when the evening air cooled the Revols moved inside and really got it on for their people.

Now that the group was attracting festival fans as well as students who were visiting from the States, they expanded their reach. Nubile and eager female students would wander over to the Pavilion on their lunch hour and embrace the driving steam-engine rhythms of the Rockin' Revols. Humid summer afternoons above the cricket fields saw Richard trilling the piano, with an icy beer tucked away just out of sight of parents and patrons. Jimmy Winkler's crushing drumrolls reverberated against the buildings of downtown through the thick afternoon air, with Till's and Kalmusky's amplified guitars the melodic sirens to entice the crowd.

Beak and the boys liked nothing more than an attentive audience of cute birds fresh from the protective nest of the Festival Theatre. These were heady times for Richard and his bandmates. Bob Kalmusky was witness to the ruckus the group would cause at the Pavilion: "Every time they played, it was packed. The dance floor was full. Whether it was faster tunes, rock 'n' roll, or the slow ballads, everybody danced to the Revols."

The group vamped on the churning rhythm of "Parchman Farm" by Mose Allison, who was a highly undervalued musical influence on Richard. He would lean into the microphone, veins popping out of his neck. The charged sounds from the band shell undressed the buttoned-up middle-class streets with youthful, fuzzy cadences. The Revols drove the Stratford kids and the visiting artistic elite wild. The Pavilion attendees and performers alike were searching for the exact same thing: a place to be yourself, get loose, drink, sweat, and dance. Alcohol was an integral element of the initial rock 'n' roll experience. The renegade adventures of sneaking around, imbibing, and then gyrating to a music that most parents could not or would not understand were exhilarating.

The Revols Live

In the summer of 1960, if you walked out of Festival Theatre and across the tree-lined ridge of Upper Queens Park and heard magic chords and the melodic rattling of R&B music from the top of the rise, you would have happened upon a Rockin' Revols performance. A typical Revols set list for an afternoon at the Pavilion or venue of a similar ilk may have contained the following songs:

"Return to Sender"	"Whole Lotta Shakin'"
"Love Me Tender"	"Hallelujah, I Love Her So"
"My Babe"	"Memphis, Tennessee"
"Three-30 Blues"	"Georgia on My Mind"
"Parchman Farm"	"I Got a Woman"
"No Sweeter Girl"	"Turn On Your Love Light"
"Share Your Love"	"Tossin' and Turnin'"
"Little Boy Blue"	"Sick and Tired"
"What'd I Say"	"Searchin'"
"Great Balls of Fire"	"Swanee River Rock"
"In the Still of the Night"	

Ransacking the R&B cuts they loved, the Revols quickly ascended to the level of real working musicians, in large part because of their constant gigging and endless practicing. Richard's church mate David Priest witnessed the change that Richard had undergone since the "teacher" had first provided him with impromptu lessons in the church basement:

> One time I was over at the Manuels when Richard was rehearsing in their living room with a group he'd put together. The band was doing all the current chart tunes, practicing for school dances all over the place, as well as a ton of other gigs.

Richard Manuel

This particular time the tune they were working on was "In the Still of the Night" by the Five Satins, and Richard's piano part was exactly the way it was on the record—even though he had mastered a whole lot of licks and phrases, which he could have played, but instead kept his part true to the original.

Beak was developing the traits of a true ensemble player as well as conjuring the enigmatic magnetism of a front man.

THE REVOLS ON THE RADIO

The culmination of Beak and his bandmates' hard work came when David Marsden, whose abilities would lead him to a fifty-year career on the airwaves, booked the group a recording date at CKSL-AM in London, Ontario.

An audio document of the session, thought to have been recorded around 1960, contains three professionally recorded songs. Marsden remembered that the band's goal was simply to get some songs on the air and pressed to vinyl. A friend of the group remembers ending up with a 7-inch record that resulted from the band's visit to the station.

The CKSL broadcast is the earliest surviving document of Richard and his pals in their rock 'n' roll element. It's a priceless artifact in telling the Revols' story. The first thing you hear is Richard's tinkling piano before the Revols tear into a rocket-fueled arrangement of the Well Street classic "Liebestraum." It's a song representative of beginnings, epitomizing the Revols era and documenting the young group caught up in the frenzy of rock music.

The lineup for the band is Richard Manuel, piano; Jimmy Winkler, drums; Ken Kalmusky, bass; and John Till, guitar (although both John and Garth Picot remember playing on the recording), with Doug Rhodes singing on both tracks. Richard wrote both of the original compositions and arranged the rock 'n' roll reading of "Liebestraum."

Winkler, who was lovingly referred to as the Hammer, is the art of youth on this recording as he deftly moves around the kit, punctuating Beak's rollicking piano figures with snap-crackle-and-pop triplets. The band is reeling and you can feel its energy. While the melody of the classical number remains, Richard greased it up with Brylcreem and plugged it into an electrical outlet.

Richard is still just a kid, laying down glissandos and chugging out left-handed piano bass like a seasoned veteran. What is particularly exciting about the recording is that the Revols are distilling their own brand of music by writing and arranging their own songs. This was not usual, since rock 'n' roll bands of this era were essentially cover groups; the songwriters were in the Brill Building in New York City, churning out hits for popular artists.

"Promise Yourself" is a Beak Manuel original, and the band smokes this one down to the butt. Of particular note is Till's (or Picot's) raunchy guitar tone and Chuck Berry riffage, which was slotted into the spaces left behind by Richard's active piano work.

The tentative lead vocals sit somewhat in contrast to the guitar, drums, bass, and piano, which are strutting with confidence. It's important for the listener to place the music of the Revols in the correct historical context to properly assess the musical strides they were making.

The last song on the recording is "Eternal Love," a Richard Manuel–penned track that his Revols bandmates recall as his first original composition. This song stays close to the popular I–vi–IV–V ballad framework of the era and illustrates the band's mastery of the form. The Revols arrangement is catchy, offering a dynamic contrast to the previous rockers. It must have been the jamming at all those school dances.

The three performances on the CKSL demo recording capture the Revols' abilities at the time. While the group leaned on deeper cover songs in live performance, the band was prepared to record original music when given the opportunity.

That visit to the radio station was the first in what would become an unbelievable yet seemingly predetermined series of events. It was thrilling for Richard and his bandmates to perform on the radio and to be heard via the same airwaves where they had gained their inspiration.

Beak and his Revols were on the cutting edge of a blade not yet realized in popular music, and Richard was the catalyst. He was writing, arranging, and performing original music.

While Richard's own voice wouldn't be heard on an official recording until 1964, he would unleash it outside southern Ontario in due time. The Revols were a mature band regardless of their age and were making their own luck. Little did John Till, Kenny Kalmusky, and Beak Manuel know that they would make lifelong careers out of these inaugural musical steps, forging a protective brotherhood yet traveling divergent paths, often intersecting through friendship and their shared beginnings in the Rockin' Revols.

"It was originally Ronnie Hawkins and the Hawks from Arkansas. Levon was the original and we were all pickup. Every one of us led our own individual group."

Chapter 3
LITTLE BOY BLUE
(1960-1962)

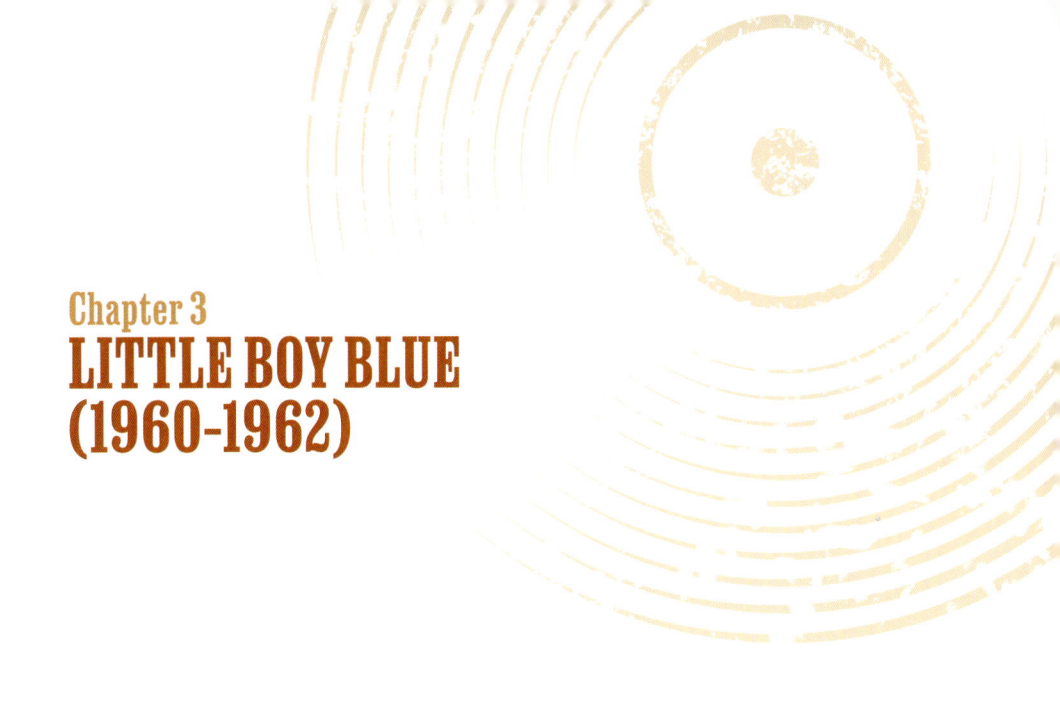

> Richard Manuel was a whole show unto himself.
> —Levon Helm

The Rompin' Ron Hawkins Quartet, a.k.a. Ronnie Hawkins and the Hawks, was a renegade Arkansas rockabilly outfit. The Hawk was the quintessential front man of the era, with a finite eye for talent and a knack for bringing any musical competition he faced into his own nest. The Hawk was keenly aware that surrounding himself with the strongest talent was the key to establishing the most powerful band.

Hawkins was larger than life in voice and stature. While he was a man who liked the finer things in life, he was an animal onstage, gyrating, duckwalking, and eying the girls in the crowd. The Hawk had developed into a charismatic lead singer while hanging around with other talented musicians stationed at Fort Sill in Oklahoma in the mid-1950s. Obviously not cut out for the military world, Hawkins decided to put together his own band. One young musician from Marvell, Arkansas, Levon Helm, was captured in Hawkins's talons and became a founding member of his Hawks.

Hawkins was a hard-ass who ran a regimented group. While he could shake it down and loved to have fun, he was serious about his craft. There were no girlfriends allowed, and no drinking or drugs, and you were expected to show up for practices when not performing, multiple practices. He was the big boss man—break his rules and you were gone.

The Hawks quickly became road warriors and played a plentiful Southern circuit of club gigs, all the while releasing several sizzling 7-inch rock 'n' roll records. Two of these singles, "Mary Lou" and "Forty Days," were trademark tracks at the turn of the 1960s. Hawkins and his Hawks had even gone so far as to make early television appearances on *The Ed Sullivan Show* and *The Dick Clark Show*.

The Hawk was always in search of a golden opportunity, and when fellow rockabilly road hog Conway Twitty mentioned to him that green pastures of gigs were waiting in the Great White North, Hawk wanted to know more. Looking forward to the chance to carve out an entirely new fan base and possibly become the "Canadian Elvis," Ronnie and the group arrived in Toronto at the end of 1958.

For the next few years the Hawks shuttled between the US and Canada and gained a deep circuit of support along the way. By 1960, they had worn a well-rutted gigging road from their home base of Fayetteville, Arkansas, up to Toronto. Crowds went crazy for the band, with its primitive showmanship and its leader's incendiary energy. As the Hawks increased their coverage over southern Ontario, it was only a matter of time before their flight path would converge with that of Stratford's Rockin' Revols.

Levon Helm was entrenched as the drummer and de facto talent scout of Hawkins's group, so by the time Hawkins first laid ears on Richard Manuel, he had already collected and caged Beak's future bandmates Robbie Robertson and Rick Danko for guitar and bass, respectively.

Robbie had joined the Hawks' ranks as a sixteen-year-old and, with Helm, became Hawkins's coequal musical arrangers and lead gunslingers. He told *Mojo* magazine in 2000, "Ronnie never thought of himself as this amazing musical entity. He knew he was an entertainer, and for him the smart thing was to surround himself with great talent."

Robbie had already fledged as a Hawk when he had his first interaction with Beak Manuel. One perfect evening in mid-1960 while hanging out between sets at the Hotel Imperial, nestled on the southwestern shores of Lake Huron, Robbie saw Richard, recalling to *Vanity Fair* in 2016: "I first met Richard Manuel when we were seventeen years old. He had been drinking that night and was somewhere between pure joy and deep sadness." He described the occasion in greater detail in his memoir *Testimony*:

> Between sets at the Imperial one night, [bass player] Rebel Payne and I wandered across the main drag in Grand Bend to a little burger stand for a snack. As we ate, a guy walked up and introduced himself, mentioning that he played piano and sang in a band that had opened for us a while back called the Rockin' Revols. I remembered him—he'd sung a terrific version of Bobby "Blue" Bland's song "Little Boy Blue." Rebel made some crack about the guy's "schnoz," his long, pointed nose, but rather than take offense, the guy laughed. "Yeah, that's why they call me Beak," he replied. "My name is Richard Manuel."

I shook his hand, but Rebel stood behind him making mocking gestures like he knew something I didn't. Then I got it: Richard "Beak" Manuel was drunk—a laughing, fun-loving sort of drunk, but drunk nonetheless. Richard's condition had puzzled me at first since nobody in the Hawks drank. We could hear Ronnie taking the stage, so we had to head back over. "I'm not old enough to get in the club," Richard called to us. "You're not old enough to be loaded either," replied Rebel.

Not long after Robbie's introduction to Beak in Grand Bend, Hawkins got involved in the musical futures of Richard and his bandmates. The Hawk was well connected and liked what he had heard about the Revols. Word was circulating through the same Canadian clubs that the Hawks frequented about the gangly kid who sang like Ray Charles and Bobby Bland.

No one with the Revols was surprised when Ronnie, Levon, and Robbie contacted manager Dave Marsden about the Revols sharing a bill with them.

Before they knew it, the Revols were taken under Papa Hawk's wing and began opening for the Hawks when they visited on their next tour. The two groups began to share stages at several well-known beach pavilions and ballrooms. One venue on the shore of Lake Erie in Port Dover was a favorite of both groups, a place called Pop Ivy's.

It was at Pop Ivy's during a steamy packed house that Ronnie Hawkins said to Levon after watching Richard, "See that kid playing piano? He's got more talent than Van Cliburn," the American classical piano sensation who was about the same age as the Hawk. Hawkins wasn't exaggerating. He observed intently as Beak's heavy barrel-aged tenor silenced a rowdy bar. He could feel Richard's emotional investment and its effect on the crowd. Patrons would cut their gossip and peer over their drinks to discern what the hell was emanating from the throat of the stringy kid with the big honker. Even though the Revols still had two singers at this time, the Hawk fell for Richard and his soulful serenades and rockin' rave-ups.

The Revols made new friends and joined in on the Hawks' already well-known lustful adventures. The bands teamed up for raging parties from Port Dover to Toronto and up to Great Bend, enjoying crazy acts of rock 'n' roll revelry. After every show were bacchanalian parties topped off with deep carousing and sexual revelry. In this age of peepholes, orgies, and after-hours sexual conquests, there were numerous backroom gang bangs and much booze-drenched debauchery.

The kids would go loony: they wanted this music; they longed for it. Both the Hawks and Revols provided it on numerous occasions. Both bands tore up and down the shore of Lake Erie on thick summer nights, playing in cramped ballrooms where kids poured like fizzy drinks out onto the beach, trailing their beer-stickied footprints into the warm sands of night.

The Hawks roosted in Grand Bend during their 1960 summer performance season, and the Revols came to visit, joining the illicit fun. Beak was often behind the wheel for notorious fast drives to the eastern shore of Lake Huron. In what was essentially a straightaway out of Stratford, he would test the limits of whatever vehicle he happened to procure.

Obscured by the mists of time, determining exactly when John Till left the group and guitarist Garth Picot joined is an inexact science. But because of his young age, Till was unable to travel for gigs that required him to miss school, and Picot, like Richard, quit school to pursue a rock 'n' roll livelihood.

Picot had woodshedded around the same haunts as the Revols and other southern Ontario musicians, in addition to being the lead guitarist of the Stratotones, out of Goderich. Picot was a tremendous player and in the loop of connected Canadian musicians. He had purchased Robbie Robertson's 1958 Fender Stratocaster when Robbie left for Arkansas on his own tour of duty with Hawkins. Picot had slowly been taking over guitar duties from Till, whose parents wanted him to focus on his studies.

Picot remembered in 2022 that "the Revols call me and they said, 'We need a guitar player.' And that was, late '60, might be early '61. . . . So, we practiced and I was part of the band." Picot ended up moving in with the Manuels at 138 Well Street for a while. He had quit school after finishing grade ten, and since he was unable to drive from Goderich to Stratford for band practice, he stayed with Richard's family. Picot remembers the move being in May or June 1961, and he was immediately included in the family's life and Beak's late-night radio sessions. A testament to the Manuels' unwavering support of Richard's ambition was how accepting they were of the additional mouth in the house. Around this same time, Richard let a neighbor boy named Danny who had fallen on hard times sleep undercover in a disabled car in the Manuels' backyard.

Picot said:

> What I remember is, at night, you could get all those Southern stations, in particular 50,000-watt stations. So we used to listen to them all at night. And that's where we picked up a lot of the rock 'n' roll. You know, not the pop song. We really hated all the stuff that was played on the radio, so we focused more on what we called real music from the southern US.

When the evening's musical excursions threatened to get too wild, the guys would nip over to their friends the Smith brothers' house.

Food, cigarettes, and strong coffee around the radio kept Richard and his pals fully enveloped in the excitement and mystery of being rockers. After the broadcast, Picot and Richard would hop in the Thunderbird for late-night ruminations and introspection. Cruisin' was not to be taken lightly in this era. Having access to and driving a car late at night was a cherished freedom and a rite of passage. Richard had his license, and his astute driving skills, or lack thereof, were becoming legendary among his friends.

Richard also took a liking to driving the car through one of Stratford's many board-flat farm fields at a moment's notice, illustrating his increasing penchant for unexpected and dangerous fun.

Though their late-night discussions could get philosophical, Richard's sneaky humor was often right below the surface. While he was a small-town guy in many ways, his comedic timing was advanced. It didn't matter if a joke was good or not; his delivery and timing were flawless. Richard's humor also reached the Revols stage, Picot remembered: "One time playing near the train station, we were onstage and Richard says to the crowd, 'Oh, here comes the train. You better stop it and let my brother Jack off!'"

By now, Beak and the Revols, with their new guitarist, had chiseled out a consistent gigging schedule around London, Stratford, and Kitchener, but with the additional shows with the Hawks, they began to have more-substantial hopes for their music.

Richard and the Rockin' Revols tearing it up, 1961. *From left*: Ken Kalmusky, Garth Picot, David Marsden, Jimmy Winkler, Richard Manuel, Doug Rhodes. *Courtesy of the Stratford-Perth Archives*

Richard and the Revols were teeming with talent and mystery. There was something street-smart about their attitude, yet innocent and full of passion. According to Levon's memoir, Ronnie Hawkins told the Revols that their exceptional abilities made him nervous. Richard modestly replied, "Thanks,

Chapter 3 | Little Boy Blue (1960–1962)

but you guys don't have to worry. You guys are the *kings*." That was a typically self-deprecating reply for Richard, blissfully unaware of how deep and fruitful the Revols vein of talent was.

Picot remembered, "Richard said he was going to make it. I remember he said that we got to be better than Ronnie Hawkins and his band. We've got to get our own sound, something different. So we were searching for the sound that would propel us into the limelight." Richard even toyed with the idea of giving himself a stage name, which was a popular trend for groups at the time. Thankfully, he stayed with Richard, and the stage name "Randy Paris" became Revols singer Doug Rhodes's nom de guerre.

Richard and the Rockin' Revols, 1961. *From left*: Ken Kalmusky, Jimmy Winkler, Doug Rhodes, Garth Picot, Richard Manuel. *Courtesy of the Stratford-Perth Archives*

At a high-profile gig of note in early 1961, when the Revols opened for Del Shannon at Wonderland in London, Ontario, it was clear that the group's hard work was paying off. The band received a boisterous response from the crowd, and the boys were feeling good about the gig. Even though Del Shannon was a well-known artist and had a hit song with "Runaway," which the Revols added to their sets, on this evening the band held its own with a popular mainstream act.

After the concert, Shannon and the Revols commiserated backstage in a dressing room. Soon after getting together, the musicians were approached by a group of female fans, flushed and breathing heavily, looking for an autograph. Del promptly stepped forward to provide his signature for his fans. One of the women, somewhat surprised, replied, "No, we want *his* autograph," pointing toward the doe-eyed, big-nosed rocker, as he casually sipped on a beer.

The Revols, 1961. *From left*: David Marsden, Ken Kalmusky, Doug Rhodes, Richard Manuel, Garth Picot, Jimmy Winkler. *Courtesy of the Stratford-Perth Archives*

Rock-A-Rama

Beak's performance at the Stratford Coliseum in the summer of 1961 changed the trajectory not only of his band, but also of Ronnie Hawkins and the Hawks . . . and in turn, rock 'n' roll history. Richard's showing onstage convinced Hawkins to rob the Revols of their most precious commodity and add the musical bounty to his already talented flock.

Revols manager David Marsden was essential to the Revols' increased popularity, as illustrated by the numerous opportunities he helped provide the group. The band was working steadily, with promotions ranging from radio shows to local newspaper ads, and a few reasonably high-profile gigs. By mid-1961, musical relationships had been solidified and the Hawks and Revols were very familiar with one another. Perhaps Marsden's most important coup was getting the Revols their biggest gig yet: a battle of the bands at the Stratford Coliseum, located at the fairgrounds on the edge of town. The scene turned out to be the launchpad that would rocket Richard's career into a twenty-five-year orbit.

Ronnie Hawkins had been circling the Revols and reached out to Marsden to discuss additional opportunities for the band. Marsden eventually traveled to Toronto, and after discussions with Hawkins and Robbie Robertson, he secured additional gigs as well as a slot for the performance in Stratford. The Hawk, who in 1986 called the Revols "as wild a bunch as you ever did see," loved to mix things up and knew that putting the Hawks and Revols head to head would make them both the better for it. Beak and his bandmates were keenly aware they were going to have to cut the Hawks in order to become their equals. With gritty playing, enthusiastic showmanship, and sonic knife wielding, they succeeded.

On June 30, 1961, at the Stratford Coliseum, Richard chiseled his musical name out of rock 'n' roll slag. The stage was set for the hometown Revols to go beak to beak with Ronnie and his Hawks. Rock-A-Rama '61 at the fairgrounds was a scene straight out of *American Graffiti*. The sprawling pastoral grounds crawled with every type of rocker in a 50-mile radius.

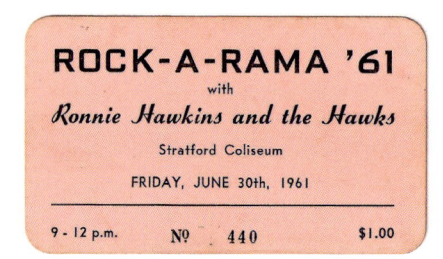

Rock-A-Rama '61 ticket. *Courtesy of Vince Gratton*

Courtesy of the Stratford-Perth Archives

Cherry cars, cigarette smoke, long skirts, and swept-up hair accessorized the tree-lined streets leading to the stone gates of the venue. A dance floor in the middle of the coliseum was packed with tables and chairs and eager music lovers. Because the show took place over Canada Day weekend, everyone in town seemed to be there.

After rousing sets by Picot's former group, the Stratotones, then Johnny and the Jaguars, the Rockin' Revols took to the stage. They dispersed a whipsaw of rocking R&B for the assembled crowd of fans and friends. The crowd was stung by their set and responded in kind with hometown love as the group blasted through the funky changes of Bobby Bland's "Farther Up the Road" and Ray Charles's "What'd I Say."

Midway through their set, the Revols ascended to another place and culminated in legendary fashion with their reading of Ray Charles's 1960 hit "Georgia on My Mind." Everyone was already familiar with the song, and Richard's rendition made them fall in love with it even more. The crowd, musicians included, absorbed every nuance of every line that Richard crooned. Girls and guys, birds and hawks alike listened intently to the flawless vocals—a performance so full of soulful resonance that Richard's singing stood in remarkable contrast to the gangly body that it emanated from.

Richard and the Revols stole the show, with a performance so powerful and poignant that attendees and rock 'n' roll historians still talk about it. Guitarist Garth Picot said, "We were very nervous, but [we] later learned they were a little nervous because of Richard. . . . It's hard to believe you were listening to a white kid." The Stratford Coliseum has since crumbled, with only its weathered ticket gates now remaining, but the spectral impressions of Beak and his Revols still haunt the festival grounds. Ronnie Hawkins was sold.

The Hawk was a top-of-the-line talent scout, and with Levon's and Robbie's assistance, his choices never missed a beat. John Till, in 2022, confirmed the Hawk's interest in Richard: "He had his eye on Manuel from the very beginning, from the first time he saw him. He offered him a job with the Hawks many times." Hawkins took the very best players he encountered on the road, recognized what they did well, and incorporated it into his own band. Richard was in his sights, and Levon agreed that now the Hawks would easily have the best singer around.

For the time being, Richard was more than content with his band of Revol brothers. If there was one thing that Richard Manuel could be counted on for, it was his loyalty. The Revols were close to breaking through, and he could feel it. A testament to how much talent was contained within the Revols is that both John Till and Ken Kalmusky would go on to rock 'n' roll success similar to Manuel's: Till with Janis Joplin's Full Tilt Boogie Band and Kalmusky with the Canadian duo Ian & Sylvia. The Revols were the farm team for a plethora of successful and vital rock groups that came from southern Ontario.

The Revols continued their dominance over the local music scene as Hawkins planned his next move. The Hawk wanted Beak in his band, but he faced a couple of issues. One, his band already had a stellar pianist and showman in Stan Szelest. The additional catch was that Richard didn't want to leave the Revols. But like any great collector and cultivator of talent, the Hawk had a plan. He was running a club in Fayetteville called the Rockwood and knew that Richard and the band could benefit from marinating in the South. He thought that by sending the Revols to play his club in Arkansas, he could kill two birds with one stone: he could fill his bar with a strong group while keeping an eye on Beak and his development.

Not long after the performance at the Coliseum, the Revols were playing downtown Stratford on the second floor of a hip venue called 42 Wellington. Manager David Marsden was scheduled to give Ronnie Hawkins a call that evening to find out whether the Revols' trip to Arkansas would be put in motion. Midway through the Revols' set, Marsden ran across the street to City Hall to use the pay phone and got the news: the trip was a go.

In one of those incredible moments of "Radio I Ching," where environment and art combine in stunning coincidence, Marsden returned to the Revols show in progress to let them know that they were going to be taking to the road and heading to the States. Marsden recalled:

> As I returned to the venue, I think I was on the first floor, I went upstairs, and as I was crossing in front of the guys playing on the stage, Richard was singing, "Tell your ma, tell your pa, I'm gonna send you back to Arkansas." It was just at the moment I held my thumb up, or whatever motion I gave to the band. At that moment in the song, that's the line that Richard was singing, and I've never forgotten that. It was really strange.

Richard and the Revols were stomping out the Ray Charles single "What'd I Say." They *were* going to head to Arkansas, a place of myth and a mystical home to the music they all idolized. This was a life-changing move for a group of middle-class Canadian kids in 1961. That they were too young to be patrons of the places they'd be playing didn't matter, because the Revols were too young to know any better.

With Hawkins's help, Marsden began preparations for the Revols' transformational transnational journey. He bought a 1956 Plymouth Fury for the band and rented a U-Haul trailer for a year. The band painted the trailer with the Revols moniker on the side and stuffed it to the top with their gear.

The final touch came through a Hawkins connection when the group went to Yonge Street in downtown Toronto to have matching suits made by famed tailor Lou Myles. They were provided a number of options, including some glassy blue silk suits that they ended up purchasing. Looking professional was a critical step in covering up the Revols' rough schoolboy look, although that's exactly what they were.

Mrs. Kalmusky was so excited for her son and the rest of the Revols that she sent the band to local Stratford hairdresser Les Debonnaire to get them perms. A photo of the group just after getting their hair done appeared in an ad in the local *Beacon Herald* on September 22, 1961, with the headline "For the smartest sport shirts in town The Revols suggest that you visit Hudson's men's wear department." An announcement for the band's upcoming Saturday night gig at Upper Queen's Park was placed in a banner across the bottom of the advertisement, where Richard is pictured "modeling a well-tailored and smartly styled dark-paisley-patterned sportshirt."

On September 28, the group was again pictured in the *Stratford Beacon Herald* with the cutline "A young rock 'n' roll group from Stratford named the Revols, who have played at various teenage dances in Stratford and district for the past year and a half, are leaving for a four-week engagement in Arkansas." To collect funds for the trip, the group continued to gig around the area, including a regular paying show on Friday nights in Goderich.

Even Garth Picot had his doubts about leaving Canada for the open road. At some point during preparations and rehearsals at Queen Street, a wishy-washy Picot was called out when Richard growled, "Hey, either shit or get off the pot." With Richard's subtle encouragement, Picot packed up his guitar in anticipation of their big move.

Another headline in the *Stratford Beacon Herald* days before their departure read, "Local Boys Make Grade—Revols Head for First US Tour." The accompanying article said:

> The boys will leave by car Sunday morning for Fayetteville, where their first engagement is scheduled for the Rockwood Supper Club on Wednesday, October 4. The band is under contract for four weeks at the club and then they plan to tour the state of Arkansas playing at various night spots.

The Saturday night before leaving, the Revols played one more engagement at a dance in Bayfield, where they were given a proper send-off. On Sunday morning, October 1, 1961, with a strong sense of anticipation in the air, Marsden and the five Revols piled into the Plymouth with their instruments and their musical hopes. The journey from Stratford, Ontario, to Fayetteville, Arkansas, covered 1,050 miles of highways and a border crossing. Richard Manuel was eighteen years old.

Barely a day into the trip, the clutch in the Fury burned up, so on Monday the band went to an all-night movie while it was repaired. On Tuesday they had to get a hotel room, and on Wednesday they finally made it over the border. At that point, all six boys slept in the car and at first light drove straight through to Arkansas. As the Fury and accompanying trailer kicked up dust close to the state line, the car finally gave up and everybody pushed the trailer to a safe location. They arrived in Fayetteville that evening and immediately set up and played for the club owners.

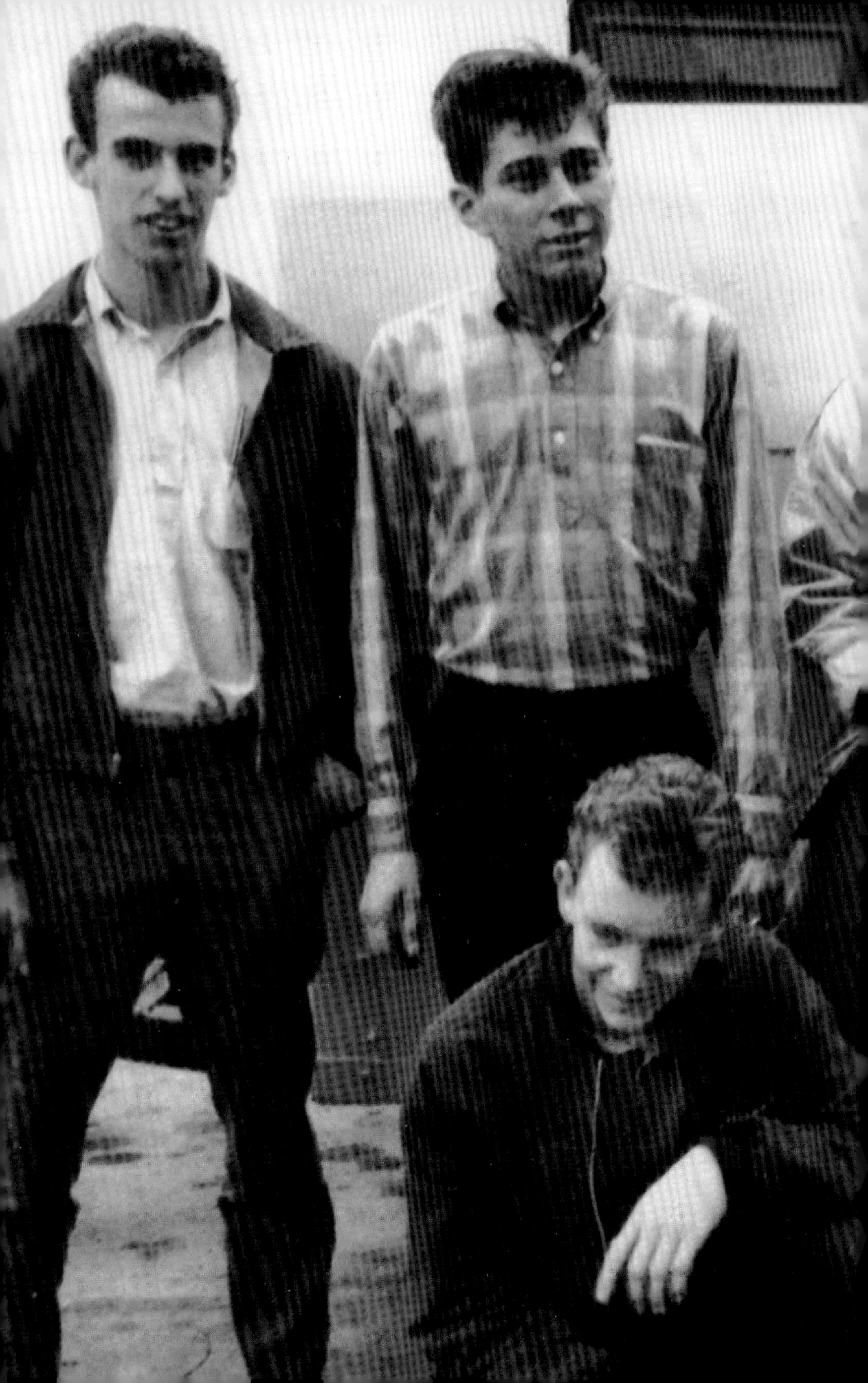

Leaving for Arkansas, 1961. *From left*: Richard Manuel, David Marsden, Garth Picot, Doug Rhodes, Ken Kalmusky, Jimmy Winkler. *Courtesy of the Stratford-Perth Archives*

Hitting the road: Richard and Ken in the front seat; Doug, Garth, and Jimmy in the back. *Courtesy of the Stratford Perth Museum*

The band arrived ready to swallow a huge dose of life as working musicians. This was an alien experience for the Revols, who had never experienced such things as segregation. Richard and his band were growing up fast, and the road was where they began their education. The boys took their exploits both musical and otherwise to extreme levels while subsisting on cigarettes, booze, and a rocker's nightlife in Fayetteville.

Hawkins bankrolled the Revols' trip and provided transportation as well as accommodations for the band in a stand-alone trailer he owned on the edge of the Rockwood property. The club was a sprawling stone building with three floors for music, dancing, drinking, and watching local sporting events.

The group left their mark on the trailer and crashed Hawkins's Cadillac just for good measure. They stayed up late, played competitive games of Monopoly, and ate Southern fried chicken and Texas chili. Richard lived up to his legend as the blue-flame flatulence king. The band rationed cigarettes and drank "White Lightning" moonshine procured by the locals. Richard would eat anything and everything; the guys called him "Garbage Guts." Hawkins was shocked at how much the Revols tore up, but they fit right in with the rest of the Rockwood rowdies. Richard was unleashed on the plentiful crop of American women who loved a good-looking rock 'n' roller. He and his bandmates were completely unsupervised in an era of unabashed sexual freedom. It was a good time to be a musician.

Letters from Arkansas

During his downtime, Richard's mind returned to the North and to his family in Canada. When the band was hopping, all was well; when given a chance to contemplate, Richard would retreat into himself. It was a theme that would become the norm when he was on the road. Not long after the Revols' arrival in Arkansas, Richard penned a series of letters home to his family, updating them on his adventures on the road. The letters held the return address of Rockwood Supper Club, Fayetteville, Arkansas.

> **October 8, 1961**: We had a little trouble at the border, didn't get over until Wednesday evening; after a good night's sleep we gave the club personnel a general idea of what we could do. They seemed pleased and we started Friday night pleasing a few more people and bagging more engagements.
>
> We phoned Ronnie Hawkins in Toronto, and from what he had to say it sounds like we'll be here for a while, he is coming here in a month with another bigger deal for us. He also mentioned something about a record contract but who knows?

A newspaper advertisement for the Rockwood from the *Northwest Arkansas Times* dated October 17, 1961, lists the Revols as the headlining act on Tuesday and Thursday evenings. The other nights of the week, the group poked around the surrounding areas for interesting and, they hoped, paying gigs.

The band had landed right in the middle of Arkansas Razorback country. On weekends, the group could find gigs at any number of house parties or fraternity get-togethers. Both Marsden and Picot remember the Revols playing several impromptu shows at local campus venues for both beer and coin. Word of mouth was powerful, and soon the Revols were playing all over Arkansas, Oklahoma, and Texas, sharpening their skills and sowing their wild oats. The group even appeared on a local rock 'n' roll television show in Tulsa a few weeks into their stay. Unfortunately, the film of this appearance no longer exists.

One crazy night at a University of Oklahoma fraternity party, things got insane. People were getting hammered, and there was an inch of spilled beer on the floor by midnight. The group played hard and fast on a raised four-post stage, which at the conclusion of their set was torn town and promptly fell on the band's heads.

Beak and the Revols continued their submergence into Southern life with gigs at the Rockwood or some witching-hour juke parties. The Revols' music drove kids crazy in Arkansas just as it did in Canada and was often the impetus for debauchery. While their gigging lives were flourishing, Garth Picot was never able to reconcile the band's bar life: "A real mystery to me is, two of us were only sixteen. I don't know why they let us play in the clubs because the age was twenty-one. Richard was only eighteen. So that's a major mystery to me."

Back at the Rockwood, after last call, is where Richard's talents started rapidly maturing. It was there that he developed and honed his craft. He threw himself into his work, even deeper than he had in Stratford. After the club had closed and the crickets would rise, Richard walked in darkness across the gravel lot from the trailer to the club steps and let himself into the Rockwood.

> **This Week's Entertainment at THE ROCKWOOD CLUB**
>
> Tues. Nite .... The Revols
> Wed. Nite .... The Del Rays
> Thurs. Nite .... The Revols
> Fri. Nite ... BoHanan & The Mint Juleps
> Sat. Nite (Dad's Day) ...... The Del Rays
>
> We think this is a week's entertainment you will enjoy. If you can find the time, come on out and see if you don't agree that good times can be had at The Rockwood Club.
>
> FOR RESERVATIONS
> Phone 2-6089 or 2-9684   **RONNIE HAWKINS**

Advertisement in the *Northwest Arkansas Times*

The Revols had a key so they could practice, and Richard took full advantage of this exclusive access. He would sit down at the piano, crack a beer, and, with no sense of self-consciousness, begin to howl and moan. He would start singing from the soft realms of sleep and move to the raspy heights of throat-shredding ecstasy. Richard sang until he was raw, flexing his muscle until it burned. He exercised it until he could control it and alter it expressively.

Revols singer Doug Rhodes remembered:

> Late at night when the club was deserted, Richard would spend hours in there alone, yelling and screaming, trying to get the raspy sound of the Black blues singers. After weeks of doing this, he developed that raspy-throated sound he was looking for.

What began as muffled pillow practice in his bedroom back in Stratford now was a rock 'n' roll reality. Nightly solo performances of the songs of Etta James, Ray Charles, and Bobby Bland at the Rockwood piano allowed Richard an additional reach into the authenticity of the blues.

Richard's formative days in the church choir and his musical education from the sonic teachings of WLAC were coalescing and exploding from his mind in Arkansas. Beak was hitting musical puberty. He was hot: he was getting laid, getting drunk, and rocking all night long. He could have stopped right at local legend. But he didn't want to be his father or punch a time clock like any other faceless factory worker. Richard was a blue-collar union man and understood there was no shame in a working-class life, yet he yearned for something deeper, something more fun.

Excerpts from letters Richard sent home to his family in October and November 1961 document the spreading of the Revols' musical wares across the South. Things were accelerating for the group, and that's just the way he liked it. A mention of both future bandmates Robbie Robertson and Levon Helm is an exciting piece of musical foreshadowing:

October 30, 1961: Last Saturday afternoon we did a TV show and it went over very well. The minute we went off the air, a club owner phones the studio and asked us if we would go to his club for an audition, which we did. He may use us the second week of November, things are looking up! I had better let you know that all of us are fine, and we are having an absolute tear here.

November 3, 1961: Our petition to the immigration came through and we are allowed until April 26, 1962. We are running into some great deals, thanks to Ronnie and the boys, and we may be touring the entire area. Ronnie has some great plans for us in the future. Today Robbie and Levon helped us to arrange a couple of our songs and give us a few pointers. Ronnie offered to let us have his entire house to use as our living quarters while we stay here. It seems we've become a division of Ronnie Hawkins Enterprises, if you can imagine that.

Hawkins's molding of Beak had been initiated whether the Revols knew it or not. The group was dizzy with possibilities. But before they could return home, they were lined up to have one additional adventure. After an evening appearance at the Rockwood, Marsden and the band traveled from Fayetteville to Memphis to take care of some business with immigration. Richard discussed the exciting misadventure in a letter home to his mother.

November 16, 1961: Last Sunday night we left for Memphis to check with the immigration people, Ron loaned us his '59 Cadillac for the trip. We got into Memphis about 2:30 in the morning when all of a sudden, we were surrounded by police cars, just like in the movies. We were charged with car theft, it was suspicious, 6 guys and a car that didn't belong to us. We were locked up for the night until they proved our story. They released us at noon on Monday, can you imagine that?

I am going to take this opportunity to wish you a very happy birthday, Mom, and I wish I were home to celebrate with you. I will try to send you a little something if I can find anything you'd like.

Imagine, indeed: six Canadian kids packed into a shiny pearl of a 1959 Caddy on a West Memphis highway in the dead of night in 1961. David Marsden takes up the narrative:

We drove in very late at night, because we had done a night at Rockwood, like two in the morning. And we were crossing from West Memphis into Memphis City. At that time, we were driving a brand-new Cadillac. Ronnie had upgraded the car situation for us. And so, we're bopping along and we passed through West Memphis on into Memphis City. As we pull onto, I think it might have been like a small thruway for the time, suddenly, we were surrounded on all sides by police cars!

The Revols, 1961. *From left:* Richard Manuel, Ken Kalmusky, Garth Picot, Doug Rhodes, Jimmy Winkler, David Marsden. *Courtesy of the Stratford-Perth Archives*

Revols drummer Jimmy Winkler remembered it too:

> So we're driving around in the middle of the night in a 1959 white Cadillac and all of a sudden four cop cars surround us and cut us off, just like you see on TV.

Unable to provide proof of ownership for the Cadillac, the fledgling Revols were arrested and taken to Memphis City Jail under suspicion of having stolen the vehicle. Additionally, Garth Picot was separated from the band and taken to a juvenile jail because he was only sixteen. After about thirty-six hours in the clink, word got to the station that the kids weren't criminals. Quite the opposite, they were underage musicians from Canada!

Oddly enough, the group's innocence was verified with the dipstick on Hawkins's Cadillac, which was engraved with his name. In exchange for the unplanned evening behind bars, the officers asked if there was anything they could do to make up for the mix-up. Richard brazenly said, "Well, we'd like to see Elvis's house."

After some quick deliberation by the police, a business card was procured, and the boys were told to present said card at the gate of Graceland when they arrived. As soon as the Revols were released, the band headed to Graceland, gave the card at the gate, and were let in. Although Elvis was away filming a movie at the time, his uncle was there and gave the Revols a tour.

Marsden remembered, "We spent a couple hours, I guess, at Elvis's house as a bunch of teenage musicians. That was a pretty big deal. We were all absolutely amazed that it happened." As a memento of their visit, Kenny Kalmusky removed a sticker from one of Elvis's many cars. The sticker was for an air-conditioning company, appropriately named "King Air."

After another month of hard gigging and maturation at the Rockwood and various Southern locales, the Revols packed up and headed home for Canada. On December 21, 1961, the Revols returned to Stratford and, according to Doug Rhodes, encountered "a great reception from our supporters." The group strutted with confidence and was primed to keep the momentum they had gained in Arkansas going. They continued to gig around southern Ontario but found getting into some of the clubs to be a bit more difficult than what they had encountered in the South.

As the new year of 1962 approached, a timely opportunity presented itself to Richard. Almost immediately after the Revols' return to Stratford, the Hawk swooped in. Stan Szelest had manned the Hawks' piano stool consistently until he decided to go to school and get married. He told the Hawk he would be leaving the group and returning to Buffalo, New York.

Stan Szelest was a legendary maniac of the highest order on the blacks and whites. He had a shimmering mound of blond hair that bounced when he trilled and boot-kicked notes out of his piano. Richard couldn't compete with Szelest's juiced jangling and onstage antics. In the end, that didn't matter, because Hawkins knew that Manuel was the best soul singer around and played proficient enough "folk" piano to take over. Richard's aesthetic was more Bobby Bland and Ray Charles than Jerry Lee Lewis and Stan Szelest. As Robbie Robertson said in his memoir, "He sang like nothing Canada had ever heard before and played proficient piano into the bargain."

Any criticism of Richard's piano playing comes only in comparison to Szelest's virtuosic abilities. They were contrasting players in that Richard wasn't a soloist; he was a collaborative player who specialized in deft accompaniment. Richard was good, but Szelest was an accomplished player. The decision to fill the void left by Szelest was an obvious one: it would be addition by subtraction with Beak. The Hawk had witnessed his onstage magnetism firsthand and was smitten with his stunning voice. Hawkins knew that those elements would negate any sort of falloff in the piano playing. He didn't delay and reached out to Richard to join the Hawks.

Richard's eventual decision to leave the Revols was difficult. He didn't just up and leave; he was faced with a terrible conflict. These were the friends that he had developed unbreakable bonds and grown musical roots with. This wouldn't be the last time that Richard couldn't muster up the fortitude to make a decision. He was brimming with ambition and was solid as bedrock, but if it came to pushing, Richard would rather take the shove.

Richard also had that long-standing pact with his best pal and drummer Jimmy Winkler, where neither of them would leave the Revols without the other. Garth Picot remembers Ronnie Hawkins calling Richard several times to convince him to join the Hawks, but Beak would only reply, "No, I've got a pact with my friend."

It was at an early 1962 band meeting that Jimmy told Richard that this was his chance and he had to go. He would be foolish not to take the opportunity, and after great discussion, Richard grudgingly acquiesced. His sister-in-law Kathryn Manuel said in 2022 that this internal conflict about leaving the Revols illustrated Richard's faithfulness to friends and family. He wouldn't step out on his own without full support of his friends, because loyalty was important to him.

It wasn't only his bandmates that Richard had to worry about; it was also his parents, Kathryn Manuel recalled:

> They [Pierre and Kiddo] were supportive of him. I think at the point when he did go and join the Hawks, I mean, he left high school. As a parent, what are you going to do? You're going to support them and "hope for the best" kind of thing. Pierre just beamed about Richard; they were so proud of him and what he had done. And wherever he went, he would always mention that Richard was his son and how well he had done. They were very supportive of all of the children.

With the unwavering encouragement of family and bandmates, Beak took the job with Ronnie Hawkins and the Hawks. By 1962, there was no doubt that he was the best singer in southern Ontario and possibly on the entire Eastern Seaboard. He was going to be a Hawk, the only issue being that Hawkins hoped his piano playing would eventually catch up with his vocal talent.

Robbie remembered, in a 1978 interview with *Rolling Stone*, what Richard's duties in joining the Hawks entailed: "The piano was used as a rhythm instrument, with solos on organ or guitar or sax. So, when you stopped playing rhythm to play a solo, the rhythm wouldn't drop out—the piano was still holding it." Richard could defiantly hold down the rhythm as good as anyone, as his soon-to-be-unearthed prowess on the drums would attest.

John Lennon and Keith Richards were also rhythm players, with approaches and unique musical fingerprints that made them essential elements in their respective bands' overall sound. It's the same in Richard's case. As every musician who shared a stage with him can attest, it was never about showing off, it was about *feeeeeeeel*. Richard had big ears and an arranger's attentiveness.

It's easy to lose sight of the fact that Richard was a very young man in 1962. The reality of living on the road with a gang of musical strangers with the potential for failure looming large was both exciting and frightening for Richard, the obvious factor being that kids just didn't quit school and leave home to become musicians. Richard was in control of a destiny he barely realized he had.

Levon wrote in his memoir that Richard told him with a sheepish grin that at age seventeen, he'd already been drinking for seventeen years. Robbie confirmed, "When I first met Richard, he was seventeen and he was already a drunk." It's important to recognize that Richard did like to get wasted. It gave him confidence; it tamped down his ugly trait of low self-esteem, either imagined or ingrained. Richard wasn't short of anything but confidence, and alcohol made that a nonissue. He'd raise a bushy eyebrow while his heavy-lidded eyes unfocused into a kind of gentle middle-distance squint when he'd had a few.

Friends familiar with Richard knew that after a couple went down, some sort of low-voiced, smart-ass drawl was close behind. There was nothing earth-shattering about Richard's vices. In this era, artists, actors, musicians, and the working man all soothed their ills with drink. Richard was living the life of a bluesman, and alcohol was a critical prop. He liked to drink a lot—beer, whiskey, and later Grand Marnier and champagne—but it was not yet his entire existence. Just a part of it.

The Hawk recalled in 1996, "Richard had the greatest voice in the world, great throat, great phrasing. I guess he must have had a drinking problem then, but he never messed up in performance; that's what mattered to me." Richard would become legendary for his ability to perform while self-medicated. But in the early days, his will was too strong and his talent too substantial to let drink take over. The alcohol was a crutch to get over his shaky confidence and was the fuel to his party attitude.

The Hawks' Beak

By the end of January 1962, Richard was a full-fledged member of the Hawks. The Revols watched him get on a plane in London, Ontario, ready to soar to his biggest musical adventure yet. Regardless of the result, the bonds between Richard and the Revols were unbreakable. The memories forged and the music created would connect the band members forever. Richard was uneasy and scared, but also focused and inspired.

He moved seamlessly into the Hawks' ranks. He was funnier than shit and as horny as they come, both prerequisites for Hawkins and his guys. Musically, as Robbie remembered in his memoir, Richard was "just a stone rock 'n' roll rhythm-and-blues head" as well as an "incredibly beautiful soul."

Rick Danko, from Simcoe, Ontario, had also recently joined the Hawks' nest. He loved country music, sang high and lonesome, and instantly became Richard's brother in mischief. Simcoe was just south of Stratford, and while Rick was a little bit more country to Richard's rock 'n' roll, they had a musical kinship.

In Levon's memoir, Rick remembered Richard's debut with the Hawks: "Richard's first night was a real baptism because Ronnie was real drunk, and he just pulled the curtain back, showed Richard the crowd, and told him, 'Let it ride, son!' . . . He brought a lot of powers and strengths to the group. He brought in gospel music from his church upbringing. Plus, he loved to play and come up with new things. It was like having a force of nature in the band."

Shortly after Richard joined, Garth Hudson left his London, Ontario, group the Capers to come on board with Hawkins. Ronnie again had to wheel and deal to get Garth into his group, bargaining with his folks to make it happen. Garth was a professional, and his parents were not so eager to have him gallivanting around the provinces with the Hawk.

The agreement reached between Hawkins and Garth's parents was that Garth would provide lessons to everyone in the band and get paid for that in addition to the group's gigs. It worked: Garth Hudson would join the band in a perfect final addition. It was the best thing that could have happened to Richard as well. He and Garth would become one keyboard assemblage. Garth would provide Richard with the exact tools he needed for success. Their individual playing ultimately complemented each other so perfectly that the resulting bacchanal of sound stamped the Hawks with a new sensibility. Garth said to the *Woodstock Times* in 1985, "When Richard and I hooked up—Richard had the voice and also this great rhythmic feel called energy piano—I went to organ."

Garth fully embraced the novel dual-keyboard attack of the Hawks and took a certain pride in teaching Richard new things on the keys. Garth is a musical genius, a term that gets thrown around frequently, but as true as blue in this case. Any discussion of Richard's success in the Hawks must be mentioned concurrent with Garth's arrival. The combination of the two keyboardists not only gave the Hawks a unique onstage look, but more importantly, a swirling cavalcade of sound from their respective stools—Richard the quirky rhythmic inertia, Garth the melodic encyclopedia. Coupled together in musical perfection, the two keyboardists invented an entire world of inspired sonics. Plus, Garth was an excellent saxophone player, so when he'd leave his perch from behind the Lowrey organ to blow, Richard could keep things moving at the piano or slip into the organ spot.

The Hawk recalled to Carol Caffin on her BandBites website in 2007 that Richard "had that throat that I liked." He continued:

> I wish I coulda sung like Richard. And so that's why I hired Garth—to teach Richard everything he could about how to play the piano properly. He put in two hours a day, five days a week. Then Richard practiced with us—we practiced two hours, so that's four hours. And then we played two and a half hours a night, so that's a lot of music. In a year's time, Richard was playin' real good and tearin' 'em up everywhere singin'.

What drove Richard's propensity to delve into the hard living, sexual longing, and religious fervor of the Black blues artists is one of the great mysteries of his talent. When he sang the blues, his vocals ignited like the frayed electrical ends that touched off the voices of Chester Burnett and Ray Charles. Richard sang as though he had lived through the dreadful wind and rain of a "Stormy Monday." With a snag in his throat that suggested a singer on the edge, he made you believe that he had been through the "Hard Times" that Brother Ray's mama had warned about.

Richard's response to the blues came from another place. He couldn't have lived that existence, though he tried. His gifts allowed him to tap a powder keg of emotional torment that in turn connected him deeply with the music's own dramatism.

Richard's musical education accelerated with Garth Hudson's direction, the constant onstage performances, and evenings filled with a strict regimen of practice. His musical foundation was built on failed piano lessons, enhanced with David Priest in the basement of Ontario Street Baptist Church, continued with the electric jolt of charged sounds from WLAC, and disseminated through his own boozy brand of blue-eyed soul.

Richard immediately took the Hawks to a new place. Levon said in his memoir, "Richard was a show unto himself. He was hot; he was about the best singer I'd ever heard. Most people said he reminded them of Ray Charles. He'd do those ballads and the ladies would swoon. To me, that became the highlight of our show."

Robbie remembered in *Testimony* that "Richard's voice was there from the start, but when I got to know him, I found he was also one of the nicest, sweetest people you'd meet. He was funny, but when someone else was funny, no one appreciated it more than Richard."

Ronnie Hawkins and the Hawks were complete, with Levon Helm, Robbie Robertson, Rick Danko, Garth Hudson, saxophonist Jerry Penfound, and Richard Beak Manuel. All the individual members, minus Penfound, had at one point led their own respective bands before joining Hawkins. Now as their talents coalesced under the Hawkins banner, they would go on to become the best band in the land.

Brian Pawley was a southern Ontario guitarist and eventual member of the Hawks who lived in Owen Sound and later London, Ontario, during this era and witnessed firsthand the power of the full-strength, newly formed Hawks. In 2022, he recalled thinking:

> "My God. This is beyond any music that I've heard in my life." But it was one of those things where I can't explain it. I think if you were there, you don't have to explain it. But it was like getting hit in the face with a blast from a turbo jet. Incredible. And then, you know Danko sang a song and it's good. And then of

course, Levon sang, and then Manuel sang. He was doing a Bobby Bland song, and I went, "Holy shit balls!" Just the improvement in his voice and his piano playing from the changeover [to the Hawks]. Incredible. The bands [Ronnie had] were always good, but that unit in itself was like going up a ladder. Ronnie reached the top of the ladder. I can't describe it. I still to this day, people say they couldn't have been that good. I say you don't even know, and you never will.

Richard's spotlight moments in the show were instantly becoming highlights of Hawks performances. He quickly factored vocally in most of the group's repertoire. When not singing lead, Richard layered harmony over and under the vocalist, creating showstopping stuff. Nothing had changed since the Revols' pavilion dances, when Beak would croon and the women would swoon. Sometimes this would get Richard as well as his bandmates in trouble with the male attendees.

In performance, the patient drawl that friends were accustomed to was transformed into a deadly serious howl, a trembling vocal tinged with the charred remnants of a previous life. Whether in the choking smoke of a lakeside Canadian club or the musty, beer-soaked ambiance of a Southern roadhouse, Richard's vocals sounded as if they were pulled from the gritty grooves of a Chess record. His throat seemed to be a coiled bundle of loose threads of influence. It felt as if one tug and they could all unravel onstage.

Richard related to the blues because he felt them. His voice was a direct conduit to his deepest emotions. One of Richard's idols, B.B. King, said in his autobiography, "To me, singing is like talking: if it ain't natural, it ain't right." Constant use made his ability only stronger and more confident. By the time he had been with the band a few months, he was a superior singer and more than adequate pianist, as proven by available recordings. Hawkins said in 2007, "We played six days a week and we practiced five; that's how come they got so good. They were probably the best white R&B band in the world at that time."

The Hawks as a traveling band was quite progressive. The group perpetuated an edgy hillbilly attitude while playing with a sophisticated feel. The Hawks' sound pushed against the popular music of the time through song choices and aggressive expression. The music was forged at the edge of chaos and didn't conform to the current trend of soft and bland radio that was championed by a number of teen idols. They were ahead of the curve as curators of blues and R&B. America didn't respect its blues players, and it took groups such as the Hawks to earn that respect for the Southern artists that influenced them.

There was a balance: Ronnie knew how to keep the crowds happy and the club owners content. But even at such an early juncture, the music trembled with a harnessed power. As a guitarist, Robbie was a serious force to be reckoned with. His Fender Telecaster tone was original, aggressive, and coveted by several groups who encountered the Hawks. The music would sometimes get too far out and intense even for Hawkins!

The Hawks played every single waking moment, often searching out gigs if they had free evenings. They could usually be found on a rickety splintered stage in a backwoods roadhouse, where the music was sexually charged, amphetamine powered, and quivering with serious attitude.

Slim in stature, Beak would hunch over the piano, shoulder cocked like an abandoned teeter-totter, and initiate a gangly dance across the keys. His boot heel pounded out time on a hollow and flexing beer-dampened stage as the Hawks cashed out the introduction to "Money (That's What I Want)." When his vocal cue arrived, he reclined to capture a deep breath and howl a reverberant cry. His inspired and gritty vocal "whoa hos" that punctuate the early Hawks recordings cut through the sonic sludge of antiquated tapes to elicit a thrill.

Richard's encyclopedic knowledge of rhythm and blues influenced the Hawks' deft cover choices such as Bobby "Blue" Bland's "Don't Cry No More," Ray Charles's "I'm Going Down to the River," and Etta James's "Something's Got a Hold on Me." While the group was obligated to play Hawkins's hits, they often dug into some off-the-shoulder-of-the-road R&B cut that they worshiped.

His already masterful use of vocal dynamics and control was stunning, a testament to his choir days. His technique could span the range from the softest whisper to the most raucous holler. His fearlessness and articulation in singing the music of both Bland and Charles, as well as of James Brown, confirms that Richard was no fool when it came to being aware of the breadth of his vocal abilities. He could sing slow and blue with a furrowed brow so the young rockers in the dance halls could press up against their dates. Then suddenly he could rave up the crowd into a fighting froth with a pulsating number. While not yet composing his own music for the stage, he chose the songs to which he related to on the deepest level.

By 1962 the Hawks were already the hardest-working group on the road. The Southern jukes were full of people who packed heat, didn't take kindly to strangers, and would pop off in a bad moment or if they got the wrong look. The bandstand wasn't immune to fighting or violence, especially with the amount of carousing going on by the band.

"The Hawks could eat and pop pills and fuck with the best of 'em," an unnamed Arkansas musician told *Rolling Stone*. Richard rocketed through adolescence and became a man in the bowels of bars from Toronto to Mississippi. His trickster attitude, jokester aesthetic, and love of women drove the Hawks to new levels of insanity on the road . . . but also instilled in Richard an unrealistic way to live.

His joyful and ambitious personality immediately fit into the group just like his piano playing. He was funny and mischievous and always up for a bit of chaos. He had an innate ability to say just the right line at the essential moment. Richard communicated with effervescence, whether speaking or singing. He kept things light and played until the lights went out, no matter how crazy things got.

One evening in Hawkins's Cadillac after a gig, Richard had taken over driving duties so Ronnie could get some sleep. Hawkins did not allow smoking in his car, just one of his many rules to keep his group in line. In typical fashion, Richard immediately lit one up and put the pedal to the floor when he got behind the wheel. While looking for a clandestine way to stub out his butt middrive, he unintentionally put the cigarette out on the sleeping Hawk's head!

No one in popular music was playing the Hawks' brand of music in the States or in the UK at this time. The Rolling Stones, Yardbirds, Animals, Bluesbreakers, and Them were still specks on a distant yet approaching horizon. Richard and the Hawks were blazing a trail toward where rock 'n' roll was headed.

It can be confidently confirmed that when Beak broke out a smoky reading of Ray Charles's "You Don't Know Me" or James Brown's "Please, Please, Please" in a Canadian beach pavilion, it wasn't the normal operating procedure of the early 1960s. For many attendees, Richard's renditions of the blues were their first exposure to this type of music.

He was authentic and tapped his influence straight from the root. Drummer Levon Helm was born into Arkansas rhythm and blues. Richard and his Canadian bandmates were as well, only through osmosis.

In the Studio

In February 1962, not long after joining the group, Richard experienced his first real studio session. Hawkins and his Hawks traveled to New York City to record a single, with Richard appearing on "Mojo Man," the B side of "Arkansas." Famed songwriter and pianist Mort Shuman was in the studio to play on "Arkansas," but "Mojo Man" can be documented as Richard's first official appearance on a record. Equally important, the grooves of the single immortalized the first time that the members of the group that would become the Band played together on a record.

"Mojo Man," though not straying too far from the ruts of the rock 'n' roll road, offers up the soon-to-be-instantly-recognizable Hawks/Band groove. Rick and Levon tighten the rhythm's hinges, while Richard swings like a windblown back-porch door. His playing, while rudimentary, establishes the endearingly rickety rhythm that would become his aural fingerprint.

Richard's wagon-wheel chording and always-on-time piano playing were driving forces behind the Hawks' musical movements. He remarked to the *Woodstock Times* in 1984:

> That's one thing I discovered playing piano: if I was unsure, if I knew I was gonna lose it [the beat], I'd keep my foot going and stay with my foot no matter what I hit and I'd get away with it. If you stop, you falter and slow up and get off the beat . . . that's what drives people crazy.

His playing, while not virtuosic, developed its own personality through his practice of quirky chord inversions and his natural knack for accompanying melody. Garth's tutelage only increased his available library of ideas. Sometimes discussed in less-than-shining terms by others, Richard's piano playing climbed a noticeable arc from 1958 through 1962. He was the dependable left-handed pulse and a wellspring of sneaky variations on a song's theme.

Richard wasn't trying to be Otis Spann or Thelonious Monk; he accompanied the Hawks with a fill-the-gap aesthetic where syncopated licks rose to the top before dropping back into the churning whole of the rhythm section. Those maturing support skills would become the sonic adhesive for all his music.

Richard onstage with Ronnie Hawkins and the Hawks, London, Ontario, date unknown. *Photo courtesy of Serge and David Daniloff*

Chapter 4
KEEP THE ENGINE CHURNING (1962-1964)

By 1962, Richard was immersed in a rock 'n' roll life: the women plentiful and willing, the booze abundant, and every night a never-ending riot. But something was getting lost in the madness. Despite the fringe benefits and amazing music, the jobs were a grind, travel was hard, and Richard was getting homesick. Even though he had long yearned to leave his hometown, he missed his parents and talked about his family often with his fellow Hawks.

To his credit, he was busy playing six nights a week to writhing crowds from Arkansas to Canada with a group that had bonded like war buddies. Though he had left one musical family behind in the Revols, he had found another just as intimate in the Hawks. He still had his doubts but figured if he had a good enough time doing it, everything would work out in the end.

The Hawks were moving at a pace that would put modern gigging bands to shame, shuttling between a base at the Rockwood Club in Fayetteville and spidering throughout the Southern states into Texas, Oklahoma, and back to Tennessee, all the while kicking up dust with Hawkins's Cadillac. Richard joined the Hawks as a kid and by 1964 was a practiced twenty-year-old professional who could play with anybody.

Ronnie and the Hawks had the seventeen-hour drive between Fayetteville and Toronto embedded in their consciousness. Back and forth they would go, pushed by the influence of the mousai . . . and girls. The band knew every heavy, whore, pisser, pothole, and truck stop along the route.

The Hawks took turns driving in shifts. Bleary eyed, Beak would get behind the wheel of Hawkins's Caddy under the buzzing lights of some lot in Illinois. The Hawk needed his rest, and Richard relished the dose of white-line fever. He would save his best moves for when the guys passed out: blowing stop signs, edging lawns, and pushing the car's engine to its rattling limits.

On these long-distance runs, the group may have performed at prebooked locales, or wherever felt like an appropriate place to land. Once the Hawks ended up at their chosen venue for the evening, then came the realities of road living: what to eat, where to sleep, and who you were going to end up with at the end of the night. For Richard, it was an adventure he relished.

The sexual conquests and self-medicating seemed like fair compensation for having to deal with the cramped quarters, long hours, rip-off artists, and constant hassles and fights. Beak avoided confrontation for the most part, but he knew when the band was being fucked over and did not suffer fools gladly. Richard knew that you could get run over by a truck tomorrow, and he would rather not waste time on matters that would take him away from his focus: music and fun.

Fused by their supreme talent and increasingly shared vision, the Hawks understood the power and possibility of their rock 'n' roll collective. They were already known on the circuit as hard-partying rockers who would fill the bar and take your girlfriend. Hawkins told author Barney Hoskyns, "Crazy as a loon he [Richard] was. He just partied, chasin' the girls with Levon. He was drinkin' all along, but in those days, he could hold it."

It was all part of the deal back then; the road was a constant test of will and endurance. Richard would try anything once, probably twice, and then do it to such an excess that it would become a badge of honor. He could handle his booze. Sure, he'd puke off the side of the stage every so often, but he always made the gig and acted the professional musician. If he didn't perform up to standard, Hawkins would have his ass and he'd be out of the group.

Musically, the Hawks' excursions were not for the faint of heart, nor were the venues pictures of perfection. There were rounders, hustlers, one-legged go-go dancers, and gun-toting roughies. Robbie said to *Rolling Stone* in 1968:

> We played some real tough joints, where the people didn't come to hear you, they came to mess with you. They'd flick cigarette butts at you and throw money at you and steal your things. And, if you got past that, then they'd listen to you.

There were fights in the parking lot, holes in the roofs, and varying degrees of illegalities taking place behind and in front of the stage. At one high-quality job, Richard and his bandmates had to sleep overnight in the club with their equipment so it wouldn't disappear.

The Hawks' music reflected the reactions of the crowds. The group was contentious and played loudly. Some evenings the music would swell with so much energy, it would threaten to split at the seams. Levon rattled glistening triplets on his ride cymbal, and Richard would rise inches off his stool while bashing away at his keys. The small clubs were ill equipped for the power of the Hawks' sound. The band had gained callouses from their constant work on the stage. Robbie succinctly summed up what the band was all about during this time: "Stomp."

Just like the members of any working group, the Hawks paid their dues. The Beatles were going through their trials of becoming a band in Germany at the Star Club, and the Hawks were earning their keep by working roadhouses in the States. It was an entirely different time to be on the road for a maturing rock 'n' roll group. It wasn't easy for a soft soul like Richard to navigate the hard ways of the music business. The early days of the Hawks weren't far removed from payola scandals and rip-offs, and desperate musicians were easy targets for shysters. Beak was open all night and welcomed everyone into his circle. Some of those friendly folks didn't always have his best interests at heart.

In contrast, the group's visits back home in Canada offered a much-needed dose of normalcy before they returned to the hardships of life on the road. Robbie's mother's home in the Cabbagetown area of Toronto was a favorite of the guys for rest and a home-cooked meal. Richard often returned to Stratford to see his parents or to play with his former Revols bandmates. Several of Richard's friends remember that he always came home in the early days and never forgot to look up his pals for a party.

Beak tore up and town the streets of his old stompin' grounds, often at unsafe speeds with a bottle in his hand. He would pick up Chuck Kelly or any of several pals and search out a watering hole where he could sit in with the locals. He never forgot where he came from, even if he never wanted to return. On one of these visits home from the road, Richard and Filbert used the opportunity to concoct a functioning whiskey still on the stove in the kitchen at Well Street.

While now performing music through most of his waking hours, Richard was still soaking up the sounds of his R&B idols and assimilating their approaches into the Hawks' sets. One reason he was able to sing so convincingly was that the songs he sang were the ones he related to deeply.

When the band was relaxing backstage, music by the Temptations and the Staple Singers was often spinning on the turntable. The Hawks worshiped the stylings of the Staples and mined their catalog for influence. Ray Charles's 1962 LP, *Modern Sounds in Country and Western Music*, as well as Bobby Bland's *Two Steps from the Blues* and *Here's the Man!*, were recordings that Richard held close and often listened to for inspiration. The Hawks added several cuts from the recordings to their stage show, with Richard injecting his own signature enhancements to the Hawks' souped-up arrangements.

Chapter 4 | Keep the Engine Churning (1962–1964)

The Hawks Onstage

The earliest audio documentation of the Ronnie Hawkins and the Hawks stage show is from a Christmas dance at Fayetteville High School on December 10, 1962. Captured by an enterprising taper who recorded the show with a single microphone, the recording offers more than acceptable sound and an array of Beak Manuel highlights. The performance finds the Hawks in full flight on the concert stage and documents the conclusion of Richard's first full year with the group.

Listening to the recording, you can almost smell the aroma of rubber gym mats and lacquered gymnasium floor. The tape is a vital representation of what Ronnie Hawkins and the Hawks were all about in this era. Members of the student body were dressed to the hilt in gowns and suits for an elegant evening of teenage dancing and petting. The Hawks, not much older than the students, were primed to provide them with an evening of raucous rock 'n' roll.

Ronnie and his Hawks were something completely out of the ordinary. Their one-of-a-kind presentation of electric blues and rockabilly music was authoritative and well respected by their traveling contemporaries. The Hawks' work ran the gamut: they could play requests, popular instrumental cuts, and authentic R&B all in the same set. It was this contrast in styles that made them such a respected group.

By the time of this particular concert, mainstream rock 'n' roll had diverted to the route of easily digestible pop confections. Even Elvis had gone Hollywood. Ronnie Hawkins and the Hawks were torchbearers, raiding the catalogs of mature blues artists, gospel troupes, and deep-cut soul singers. They reveled in paying homage to their musical heroes while developing an exclusive tactic for expressing their craft.

While the Hawks were just musical interpreters, albeit stellar ones, at this point in their development, they were using their interpretations to navigate their way to becoming true artists. Almost every band of this era focused on interpretation as opposed to composition. Garth Hudson told *Something Else! Reviews* in 2015:

> At first, we played what you would call cover material, but the very best that could be found—from Delta blues through the guitar and harmonica tradition and up through the uptown players. . . . Richard admired Bobby "Blue" Bland as a singer, for example, and Ray Charles. We had all our sources.

The debut of Beak Manuel in the spotlight on the Fayetteville High tape comes a bit into the first set with a steamy version of T-Bone Walker's "Stormy Monday." It's fitting that this cut is the earliest available documentation of Richard onstage with the Hawks. He deftly and confidently navigates the blues changes, learned via Bobby Bland's 1961 rainy foreboding of the dreaded weekday.

Rick Danko and Levon Helm are rhythmic rain on the glass, dynamic in their response. Richard pleads for mercy from Monday in a voice of restrained power. The verses gradually gather in intensity before tumbling fearlessly into a vocal downpour. Richard can be heard answering his own appeals with trickling melodic keystrokes and by emulating Bland's standard aside, "and this is what I say."

When he begins the second verse, Richard plays it cool at first. He then moans out a more serious demand for mercy. Hudson answers this emotional outburst with impassioned splays of Lowrey organ. The performance is so astonishing that it's hard to believe that musicians so young could be so authentic.

The double banger of "Hey Bo Diddley" segued into "Who Do You Love?" elicits a full-band orgasm. The group completely grasped the timeliness of "Who Do You Love?," and not long after this performance they headed to New York to record it as a single. On this performance, the group is as tight as a jailhouse gate, blowing out some of the most primal rock 'n' roll that has ever been committed to magnetic tape. Robbie strangles his Telecaster while Richard thumps out a jacked-up Bo Diddley beat on the upper registers of his piano. Levon, the pulse of the band, keeps everyone on the straight and narrow while Rick slides around his fretboard with airy moans.

On an up-tempo reading of Howlin' Wolf's "Howlin' for My Baby," Richard clobbers out woody sets of splintered triplets, encouraging the groove forward as Robbie and Rick take a stroll out to the yard to sip cherry wine and look at the moon.

There is no better example of the Hawks at their best than to hear them blasting through Etta James's religious proclamation "Something's Got a Hold on Me," featuring some raucous Beak Manuel howls. The song was a favorite of the band and remained in their arsenal of songs until they stopped playing clubs. Richard pushes the musical tension to its limits in the preamble, vacillating between two vocal timbres over Garth's righteous chording. The band celebrates its newfound faith by ripping through the high-tempo verses before culminating in a closing crescendo of Richard's exultations and Garth's exclamations that fight over the group's collection plate.

Richard plays honky-tonk piano while Hawkins takes over the vocals on a chugging version of "I Got a Woman" before playing what would become the first available recording of Richard Manuel singing "Georgia on My Mind." This rendition is exactly what you would expect, a soft and gracious Richard emulating his idol in flawless tribute.

THE **HAWKS** ONSTAGE

It was only a bit over a year removed from his career-changing performance with the Revols at the Stratford Coliseum, and it is easy to understand what all the fuss was about. Richard's vocals are visceral and the Hawks' orchestrated arrangements increasingly intuitive.

The Fayetteville recording is a prime example of a Ronnie Hawkins and the Hawks concert of the era. The set, built around blues, instrumentals, and hoochie-coochie, gives us a fantastic insight into the originality of the group in its prime. After a chug-a-lug instrumental jam on the "Peter Gunn Theme," Richard plays fast and hard on a killer version of "What'd I Say," a cut he sang during the Revols days.

The Coasters' "Searchin'" grooves so hard it hurts. While Hawkins takes the lead vocal, it is the Manuel-Danko-Helm backing vocals that foreshadow a late '60s Band rehearsal. They stir up a formative pot of what would become the group's famed three-way vocal blend, while the Hudson-Manuel keyboard work spices up the sauce. This successful approach is also used to stellar effect on a version of Sam Cooke's "Bring It on Home to Me."

At points during the show, Hawkins would leave the stage to take a breather and prowl the venue, giving each member of the Hawks a moment in the spotlight. Richard always took full advantage of these opportunities. On Bobby Bland's "Don't Cry No More," he switched into his late-night Rockwood Club throat. While the vocal track feels distant on the recording, the power in his delivery is evident.

Ray Charles's "Hard Times," from 1961's *The Genius Sings the Blues*, a song Richard would sing until his final days, is given a magnificent reading. Hearing him unleash such a chilling and world-weary vocal is astonishing. The fervent emotion and soulful conjuring are stunning. His dynamic mastery of the mood and channeling of Charles's intent is one of the vocal gifts that separated him from other singers.

The first and only recording of the Hawks performing Ray Charles's "I'm Going Down to the River" is a powerful exclusive. A dusty Danko-and-Helm groove frames what is Beak's finest early live vocal. When he testifies that he's going down to the riverside to jump in, believe it. The sonic alchemy of the Hawks' instrumentation rattles off the recording.

Someone in the crowd cries out, "Yeah!" when Richard shreds his throat to soul-bearing smithereens in the middle eight. Robbie lightly adds shading as Garth blows the doors ajar with a drafty solo. Richard returns for the verse, veins in his neck like taut lines, and lets one go from the pit of his gut. The band lands perfectly on the rocky shoreline, with Penfound's and Hudson's honking exclamations concluding a superb display of musicianship.

THE HAWKS IN THE STUDIO

Not long after the performance and into the new year of 1963, Ronnie and the Hawks headed to New York for another single session. "Bo Diddley" backed with "Who Do You Love?" is one of the most incendiary slabs of rock 'n' roll the Hawks ever served up.

The A side is all serrated edges, and the Hawks engage aggressively, even though Diddley's famed original single quivered with chorused strums and sneaky percussion. Robbie's guitar playing is molten distortion, his rhythmic approach a crosscut saw throwing sparks. Richard contributes an excitable upper-register piano part that quotes the central rhythm against Levon's alternating primordial groove.

"Who Do You Love?" on the flip side was a stage standard for the Hawks and perfectly encapsulates what they were all about in 1963. Richard again thumps out the Bo Diddley beat in the higher register. Hawkins growls from the recesses of his being, the guitar work starts to leak around the seams, and before long the lid has blown off. Richard powers up the groove, as Robbie's string bending screams skyward before falling back into a bluesy sliding roll.

Surprisingly enough, Garth Hudson doesn't appear on either side of the single. Rick Danko plays rhythm guitar while Ray Buchanan takes over bass duties. The single disappeared in the US but did reach No. 8 in Canada. Ronnie Hawkins and the Hawks were legitimate, and it seemed like only Canadians knew it.

Richard Manuel

Postcard from Richard to his parents, postmarked May 5, 1963, as the Hawks were headed to Nashville to record. *Courtesy of the Richard Manuel family*

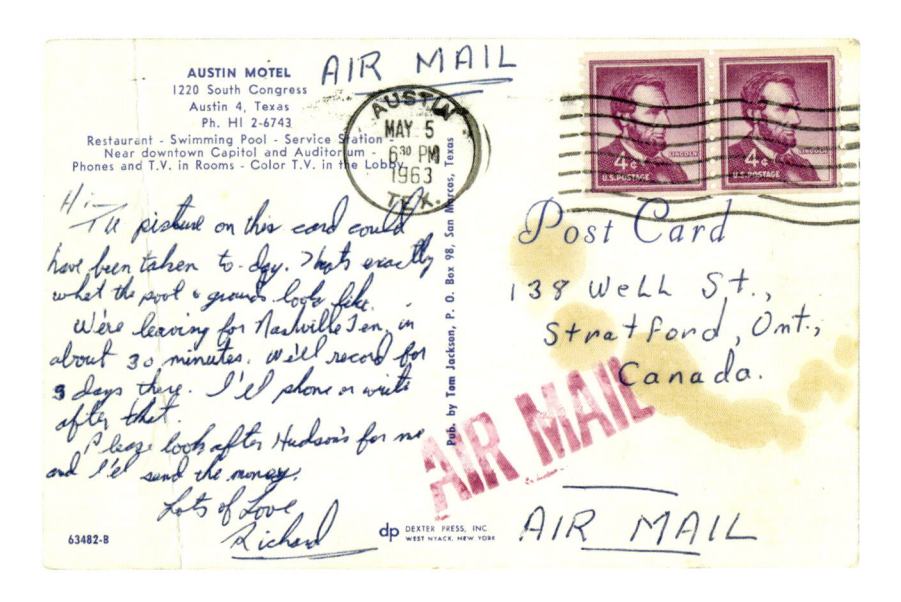

The Rules of the Road

Hawkins kept the Hawks busy throughout 1963, keeping them on the road for long stretches of time. When they returned to Toronto for concerts at the famous Le Coq d'Or at 333 Yonge Street, Richard's brother Filbert and his wife, Katherine, drove down to visit him.

Everywhere he went, there always seemed to be something happening, and he suddenly had a little bit of money from the gigs. He also had a group of adoring fans, including a sixteen-year-old girl from Aldershot named Cathy Smith, who started to follow the band around southern Ontario after seeing them in Hamilton earlier in the year. Richard had quite a few girlfriends, and Smith was involved with other members of the Hawks. At seventeen, she gave birth to a baby whose father was never identified, even though she maintained that it was Levon.

When Levon told Smith he didn't want anything to do with the child, it was Richard who was the most caring and understanding. Richard even sincerely told Smith one boozy late night that he would happily marry her. She graciously declined because she was in love with Levon, but she treasured Richard's unabashed sweetness toward her. She remembered Richard in her memoir as "just like his singing voice—sad, sweet, and soulful, a little boy lost." They would meet again.

By sundown, Le Coq d'Or had curvaceous go-go girls dancing in cages and stiff drinks being served up by the gallon. Le Coq d'Or would rise to prominence in downtown Toronto in part because of its connection with Hawkins and his band. The venue was famous for its chintzy western theme, including faux saddle seating and blood-red walls. It was Ronnie and his Hawks who were bringing in the crowd. One musically inclined and sharp-dressed patron of Le Coq d'Or who dug the Hawks sound was Mary Martin.

Martin lived and worked in Toronto and just happened to be Albert Grossman's secretary. Grossman was the manager for several artists, one being a famous folk singer named Bob Dylan. Martin, who loved a good band, took a special interest in the Hawks and the music she was hearing from the Le Coq d'Or stage. She was smitten with the entire group but took particular notice of the handsome man with the incredible voice seated at the upright piano.

Often the crowds that attended the Toronto performances were the same people partying with the group after hours. Word of mouth kept the room packed and the band well fed on temptations. Richard remembered the insanity of the Hawks' days at the Coq, telling *Time* in 1970, "Lots of bring-out-the-wine-and-turn-up-the-music parties, lots of people in one room sweating."

It's impossible to overstate the steamy rave energy kicked up when the Hawks really got it on at the Coq or Friar's Tavern. The group conjured swells of onstage catastrophe that were unheard of on live musical stages in this era. The go-go dancers stood in suspended animation in their cages when the Hawks shoveled sound from a quarter-moon formation on the small stage. It was as if the Hawks forgot they were a hired dance band until Hawkins demanded them back to earth with a stern reminder of who was paying the bills.

The band was pissing off club owners, riling up college kids, and surprising themselves on a nightly basis. Part of the reason the group would eventually move on from Hawkins was the astronomical musical growth that they were experiencing. As Richard said in the film *The Band Is Back*:

> It was kinda like boot camp. We drove ourselves to as near perfection as we could get, to the point that we would really thrill each other. Where there was almost a clairvoyance and we'd know before it happened if someone was gonna do something different.

The group developed a musical empathy that was driven by subtle signals and eye contact. Onstage there was a gestalt linkage between the musicians. These recurrent interactions would cement tacit musical agreements that would serve the group in the years to come. Richard said to *Rolling Stone* in 1968, "There are five of us, but we think like one." While the band was thinking as one unit, the chatter in the crowds was also about the guy who could sing better than Ray Charles.

Ronnie Hawkins was slowly being left behind by the rock 'n' roll Frankenstein's monster he'd created. By piecing together the best and most-talented musicians he encountered, they became more powerful than he could ever have imagined. The group wished they could play more blues under Hawkins, and his rules and regulations regarding girlfriends, drugs, and music tied the band up in knots. Ironically, it was this discipline that molded the group into a musical power.

The group was continuously taking a crash course in life lessons onstage and off. Hawkins and the Hawks made local connections in the towns they visited, for varying means of protection on the road. Town after town and club after club were dotted with various hookups for numerous needs. Rick said in *The Band Is Back*, "We were kids, you know, playing in bars that you were supposed to be twenty-one to play in, and we were seventeen, eighteen, nineteen. It can get outrageous when you're out there that young."

Richard got the girls flush when he would croon "Share Your Love" to the front row, which often caused issues with attending boyfriends. Hawkins always referred to Richard as a homewrecker, and for good reason. No matter the relationship status of a chosen female, Beak would move in. There were several close calls, pregnancy scares, and fights. While Richard would discreetly avoid confrontation, Levon would engage, deploying a steely look that would seat even the most aggressive patron.

Hawkins recalled to *Rolling Stone* in 1969, "They were boys when they started, but they were men when they finished. They'd seen damn everything there is to see. They practiced, played, and fucked in every town you care to name. Real dudes, man."

As the Hawks matured, the music got increasingly good, or as Robbie said to *Rolling Stone* in 1968, "hard, fast, and tight." The group was making around $1,000 a week and living well. Ronnie was the star, but the group's members were the aural magicians. It wasn't easy work. The group was reaping benefits, but they were also grinding the stone to dust at the same time. The endurance to perform required youthful stamina and deep ambition; the hard traveling took a toll.

Ronnie Hawkins and the Hawks at the Cedar Crescent Casino in Port Elgin, Ontario, summer 1963. *From left*: Garth Hudson (*behind pillar*), Ronnie Hawkins, Levon Helm, Robbie Robertson, Jerry Penfound, Rick Danko, Richard Manuel. *Courtesy of Wayne McGrath*

Not Just an Ordinary Bar Band

The group was constantly driving from Arkansas to Texas, Tennessee, and Oklahoma, across the gritty back roads and through the whipping dust devils of the South. While they were still a club act, contemporaries the group met on the road were taking note of the group's abilities. Carl Perkins was impressed by them, and another admirer was Harold Jenkins, a rockabilly singer who was touring the greener musical pastures of Canada. Jenkins, later known as Conway Twitty, picked up on what the Hawks were laying down. Word spread like a tipped drink on the bar when club owners and fellow artists were impressed by or, alternately, scared of their competition. Unlike the music world of the twenty-first century, fueled by social media, most bands of the Hawks' era were forced to develop a following through grassroots efforts and street cred.

The variety of music that the Hawks were playing was designed to keep people dancing, the booze flowing, and the customers having a good time. The club stages weren't the place for creative indulgence. The start of the musical conflict between Hawkins and his fledges began here: he wanted to maintain a delicate balance in his stage show. His job was to keep the bar filled. The crowd expected to hear certain songs, the club owners demanded it, but the group was opposed to playing the current chart hits.

Whether they were playing instrumentals, gutbucket R&B, high-octane rockabilly, or back-seat ballads, the Hawks were, in Hawkins's words to *Goldmine*, "probably at one time the very best rock-and-roll band in the world." The group knew it too, and they were steadfast in their belief that they had something worthy of deeper inspection.

It was during this time that Richard began to expand his palate from beer to something of a higher standard. Not unlike one of his musical idols, Bo Diddley, Richard had taken a liking to drinking the French liqueur Grand Marnier to smooth his edges. Mr. Diddley was a great proponent of the sticky-sweet, orange-flavored beverage, since he advised that it prevented his singing throat from drying out in smoky environments (see *Bo Diddley's Guide to Survival*). Richard was all for trying out whatever Diddley recommended.

Grand Marnier soon became Richard's essential beverage of choice. He began to carry the long-necked bottle in a crooked finger, dangling like a pendulum, occasionally pulling it to his lips for a hearty gulp. With a toothy grin and low-key drawl, Beak would lean in, telling anyone who'd listen the important facts behind his new favorite drink.

The Hawks' flock began to drift. Hawkins was changing too; he was starting a family, and priorities were shifting. His inflexibility was also beginning to grate on the other members. The Hawk brought in an additional vocalist in Bruce Bruno to help cushion his more-frequent absences. None of this mattered to the tight-knit group of Hawks. Levon, Richard, and Rick knew that they could vocally carry the performances just fine on their own. Levon was certain of it and felt that with Richard Manuel they had the best singer around.

LIVE AT THE WINDJAMMER

There is a circulating reel-to-reel field recording from February 1964, very close to the conclusion of the Hawks' run with Hawkins. In the limited scope of the tape, you can hear a definite pulling away from the usual Hawks set both in song choice and musical attitude. Richard has undoubtedly taken on a greater focus as the lead singer.

The recording from the Windjammer in London, Ontario, carries a sense of the room's stagnant air of perfume and cigarettes, underscoring the ribald ambiance of the event. You can almost feel your feet sticking to the floor and see Hawkins leering at your date from the stage.

The tape begins with an essential and vicious version of "Who Do You Love?," brimming with the sonic debris and sexual energy that let a listener discern the slow molt of the Hawks' current feathers. When the Hawks kicked up dust with the detonations of "Who Do You Love?" in concert, the song wasn't a question but a serious and pointed threat.

The band idles with a restrained power, percolating with edgy energy, recoiled and ready to strike. The crowd responds to the propulsive churning with exclamations of inebriated ecstasy. Beak's rubbery chords punctuate the pounding groove.

The Hawks are tight and sound like they're going to burst. The music is dangerous and the drama thick while the band plows through the verses. Hawkins begins to moan over the seething froth. The Hawks grab on to this encouragement and race into the song's change with an array of angry Robbie Robertson phrases and excitable responses from Richard.

In performance, the Hawks cracked "Who Do You Love?" like an egg, revealing its insides and using it as a vehicle for their own musical aspirations. Their furious and frenetic playing acts as a statement of gaining their independence from Hawkins and a declaration of their fast-developing musical personality.

Robbie recalled in a 1978 *Rolling Stone* interview: "When the music got a little too far out for Ronnie's ear, or he couldn't tell when to come in singing, he would tell us that nobody but Thelonious Monk could understand what we were playing."

Surpassing ten minutes, the "Who Do You Love?" jam includes demented Hudson playing and concludes in a wire brush jumble of string scrubbing by Robbie and thrashing instrumentation by the rest of the band. During this vamp, Hawkins lends the embarrassing aside, "Beak! She's only fourteen.

That's your speed . . . I'm second!" At the song's conclusion he adds, "We got a lot of requests. We gotta do some slow ones for the sake of the people who're kind of rubbing around on one another out there."

Richard then gives the assembled throng the opportunity to bump bodies. His tender reading of Bobby Bland's "Share Your Love," with his voice as emotive as Bland's, shows him completely in touch with something deeply personal. "Share Your Love" was the song Richard always returned to, and he never failed to nail it.

Things get funky with the sonic showcase of Bland's "No Sweeter Girl." Richard drives the group into a waist-deep groove. Levon rides the bell of his cymbal, lending the cut a hip swing. Beak "whoa-hos" his way through Bland's verses, and after a double-snare crack from Levon, the Hawks fall deep into the pocket. The tape carries some high distortion, but Richard's voice audibly rattles light fixtures. Levon and Rick keep it cooking while the horns blow well-placed punctuations. The Hawks are R&B thumping at its finest, slick as oil and taut as leather.

A beautiful moment takes place at the first big break, when Richard plays a descending line on the piano, hitting the boogie-woogie button just in time for a sax solo. Near the song's conclusion, the band drops completely out, leaving Beak to really get into it, vocally fanning the flames while accompanied only by Levon nailing a beat to the floor with his right foot.

While the levels on the recording are unfortunately hot, the tape is really kind to Richard. It aptly documents that he was becoming something more than a proficient rhythm player. He had acquired the ability to insert the appropriate melodic quote in precisely the right spot. It was a gift that when given the chance to fully develop would inspire his own songwriting.

The Hawks Leave the Nest

By the time of the next available recordings in June, Hawkins was well in the rearview mirror and the Hawks were busy developing a new stage show, one where Richard became the undeniable lead vocalist. The music's shift was subtle yet perceptible. The group still played full-throttle rockabilly and blues, but there was a movement to a more attentive and jazzy sensibility. The Hawks were developing patience, finessing dynamics, and finding space for each of their respective sounds. They could still blast holes through dance hall walls with "30 Days," but they could also drop like a feather into water with "A Theme from 'A Summer Place'" or Nat Adderley's "Work Song."

After Hawkins's departure, the group gigged for a bit under the name the Levon Helm Sextet before deciding to keep the recognizable Hawks name and settling on Levon and the Hawks. It wasn't an easy proposition for the group to break free from the protection of the Hawk, but they knew their own destiny was too good to deny. Bill Avis, who had met the Hawks in Toronto, took over managing the guys, and before long the band was getting steady gigs without Hawkins. Robbie remembered in his memoir *Testimony* that "our set list of songs and our whole stage presentation were shaping up, and our confidence grew a little bit each night."

During early to mid-1964, into the beautiful chaos of Beak's musical development came another important name: John Hammond Jr. Hammond was an acoustic blues player and son of John Hammond Sr. of Columbia Records fame, who, ironically enough, had discovered Bob Dylan, Michael Bloomfield. and a host of other musicians. Hammond Jr. was performing a solo acoustic blues show in Toronto at the Purple Onion and, at the insistence of a friend, went to see the Hawks onstage just up the street.

Hammond recalled seeing the band at the Concord Tavern at 925 Bloor Street. He was introduced to the group, dug their authenticity, and joined them onstage to play some electric blues. Hammond was a purist and felt that the group also shared a sturdy awareness of and respect for the genre. He was knocked out by the Hawks' abilities and walked away impressed with Richard's vocal prowess.

He recalled in 2022, "Richard Manuel, I felt, was one of the main cogs of the group. He could sing, I mean he could *really* sing. And he could really play. . . . He knew all the good stuff. He was a blues guy."

Hammond approached the Hawks' music from an alternative musical space—oddly enough, a space shared by his friend and contemporary Bob Dylan. Dylan and Hammond were predominantly acoustic players and had just started to brainstorm ideas to front electric bands.

Hammond continued, "The band was just tight. They were really good. I was so impressed." He was impressed enough that the Hawks were the guys he wanted to back him when he began to hatch his plans to record an electric blues LP.

Not long after the kindling of that musical friendship, the Hawks headed to New York City for a big bite of what the metropolis had to offer. Levon's memoir, *This Wheel's on Fire*, relates how the Hawks played a two-week residency at the famous Peppermint Lounge, where they performed from 9:00 p.m. to 3:00 a.m. The Hawks in a twist joint? What a combo!

Robbie remembers Hammond showing up to the Peppermint Lounge and jamming on Billy Boy Arnold's "I Wish You Would" and Howlin' Wolf's "Spoonful." For some reason, the club's ownership wasn't cool with these blues shuffles; they pulled Levon aside to ask, "What is this shit you're playing!?"

The boys got themselves into all sorts of trouble in the Big Apple. But when they weren't chasing women or a good time, the Hawks assisted their friend John Hammond with his upcoming record. These sessions resulted in an electric blues album released in January 1965, *So Many Roads*. Richard and Rick Danko were not involved in the recording, but through no choice of Hammond's. "I had a deal with Vanguard Records," Hammond said. "I had recorded a year before with a band put together by a guy named Herb Corsack. There was no piano called for on the session."

If it would have been up to Hammond, he said, he "absolutely" would have taken all the Hawks as his band. That idea would ultimately be undermined when a folk singer named Bob Dylan cast his eye on the Hawks, especially guitarist Robbie Robertson.

It's hard to know whether Richard was disappointed about not making the Hammond session, but he had to have felt slighted a bit. Regardless, he and Rick, who had formed a bond as the younger guys in the group, took solace in the fact that they were in New York doing what they loved to do.

Summer Nights at Port Dover

By the summer of '64, the Hawks were back on the circuit, playing almost every night. There are two famed audio documents of Beak and the Hawks soaring on the stage post-Hawkins. These recordings from July 1964 feature Jerry Penfound still with the group and contributing saxophone. As the audio attests, the band is fully ripened on the vine.

Fan Bryan Davies attended the Levon and the Hawks performances at Pop Ivy's Ballroom in Port Dover, Ontario, on a July evening and decided to take along his Philips reel-to-reel to capture the show. Davies remembered in 2021, "I set the recorder up backstage with the mic draped over the band's column speaker to capture the balanced mix of voice and instruments."

Levon's biography relates how after the Port Dover shows, the group drove to Quebec City for a weeklong run, then back to the Embassy Club and the Grand Hotel, and finished at the Brass Rail in London, Ontario, by the second week of August 1964.

Davies picks up the story:

> A few weeks later, when the boys were performing at the Brass Rail in London, I was able to visit their motel and set up my recorder to play back the Port Dover tape. As Levon, Richard, and Rick listened, they were awestruck with their performance, and I have heard from a reliable source that after the guys heard how good they sounded, they made a firm decision to proceed on their historical journey to become the Band.

The recordings that Davies made of those wild formative evenings are forensic musical documents that help listeners more fully appreciate Levon and the Hawks in performance—and the power of Richard Manuel live onstage.

One of the July Port Dover reels begins with a stimulating version of Buddy Holly's "Not Fade Away." Richard can be heard percussively entering a jittery call and response with Robbie during the first solo break. The first vocal highlight, Bobby Bland's "No Sweeter Girl," is much like the Windjammer recording, which Levon introduces as a dance tune. Once again, it's a performance decorated with dual horns and a grindy groove.

Chapter 4 | Keep the Engine Churning (1962–1964)

SUMMER **NIGHTS** AT **PORT DOVER**

After a good-time blast through the instrumental "Peter Gunn Theme," once again focusing the dual horns of Penfound and Hudson, the Hawks peel through a fat roll of hundreds with a loaded reading of "Money (That's What I Want)." The lineup for "Money" is Garth on organ and Jerry on saxophone, which leaves Beak to play the excitable piano work. A close listen reveals Richard grooving double time during the verses and lending music box glissandos during the Penfound solo spot.

"You Don't Know Me" is another crystalline example of how Richard made his name by singing Ray Charles. He sings the song as though he wrote it and expresses the gamut of emotions contained within Charles's narrative.

A song from their former leader's set, "Hey Bo Diddley," is given an incendiary reading, with Robbie shearing off jagged pieces of guitar metallics and rhythmic riffing. Richard is on his game, forcefully banging out variations on the Bo Diddley rhythm. "Forty Days" quickly follows and is given the same stamp as "Hey Bo Diddley," with emphatic playing by everyone in the band.

"Hoochie John Blues" is a testament to the group's diversity at this juncture, their catalog ranging from thematic instrumentals such as the "Peter Gunn Theme" to horny burlesque blues. The Hawks' penchant for horns was already well entrenched in their early repertoire.

Each member gets a focus for "Robbie's Blues," a straight twelve-bar spotlight. Despite some spotty audio quality, Beak's solid piano underpins the foundation, while Garth and Robbie strut their stuff. Each soloist shows off his abilities, but the gold star goes to the song title's principal. Robbie illustrates the talent that would make him a legend with atmospheric and shredding guitar work.

Richard takes the lead vocal on the Leiber and Stoller classic "Kansas City," played as a spicy shuffle with heavy brasswork. He then puts forth another goose-bump moment on James Brown's "Please, Please, Please" with soul-stirring vocals that make you accept his plaintive begging. It's a tall order to cover the great James Brown, but Beak doesn't back down. The Hawks crack it open and cook it. Levon and Rick support in vocal harmony while Richard sands his lead lines into dust. Garth could have come out from behind the Lowrey and placed a cape over Richard's shoulders, for each time he begs his baby to stay, the group ratchets up the intensity.

Bobby Bland's "Turn on Your Love Light" was a standard of early Hawks sets. Here we get an intense reading introducing bacchanalian Garth Hudson organ, while Richard does his all to encourage the assembled crowd to fire up their own love lights. It was an ambitious addition to their set and an obvious crowd-pleaser, stirred up and served by Beak. Levon later said that if there was anybody that the Hawks wanted to emulate, it was Bobby Bland's band. Here, they come close.

A series of tight blues instrumentals marks the recording. Garth, Robbie, and Penfound illustrate their instrumental prowess while Levon and Rick crank down the top of the shuffle. An attentive ear will notice Richard's very Bobby Bland–like piano accompaniment with some off-kilter trilling and well-timed single-note dressings underneath Garth's wild sonic excursions.

As a testament to the group's obscure music tastes, Marie Adams's 1951 Peacock single "I'm Gonna Play the Honky Tonks" receives a churning reading. Once again, the horns blast out a brassy accompaniment while Richard sacrifices his voice to the blues gods. His inaugural scream snatches the crowd's attention. The band must have realized that this cut was a fine representation of what they did well, since they would later attempt to lay down a studio version. A cleaned-up and speed-corrected version of this live reading can be heard on the out-of-print 1994 Band box set *Across the Great Divide*.

Concluding the recording is another preserved version of "Georgia on My Mind." Richard's effortless vibrato and emotive singing press against historic glass, leaving a steamy imprint decades later. Unfortunately, the last two songs on the Port Dover tape are cut, so we are left with just a snippet of one of Richard's most beloved songs, Bobby Bland's "Share Your Love with Me."

The second Davies tape was purportedly recorded at Crang Plaza in Toronto in August 1964, though it could have also come from Port Dover. Internal evidence on the tape suggests it was recorded about a month after the Pop Ivy performance.

As the recording begins, the band is in the throes of an incandescent "Turn On Your Love Light." Richard sings with a sly grit and shows an urgent sense of control in his onstage vocal approach. The group is churning hard and scales a properly raved-up and Manuel-inspired conclusion.

There quickly follows a thrashing version of "Not Fade Away" sung by Levon, which precedes the set break. The tape picks up with a Rick-led reading of the Isleys' "Twist and Shout," with Richard and Levon lending the joyous responses to Rick's calls.

A hard-driving cover of the Chess single "(The Story of) Woman, Love and a Man" not only spotlights the Hawks' hip taste but also their deft arranging. Tony Clarke's original version was split over two sides of the single, and the Hawks play both sides as one piece. Levon takes the lead, while the chorus features hearty group vocals. Levon's, Richard's, and Rick's voices commingle in celebratory confirmation that everything is going to be all right. When the song drops into the second segment, Levon hollers for some piano, and Richard answers on time with a gallop across the keys.

Sam Cooke's "Bring It On Home to Me," similar to the performance in Port Dover, spotlights the emotional simpatico of the Richard Manuel and

SUMMER **NIGHTS** AT **PORT DOVER**

Rick Danko vocal blend. In these early performances, they sing in a way that makes them sound like long-lost relatives. Richard is on bottom and Rick sings angel harmony, though they were both nimble enough to flip at a moment's notice. Reminiscent of the vocal blend of the Davies brothers of Kinks fame, it's hard to tell where one voice ends and the other begins.

"Kansas City" is marinated in confident Manuel lead vocals, with Richard sounding the part, kicking back on the corner of 12th and Vine. Garth and Richard mesh like golden gears for the break while Robbie takes a silvery solo.

The nightly appearance of "Georgia on My Mind" gets a fully invested and carefully caressed reading. One interesting note on these Levon and the Hawks tapes: while Beak takes most of the lead vocals, each song features a particular member bobbing to the surface for their moment. The group is adept at passing the ball around the stage, stepping forward, then falling back into the whole. Whether a Rick bass run, a Robbie lead part, a Garth mini orchestra, a Levon screamer, or Richard moaning an introspective blues, the group was at its best when every position was firing.

James Brown's "Please, Please, Please" gets another concert showcase, and Richard plays up the dramaticism of the track with well-timed caesuras and playful dynamics throughout the verses. His piano rattles along with his alternating vocal crescendos. Richard emulating James Brown offers an excellent snapshot of his sense of histrionics and stage presence.

The two circulating concert recordings from the Levon and the Hawks summer of 1964 not only illustrate Beak's quickly ascending vocal prowess, but his important contributions to the overall sound of the band.

LEVON AND THE HAWKS AT ROMAN RECORDS

In the fall, Richard and the Hawks logged studio time at Hallmark Studios in Toronto for Duff Roman's Roman Records. They laid down six songs from their stage show, as well as some original music.

Recorded that day were versions of James Brown's "Please, Please, Please," along with "Robbie's Blues," the Hudson/Robertson composition "Bacon Fat," and "Uh, Uh, Uh," a Robertson original. "Robbie's Blues" and "Bacon Fat" were officially released on the 2005 box set *A Musical History*, but no additional audio has surfaced from the sessions.

The Hawks sound strong and focused. "Bacon Fat" comes off as a soulful strut, with Rick immediately marking his territory with heavy stepping. Richard busts in with a raucous vocal, brimming with smoky exclamations. Peak Beak, and his voice is the perfect bluesy clarion call. The cut is one of the best officially recorded examples of the Levon and the Hawks stage show.

Additionally important is that while the Hawks are swinging hard, it's to their own original music. "Robbie's Blues" is just that, a blues vamp, a band collaboration, a shady instrumental number to show off their chops. This is the Hawks at closing time, with each member getting a moment to display his wares before last call. Garth and Robbie are the stars, and Penfound takes a breezy flute solo. Richard plays tastefully on this cut. He accompanies the soloists professionally, all the while using appropriate portions of his piano seasoning for the bubbling blues stew.

Richard didn't contribute any of his original songs to the Hawks session. It wasn't his place yet. Robbie had been writing songs for Hawkins since '58 and took care of procuring the group's studio time with Levon. They were the senior members of the organization. Richard tinkered with phrases and melodies during rehearsals and after shows but had nothing ready for presentation to his Hawk bandmates . . . yet.

After their brief foray into the studio, the Hawks continued the road grind and further developed their abilities in front of a live audience. That autumn saw the Hawks playing the Concord Tavern from September 28 through October 10. They were back at the Friar's Tavern for a series of performances through November and the beginning of December. Mixed in were some rowdy one-offs at the Embassy Club, Brass Rail, and other familiar venues.

With the Ronnie Hawkins name not consistently pulling in crowds, things were rough for the Hawks. While they were busy, there was no sense of upward mobility. The band wasn't immune to discouragement or setback, and Richard struggled with bouts of crippling self-doubt. Levon remembered in his memoir that by the end of 1964, the entire band was feeling down, waiting for something to happen. Richard had told him, "I'm tired of being a rankster. I wanna move on up out of this rankdom we are in."

While the band loved playing, they longed to break out of the endless parade of bars and jukes. They heard the music on the radio and knew that they were just as good if not better than the hit parade. Something had to happen. The Hawks were living hand to mouth, and it was getting old. If they weren't careful, they would end up becoming a lounge act.

The rock 'n' roll world had changed since the Beatles landed in America in February: they wrote their own songs, curated their own sound, and were completely original. The Hawks felt they checked these same boxes. While not directly affected by the Beatles' influence, the Hawks couldn't help but feel the repercussions of the music being created by their contemporaries.

The Hawks flew against the jet stream yet couldn't escape its pull. Levon said in his memoir, "After a while, it got to be a drag. It was just reproduction, and when you do that, you end up just being a house band."

The first positive change in escaping the "rankdom" as 1964 turned to 1965 was Richard meeting his future wife and the mother of his children, Danish model Jane Kristiansen. Jane was an innocent nineteen years old when she first encountered Richard in his element at the Friar's Tavern. Jane attended the show when a mutual friend told her there was a band that she needed to check out. Jane remembered the group as tall and clean cut; Richard the joker, making sly comments, and acting out, trying to capture her attention.

Richard was familiar with Jane and had tried to pick her up before. Later that evening in between Hawks sets, Jane, her friend, and others in the band headed up the street to take in a Muddy Waters performance. Jane was denied entry to the club because of her age, so Richard stepped in and offered to take her out for coffee instead. Jane later thought that maybe their meeting had been a setup all along.

Over steaming cups of coffee and looking out onto the bustle of Yonge Street, Jane found Richard's company lovely. She enjoyed his gentle smile and his soft attentiveness. In her presence, he acted in total contrast to how he was onstage and with his rock 'n' roll mates. Richard mused about his family and home, Jane about her being born in Denmark and how she came to be in Toronto. By the end of the evening, they were both intrigued and smitten. Jane enjoyed her time with Richard and even considered seeing him again.

"I know my thing now. I know what it is. It's hard to describe. I don't know what to call it, because I've never heard it before."

—Bob Dylan

Chapter 5
GHOST OF ELECTRICITY (1965)

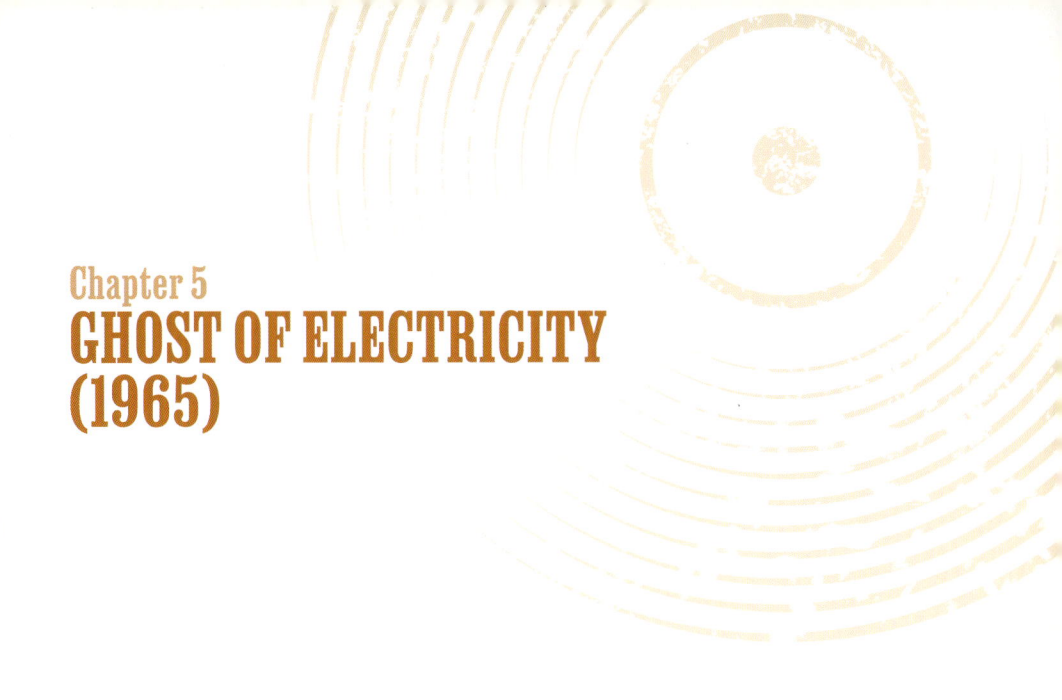

> Everybody wants to be my friend, but nobody wants to get higher.
> —Bob Dylan

Levon and the Hawks concluded their first year without Ronnie Hawkins with a two-day New Year's concert at the Dallas Memorial Auditorium. The Texas performance was part of the group's return to the Southern circuit after spending the autumn in Canada. Being transcontinental purveyors of rock 'n' roll was a difficult proposition and a drain on the group's creativity and general well-being. Richard had fleeting thoughts about simply heading back to Stratford and jamming with some of his old Revols pals.

Running the same roads, booking the same gigs they had with Hawkins, the Hawks were ready for something new. Some of the local gigs had dried up, and times were getting tight. To eat and sleep, the band depended on well-placed girlfriends, musicians, and friends. The Hawks, as Richard would boozily pantomime in the 1976 film *The Last Waltz*, had taken up gang shoplifting, using subtle diversion and Canadian overcoats to stash food and stuff bologna, while shaking down cigarette machines for creature comforts. As Robbie remembered in his memoir, "Breaking out on our own as Levon and the Hawks was a struggle and we were feeling it. Survival was hand-to-mouth and week-to-week. This was not glamorous work; the struggle was real."

Richard and his bandmates were not modern-day pop stars cultivated for mass consumption. The guys were down-to-earth, hardworking music lovers. With these cats, there was no pretense, no bullshit. Every single action was an intentional move to get closer to their goals. The Hawks' refusal to kowtow to musical trends made their journey difficult, but it also created an air of authenticity around the band. The eventual payoff was not yet visible, but the guys knew they had *something*.

Artistic expression and authenticity were foremost on the Hawks' minds. They understood that if they kept playing the same old haunts, they would never be more than a bar band. This self-awareness and increasing maturity can be heard on their 1965 live recordings. Levon and the Hawks were growing up and developing as musicians. Their increasing affinity for jazz—including but not limited to Cannonball Adderley—began to smooth out and mature their instrumental excursions. Beak loved listening to the 1964 *Getz/Gilberto* LP and its Brazilian rhythms.

LIVE AT THE FONDALITE

Musically, the Hawks were sharp as a shank, as evidenced by a recording from early 1965. This concert tape from the Fondalite Club in Tulsa, Oklahoma, was released in 2022, and it documents a critical time in Levon and the Hawks' maturation and, in turn, Richard Manuel's development.

Dayton Stratton, who booked gigs for the Hawks, gave permission to local Tulsa musician and Hawks friend Connell Miller to record the show on his Wollensack reel-to-reel. The January 1965 performance finds Levon and the Hawks near the corner of 11th and Denver at the Fondalite, a local hotspot frequented by musicians such as Jesse Ed Davis, Leon Russell, and J. J. Cale.

The recording is a glimpse into the diverse showmanship of the post-Hawkins Hawks, and it highlights Richard's contributions to the group during this era. The group's revamped set runs from jazz and blues to instrumentals to dance floor ballads. Richard is featured on vocals or covocals on over half of the tracks, which is consistent with all the recordings from 1965.

The recording begins with a jumpy reading of James Brown's 1960 cut "I'll Go Crazy," with the Hawks in edgy syncopation and Richard's lead vocals slyly sinister. The Hawks' orchestrated sound pops off the tape, despite some minor technical shortcomings with the reel. While much has been said about Richard's affinity for Ray Charles and Bobby Bland, he could sing the shit out of James Brown. Hot as Southern fried chicken, he leads the Hawks into the chorus chant, "You've got to live for yourself, yourself and nobody else!" Punctuated by a popping Helm snare crack, for Richard, truer words have never been sung.

A tender version of Sam Cooke's "Bring It On Home to Me" follows and features the Levon-Rick-and-Richard rustic three-way vocal blend that would be featured on a decade's worth of Band recordings. It's a treat to hear each vocalist discovering his individual strengths while singing in perfect union: Levon, the Southern grit; Rick, high harmony from the Canadian tobacco belt; and sweet Richard's sturdy northern angst. Their voices have a synergy that renders each principal element essential to the greater whole.

The recording finds Richard swinging heavy-handed rock 'n' roll piano on a rubber-burning "Hi-Heel Sneakers," where Levon and Robbie each nail their parts to the wall. While Robbie burns, Richard can be heard trilling energy piano underneath the solo.

He doles out a glistening Hawks standard with a delicate "Share Your Love," a song he made his own and always performed splendidly. He then gets the crowd worked into a froth with another Bobby Bland cut, a rave-up rendition of "Turn On Your Lovelight" from his *Here's the Man!!!* LP.

Smooth as a frozen Canadian lake, Richard smirks while singing lead on a chugging version of "Kansas City," followed by what was always a Hawks onstage smoker, "Don't Cry No More," yet another Bobby "Blue" Bland cut. The Hawks even open the shades to reveal the breezy nod to "Summertime" found on Bland's original single.

Part of the recording of "Georgia" is missing, but what remains is a crystalline reading of the song that illustrates great attention to detail by the group, with Richard's voice hardened from constant use and aged to perfection.

"Money" has only gotten better since its last appearance on the August 1964 tape. Levon and Richard first share the lead vocals like a matched pair. Richard and Garth take over the gassed instrumental breaks with a one-track mind.

The definitive peak of the recording takes place at the end of the set. The tape cuts to the in-progress slow, cautionary blues of "Your Friends," another song from Bobby Bland's *Here's the Man!!!* The Hawks play it on a razor's edge, expressing it as a shifty blues, replete with the now-trademark and soulful Beak "woah-hos." The Hawks lay down a dramatic tribute to Bland, with Richard dueting instrumentally with both Robbie and Garth. Cutting through the extraneous noise of the tape, Richard can be heard emulating the dark and skittering piano lines contained on Bland's studio version. Garth orchestrates a spacious sonic wash, while Richard's voice reverberates around the small room. Robbie's sweetly overdriven guitar replaces the saxophone lines of the original arrangement. Immortalized in this sublime moment, the Hawks illustrate why John Hammond wanted them for his electric blues band. Additionally, "Your Friends" shows why in less than three months, the Hawks would be perfectly at home jamming with and hatching plans to be the backing band for Sonny Boy Williamson II.

Similar to his performance of Ray Charles's "I'm Going Down to the River" on the 1962 Fayetteville tape, Richard plays the hardened narrator; both of these song choices are a musical translation of his own submerged emotions and apprehensions. Richard's idol Ray Charles said to *Life* magazine in 1966, "Soul is when you take a song and make it part of you—a part that's so true, so real, that people think it must have happened to you."

Therein lies Richard's own power as a performer: his ability to make the audience believe what he was singing about. "Georgia on My Mind" in Stratford, "I'm Going Down to the River" in Fayetteville, or "Your Friends" at the Fondalite all manifest his innate ability to connect with a room of people. Audiences can detect when they are being bullshitted. Richard's convincing tone and investment in making a connection ultimately puts listeners in the palm of his hand.

After the Fondalite performance, the Hawks returned to Canada for a run of February shows at the Friar's Tavern. The Hawks piled in the Caddy to head back to Toronto, and on the way, the car was searched for drugs. The headline in the February 1, 1965, *Toronto Daily Star* read: "Mounties Nab Six Musicians on Dope Charge." In Richard's local paper, the headline was "11 Arrested, Stratford Address Given," with his name in black and white. The Hawks liked to smoke dope, a lot of it, and someone had tipped off the Mounties that they were coming home. When marijuana was found in the vehicle, the Royal Canadian Mounted Police arrested manager Bill Avis and the Hawks for importing narcotics.

The catalyst for the bust was a jealous girlfriend of Rick's who had decided to get revenge by having the band arrested. The troublesome brush with the law hung over the band throughout the year. A bigger issue for Richard and the guys was explaining the situation to their families.

After the arrest, the group played to their people at the Friar's Tavern in a series of shows from February 22 through 27. Soon after, the Hawks migrated south in April 1965 for additional performances. The guys continued to live hand to mouth. This was not a glorious life on the road. There were plans of thievery, and covert operations were always afoot to get food, get paid, or get laid. Richard was usually in charge of the latter.

Since Hawkins's departure, the band had shifted operations closer to Levon's home in Marvell, Arkansas. One morning while they were lounging in their rehearsal space at the Rainbow Inn on Route 20 in West Helena, the radio blasted out a familiar refrain: "It's King Biscuit Time!" Knowing exactly what the exclamation meant, everyone in the Hawks craned their ears to hear *The King Biscuit Flour Hour*. This was the stuff that Richard cut his teeth on while beaming in the WLAC radio waves to Well Street. According to Levon's memoir, when the radio issued the clarion call, Richard replied, "Holy shit! I can't believe these guys are still doing this."

One of the more interesting turns of the Hawks' tale is their meeting and eventual playing with famed blues artist Sonny Boy Williamson II, a fixture of the King Biscuit show. Word around Phillips County was that Williamson had just returned home from touring England, where the British blues boom was drawing attention to the original blues greats. In a fantastic story told by Levon in his memoir and reiterated by Robbie in his, the Hawks were inspired to go look around West Helena for Williamson.

Rick remembered in *The Band Is Back* in 1983, "We went to look [Williamson] up, down on Yazoo Street. He took us to a booze can. We played with him, drank some moonshine." Williamson told the Hawks that he had been playing with the rock groups in the UK and that they just didn't measure up to the bands back home. The group eventually headed over to the Rainbow Inn to play together.

Chapter 5 | Ghost of Electricity (1965)

Richard Manuel

The Hawks tuned their instruments, lit their cigarettes, and did their best not to be in awe of the legend. The group waited nervously for Williamson's cue and followed him into the serpentine blues of "Fattening Frogs for Snakes." Williamson tipped his bowler hat and pulled his harp out of his coat pocket.

Robbie recalled in his memoir, "Pretty soon sparks flew. He [Williamson] looked around the room at each of us, showing his wide, crooked smile with a couple of missing teeth."

Williamson and the Hawks jammed throughout the day, intoxicated by both their music and the moonshine. The prospect of their potential collaboration excited them all, and tentative plans were made to hook up again. For Levon and the Hawks and Sonny Boy Williamson II, the possibilities were endless. According to Robbie, Williamson told the Hawks, "You fellas as good as anybody I ever played with."

Later in the spring of 1965, the group traveled to New York to record a single for independent producer Henry Glover. Their visit to Bell Sound Studios, under the new moniker the Canadian Squires, resulted in a single for Apex Records that went nowhere. While the advice to change their name was certainly misguided, since the Hawks had much-greater name recognition, one positive thing to come out of the session was that the group was recording original music.

The resulting A side of the Squires single, Robbie's "Uh, Uh, Uh," snaps along in a perky way, spotlighting both Richard and Levon verbalizing band bragging rights. A simplistic harp overdub by Robbie stays the course throughout the song, punctuated by big, reverberant tom-toms at the breaks. While the lyrics initially seem basic, the song is actually rock 'n' roll perfection for the era, when a philosophical and literary lyrical approach was just starting to take hold in the mainstream.

The flip side, "Leave Me Alone," is a definitive statement on the group's existence as separatist road warriors. Ushered in on a sturdy Bo Diddley beat, Robbie composed a semielitist attitude toward the fast-developing rock scene. Levon and Richard again alternate lead vocal duties in a call-and-response warning to those who dare interfere with the Hawks' flock. Richard plays a high-tempo pulsating piano that alternates with Levon's snare cracks, powering the song's highfalutin tempo.

Taken in context with the artists behind the singles at the top of the Billboard charts at the time—Herman's Hermits, Freddy and the Dreamers, the Beatles—the Hawks were laying down an original, edgy, and honest form of rock music. While the public at large wasn't yet aware of them, their work wouldn't escape the notice of another artist who was looking to take his own compositions to an unrealized electric level.

The constant performances and street-style networking were starting to pay off. It was a small musical world in the mid-1960s. The Hawks jammed with

Butterfield in Chicago; hung with a young Jesse Ed Davis, Leon Russell, and J. J. Cale in Oklahoma; and rubbed shoulders with connected people in the studios and at the Brill Building in New York. Rockabilly contemporary Conway Twitty loved the guys and pushed their wares onto club owners whenever he got the chance. Robbie Robertson was a driven man, a mover and a shaker, and had been the impetus for securing the John Hammond sessions while in New York. He was always active in securing his future—and in turn, the Hawks'.

Another fortuitous meeting for the Hawks was a connection made via a fan of the group. Mary Martin was raised in Toronto and worked as a receptionist in one of Albert Grossman's offices. Grossman was the manager and representative of a number of artists, including Bob Dylan, Odetta, and Peter, Paul and Mary. Later in her life, Martin would go on to represent artists herself, including Van Morrison, Leonard Cohen, and Emmylou Harris—proof that she had an ear for talent and knew a good musician when she heard one.

Martin and her friend Toni Troe frequented the downtown Toronto clubs, where cultures and musical styles were colliding head on. It was on Yonge Street where Martin and her sidekick's adventures led to the discovery of their new favorite band: Levon and the Hawks.

Martin frequently settled into Le Coq d'Or, posting up near the stage close to the stand-up piano, and listened. She recalled in 2021, "They were a really mature and loving and dedicated bunch of boys who loved the music they were doing, and they executed it with passion. I would swoon when Richard would sing a Ray Charles song. I think we all would swoon."

Referring to herself lovingly as a groupie, Martin remembered that she "loved Richard Manuel" and wanted nothing but the best for all the boys in the band. She recalled, "Richard had a girlfriend. But he was who I sort of took a fondness to. He was a charming, good-looking, talented young man. . . . We relished every single moment when they performed. I guess we became sort of friends with them. Some were more friendly than others. I'm not going to say who was more swell than the others. Richard Manuel was indeed a really truly good man, and he was good-looking!"

Richard was suave, his duckbill maturing into a sweetly swooped-up dome framing his classic features and sturdy nose. His clothes hung well on him, and his impeccable choices in suit coats were hard to beat. When he leaned in with a speaking voice as attractive as his singing, the girls were all ears . . . and other things.

When asked what she thought made the group work internally, Martin replied:

> I think what drove them was their relationships with one another, and the end result was making fabulous music. . . . I adored their presentation and their skills. They had their musical act together, and each one of them had a viable piece for

the audience. Richard was a true member of that group. They [People] would be drawn to his absolute devotion to music.

Martin and her friend Toni hung out with the guys after sets and became a source of comfort for them: "We taught them about Bob Dylan, and they taught us about the real value of the Abyssinian Baptist Choir." Bob Dylan's *Bringing It All Back Home* spun on the communal turntable as Martin's two worlds of work and pleasure collided in fantastic syncopation.

Summing up what the Hawks were all about in this era, Martin said, "They were the band to take your blues away." Because of how the group made her feel, she was about to become their biggest advocate and a critical voice in the ear of both Albert Grossman and Bob Dylan, who told *Rolling Stone* in 1969 that he felt like she knew all the bands and singers from Canada . . . and kept pushing the Hawks on him.

In an era filled with valiant attempts at authentically emulating rhythm and blues by lesser and often-more-famous rock groups, Levon and the Hawks were legitimized by their relationships with respected musicians such as John Hammond Jr., Conway Twitty, and Sonny Boy Williamson. Mary Martin's connections meant nothing without the Hawks' hard work, talent, and ability to dig into a number of genres that they weren't born into, and to do it authentically.

The Hawks Soar to the Shore

An underrepresented connection when discussing the Hawks' musical destiny was their friendship with Harold Jenkins, later known as Conway Twitty, who not only was a fan of the band but was working the same circuit as the Hawks, often sharing the bill. Levon remembered how vital Twitty was to the luck that was to find the Hawks when Twitty recommended that the band go see Tony Marotta for work.

Tony Marotta was a New Jersey club owner whose iconic venue, Tony Mart's, was one of the most influential venues in early rock 'n' roll history. His son Carmen Marotta confirmed Levon's story in 2022:

> Conway asked Dad to give them a shot, and basically what was said to Dad was "Look, Tony, these guys are great. They are one of the greatest rock 'n' roll bands you are gonna hear. Just give them two weeks, and if they don't do well in two weeks, you can throw them out." Because my father was infamous for throwing bands out.

Tony worked with a Canadian booking agency run by Howard Kudlets, so when the Hawks ended up on the Jersey Shore, the connection was a natural one for both parties. An August 1965 article in the *New York Times* called Tony Mart's *the* nightspot in Somers Point, New Jersey. Furnished with seven bars, twenty cash registers, and over forty bartenders and bouncers, Tony Mart's was a key element of the town that the *Times* called "the wildest spot on the New Jersey shore and perhaps the entire Eastern Seaboard." Its central location pulled college kids from New York City and Philadelphia as well as rounders and music fans from Atlantic City.

The Point was a youth-filled hotspot on the cusp of exploding, a bastion of cultural upheaval, rooted in freedom around music, drugs, and sexuality. Levon and the Hawks showed up at just the right time and took the Tony Mart stage as a practiced, confident, and well-oiled musical machine. Tony Mart's was just fifteen minutes away from the bright lights of Atlantic City, where Robbie remembered in his memoir that the guys "would slip over to the Wonder Garden club in Atlantic City where we caught some of the best jazz-organ combos going." In between, Levon and the Hawks played three shows a day, seven days a week while living on-site or just around the corner. It was perfect, a consistent gig, close to New York City, and a place to settle while planning their next move.

Robbie talked about Somers Point in an interview with Kurt Loder on Sirius/XM Radio in 2020:

> We were back to back. . . . We weren't doing what anybody else was doing. From the very beginning. And a lot of people at Tony Mart's, a lot of people were like, "You gotta go and hear these guys. You gotta hear this band. There's something about them. They're hot."

Carmen Marotta concurred to *Atlantic City Weekly* in 2005:

> It was incredible because so much of what was going on at Tony Mart's at that time was more like schtick and pop music. Levon and the Hawks may have dressed for a 9-to-5 but they played a ragged and dirty mixture of blues, gospel, rockabilly, and country funk.

The first appearance of Levon and the Hawks at Tony Mart's came on May 8, 1965. Carmen Marotta had a unique view of the Hawks at his father's establishment, since he was a boy who often posted up right in front of Beak's piano. Carmen recalled that Richard was the type of guy who would take the time to be nice to a nine-year-old.

In the same way that the Hawks would woodshed with Hawkins, Tony Mart's gave the Hawks another dose of what was proving to be their best formula for success: complete musical immersion through working together, playing together, and fucking together resulted in the band becoming melded, young brothers joined in cahoots. Whatever you want to call it, it was a bond forged

Chapter 5 | Ghost of Electricity (1965)

out of the hardest rock 'n' roll steel. Richard had found his home and his place in the Hawks. Levon told *Razor* magazine in 2004, "Richard swore he'd pay for laughs if he could buy them, and then he'd raise his glass and toast you with his trademark grin and say, 'Stand tall brother. Stand tall.'"

Marotta remembered in 2021:

> They lived over the top of the Mart. Dad had four apartments over the top of Tony Mart. That was part of the deal: you got paid and you got the apartment. There were three or four bedrooms in the apartment. It was, as you might imagine, a complete bordello with parties, crazy shit going on. There was no problem pre–sexual revolution at Tony Mart's; that's part of the scene I'm trying to describe to you. Eventually they [the Hawks] rented a little house that was next to our house, which was down the street from Tony Mart's. They rented it because they had so many friends and so many women and so much partying and carousing that they needed a second place!

Something was happening down at the Jersey Shore in the summer of 1965. John Lennon used to compare the after-hours fun on Beatles tours to Fellini's *Satyricon*. While the Hawks were still working their way up the popular-music ladder, their postperformance hijinks were not unlike what Lennon was experiencing. Especially for Richard, meaningful female companionship on the road sprung from licentiousness, and the Hawks' scenes were steeped in debauchery.

The Tony Mart performances were love fests. They were heavily attended, and the Hawks had developed a cadre of hard-core fans. Tony loved the Hawks, and the crowd responded the same way. The band had fallen into an environment where there was a reciprocal love between the performer and the entire neighborhood. The club had a legal capacity of 1,300 but on the weekends, as Marotta remembered, "Fuhgeddaboudit"—the place bulged at the seams. He continued, "The pulsating pandemonious kind of ambiance and atmosphere when a band that good is killing it in a club like that. Where all these young people were going crazy. And there were plenty of girls where Beak was concerned."

But at one point during his time in Somers Point, Richard thought more about Jane Kristiansen from Toronto than anyone else. He knew that she wasn't like other girls, and called her to ask her to join him down on the shore. Jane accepted his offer and stayed with Richard for a bit, even traveling with the Hawks when they left for performances in the South.

The Tony Mart stage was a postage stamp, and the group set up in a crescent with Levon and Richard across stage from each other at the points. Tony Marotta procured a stand-up piano for Richard, which he promptly modified and had set up near the brass railing that ran along the outside of the stage. After taking off the back and banging around inside, he gave a big wink to the guys, nodding his approval.

The Hawks moved like a freight train from Memorial Day to the end of July, playing to an endless stream of packed houses. Nightly, a mass of sweltering bodies swarmed the stage, and the Hawks, a musical group of steel-driving men, pounded their sound into shape with 9-pound hammers, while knocking out the sunburned crowds with well-timed and weighted blows.

One famous night at the Mart, fired up on a rocket fuel mixture of speed and alcohol, the Hawks were jamming so fast and furious that they failed to respond to numerous requests from the club bouncers to cut the music. They had already surpassed the 2:00 a.m. curfew, and the police were threatening to act if the band didn't cease.

The Hawks continued to play hard, quivering waves of sound shaking the club, oblivious to anything but their own artistic will. Finally, someone got up the gumption to climb up to the stage and shake Levon's arm to clue him into what was happening. Levon snapped out of his musical trance and the group escaped unscathed.

Unfortunately, no audio documentation exists of these legendary nights on the Jersey Shore, only Kodachrome images locked in the minds of those lucky enough to see the group peaking at the Mart: Beak singing "I'll Go Crazy," head leaned back on a hinge, raring back for a deep breath, eyes to the rafters, conjuring from his gut to throat a primal roar into the mic. Or, posted on his stool Fats Domino style, tearing open a funky reading of Otis Redding's "Mr. Pitiful." Arms, shoulders, and head all in movement, bobbing, weaving, and coming in for the knockout on the downbeats.

Tony Mart's in Somers Point, New Jersey, with the Hawks featured on the marquee, summer of 1965. *Courtesy of the Richard Manuel family*

Chapter 5 | Ghost of Electricity (1965)

The mind's-eye view of what exactly was going down in the summer of '65 included Rick and Levon stepping in each other's footprints, an unbreakable bond of rhythm in "Money (That's What I Want)"; Robbie, fighting his instrument to the death, bowing the neck to signal the changes in "Robbie's Blues" or "Hi-Heel Sneakers"; Garth standing stoically on one of the Mart's sticky bar tops, blowing sax to Junior Walker & the All-Stars' 1965 dance classic "Shotgun."

In between sets, the most-beautiful girls in the world spilled out onto the boardwalk, browned, thigh-high minis, and hair to the stars. The thick salty air sliced by the cries of hot-rodding young studs and their cars streaming into the night . . . with Levon and his Hawks as the soundtrack.

Carmen Marotta summed up Richard's time at the Mart:

> I don't give a shit. He was one of the best damn white blues singers that ever lived. I got to see it firsthand. Everybody loved Beak. He was an icon. Tremendous piano player, such an unbelievable blues singer. He was the go-to guy. When you had to go to your heavyweight, to your guy that was going to blow people away, mesmerize them, make their jaws drop, that's when it was Beak's time. We had Black performers coming up to Somers Point to see Beak. Because that's how great he was.

By mid-1965, Richard was a practiced entertainer and had developed a flair for onstage dramatics. During performances of James Brown's "Please, Please, Please" or Etta James's "Something's Got a Hold on Me," he elongated the verses with effectual vocal dynamics while punctuating the verses with theatrical caesuras. He ratcheted up the musical tension by shifting the timbre of his vocals. He taffied the workings of a song to create anticipation before dropping into a verse full steam ahead. He later used this showman's approach to great effect on much-larger concert stages.

The Hawks owned the Jersey Shore in 1965, and their performances there left an enduring aura. A fictional yet lasting snapshot of these free-flowing evenings can be viewed in the 1983 film *Eddie and the Cruisers*, which was shot on location at Tony Mart's. The "Wild Summer Nights" scene of the film epitomizes the horny and joyous vibe of the summer of 1965 on the shore.

Just as Levon and the Hawks' residence at Tony Mart's was heating up, word came that Sonny Boy Williamson II had passed away in Arkansas on May 26, 1965, only a month or so removed from their jam session. The group was disappointed and saddened by the development but still had their eyes on playing for themselves. Even so, they couldn't help thinking of what could have been.

The band lived at Tony Mart's for most of the summer of '65. They split every couple of weeks to play a one-off gig or to return to the Southern circuit.

Of course, there was the usual booze and a plethora of women, pills, and pot—heady stuff for youth unchained during a musical, cultural, and sexual revolution.

On the flip side of all this hard work and intermingled adventure, Richard still took joy in the things that reminded him of home. Marotta remembered, "They were not bigger than life. They were just the opposite. They were very real, warm people. There was no pretense of any rock star stuff. Because there was no rock star stuff."

One of the ways that Richard got through the long hours and his intermittent homesickness was at the Coaches Corner. The small roast beef stand was family owned and operated and offered Richard and the guys a place to refuel and take stock after charged evenings of madness. Sharon DeFilippo, a then-twenty-one-year-old waitress and daughter of the owners, remembered in 2021 the Hawks becoming consistent patrons of the establishment:

> They were all just incredible. Just incredible. We had a restaurant that was about 30 feet away from where they were playing. So it didn't open until four o'clock. But my mother used to cook all day. So these guys started to come over there for breakfast, because she would make them breakfast. They would sit and have breakfast and coffee. And it was like their personal restaurant.

Richard nipped over in the morning for his coffee, Irish style of course, specially enhanced with his own pocketed bottle of Grand Marnier. He posted up at the counter to commiserate with Mrs. DeFilippo. He spent a lot of free time at the Corner, and no one ever had a negative word to say about Beak.

Sharon saw the guys almost every day during their summer stay on the shore, and in her words, Richard was "a gentleman and easy to get along with." The DeFilippos acted as a surrogate family to the guys during their stay in Somers Point and enjoyed their company. The DeFilippos had three young and attractive daughters, including Sharon, working the counter at the restaurant through the summer, and Richard and the rest of the Hawks showed nothing but respect to the girls and the family. Though in what seemed to be a more and more common occurrence, random young fans would sometimes try to enter the closed eatery to get at Beak and the debonair Rick Danko.

Sharon remembered:

> Richard had what I call a preternatural smile on his face. I don't know that it didn't have something to do with the structure of his face. But he always looked as though he was smiling. It was part of him. You know how we have to work to make a smile? He had to work not to smile.

Richard relished the home-cooked goodness and warm sensibilities.

Richard Manuel

Levon and the Hawks at Tony Mart's, 1965. *Courtesy of Bill Avis and Jerome Levon Avis*

Sharon continued:

> They were the kind of people, they came into town and they were Everyman. Everybody in town loved them. The cops, the waitresses, the gas station attendants. They just descended on this town, which is a little, I would call it like a little Peyton Place. And for the year, the summer that they were there, there was no other gossip. There was nothing. There was just them.

While Sharon and her sisters didn't always get to make the evening Hawks performances at the Mart because the restaurant opened at 4:00 p.m., she did get to experience Richard Manuel in his performing element several times:

> The first time that I heard Richard sing, it was like he had a fire in his brain. He just would corral people, you know? Most of the time, the guys are trying to flirt with the girls that are there. Not to say that they didn't pay attention to everybody singing. But Richard would get up there and wail, and it was like he could stop the clock. Because people were just "Wow," you know? Everybody recognized that there was something amiss, but it was just filled with talent. Richard was just one of those guys you could never ever forget if you met him.

Offstage, the lasting memory of Beak in Somers Point is his standing on the flat apartment roof at parties, fist wrapped around the neck of his Grand Marnier bottle. Sharon said:

> Whenever he would bring that up to his mouth, you didn't see the opening of the bottle, you just saw the circle in his fist. And it was almost like there was a little brewing factory going on. And it just was made for him. For eternity that he could have his Grand Marnier pour right out of his fist.

Chapter 5 | Ghost of Electricity (1965)

The Hawks' Tony Mart shows were as relevant as any taking place in the greater New York area at the time. When you're that good and other musicians are traveling to see why, the word gets around quick. With an excitable new group of fans, many hands were pointing fingers at Levon and the Hawks. Additionally, two sets of eyes were beginning to take note: Albert Grossman and Bob Dylan.

In a broader historical and cultural scope, 1965 in New York City and its surrounding areas was beginning to blur the lines between artistic fields. Musical genre, film, literature, and performance art were combined into an awe-inspiring conglomeration of revolutionary thinking across the entire spectrum of creative exploits. The Hawks, only a musical arm, were a square peg in a musical industry full of round holes. The first strike against them was being Canadian. The second was their originality and authenticity. The unfortunate reality was that their cultural backgrounds and nonconformity had a negative effect on their music reaching a mainstream audience.

Their regimented run of performances with Ronnie Hawkins left the Hawks locked in, as Richard told the UK magazine *Disc and Music Echo* in 1971: "That was like an apprenticeship, really. That was like boot camp." Everything Richard and the Hawks had experienced with Hawkins prepared them for anything they could face as musicians down the line. An underground collective knew what these guys were all about, and that led to the breakthrough Richard and his bandmates were waiting for.

The group still needed to eat, so any idle time that summer was used to get additional gigs. Miles upon miles of swapping seats, side-of-the-road pisses, and cigarettes flying back into the car window marked the journey. In July, they headed back to the South yet again, and when they returned to New Jersey, Levon and the Hawks would be faced with the decision of whether to back yet another lead man in need of a band.

On the Road
to Texas and Oklahoma

Two final Levon and the Hawks live recordings, both dated July 1965, circulate. Taped less than a month before they would leave Tony Mart's, the recordings reveal Richard at his best.

The tapes spotlight the group as fully formed and ready to level up. The group has stockpiled new music as well, with a limited number of original songs credited to Robbie Robertson, who had been practicing his songwriting craft since joining Hawkins. Richard's attempts followed soon after, once given the time and inclination.

These two recordings, from Dallas and Oklahoma City, feature the solidified Levon and the Hawks lineup that later came to be known as the Group, the Honkies, the Crackers, and, eventually, the Band. While the dates for these recordings are debatable, the strength of the performances is not. The Oklahoma City show circulates as July 28, 1965. Audio documentation by Levon on the Dallas tape does confirm that the Hawks played Oklahoma City "the week after next on the 27th and 28th." It appears that these shows took place just weeks apart.

These recordings are critical in documenting a significant turning point in Richard's development. By the next week, the band would be back on the stage in Somers Point. Within a month, their entire musical existence would be hanging in a precarious balance.

The Dallas recording is the worst sounding of all the circulating Hawks tapes, but the performance is a heater. It's distant and slightly muffled, but the group's performance is ace, and Richard is highlighted on every single track.

We are placed midway into the opening set, where a large crowd can be heard rumbling. Robbie's guitar spills from the speakers ferociously as the Hawks tear into Muddy Waters's "She's Nineteen Years Old," with Levon sneering the lead vocals. Richard's piano is immediately discernible on the tape. He alternates a wobbly shake under Levon's vocal and keeps his right hand pumping the twelve-bar. Bluesy tremolo licks and trills are an important hallmark of Richard's piano playing and often accentuate important moments in a full band arrangement. Tickling the sevenths of a chord during a hot solo is a technique Richard mastered to great effect and relied on often.

The Dallas performance moved immediately into a frantic version of "Don't Cry No More." It could be the tape speed, but this version sizzles over Sterno.

ON THE ROAD TO TEXAS AND OKLAHOMA

It's a charged tribute to Bland's 1961 Duke single, with Garth's Lowery organ playing the horn lines.

A twelve-bar instrumental follows and finds Beak pushing the tempo, in addition to taking a sweet solo alongside Robbie's measured riffing. Once the jam gets legs, it starts to run downhill and surpasses five minutes. Richard and Garth blend seamlessly, each nudging the other for melodic ideas.

Two crown jewels to be retrieved from the sonic sludge of the Dallas tape are the fully realized and mature readings of "Georgia on My Mind" and, later, a fortuitously captured version of "You Don't Know Me," from Ray Charles's 1960 album *The Genius Hits the Road* and 1962's *Modern Sounds in Country and Western Music*, respectively. "Georgia" spotlights Richard's now-recognizable "Geor-ja" in the first verse.

Introduced as a folk tune by Levon, Rick Danko's walking bass line kicks off the intersecting vocals of "Go Go Liza Jane," the genesis of the Band's blend in all its rockabilly glory. Rick, Richard, Robbie, and Levon all take a shot at passing the vocals around. It's a traditional song going back to the early part of the twentieth century, and the Hawks rearranged it into a real shitkicker. Breathless call-and-response vocals and overlapping melody lines highlight the perfect good-time Hawks number.

Richard heats up the second set with the deep and funky syncopation of the Garth Hudson / Robbie Robertson cut "Bacon Fat." The frothy groove of this Hawks song sounds suspiciously like Big Daddy and His Boys' 1957 single "Bacon Fat," which obviously someone in the band had a copy of. But it's Richard's piercing vocal that brings this version to a sizzle with heady Bland-inspired "whoa-hos" and soulful howling. Additionally, he lends more than a few falling-water glissandos on his piano for good measure during Garth's soloing.

After he tinkles out "Happy Birthday" on the piano for a friend of the band, the Hawks slip into a funky reading of Nat Adderley's "Work Song." This version takes on Oscar Brown Jr.'s reading, with lyrics featured on his 1961 LP *Sin and Soul*. This is exactly the type of song choice and performance that separated the Hawks from the mainstream of the hit parade.

While Dylan and the Byrds may have been combining folk and rock, the Hawks were combining rockabilly and rock with jazz and R&B while developing their varied palette. On this version of "Work Song," Levon's groove is delectable, Rick struts out a prolific bass line, and Richard stops time with his clarion call of the working man's angst.

Giving the crowd a chance at taking someone home for the night, Richard croons Ray Charles's "You Don't Know Me." It was a song that he would sing until his very last days, and here the youthful Beak sings out from a place older than his years. Documented via delaminating magnetic tape for us to hear are

Richard's famed vocals, captured like lightning in a bottle. Despite a small cut in the recording, it immortalizes Richard and Garth singing to each other through a shared melody, resulting in a performance that levitates just inches off the ground.

An important segment of Hawks live performances after their separation from Hawkins was the instrumental excursions. Robbie was a guitarist who could cut you, and his playing was highlighted through various instrumental blues that gave him the opportunity. Garth's abilities enabled the group to play anything—standards, dance songs, jazz, blues, or rockabilly—with a sonic strangeness that separated the group from any other of the time. This Dallas recording features several instrumentals that run the gamut from blues structure to dinner music. The musicality expressed by the Hawks is stellar from either side of the aisle. Richard's piano playing on these instrumental cuts traverses difficult jazz changes and shifting time signatures, and he's on point for all of them.

Richard takes the lead vocal on "Smack Dab in the Middle," a song he learned from Ray Charles's 1964 CBS single, though the original 1955 version from Charlie Calhoun and his Orchestra and Chorus has an arrangement similar to the Hawks'. Richard injects the reading with a vocal strength that pierces through the ages. The tape closes with a bulging wad of "Money" that rollercoasters on Garth's organ and the collaborative three-way vocals of Rick, Levon, and Richard.

Two weeks later, the Hawks were at the Onyx in Oklahoma City for a two-night stay on July 27 and 28. Similar to the Dallas recording, there are many Richard highlights. The vocal dominance that Levon often referred to is proven on the tape as Richard takes the lead vocals on no fewer than ten songs while lending supporting vocals on the rest. The sound quality is much improved from Dallas, and the group is playing at a fiery and consistent level.

Levon remembered in his memoir:

> Rick and myself in the beginning were just there to rest Richard up. I would do the novelty songs, and Rick would do some Sam Cooke, and then we would go back to Richard, and Richard would sing the shit out of something!

The Onyx recording opens with another version of "Work Song," with its hard-hitting groove that rivals the 1966 Paul Butterfield Blues Band reading. Richard pleads his case with a rough-hewn recitation. You simply must believe him as he testifies the harsh realities of the chain gang with an authenticity that can be heard through almost sixty-year-old tape.

An unfortunately incomplete version of Bobby Bland's "Your Friends" spotlights tasteful Robertson guitar work and Richard flirting with brittle perfection on the vocals. From a lustful whisper to a painful exclamation, his singing covers the range of emotions. When Robbie comes in for his solo spot, Richard tinkles out professional piano lines pulled right from the grooves of Bland's LP.

ON THE ROAD TO TEXAS AND OKLAHOMA

Etta James's "Something's Got a Hold On Me" follows and has become a Hawks highlight. James cowrote the Chess Brothers–produced track and released it as a single in 1962, when Richard immediately co-opted the song into the group's onstage set. Beak and the boys take the pious cut and make it a carnival rave-up while spotlighting call-and-response vocals underpinned by glorious Hudson keyboards.

The Hawks squeeze the arrangement until juice comes out, the nimble groove hanging on for dear life. Richard sings James's soulful lines in his own bluesy dialect. You can't fake this type of soul; you have to pull it from some part of your inner being. The conclusion of the song finds Garth and Richard entering a hand-raising organ-and-vocal volley that brings the track to a proper peak and conclusion.

Bobby Bland's "Don't Cry No More," as on the Dallas tape, is hot to the touch. Every single element in the group is working at top velocity. A testament to the Hawks' exclusive song choices and hip taste is their take on the 1955 Mills Brothers track "Smack Dab in the Middle." Unfortunately cut at the beginning of the tape, this may be Beak's best vocal of the evening. A funny song about decadence and living life to the highest levels possible fits Richard's ideology to a T. Levon and Rick lend the well-timed "do do do dos" on backing vocals, and Richard places personality into every syllable. Toward the end of the song, he tosses in a soaring "oooooooooh" for good measure.

A crowd request for "Go Go Liza Jane" encourages a version so off the rails that Levon can't help but giggle when the song is over. Everyone in the group except Garth joins in on the lead vocals, and the joy they all get from performing this gassy slammer is infectious.

Introduced as "Oh, Baby, Why Do You Bacon Fat?" and played with a groove one could refer to as Southern slouch, Richard bellows on this cut just as he did in Dallas. Hard syncopation by the rhythm section and lustful screams highlight a performance that encapsulates 1965 Beak Manuel and the Hawks. When Richard screams, "One more time, yeah!" as a lead-in to Garth's sizzling organ swell, you want to bacon fat too.

"Georgia, oh Georgia!" The song that got Richard his gig and made his name is played on the Onyx tape as a dynamic and gentle tribute to Charles's version, every instrument audible and every nuance caressed by the band. Richard strikes pulsing eighth notes on the piano, and Garth makes the bed over the top. The Hawks rendition drifts more than swings, allowing the emotional landscape to come alive, every one of Richard's breaths perfect.

"Rockin' Pneumonia and the Boogie Woogie Flu" and "Money" also feature Richard, while sharing lead vocals with Levon in high-octane renditions. A cut snippet of "Bring It All Back Home" reveals Richard and Rick sounding like blood brothers. No matter the song, Richard is there, leading or supporting vocally.

James Brown's "I'll Go Crazy" and Bland's "Turn On Your Love Light" are, again, both Richard lead spots. "Love Light" is available on both circulating 1965 tapes but sounds the best on the Onyx tape.

"The Feeling Is Gone," from Bobby Bland's 1963 *Call On Me / That's the Way Love Is* album, is a major highlight. Featuring deft Robbie Robertson soloing that foreshadows *Music from Big Pink* and its minimalist playing, everything the Hawks are about is contained in this cover. Richard's voice and playing are imbued with meaningful sentiment. The group's future sound comes through on the magnetic tape as they raise the song into the light for all to admire before settling back into the final verse.

The Hawks' 1965 recordings not only capture Richard's ascending abilities but also display the musical intelligence and diversity of Levon and the Hawks. Their sets comprise a strange conglomerate of blues, country, jazz, gospel, rock, and novelty songs. Onstage, unselfishly passing around the parts, retreating, and coming forward for their respective spotlight moments, each musician is an essential part of the greater whole.

A tale that has been repeated as many times as this one could make for a decades-long game of rock 'n' roll telephone. It was in the dimly lit backroom at Tony Mart's where the phone in the booth started to ring. Someone answered and handed the receiver to Levon Helm, who heard Bob Dylan on the other end.

Dylan called Tony Mart's payphone on a mid-August night in search of a guitarist and drummer to join him for gigs at Forest Hills Stadium and the Hollywood Bowl. Dylan warned of a confrontational experience and wondered whether the Hawks were up for it. It's been said that Mary Martin had already given Levon and Robbie the heads-up that Dylan was interested and wanted to speak to them. Regardless of how this information was communicated, Robbie ended up meeting with Albert Grossman to see what was up. The group's self-made buzz and a heavy dose of word-of-mouth resulted in another opportunity for Richard Manuel and the Hawks.

According to Robbie's memoir, at first, "Richard was the only one who showed any interest in exploring what might be stirring on the Bob Dylan front." Though Richard had referred to Dylan as a "strummer," he also had likened Dylan's "Subterranean Homesick Blues" to Chuck Berry's "Too Much Monkey Business" when talking with his bandmates.

Oddly enough in the situation presented to the Hawks, Dylan already had a keyboardist in Al Kooper and a bass player in Harvey Brooks, so he wanted only Robbie and Levon for the gigs. As with the Hammond Jr. *So Many Roads* sessions, Richard would be sitting this one out.

Leaving a steady-paying gig at Tony Mart's was another huge leap of faith for the Hawks. Even more so for Richard, Rick, and Garth, who weren't going to be playing in Dylan's band. But Richard was loyal to the end and had come too far to stop now. He was going to take the ride until he ran out of road.

Levon and the Hawks' last evening at the Mart was Sunday, August 19, where a large contingent of friends and followers gathered to wish them well. Tony Marotta brought the guys a large and overly ornate going-away cake, which the band got a tremendous giggle out of. The DeFilippos and the Tony Mart family had one hell of a party for the band.

Other than Levon and Robbie committing to Bob Dylan, things remained the same, and the group was scheduled to be playing back in Toronto at the Friar's Tavern in September. Beyond that, the Hawks were still biding their time on the club circuit. A great deal of uncertainty surrounded Richard and the group, including their still-unsettled charges from the marijuana bust in January. Things were moving at a furious pace, but lacking a specific direction.

Levon and the Hawks loaded up their gear and pulled out of Somers Point not knowing what would happen next. Within a month, the band would mean something else completely to an entirely new audience.

"Dylan is like a ball of fire and is filled with a hyped energy. He never ceases to amaze anyone."

Chapter 6
GALLANT KNIGHTS (1965-1966)

August 28, 1965: Richard Manuel is immortalized in a summery black-and-white Daniel Kramer photograph. It's just before Bob Dylan's Forest Hills concert, and Dylan, Levon Helm, and Robbie Robertson wait in a semicircle backstage. Standing in the background, Richard looks on, interested and especially dapper and hip, sporting side-parted hair and a midday shadow.

The stadium was packed, and as Levon Helm remembered in his memoir, "The whole band had come up from New Jersey. I wanted everybody to feel part of the show because I had an inkling of the way things would work out." Richard, Rick, and Garth watched from the wings of the stage as their bandmates played for the biggest and strangest crowd they had ever seen. It's not a stretch to say Richard wanted to perform. He was a player, not a spectator. He felt like a benchwarmer waiting patiently to get on the field to show his stuff.

The two opening shows of Bob Dylan's electric tour changed rock 'n' roll performance forever. Conflict between folk music purists and Dylan's new direction created provocative theater. Dylan was an artist in complete command of his vision, and his band was the central element of this combative musical mixture.

The two confrontational yet successful performances with Levon and Robbie, the first at Forest Hills and then at the Hollywood Bowl, were insane. The crowds were rowdy, Dylan unapologetic, and the music rough hewn and exciting. After the Hollywood Bowl concert on September 3, Dylan's management broached the inevitable: Would Helm and Robertson sign on for the rest of the tour?

Who exactly took a stand for the Hawks brotherhood is irrelevant. The act itself is an obvious testament to the deep friendship and shared confidence in their music. Levon and Robbie told Dylan Inc. that all the Hawks would be coming along for the musical ride—or none of them were coming. Robbie remembered in his memoir that he told Dylan, "It's kind of an all-or-nothing situation." Levon concurred in his book: "Take us all or don't take any of us." With that ultimatum to Dylan's management, Bob himself decided to head to Toronto to watch the band play and decide whether the rest of the guys could cut it.

THE MIRA SOUND SINGLE

Before their rendezvous with Dylan in Toronto, Levon and the Hawks had another studio date to make. The Hawks had a session booked at Mira Sound in Manhattan to cut a single. For the session, Richard took the lead vocals on two Robbie Robertson–penned songs, "The Stones That I Throw" backed with "He Don't Love You (and He'll Break Your Heart)." That B side is as weighty a slab of funky R&B as the group ever cut. Richard pleads with a typically invested vocal attack, the cut bobs with a weighted bottom, and the Hawks never sounded better on tape. The track sums up an entire fantastic era of the group in a tight, crisp package.

Similar to his stunning vocal performances on Bobby "Blue" Bland's "No Sweeter Girl," from the London and Port Dover 1964 field recordings, Richard navigates the hard changes with deft precision, the only difference this time being that the song was an original composed by one of his very own bandmates. Richard and the Hawks captured lightning in a bottle on the song.

The A side, "The Stones That I Throw," was also quirky in its approach both instrumentally and lyrically and was another of Robbie's original compositions. The arrangement finds Richard taking the lead vocals against a solid secular backdrop of lacy Hudson church organ and wistful harmonica. The verses are a bit stiff, but the chorus opens to reveal the swinging depths of Richard and the Hawks' gospel influences.

On 2005's *A Musical History*, a demo recorded while the group was in their apartment in Somers Point illustrates the work being done by the band. Robbie plays the framework of the song on acoustic guitar while Richard navigates the vocal melody, a gentle sense of wonder tangible in his tone.

Guitarist Brian Pawley remembers hearing the song when the single dropped, and thought back to spinning records by the Impressions with the Hawks in London, Ontario: "When they came out with that song, 'The Stones That I Throw,' and I heard the harmonies . . . yeah, you can hear the [Impressions'] influence."

Returning to Toronto and the Friar's Tavern, Levon and the Hawks got back to work and awaited Dylan's visit. The Hawks had sharpened their skills night after night, working toward a common goal of *not* having to back anybody. But opportunity knocked hard, and the Hawks owed it to themselves to answer.

On the afternoon of Wednesday, September 15, 1965, Dylan landed in Toronto to watch the Hawks play. What he witnessed was a group as tight as Booker T. and the M.G.'s, as loose as Howlin' Wolf's band, and as adept at playing R&B and blues as they were hit-parade rock 'n' roll. Dylan heard the ramshackle vamp of the rhythm section and Robbie's aggressive mathematical dressings. Especially powerful was the way that Richard and Garth initiated a complex and billowing wash of sound over the big beat. Dylan was sold.

On September 18, 1965, the *Toronto Daily Star* reported:

> Dylan was in Toronto this week to spend a few hours rehearsing with Levon and the Hawks, the group at the Friar's. Dylan came here from New York in his private plane Friday evening. At midnight Dylan went to the Friar's to hear Levon's group, and when they finished, he rehearsed with them till six. The next night he repeated the process and then went back to New York at noon Friday.

Dylan hit it off with Richard, whose soft intelligence and humble humor appealed to him. He got along with all the Hawks, but what really mattered was whether they could relate musically. They rehearsed into the early hours after the Hawks sets. Dylan ran through some blues tunes and then some originals. Roughshod renditions and squeaky-wheel readings of "I Don't Believe You (She Acts Like We Never Have Met)," "Just Like Tom Thumb's Blues," and "It Ain't Me Babe" made up the haphazard rehearsal.

The Hawks had mixed feelings about moving forward with Dylan. Richard was Richard, always up for an adventure. He was excited about the possibilities Dylan would afford them, yet he was concerned that the rehearsals were sloppy. He felt that sometimes Dylan and the Hawks were playing different songs. Robbie recalled in his memoir that Richard offered the following critique of Dylan after rehearsals: "He seems like an OK guy to me, but that run-through wasn't very good on our end. We have to start by really learning these songs." If they were going to do this thing, they were going to have to put in the work to make it right.

Dylan was immediately convinced that the Hawks were his band. Right after those introductory rehearsals, he told the *Toronto Daily Star*, "I know my thing now. I know what it is. It's hard to describe. I don't know what to call it because I've never heard it before." Dylan and the Hawks had invented a creative cacophony of sound that night on the Friar's stage. While neither Dylan nor the Hawks could figure out what exactly happened when they played, they all knew they had to pursue it.

From militant practice and self-discipline, the Hawks had mastered an error-free professional presentation and a viselike grip on their respective arrangements. Dylan famously worked in the opposition. As Richard explained to his hometown newspaper in 1966, "Dylan is like a ball of fire and is filled with a hyped energy. He never ceases to amaze anyone." He revealed that "he even took awhile to accept our group. Dylan has no patience for rehearsals and expects a certain spontaneity from us."

Therein lies the conflict in the collaboration between Dylan and the Band: Dylan, a troubadour assimilating a solo acoustic show into a full band, and a group learning to disregard everything they had learned in order to find the music in beautiful chaos. What was born from the union was beyond any of their expectations or dreams.

Richard put a lot on the line to find the music. Just as he got comfortable in leading the Hawks with his voice, he silenced it for opportunity. He set aside his most prolific gift and became a better bandmate and instrumentalist because of it. Richard recalled the Hawks' initial collaboration with Dylan in a rare May 1971 interview with *Disc and Music Echo*, saying, "We were just starting to work on our own material at the time, but I'm glad we did it."

Listening to their live recordings and studio singles confirms it: the Hawks were a band operating on the fringes of the industry. Dylan provided an opportunity, no matter how strange, for the band to be seen. Richard continued:

> I hadn't heard much Dylan stuff before then. I'd heard other people's albums but prior to that, we were very much into nightclub rock 'n' roll. When Bob recorded his first electric album, *Bringing It All Back Home*, most of the musicians on it were studio musicians; they weren't a group as far as traveling around was concerned. After we'd heard **that** album, it wasn't so much a surprise he asked us. . . . Being with Dylan probably did help us; it would be silly to say it didn't, but I'd hate to say that we wouldn't have made it otherwise. It would have probably just taken us *longer*.

Plans were hatched to have the entire flock of Hawks, as well as manager Bill Avis, join Dylan for his upcoming fall dates. Garth Hudson would recall in a 2003 interview on the Canadian television show *Studio 2*, "We went from the bar to the stars." The ascent was a blur of wild mercury music. The Dylan tour was idling and scheduled to run from September 23 through December 19, with breaks for studio sessions penciled in. Only four years after loading up the Cadillac and heading to Arkansas with Ken Kalmusky, Jimmy Winkler, Garth Picot, and Doug Rhodes, Richard got on a private plane and toured the United States.

The transition was not seamless for either party, as Robbie explained to *Rolling Stone* in 1978:

> It was an interesting challenge. It was easy to play with him, but it was hard getting everybody to play with him at the same time because he would break meter and all of a sudden you wouldn't know where you were, you'd get mixed up. Sometimes we didn't know if we were playing great music or nonsense.

Levon echoed these sentiments in his memoir: "It was a hell of a challenge, because he was still learning about a band. He would suddenly stop and break the beat, and we'd get confused and not know where we were."

Richard's role as the pulse of the Hawks became even more important as they teamed up with Dylan. Levon and Richard locked eyes to feel the changes. Rick focused on the root so that the changes were true. Robbie and Garth would leave the songs in a flourish of melody and look for gentle returns to Richard's solid underpinning.

Dylan's electric-guitar approach needed direction. Keeping tempo with a rock orchestra like Levon and the Hawks was a far different proposition than playing as a solo performer. Richard and the Hawks were practiced pros at electric music by this juncture. Perfectionists. When the Hawks worked out the arrangement of a song, they ground it until the corners were rounded. When success was reached, the group would exclaim, "That's official!," which meant that they had the groove nailed to the floorboards. Leading up to the Dylan tour, they knew they might get only one shot at playing a song, and it might turn out differently the next night.

Audio documentation of Bob Dylan and the Hawks' introductory autumn 1965 concerts is limited, which is unfortunate because of the obvious importance of the shows in rock history and in tracing Richard's musical journey. Fortunately, by the time Dylan and the Hawks hit Australia and Europe in April and May 1966, the effort was made to record every single night of the concert tour in pristine soundboard quality both for review and documentation.

The fall US tour began in Austin, Texas, on September 24, 1965. The Hawks had played often in this region, but their name wasn't noted at the performance. To kick off the tour, Dylan and the Hawks flew by private jet, a thirteen-seat Lockheed Lodestar that Rick called the "Volkswagen Bus of the Sky."

The performances on the Dylan tour were broken into two sets. The first featured acoustic Dylan, the troubadour, rising to meet the crowd's expectations and leaving them dizzied and contemplating the smoke rings of their mind. Wistful and thought provoking, the focus was on the words, the message, Dylan.

The second portion of the concert was unexpected for many in the audience. The Hawks—dressed street casual, with tight hair, sport jackets, and slacks—plugged in. Richard, wearing a gray suit coat and drainpipe trousers, his hair swept in the front and sideburns just below his ears, pulled up a stool to the piano. On the darkened stage, the Hawks took their battle positions: Richard stage right / audience left, Rick just offset in front of him, Dylan center stage, Levon on a riser center stage behind Dylan, Robbie stage left, and Garth just offset behind Robbie. The amplifier dials emitted an eerie glow, and a humming chorus of electric guitars charged the air with an alien anticipation.

In a face-off, Dylan and Robbie, guitars kissing, would stomp their feet to the rhythm of the opening number, and with a snare crack the group would tear into "Maggie's Farm"—a screaming, teetering, runaway rockabilly hybrid, Dylan's vocals too fast, rhythmic, chanted, flying by unintelligibly like a hopped-up derivative of an Elvis Sun side. The Hawks were in full churn, the dual keyboards sending a whirling and disorienting array around the arena, Robbie pulling off his strings like the guitar was 1,000 degrees, and Rick visually illustrating the groove of the music by gyrating his body to every downbeat.

One thing that can be confirmed from eyewitness accounts is that Dylan and the Hawks were LOUD. Seriously loud. Devastatingly loud.

The Texas crowds were accepting of Dylan's new direction and offered positive feedback to the performances. When the tour moved north, the booing and jeering became a nightly ritual. The electric sets comprised reimagined Dylan "folk" songs as well as new Dylan compositions written with a full band in mind. Regardless of the choice, the crowd was often disappointed.

There are no existing recordings from the Dylan fall tour's first three shows, the two in Austin and a single show in Dallas. There is allegedly an audio copy of Dylan and the Hawks' now-legendary performance at Carnegie Hall, which was the first show of the East Coast portion of the tour on October 1, 1965. Unfortunately, copies of this recording remain elusive, so the earliest accessible tapes are from the end of the month.

According to multiple accounts, the Carnegie Hall concert was the highwater mark of Dylan and the Hawks' first iteration. It proved to Richard and his bandmates that the uncertain mission they had embarked on was irrefutably relevant and musically important. Mary Martin attended the Carnegie Hall show and witnessed Dylan beaming because of the way the evening had transpired. Future Band manager Jonathan Taplin was also at the show and remembered, "It was astonishing. They were louder than any band I'd ever heard." In the program for the evening's performance, Levon and the Hawks are listed both individually by name and as accompanists.

After an October 2 performance at Newark Symphony Hall in New Jersey and still high from Carnegie, the Hawks hit the studio with Dylan to see how their onstage alchemy would translate to tape. This session was the first time Dylan and the Hawks attempted to play music in a studio setting.

THE CUTTING EDGE

On October 5, Dylan and the Hawks visited Columbia Studio A for a pair of three-hour sessions, where they attempted four Dylan originals and two instrumentals. The entire day's work was eventually released on the 2015 deluxe box set *The Bootleg Series Vol. 12: The Cutting Edge, 1965–1966*.

Richard's piano personality and tone when played on a professional studio piano is a revelation. His trademark saloon roll and well-placed rubato are a joy to hear. The session reels begin with two attempts at an unreleased Dylan track called "Medicine Sunday," which results in two incomplete versions. The group settles in with a jerky period-appropriate "Ticket to Ride" type of rhythm before moving on.

Richard percolates to the surface on the next take, the first iteration of "Jet Pilot." It's only a song fragment, but it gives us our first glimpse of the Hawks as a full performing unit behind Dylan. While lasting only a bit over a minute, the song begins as a lumbering airplane taking a slow taxi, but by the time the instrumental section hits, the Hawks are screaming down the runway.

Richard remains the mucilage that connects the duo of Danko and Helm. While he was vocally silent in Dylan's band, Richard's inventive chord inversions and melodic snatches are his vehicle for expression. Dylan and the group are searching for the perfect sound, and the journey is fascinating to hear.

A legendary and initially unreleased Dylan original follows, with six takes of "I Wanna Be Your Lover" in which Richard's playing is strong and worthy of inspection. The first take finds Richard working in the upper register of the piano with heavy accents. It captures the band discovering the song's center, with Richard and Garth swinging with an urgency reminiscent of "Bacon Fat." There is a definite enthusiasm on the reels in the creation of this Dylan/Hawks hybrid.

Take 2 of the arrangement turns on its heel into a rockabilly thump with killer Helm/Danko interplay while Richard plays with restraint. After that complete take, there's some discussion regarding the arrangement between Robbie and Richard, who then practices some roly-poly chording as the tape runs out. Before take 3, Richard and Garth work out their parts together; Robbie then joins in as the Hawks discuss their approach.

The third attempt keeps the same arrangement and smokes like a campfire after a downpour. Dylan raps with a *Blonde on Blonde* urgency that culminates with howls at the end of every stanza. Three additional complete takes, similar in scope, follow, with Richard actively finding his place in the instrumental mix.

The band finishes the session with two instrumental takes listed as "Number One" on session sheets, one a fragment and the second a complete take. A strange power emanates from this groovy instrumental. Midway through, Levon bangs on the tom-toms and Richard clip-clops down the steps to a place where Robbie is indulging in string bending. This is a mysterious track that blends the best of both the Hawks' and Dylan's abilities in a melodic meshing of what was yet to be. The day's work ended up a productive initial session for Dylan and the Hawks, though it's almost unbelievable that nothing was released from this day until 2015's *The Cutting Edge*

Returning to the road, Dylan and the Hawks finished up their East Coast engagements before heading to the Left Coast for additional dates. The crowds that attended the concerts were mixed in their reactions to the electric portion. The folk purists were angry and confrontational, but others allowed themselves to be taken away by the new music. Richard and the Hawks didn't give a shit. Chiseled from the Ronnie Hawkins School of Hard Knocks, the Hawks completed their jobs, collected the loot, and swooped into the next city. Dylan's attitude rubbed off on the guys, and a collaborative "fuck you" mentality started to come out in the music.

As an addendum to 2015's *The Cutting Edge*, Dylan's team included over ten hours of live recordings from 1965. It includes snippets of tape from the October 29 and 31 performances in Boston, as well as a more complete recording of Dylan and the Hawks from October 30 at Bushnell Memorial Hall in Hartford, Connecticut, which split the Boston shows. These renegade field recordings allow an audio verité glimpse into Richard Manuel's musical majesty in the making.

On the tape from Hartford on October 30, while the band sounds tentative, there are moments that foreshadow the musical monster ready to reveal itself. Highlights include Richard's triumphant piano exclamations throughout "It Ain't Me Babe" punctuating each of Dylan's choruses. His playing is the work of a man giving his all to develop the framework of the song. While not a virtuosic approach, it is one of attentiveness. Richard had committed himself to improving his listening abilities, and playing every single night on the precipice of sonic ecstasy helped his ascension to a more-than-serviceable accompanist.

A destructive "Maggie's Farm" jumps off the Boston tape, where Richard's road-graded boogie-woogie can be heard answering Robbie's overdriven guitar tone through the aural sludge.

The musical difference between Dylan's first electric shows with Al Kooper and Harvey Brooks and the subsequent shows with the full Hawks is astonishing. It's immediately obvious that Garth Hudson and Richard Manuel's dual keyboard attack would take Dylan's lyrical landscapes to previously unattainable horizons. The music, once colorless, now shivered with vibrant energy. This is especially evident on a dynamic reading of "Positively 4th Street," where the Richard and Garth teamwork is a highlight.

Richard has taken over the piano stool with a fierce determination that is supported by the available recordings. His rhythmic sophistication and attentiveness to the songs make up for any lingering technical shortcomings. His willingness to assimilate himself into the arrangements selflessly and with soulful intent is a testament to the long hours and on-the-job training he'd had since 1957.

After a month on the road together, changes began to take place in the performances. Dylan and the Hawks were no longer a clunky folk-rock test project made up of disparate elements. They transformed onstage at a furious rate in front of paid spectators.

Richard threw himself into Dylan's leaden aesthetic as quickly as he did with Hawkins, the only difference being that Dylan was as off the rails as his new bandmates. Richard jumped into the supersonic pace of Dylan's existence with aplomb. Every night was a journey into the unknown, artistically, culturally, sexually, and psychologically.

After two months on the road with the Hawks, the changes taking place in the performances became discernible. By November, the band had tightened down the musical bolts and was starting to run with a polished efficiency . . . but one that threatened to collapse at a moment's notice.

Richard and the band returned home for a performance at Toronto's Massey Hall on November 14 and 15. Canadian DJ John Donabie attended the first night and recalled, "The sound was wild and unleashed. I had never seen a band play this way before. I would say that they were the tightest, loosest band I had ever seen." Despite the prolific creativity taking place onstage, Levon was nearing the end of his rope, sick of the moody crowds, loose arrangements, and the looming loss of his band.

After that show, Levon's second thoughts about his place in Dylan's group were impossible to hide. The Toronto press called the Hawks "a second-rate Yonge Street band." Levon was discouraged, he was sick of the booing, and he was tired of the insults and anger directed at the group. He spoke with Richard about his plans to leave, and Richard was supportive of his friend and understood Levon's misgivings about backing Dylan. On the other hand, Richard liked the chaos, enjoyed the fringe benefits, and was going to ride the opportunity till the wheels fell off.

Over the next year, battle lines were drawn between folkies and rockers, and the Hawks were the central focus of angered Dylan supporters. The Boston crowds were the beginning of the end for Levon, but Toronto pushed him over the edge. This was the Hawks' crowd, and to be booed and criticized was too much for him to bear.

The band loved Levon and understood his plight but knew that they now had a responsibility to the music and the muse. In his memoir, Robbie remembered Richard being matter-of-fact about his friend's departure: "Hey, not everybody's cut out for a big, strange, unusual challenge. He hated it, I know. He just doesn't dig this music like we do, and I'm liking it more every day."

There is a partial audience recording from Chicago's Arie Crown Theater on November 26, 1965, only days before Levon's defection from the group. The concert begins with an enterprising taper preparing his gear for the increased intensity of the electric portion of the concert. The taper, who lends his own narrative to the event, speaks into his microphone: "Bob's tuning up with the orchestra right now. He's playing electric guitar." "Tombstone Blues" starts the show as an undulating swing, with Dylan singing classically over the groovy din. With earphones giving Richard a particularly careful focus, his trembling thump works in perfect conjunction with Rick's hearty pulse, audible through the magnetic tape like spying a silhouette through a steamy shower curtain.

Bruce Plowman of the *Chicago Tribune*, after attending the first evening, wrote, "Throughout the second half, or second concert, Dylan was booed by the purists who wanted him to unplug his guitar, send his cohorts off of the stage, and start singing the way he did before intermission."

The Chicago show was Levon's last. He spoke with Robbie about his struggles with playing behind Dylan and his decision to step down from the drum riser. He asked Robbie to let his bandmates know, and caught a bus out of town in the middle of the night. Unfortunately for Dylan, and the Hawks, just after Levon's departure they were immediately due in the studio. Levon's absence definitely was a contributing factor in the band's inability to ever truly get it together.

On November 30, 1965, Richard and the Hawks entered the studio for their second session with Dylan. The group ran through multiple versions of Dylan's opus, "Visions of Johanna," which at that time was titled "Freeze Out," as well as several attempts at a recording of "Can You Please Crawl Out Your Window?" Dylan was tasked with getting a single ready for release, and the pressure was on. His frustrations boiled over and can be heard on the recording, with most of the venom directed at the drum stool, which was occupied by an unnamed session drummer thought to be Bobby Gregg.

Dylan and the Hawks did get something captured for public dissemination, since take 6 of "Can You Please Crawl Out Your Window?" was earmarked as Dylan's next single. Both Paul Griffin and Richard are listed in session notes, though Richard's playing is instantly recognizable on the mono single. Additional audio evidence has Dylan referring to Richard by name on the session tapes.

The resulting single is a funky rocker with Richard highly active in the mix. The Hawks' double-barreled keyboards fire off alternating streamers of melodic variations, with Robbie's guitar an aggressive anomaly for the era. But in the end, the song did nothing on the charts, and once again Dylan and the Hawks couldn't properly capture their alchemy in the studio.

The band headed back out on the road in December minus Levon and with a degree of uncertainty of what they would encounter next. Richard, on the other hand, was in the mood for some science fiction. He didn't give a shit about being booed. Being in the center of such a freak show was what was so appealing. He dug the jet-setting, high-speed environment. He loved the flowing drink, he *really loved* the girls, and he was willing to take a chance on the music, with the hopes of being able to stay on the path he was traveling for as long as possible.

The Ginsberg Tapes

The final available recordings of Richard onstage with Dylan in 1965 come on the "Ginsberg" tapes, which poet and Dylan friend Allen Ginsberg dutifully recorded with his newly purchased reel-to-reel. The immortalized West Coast performances in Berkeley on December 11 and San Jose on December 12 are playful and purposeful and were well received by the crowds. The tapes are also the best sounding of the 1965 performances.

The San Francisco concert is powerful and well played, highlighted by an orchestrated "It Ain't Me Babe" and a sneering "Positively 4th Street." It's at the San Jose show where you can really discern what Richard is laying down. In spite of having to work with another drummer in Bobby Gregg, the Hawks continue to flex their musical muscles.

During the opening "Tombstone Blues," Richard and Garth agitate themselves into a vortex. Richard spackles up emotional cracks throughout the syncopated start-and-stop arrangement of "It Ain't Me Babe," a song that would unfortunately disappear from Dylan sets before the end of the year. Richard really ups his playing with sparkling filigrees. His roly-poly chording concludes each Dylan verse.

A highlight of both available December performances is a song the Hawks would later make their own attempt at in the studio, Dylan's "Long Distance Operator." Never officially released by Dylan, the bluesy stomp made a connection with Richard and the Hawks. The band expressed a kinky style of playing that conveys Dylan's painful inability to get an important message through.

Richard plays off everybody in the group, responding to all nuance with timely rhythmic tidbits. Rick and Richard lock in on a groovy thump as Robbie and Garth toss off copacetic riffing. The interplay is delectable. Perhaps the new addition to the set was Dylan's way of working more toward his band's strengths.

The tour concluded in Santa Monica on December 19, and Dylan and the Hawks separated for the holidays. The plan was to reconvene for another studio visit in January before starting a world tour in February. Richard returned to Stratford to take stock of what he had just experienced and to prepare for round 2 with Dylan.

The band's inability to get anything down in the studio was a problem both for Dylan and his management and planted a seed of doubt with Dylan as well as the Hawks. After their whirlwind escapades with Dylan, the Hawks brought in New Year's 1966 at the Friar's Tavern with family and friends.

In January, the band met with Dylan for sessions for what would eventually become *Blonde on Blonde*. There were issues all around, the biggest being Dylan's volcanic creative dysfunction. When one listens to the session tapes, it's obvious that Dylan is erratic in his decisions . . . and the group stubborn in as attempts to accommodate his whims.

Unfortunately, the onstage success of the band still couldn't carry over to the studio. Dylan's consistent impatience and blurred vision and the Hawks' constant search for perfection collided in messy sessions. The impact of the loss of Levon Helm cannot be overstated, as a multitude of issues stemmed from the efforts to develop a consistent groove among the six musicians. Dylan and the Hawks reconvened for one final studio call on January 21, 1966, where they attempted sixteen takes of "She's Your Lover Now." This entire session is available to review on *The Cutting Edge*.

It was a missed opportunity as Dylan and the band worked for twelve hours on a song that remained unreleased. They got down an almost complete sixth take that featured moments of note and some probing playing by Richard. By take 7, the arrangement changes, and Dylan did most of the piano playing; by take 12, Dylan explained to Richard what needed to happen just as the tape cut off.

On take 14, Dylan pleaded with Richard to "just do that, please just do that," to which Richard responded, "But sometimes you're doing long breaks," before the tape ended. It would take dedicated hard work and compromise on both sides of the aisle for this music to get off the ground.

By the next session on the 25th, only Robbie and Rick were on hand while Richard and Garth cooled their heels until the tour started on February 5. When asked by *New York Times* music critic Robert Shelton why the sessions with the Hawks failed to yield any fruit, Dylan was frank: "I mean, in like ten recording sessions, man, we didn't get one song. It was the band. But you see, I didn't know that. I didn't want to think that." Dylan then moved the remaining sessions for what became *Blonde on Blonde* to Nashville, using session musicians, and the Hawks remained his road band.

When Richard Manuel embarked on the 1966 portion of the Dylan tour, there was no rock band on earth that could touch the Hawks when they mixed up the medicine onstage. Whatever misunderstandings had taken place in Columbia Studios went out the window on the road. Richard and Garth had developed a slippery aerodynamic telepathy in their playing and a second sense that turned previously acoustic-based tracks such as "I Don't Believe You (She Acts Like We Never Have Met)" into a new genre of music beyond description.

Butch Dener, who would later go on to be road manager for Levon, remembered in 2022 seeing Dylan and the Hawks at the Westchester County Center on the second night of the tour:

> So when they set up and started to play, it was like a thunderbolt. Wow, Bob Dylan, you know, amplified with this band. And Richard and Garth . . . I mean, Robbie was Robbie, but two keyboards. Man, that was awesome. That was just amazing. And you couldn't get enough of either one of them.

The musicians took a short break after the opening US concerts before heading out to aurally assault Hawaii, Australia, and then Europe. Oddly enough, part of the respite included the Hawks lending their instrumental talents to the song "Moulty" by the Barbarians, a Boston rock 'n' roll group. The track is a quirky inspirational novelty, and the Hawks' instrumental aesthetic fits it perfectly. The group joins in on the bombastic vocal choruses, and a close listen reveals Richard's recognizable piano jangling underneath the weighty beat. The circus tent groove and straight-up strangeness of the song foreshadow the goofy excursions that the band would become involved in throughout the next year.

Richard, possible passport photograph, 1966. *Courtesy of the Richard Manuel family*

The electric sets of the 1966 Dylan world tour are some of the most original and visionary music played on a rock 'n' roll stage. It changed music presentation, audience interaction, and how rock 'n' roll music was written and shared. Dylan and the Hawks were creating a new genre in real time and force-feeding folk audiences a lethal dose of what Dylan later called "that thin, that wild mercury sound."

A series of intimate theaters were booked in Australia and then throughout Europe for 1966. The framework of the fall 1965 performances remained, with Dylan first playing a narcotics-soaked acoustic set followed by an intermission, and then the radical electricity of Dylan and the Hawks.

As it did in the States, the nervous buzz of electric amplifiers elicited an eclectic anticipation. The European crowds squirmed in their seats, unsure of what to expect. Richard would nestle at stage right with a cross-stage view of the remaining band members: Rick just in front of Richard, new drummer Mickey Jones on a riser center stage, Dylan in the spotlight, Robbie close at hand, and Garth obscured in darkness far stage left. An attendee of one of those European concerts recalled the Hawks' stage entry: "They all looked a bit mad. Tough. As if to say, 'Let's see what reaction we can get.'"

Fortunately, the entire tour from Australia until England was documented and is available to those who wish to take the deep dive. Soundboard line recordings of every night are available for inspection and analysis. Unbelievably, the tapes were released in November 2016 in a comprehensive box set by collecting all the available soundboard recordings made by Dylan soundman Richard Alderson, who experienced every epic night firsthand. When asked to describe life on the tour for the box set's release, Alderson used such terms as "hectic, hard, sleepless, driving, and crazy." He recalled, "The audiences were hostile. The band responded to the hostility of the audience by playing more aggressively. The band played their asses off."

For many years, the only official documentation of the tour was the version of "Just Like Tom Thumb's Blues" from Liverpool on May 14, 1966. Richard's playing is special; he dances up to and around the central melody, working against Dylan's fluctuating vocal current. He and Garth play a matched pair and take turns meshing dynamically into a radiant wall of sound. Dylan obviously felt that the moment was important enough to warrant an official document of his adventures with the Hawks. It was placed on the B side of the "I Want You" single in June 1966.

Dylan and the Hawks landed in Sydney, Australia, on April 12, 1966, to kick off a month-and-a-half-long vision quest of revolutionary rock 'n' roll music. The preliminary Australian shows were gritty, loud, and an instant shock to the inhabitants of the continent. Dylan and the band would play seven shows through April 23. On flickering black-and-white newsreel footage of Dylan, his entourage, and the Hawks landing, Richard can be seen walking across the tarmac, beaming, wearing shades and a now-constant chapeau perched high upon his head, all the while balancing a precarious stack of tambourines.

Bob Dylan and the Hawks onstage in Melbourne, Australia, 1966. *Courtesy of Photography by John Collings*

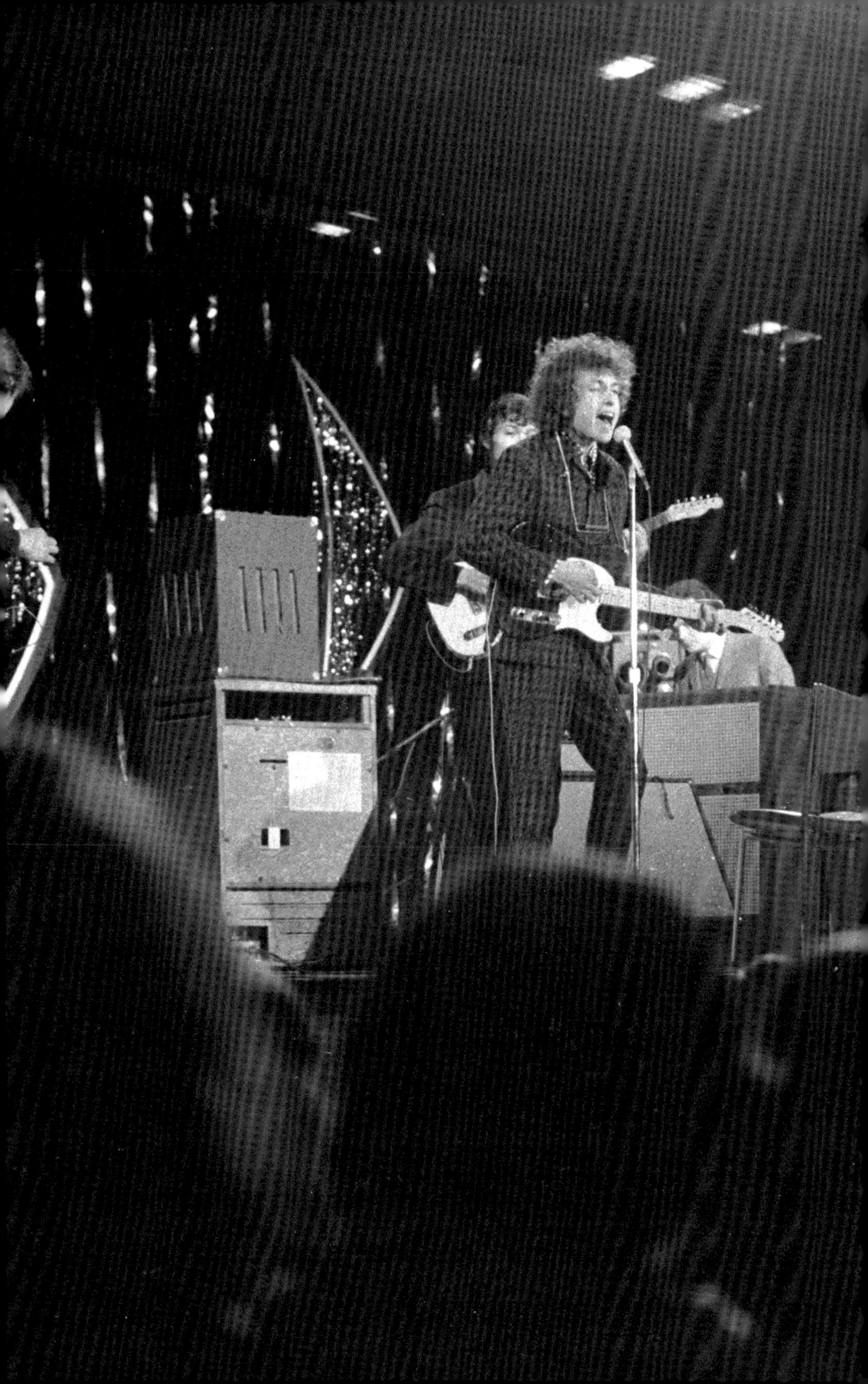

On the Sydney soundboard recording from April 13, where the band played on a rotating stage, the spacious mix reveals confident playing by Richard on "Positively 4th Street," which quickly disappeared from the set when the group left the continent. Concert attendee Terry Darmody recalled the Sydney concert in *Isis* magazine and remembers Richard wearing a maroon silk shirt with long sleeves and maroon chalk-stripe woolen pants. The band was "exploding all over the stage in their carnival-type clothes," Darmody said, "and I thought, 'This is a musical circus played by incredibly good players.' It's hard to describe why it didn't sound like an assault, but the music breathed in a way a good orchestra breathes together. It entrances you in an aggressive, masculine way."

The carnival continued its run across Australia, landing in Brisbane for the next show. Local photographer Frank Neilsen recalled the Hawks' arrival at the airport in *Isis*:

> People smoked in airplanes in the day, and I think that some of the members of Bob's band may have been smoking hashish on the way up from Sydney. They were certainly in high spirits as they burst into the almost-deserted terminal and proceeded to ride the children's coin-in-the-slot rocking kangaroos.

Richard was still a kid, and he took every opportunity to laugh. He and Rick took their comedy to new levels and kept bumpy bus rides and boring hotel stays full of chuckles and smiles. Richard was not a cosmopolitan, and though his hometown of Stratford instilled in him an artistic sensibility, he was a working-class man, who was flying by the seat of his rock 'n' roll pants. He was unsupervised and undereducated in the ways of travel arrangements and schedules. He was learning, but trying to navigate the press was one thing Richard quickly removed himself from.

Reports indicate that the Brisbane performance was full of angry folk purists and fans who also disliked the look of the band. In what would become a theme for this portion of the world tour, Dylan and the Hawks blasted their way into town, ravaged the townspeople, crashed their parties, and moved on to their next conquest.

The group returned for a second performance in Sydney (of which no recording circulates), where the Hawks were described locally as looking like "greasers with truck drivers' haircuts." The Dylan cavalcade was involved in some behind-the-scenes madness as Hawks manager Bill Avis was removed from the tour after some unfortunate circumstances with the Australian authorities and a pot party. Onstage, the band continued its aggressive dissemination of sound art with two shows at Festival Hall in Melbourne.

Dylan had issues in Australia: his throat bothered him, and his acoustic guitar had been broken in transit. The Hawks played gritty and loud, though they were still struggling with Dylan's folk strumming in the electric maelstrom. Eyewitnesses report Robbie unplugging Dylan's guitar from the amp while onstage in Melbourne. Regardless of the on-the-fly adjustments, there is gradual and traceable expansion of the songs from Australia to Europe.

Richard's playing was quickly becoming a key element of the Dylan and the Hawks' onstage mix. His piano playing, much as it was during his time with Ronnie Hawkins, not only acted as the pulse of the group when their instruments throttled into the stratosphere but was the bed in which Garth could drape his keyboard magic while Robbie stabbed holes in the sky. Richard had graduated from block chording and percussive accompaniment to delicate runs and all-around confident playing.

As wide eyed as Richard was leaving Canada for Arkansas, leaving for Australia and Europe was a completely different experience. Drugs and alcohol figured into the musical equation. Smoking hash was a favorite pastime for the Hawks. Medicine, as Dylan called it, was the only way for anyone involved in the tour's madness to keep up with the tempo and the traveling. The music reflected this reality in its detached attitude. By 1966, the result of the Dylan/Hawks union was a group of road-tested musicians from contrasting artistic spheres hitting their stride, collectively and individually.

The film crew that accompanied Dylan's silver streak around Europe often caught Richard as foil to Dylan's surreal escapades of absurdity. Richard, like Robbie and Dylan, donned an impenetrable shield of dark shades and often spoke in jokes, non sequiturs, and asides that only members of Dylan's exclusive club could translate. The entire entourage moved through a fish-eye world in a prolific haze.

Musically, the Hawks were beginning to find ways to express Dylan's lyricism through nuance and dynamics. The group's constant high-pressure and maximum-impact concerts had provided them with a fighter's stance and a collaborative kinship that only strengthened their resolve. Dylan had learned to accept any real or imagined shortcomings in Richard's and Rick's instrumental prowess and just plain liked hanging out with the guys. Richard had earned his stripes, made the big man laugh, and was a full-blown, world-travelin' rock 'n' roller.

On the best nights of the 1966 tour, the music is lustrous chrome, street music, renegade shit. By May 1966, Richard was a critical member of the best band on the planet. The 1966 live stages of the Beatles, the Rolling Stones, and the Who paled in comparison to the defiant onslaught of sound alchemized by Bob Dylan and the Hawks. United States or Europe, Dylan and the Hawks blended the best songwriter with the most diverse rock 'n' roll band into a melodic maelstrom of mathematical chaos.

The crowds were belligerent. The British reacted even worse than the folk purists in Australia and the States. Concerts in Liverpool, Newcastle, and London were especially rowdy. In Dublin, Dylan was called a traitor. In Paris, the curtain opened to reveal Dylan and the Hawks playing in front of an American flag. The resulting interactions with the crowd were tinged with aggression. There were walkouts, shouting matches, and things thrown at the stage. The Hawks were the center of the ire, the cause of the madness, as if *they* were responsible for Dylan's insane change of artistic direction. The synergy of the sound, the crowds' angst, and Dylan's bizarre behavior made for an uneasy evening of music and art.

Watching footage of the performances is surreal theater. The venues are classically ornate, the stages barren, Richard and Garth tucked away stage right and left, respectively. Dylan moved in, initiating a strange erotic dance with Robbie while conducting a guitar pantomime. The audience, not quite sure who's playing what, is pummeled by the sheer volume of the instruments. Robbie put it succinctly to Rob Bowman in 1991: "By the time we did the Australia and Europe tours, we had discovered whatever this thing was. It was not light; it was not folky. It was very dynamic, very explosive, and very violent."

Richard boarded a rocket from the Blue Water Lounge to Desolation Row, while balancing on the salient razor's edge of the music of an electric prophet. The European portion of the tour was captured in a still-unreleased film (as of this writing) by director D. A. Pennebaker. Originally titled *Something Is Happening* and later presented in altered form as *Eat the Document*, the tour is illustrated in a cut-up, fragmented, and jittery series of images juxtaposed against the backdrop of incendiary musical performances by Dylan and the Hawks.

The opening salvo of the film finds the giggling Richard alongside a hysterical Dylan, who's conspicuously imbibing some sort of illicit powder off the top of a piano, assumed to be methedrine, cocaine, or some other snortable amphetamine; drugs are an obvious and overwhelming influence that must be discussed when analyzing any sort of music and musicians in the 1960s. Pennebaker recalled to Barney Hoskyns, "I may have made a movie about drugs without realizing it."

While many if not all the performances in the *Eat the Document* film are incomplete, the footage is an invaluable document of the most important tour of the 1960s. Color professional footage of peak Dylan screaming lyrics through cupped hands while dressed in a houndstooth suit is priceless.

In the case of Dylan's 1966 tour, amphetamine was the shimmery sheen covering all the various ephemera of Dylan and the Hawks' travels. Back at Tony Mart's, the group chased handfuls of diet pills with trays of ale. The guys were no strangers to the chemical temptations they encountered on the road. They were no angels, either. In the case of their travels with Dylan, it was the abundance of and the ease with which they could get anything they wanted. It was part of the mixture that allowed everyone to keep up such a pace. For Richard, it also was part of experiencing everything to its absolute limit.

Once the show landed in Europe, the experience intensified. Robbie explained the Hawks' way of thinking at Lower Canada College in Montreal in 2018: "We started playing louder, harder, bolder and sort of preaching our sermon of music." Dylan and the Hawks landed in Stockholm on April 29, 1966, for the European leg of the tour, and Richard is captured by the press clowning for the camera, guitar in one hand, paper bag in the other, cowboy hat perched on his head.

In footage from *Eat the Document*, both Richard and Dylan barter for a young Swedish man's girlfriend. In a surreal and awkward bit of comedy for the camera, Richard offers his jacket, a can opener, and eventually his ChapStick for the young man's blonde girlfriend. While the girl laughs nervously, the man declines. Richard, with a sly grin and youthful glimmer, replies, "If she smokes cigars, I'll throw in my shirt too." When the man declines again, the woman slides farther away, and Richard quips, "Swedish girls don't have any business sense." One last attempt is made in which Richard offers his smokes, but again to no avail. Dylan looks on in amusement, obviously stoned to the gills.

Two days later, on May 1, Richard caught up with Jane Kristiansen, who was in her native Denmark visiting family. The two had stayed in contact after their last meeting in Toronto, before he joined up with Dylan, and would connect again in the States.

Richard bartering alongside Bob Dylan in *Eat the Document*, 1966.
Courtesy of Grey Water Park Productions

Dylan and the Hawks quicksilvered their way through Ireland, England, and France in a series of high adventure and tightrope walks through the hallowed theaters of Europe. In a letter from mid-May, Richard wrote to his mother

Chapter 6 | Gallant Knights (1965–1966)

Richard bartering alongside Bob Dylan in *Eat the Document*, 1966.
Courtesy of Grey Water Park Productions

on Albany Hotel Birmingham stationery, where he outlines that Dylan and the Hawks have ten shows left in the tour in England and Scotland and one in Paris. He wrote:

> The Beatles came to our hotel in London one-night last week and we had a bit of a party. Before the night was over, Johnny Cash dropped in and some of the Rolling Stones got drunk and started a big argument and had to be sent home to bed.

Richard had also been shopping and collecting hats; he alerted his mother that he might send a box of clothes home, and she shouldn't be surprised if a suitcase were to show up without him attached.

Just as the Hawks had sharpened their musical talons traversing shitholes, honky-tonks, and dance halls from Canada to Arkansas, they had now ascended to sonically violating ornate and famed theaters of Europe replete with classical paintings, velvet ropes, and regal mezzanine seating.

The collaboration between Dylan and the Hawks was a volatile concoction that raised the game for everyone involved. Richard was soft; touring was hard and decadent. But his ambition still outweighed any issues he might have had around confidence. Dylan, like Hawkins, pushed him to greater things. His youthful energy and the collaborative gang of rockers created a shield of armor against anything they encountered.

Dylan and the Hawks' legendary electric sets on the 1966 tour were consistent and incredible. Every night was an experiment in musical fortitude. While the songs in the set didn't change once the band left Australia, the attitude of dissemination did. Concerts developed their own personality on the basis of several internal and external elements. Acceptance or rejection by the crowd was the defining factor of the attitude of the music. Some nights, such as May 10 and May 20, could be funky, while some, such as May 12, were playful, but most dates were defiant, such as those in Liverpool, Paris, and London. Cardiff and Manchester were celebratory, and every evening revelatory.

Richard played his ass off, as evidenced by the available recordings. He was solid, dependable, energetic, and an important coagulant in Dylan's chaotic expression of art. Richard and his bandmates had battled hard for musical relevancy. They proved it night after night in front of their contemporaries, judgmental crowds, and smug critics.

Richard onstage in Europe, 1966. *Courtesy of Grey Water Park Productions*

THE 1966 ELECTRIC SETS

What follows is the basic makeup of the electric sets that Bob Dylan and the Hawks played every night of the 1966 tour, with only minimal deviations. Important Richard Manuel musical moments are noted, and highlights are listed.

"**Tell Me, Momma**": An officially unreleased song obviously curated with the Hawks in mind. A hard-driving steam drill of a number and the show opener for every night of the 1966 tour, this song contains a litany of imagery both sexual and conceptual. The song was constructed in such a way that the Hawks could really get down and blast.

The tune evolved to become harder and more defiant as the tour progressed, with the lyrics morphing from improvised syllables into something more coherent. The electric set from May 10, 1966, in Bristol spotlights a limber Richard, who plays one of his finest sets of the tour, with "Tell Me, Momma" being one of many highlights. On May 12 he brought the funk with sharp riffing. The combative May 24 Paris performance also captures the Hawks in fine fettle, where Richard plays with a more melodic assertiveness. In color footage of this performance, Richard looks crisp in a hip gray suit. The clip captures him lending horny left-handed rolls while sitting cross-court from a beardless Garth.

"**I Don't Believe You (She Acts Like We Never Have Met)**": An acoustic number re-imagined from Dylan's 1964 *Another Side of Bob Dylan* LP and a song he introduces nightly as "It used to go like that and now it goes like this." The song puffed out its chest on the European tour after Richard and the Hawks had broken it in on the fall '65 run.

A true beneficiary of the Hawks' approach to arrangement, the song was an experiment and success in rock dynamics. It rises, falls, races, and slows while Dylan's harp wails, piercing notes over the artistic din. Search out the majestic version from Belfast on May 6, which was officially released on Bob Dylan's *Biograph*. The Hawks roll out the red carpet, and the performance contains all of the majesty one wants from the best versions of the tour. The concerts on May 24, 26, and 27 are also worth a listen for Richard's welcome contributions. The version believed by many to be definitive, May 17, can be heard on *Bootleg Series Volume 17*.

"Baby, Let Me Follow You Down": Richard's playing was consistently resplendent on this traditional folk song, originally recorded for Dylan's 1962 debut. The Hawks plug in the strummer's arrangement and go full-on Reddy Kilowatt. They changed the song from the twinkling recitation that Dylan had learned from folkie Eric Von Schmidt into an undulating and slippery rock song. By the time of the performances on the 1966 tour, Richard and his bandmates played through the changes with a second sight. The version on May 1 in Denmark is a beast, as well as a full team effort. The Paris performance is a free fall containing a spectacular Richard performance and solo. At the final Royal Albert Hall concerts, Richard grew confident enough to deal out short countermelodies spread out along Dylan's verses. He also took a nightly solo break, of which he took full advantage with a tottering run across the keys.

"Just Like Tom Thumb's Blues": The centerpiece of the 1966 tour's sets. Over the course of the tour, Richard developed a stunning descending series of chords that rolled beneath Dylan's verse melody in beautiful contrast. The spacious Hawks arrangement allowed ample space for Richard to creatively voice his melodies pulled from Dylan's chord changes. The song was a showcase for the Garth and Richard keyboard jamboree, stirring up a whip-poor-will of sound.

For many years, the only official documentation of the 1966 tour was the version of this song from the confrontational Liverpool concert on May 14. In addition to this perfect example of the Hawks in action, Richard plays especially well with a bluesy underpinning on versions taking place on May 11 and once again in Paris on May 24. Both are substantial renditions showcasing Richard's frisky finger dancing under Robbie's furious riffing. Also of note is the frantic version from the closing night of the tour on May 27.

"Leopard-Skin Pill-Box Hat": A crooked and twisted Dylan twelve-bar that allowed Richard and the group to perform like they were on the stages of the Rockwood Club. Richard was all over this number with staccato trilling and fortissimo riffing, the groove right in his sweet spot. His performances of note can be found in the stellar sets on May 10, 12, and 17. The *Blonde on Blonde* song was an essential element of the show, and a rock 'n' roll saloon blues that nestled right in Manuel's wheelhouse . . . or pub.

"Ballad of a Thin Man": Richard vacated the piano stool for Dylan when this song was performed.

"One Too Many Mornings": Another old song transformed by Dylan, which in the rough hands of the Hawks became an epic devotional. Richard lent pious chording to the song, becoming a key element in the cinematic aspect of the arrangement. Rhapsodic contributions from Garth took the panoramic melody over the top.

Rick Danko would join Dylan on the microphone for high harmony on the "behind" line every night. Richard's playing on May 26 and 27 reached a peak that he had been stacking up over the course of the tour. His performance culminates with glorious, sustained chords that ring down from some lofty reach.

"Like a Rolling Stone": The oft-extended conclusion of every set in Europe. Richard enthusiastically expressed himself nightly with the recognizable opening salvo from Dylan's studio single. Even on the most-confrontational nights, the song could sway the most jaded crowd. During the song's extended outro, the Hawks got into it like they hadn't since they last incinerated steel on "Who Do You Love?" Both Dylan and the Hawks used the song as therapy, and the readings matched the vibe they received from the crowd.

After a gunshot snare crack, the band crashed in and Richard would rattle out the recognizable introductory lick. They would start the long roll downhill, and while picking up speed, Richard would play his way through the verses while taking on short staccato improvisations during the chorus.

The incredible version from Manchester on May 17 contains Dylan's famous onstage threat, "Play fucking loud," which occurred after an angry concertgoer called him Judas. The group takes the request seriously, strikes a match, and lights the fuse.

Also worthy of note are the heavy-handed versions from both Paris and the Royal Albert Hall, which send destructive sound waves and a sonic "Fuck you" through the respective theaters.

Footage of the Newcastle "Like a Rolling Stone" from May 21 is featured as a bonus track on the *No Direction Home* film and is definitive.

After an intense roughshod performance and the bombastic conclusion of "Ballad of a Thin Man" on May 27 at the Royal Albert Hall, Bob Dylan, for the only time on the tour, introduced his band, the Hawks. He said:

> I've never done this before, but I want you to meet Robbie Robertson . . . here and Garth Hudson, Mickey Jones, Rick Danko, and . . . *Richard!* It doesn't mean a thing, but they're all poets, you understand? If it comes out that way, it comes out that way, all poets, you know?

Dylan and the Hawks then proceeded to pull their beastly tails through a loud and thick "Like a Rolling Stone" that slammed a stainless-steel door on Tour '66. Richard Manuel walked off the stage at the Royal Albert Hall having just taken part in a musical movement that shifted the entire course of rock music and concert performance.

Dylan commented in 2005 for *No Direction Home*:

> The guys that were with me on that tour, which later became the Band, we were all in it together, putting our heads in the lion's mouth. And I have to admire them for sticking it out with me. Just for doing it. In my book, they were, you know, gallant knights for even standing behind me.

Dylan and some of the Hawks at dinner on the 1966 tour.
From left at the table: Garth Hudson, Bob Dylan, Richard Manuel, Rick Danko. *Courtesy of the Barry Feinstein estate*

Richard, Rick Danko (*with Telecaster*), Bob Dylan (*with coonskin cap*),
Woodstock, New York, March 1967. *Courtesy of the Arie de Reus archive*

Chapter 7
OPEN THE DOOR, RICHARD
(1966-1967)

I'm tired of everything being beautiful, and I ain't coming back no more.
—from "Orange Juice Blues"

After an inspiring and amphetamine-fueled jaunt through the United States, Australia, and Europe, Richard and his bandmates had earned a respite from the circus. Richard returned to New York City in June 1966 and awaited his marching orders. The Dylan tour had been a nightly musical epiphany, personally and professionally. Everything that the Hawks touched, they took to the absolute limit. Richard was open to anything and everything—and it was all available to him.

He was pushed along by the swell of creativity that seemed to be happening everywhere in popular culture. Richard was blissfully unaware of his integral part in the musical revolution because he was so completely immersed in it. Dylan and the Hawks altered the artistic direction of popular music every time they plugged in their instruments.

The Dylan entourage had blown into city after city, venue after venue, with cool attitudes and chrome-plated songs. They administered lethal doses of the Hawks' sound and Dylan's flash-point poetry to squirming masses of conflicted youth.

Musically, Richard's playing had advanced to another level while on tour with Dylan. His constant search for a sound placed him on the anticipatory edge of brisk ensemble playing. Practicing and performing Bob Dylan's songs—with their uncensored content, rhythmic diversity, and fearless originality—offered Richard a brand-new insight into the possibilities of music.

Like absorbing radiant heat from a flame, Richard was inspired by Dylan's insane creativity. While Robbie and Dylan had been composing nose to nose throughout the Australian and European legs of the tour, Richard too had been forging a relationship with Dylan. Though those moments were ostensibly based in fun, he was filing away mental notes on how Dylan built his songs.

By seniority and necessity, Robbie slid into the leadership void created when Levon split in November 1965. It never occurred to Richard to do anything but keep on keeping on. The succession in the Hawks was a logical one, but the dynamics of the group had undeniably shifted.

Robbie was ambitious. He mixed it up, liked to name-drop, and was sharp as a tack. His critical thinking was essential to the Hawks' flight path. Richard, on the other hand, wasn't going to fight; he was going to flow. He didn't care about schedules, contracts, or the redundancy of business matters. He wasn't going to elbow his way into anything. Richard let things happen. He wasn't uptight; he wasn't going to get serious . . . ever.

After the European tour, Albert Grossman and Dylan kept the Hawks on retainer. Richard took up residence in a suite at the famed Chelsea Hotel with Robbie while cooling their heels waiting for Dylan's next move. Robbie said in *Testimony*:

> Richard was so easygoing, the perfect roommate, game for anything. Whatever I suggested we do, see a movie, catch a show—I'd ask Richard and the answer was always yes, and we always had a blast. Plus, I could talk to Richard about the big dream. Getting a place where we could play and write and where we could invent the sound, the music we were meant to make. I could talk to Rick or Garth about it and they'd be excited too, but with Richard it was something more. Talking to him made the dream seem real.

Richard's willingness to take chances is what got him every gig he had. It's what gave his singing its hook, and what gave his piano playing its quirky soul. He was turned on by the opportunities presented by the relationship with Dylan. He understood how the reciprocation allowed the Hawks to advance their own musical aspirations while helping Dylan achieve his.

For Richard, living in New York City was essentially the same as being on the road, except now the band had nothing to do. The city was hustle, bustle, strangers, and skyscrapers. Summer in New York was equally stressful, with no break from the sun-heated stone of Manhattan. Richard holed up in the Chelsea with a good book and a stiff drink, spaced out on some random local television channel.

While waiting for their next move from Dylan & Co., word came that there was trouble in Woodstock. On July 29, 1966, Bob Dylan crashed his

Triumph motorcycle when he sped around a corner and was blinded by the sun. The Hawks were notified that Dylan had broken his neck and was in traction. The Hawks, too, were placed in suspended animation and wondered what was going to happen next. Everything was put on hold, including live performances and studio time, until further notice.

Richard continued to simply hang out and, in what would become a theme when faced with free time and no direction, swung between inspired positive energy and lackadaisical self-loathing. He chain-smoked cigarettes and drank beer while contemplating an uncertain future.

In an article headlined "The Band: An Outsider's Insights" in the *New York Sunday News* on December 2, 1973, Al Arnowitz, the godfather of rock journalism, wrote:

> Sure, Richard drinks a lot. Maybe it comes from the colorful nuttiness and artistic pride that runs through his veins. His father was an automobile mechanic in one garage for 30 years. Drunk or sober, Richard always has a smile for you. I remember visiting him one Sunday in his room at the Chelsea Hotel. He hadn't been out for days and was reading a book on hypnosis. It was 1966 after Bob Dylan's motorcycle accident and just about everybody I knew was all freaked out, spooked by some mystic onslaught that had caught all of us in its grip of weirdness.
>
> As for me, I kept imagining I was dodging God's thunderbolts. The sinners were being weeded out. I got Richard into the fresh air that day. It was good to have a friend in that cold, bleak, hostile city, good for him, good for me. We took a walk in Riverside Park, through the brittle fall leaves spiritually hanging on to each other like two frightened babes in the unknown of a new dimension that had been revealed to us.
>
> As I say, those were weird mystic days of 1966. It was as if everyone had been given a piece of some vast common vision and nobody wanted to crack about it. And yet everything seemed connected. You'd find yourself thinking a violent thought and a piece of plaster would fall from the ceiling.

While trying to think their musical futures into a reality, the first inklings of a creative workshop for the Hawks were developed in a local artistic space. Barry Feinstein, a photographer and Dylan friend, had a studio on East 73rd Street, close to Albert Grossman's office, and offered space there. The guys were desperate to get some music out of their system, and it was at Feinstein's photo lab that Richard recorded his first known original song demo for the Hawks.

"Beautiful Thing" was Richard's first documented composition since the Revols days. Recorded on a reel-to-reel, it is marked by sparse instrumentation, with Richard on piano and vocals and Rick on bass. A Rick Danko songwriting credit was added when the song was later recorded for Eric

Clapton's 1976 album *No Reason to Cry*. The "Beautiful Thing" sketch track was first found on basement tape bootlegs, then later released on *A Musical History*.

"Beautiful Thing" was played on electric piano, and Richard sets a circular melody in place. The song lilts wistfully, swaying on Rick's loopy bass lines and a central descending piano lick. Richard sings with a gentle resignation only previously heard on covers of Ray Charles's "Georgia on My Mind" or "Hard Times." While the melody is undeniably strong, the song lacks completed lyrics.

Richard was twenty-three years old in the summer of 1966, living in Manhattan and coming into his own. While on tour with Dylan, freed of any dress codes, Richard cultivated a hip individual style. He dug buttoned-up, high-collared shirts in a multitude of colors and paisleys. He donned colorful suit coats that hung well on his long frame—even though he usually had the chest pockets stuffed with bills or random scraps of paper. Coordination didn't matter to Richard: if it was fun, he wore it. He was especially fond of an orange corduroy jacket that he had scored on the first Dylan tour. He topped off his effortless cool with black shades and a collection of fancy hats.

In addition to being perched on his head, Richard's hats could often be found accessorizing lampshades, guitars, or chairs. His hair had grown out into a side-parted tuft with an impressive pair of matching sideburns. He sported an on-again, off-again beard, but in typical Richard fashion, his was a neck beard, a special type of facial hair tucked beneath the jaw line. He was turning into an effortlessly groovy Amish hybrid.

During the summer respite, Richard returned to Stratford to visit friends and family. The city was fun, but he missed home and needed to do something. The void after nine months of jet-setting was bringing Richard down. The trip home was a big deal for the town, and his hometown paper highlighted his musical journeys since leaving at the end of 1961 with the headline "Join Dylan—See the World."

The short article focused on the last tour with Dylan, noting, "He is Richard 'Beak' Manuel, piano man for Bob Dylan's background music." A moody black-and-white image of Richard at the family piano accompanied the article, with the caption "Richard, who plays piano with Bob Dylan, just can't get away from it all, even at home at 138 Well Street."

Back at home, Richard acted like he never had left. He never forgot who he was or where he came from—one of the many things that endeared him to those he left behind. Chuck Kelly recalled a visit from Richard:

> I remember once, when he was with Dylan, he came around my house. And we drove up to Goderich because there were some guys playing up there, I think Garth Picot. And Richard had this big car and the speed that we drove up there being young, you know!

After the visit home, Richard returned to New York, and the Hawks played on an early Albert Grossman–produced Carly Simon session. Shortly after this, the wait ended, and the Hawks bore witness to the "Bob Signal" shining in the skies above Gotham. They set their compasses north of Manhattan, toward the artists' hamlet of Woodstock, New York. Grossman wasn't going to keep the Hawks on the payroll forever if they weren't being useful to Dylan or his endeavors.

Robbie had been updating the Hawks after scoping out the situation in Woodstock. Rick and Richard followed Robbie's lead in early February 1967. They arrived in the cold sun and intoxicating air of the Catskills and immediately took up residence in the Woodstock Hotel. Richard saw southern Ontario's reflection in the Ulster County landscape and quickly made himself at home. By March, the guys were firmly embedded in Dylan's stony filmmaking adventures with coconspirator Howard Alk. Rick and Richard hung around, got high, and made surreal movies that have never seen official release.

The group also offered its talents to a quirky project that had come along as a result of connections in Dylan's circles. The 1968 film *You Are What You Eat* was the brainchild of musician Peter Yarrow and the Hawks' photographer friend Barry Feinstein. The Hawks were enlisted to play on the soundtrack of this surreal bit of rockumentary.

TINY TIM AND THE HAWKS

For what would be the final time, the Hawks backed a front man, Tiny Tim, for two songs on the soundtrack of *You Are What You Eat*. Tim was a folk singer who had become known for his fluttery falsetto and ukulele in Greenwich Village. The marriage between Tim and the Hawks was an odd one but resulted in some enjoyable music.

Both Garth and Richard pop from the grooves of "Be My Baby," as the Hawks' dual-carbureted keyboard flex is up front and in full swirl mode, and then Richard takes a sweet slice of playful chording during the outro. "I Got You Babe" finds Richard playing a music-box waltz on his piano while Robbie twists up some twangy Telecaster bends.

Two additional tracks from the soundtrack sessions circulate unofficially. "Memphis, Tennessee" and Tiny Tim's "Sonny Boy" are both worth a listen, with the first recalling the Hawks on the stage at Le Coq d'Or. Both cuts feature a bulging bag of shredded Robertson guitar work. Of note is "Sonny Boy," which is played with an attentive and regal approach that recalls the penultimate dates of the 1966 tour.

The Hawks made another well-timed connection through the film project in meeting musician John Simon. Simon, who acted as musical director, immediately cultivated a natural rapport with the Hawks and became a confidant of the group.

Fascinating clips from this period were used during promotional activities for the Bob Dylan *Bootleg Series Vol. 11: The Basement Tapes Complete* box set. A neck-bearded, mustached, and glowing Manuel is filmed outside in sun-prismed snow and brisk Technicolor. He is beaming with the joy of a man doing what he loves and is in the prime of his days. The camera rolls as Richard stands by Dylan at the piano while Tiny Tim peeks through a frosted winter window, witness to a permeating spring of creativity thawed in the icy Catskills.

In a series of previously unreleased images from March 1967, Richard is photographed in an unidentified Woodstock locale, reclining on a bed and blowing harmonica during a surreal shoot for *Eat the Document* cut-ins. He is dressed in tall boots and slumped in an oversized wooden chair, looking as if the weight of the world has been taken from his back. He also looks a little drunk. Rick is there, and Dylan strums an acoustic guitar with a coonskin cap perched upon his head. The random filming of druggy antics and blurry nonsensical card games, featuring Dylan and Richard getting red eyed and weird for the camera, documents the winter of 1967.

By this time, Rick and Richard had grown tired of the Woodstock Hotel and made a decision about a more permanent living situation. Rick remembered in his final interview with Robert Doerschuk in 1999:

> I went up to work with Tiny Tim and Richard Manuel; we all worked together on Bob's movie, *Eat the Document*. The restaurant where we ate, the woman's husband died. They were from Long Island, and she didn't want to stay there after he died. So she went back to Long Island, and that's how we got the house. It was, like, a three-bedroom house for less than $300 a month. Bob had us on a small retainer, and we got to live like kings. We bought a '47 Oldsmobile and a '49 Hudson.

Richard and Rick moved, Garth joined them, and so began the legend of what lovingly became dubbed Big Pink. Located at 2188 Stoll Road in West Saugerties, Big Pink was a three-

Richard, March 1967. *Courtesy of the Arie de Reus archive*

bedroom home with a walkout basement nestled on 100 acres of Catskill Mountain bluestone and sided in what Levon Helm called "Saturday night pink." The quaint home provided the Hawks with solitude, a sense of responsibility, and, eventually, inspiration.

Richard took the master bedroom in the back of the house, Garth the second, and Rick upstairs in the loft. Robbie had a place with his girlfriend, Dominique Bourgeois, over on the Grossman estate and drove over to see the guys with Bob almost every day.

Richard embarked on his own personal journey in Woodstock. He hadn't experienced any sort of domesticated normalcy since he was a kid. He was now an adult who hadn't learned to properly take care of himself. Richard's hippie home-economics training included cooking dinners and reconnecting with Jane Kristiansen, whom he invited to Woodstock. Jane remembered Richard being "very present" with her while exhibiting a gentle sensibility. Living at Big Pink was simple.

Richard walked out the front door of Big Pink, cracked a beer, and strolled down to the pond and followed the game trails around the water's edge. The area was magical, the days endless. On some heady afternoons, Richard wandered as far as the rocky pine-dotted slopes of Overlook Mountain, climbing while buzzing on Catskill air, fueling his creative hearth. He'd lounge in the sun, dozing, often residing in the space between sleeping and waking, the same place inhabited by the songs bouncing around in his head.

Garth recalled in *The Last Waltz*:

> We got to like this lifestyle. Chopping wood and hitting your thumb with a hammer, fixing the tape recorder or the screen door, wandering off into the woods with [Dylan's dog] Hamlet. . . . It was relaxed and low key, which was something we hadn't enjoyed since we were children.

Big Pink was a hard left turn onto a rutted dirt road, running in contrast to an expressway career of bars, jukes, and concert halls. It was time to nurture creativity, to reflect and reload. Richard cooked the meals at Big Pink; Garth did the vacuuming. Rick assisted with keeping things in order on the property. Both Garth and Richard enjoyed tinkering, so boredom wasn't an issue. Richard was constantly pulling apart electronics, with varying degrees of success. In the evenings, the guys retired to the living room to play music.

"Things were easy in the hills," Richard told *Time* in 1970. "Well, we were shooting films up here, and then we were shooting vodka, and first thing you know, we took to shooting fresh air. What a habit." A turntable and stereo gear had been installed in the living room, and the Hawks were constantly mining a box of classic late '50s 7-inch singles that belonged to former manager Bill Avis. Garth told writer Sid Griffin in 2014 that Richard liked a Caravans single called "To Whom Shall I Turn" that he spun constantly.

From March 1967 through that fall, while the rest of the music world basked in the dayglow of the Summer of Love, the Hawks sat in the algid shade of Overlook Mountain and explored the maturing musicality of their friendships. The Hawks, content in their new digs, were operating at a different pace than the rest of the rock world. Time was suspended for a few months in 1967. The shared creativity of Dylan and his Hawks eddied like the pools of Esopus Creek as it wove its way through Ulster County.

While filmmaking was a trip, the natural thing to do was to make music. Jam sessions developed organically from the movie shoots and loose hangouts at locations around town but began formally in the Red Room of Bob Dylan's home in Byrdcliffe, an artist's colony outside Woodstock.

Greil Marcus told the *Dallas Observer* in 1999 that folklorist John Cohen called him and said that in 1967, Dylan had invited him to a get-together at Byrdcliffe to commiserate with the guys. Cohen told him that Dylan had called him up and asked him to bring a banjo, then a few days later to bring a dulcimer. Marcus wrote, "It turned out Dylan wanted John to bring all his traditional instruments because he wanted him to play stuff in a casual manner, so Robbie and Richard [would] get interested."

The musical meetings that started in the Red Room and later moved to the basement at Big Pink were ragged glory. Dylan thumbed through the back pages of his past and introduced the Hawks to an entire side of music that they weren't accustomed to, nor had they been exposed to. The Hawks, sympathetic coconspirators, in turn gave Dylan new instrumental and vocal options. The documentation of the disparate elements famously came to be known as the "basement tapes."

While the Hawks had been playing together loosely in the living room of Big Pink, the downstairs was soon outfitted by Garth and Robbie with instruments, microphones, and recording equipment. While the basement wasn't the ideal location for a studio, the intimacy of the space encouraged attentiveness and collaboration.

Dylan and the Hawks fell into a bucolic schedule perfect for making music. Rick told *RPM Magazine* in 1985, "Bob Dylan would come over for a year, seven days a week, and we would spend four or five hours together playing. We must have come up with 150 to 200 songs in that time."

Robbie, who was living in Bearsville with Dominique, drove over to Big Pink, sometimes picking Dylan up on the way. On other days, Rick or Richard sped alongside cobblestone retaining walls at unsafe speeds to pick Robbie up. A routine was coming into focus, and the Hawks now had a space to work on their own artistic vision. Richard woke up (not too early) at Big Pink to the aroma of Bob Dylan's notoriously high-octane coffee, followed by the rhythmic click-clacking of the Olivetti typewriter. Richard made his way across the hardwoods for greetings before he descended the steep basement steps, where the musical day commenced.

In the book *Million Dollar Bash*, Garth told writer Will Hodgkinson:

> Dylan would be coming 'round the house three or four days a week, and there was a little typewriter on the coffee table in the living room that he would bash away on while we were in the basement. Richard wrote a song about that, "Upstairs Downstairs." As far as I know, that's one of those few basement tapes songs still in the locker.

Everyone in the house could add a line or a word to the stream-of-consciousness typewriter scrolls. There were no set rules, which explains some of the more surreal and nonsensical verses contained among the cache of songs recorded.

Creativity on both floors had Big Pink buzzing. Levon said in a 2004 interview with *Razor* magazine:

> We set up a typewriter on the coffee table at Big Pink with paper in it, ready to rock at all times. Bob would sit down every so often and type a couple of lines. I'd come along, read it, grin to myself on the way down to the basement studio. Richard would mosey through with a cup of coffee, stop and sit down at the typewriter, he'd start laughing while he typed out a few lines of his own for the equation. When it came to "slanging the lingo," Richard was the only one who could play pitch and catch with Bob.

The clubhouse environment of the Big Pink basement was a familiar one for Richard. His musical growth had its roots in the basement on Queen Street back in Stratford. Playing piano and commiserating with a close-knit collection of friends gathered in the Kalmusky basement was the best way to play, enjoying revelry while sharing musical creativity.

Collaboration stirred something inside Richard. His enthusiasm smoldered as joints were passed between hands, instruments shared among friends, and songs birthed in a frothy mountain spring of inspiration. Stripped of the mythology, what occurred between Dylan and the Hawks in Woodstock in 1967 was based on musical respect and mutual friendship.

From March through November, Dylan and the Hawks recorded about twenty reels of tape. One can only speculate about the music that wasn't captured by the reel-to-reel, those late-night living-room jams that inspired the work on the lower level, witnessed only by the walls and floorboards.

Levon explained the group's process to *Hit Parader* magazine in 1971:

> We'd get together, maybe two or three of us, and we'd just sit around and sing a lot of tunes that we remember. Just for our own amusement really, but it keeps our hand in. If you can take a tune, a country tune maybe, and play it with a suburban flavor, that's the kind of thing we do. Or take a Motown tune and play

it on country instruments, see how a fiddle might work out. I guess it does get through in our music, it makes our harmonies tighter. If it's a nice day though, we'll go across the park and play some football.

The Hawks were eager pupils, and Dylan drove them to express themselves musically in surprising new ways. It wasn't "Turn up and stomp" anymore for the Hawks; it was "Turn down and listen." Richard had fully come into his own. His piano is central on most of the circulating basement recordings. If he wasn't playing piano, he was just as likely to pick up a harmonica, saxophone, or percussion instrument.

Just as Richard's piano had been the rhythmic constant in the Revols, and then the Hawks, his playing was now the essential ingredient in what was being stirred up in the basement. Garth told *Something Else Reviews* in 2014:

> His piano work is a study in itself. Richard was the finest of the energy accompaniment players, and behind all of the tapes, almost all of the basement tapes, you will hear Richard Manuel's piano.

Richard in Woodstock, March 1967.
Courtesy of the Arie de Reus archive

In 2014, most if not all the available Dylan and the Hawks basement reels were officially released as *The Bootleg Series Vol. 11: The Basement Tapes Complete*. Sonically scrubbed, the Hawks' detailed playing comes through the restored reels. The recordings feature Richard's contributions fully audible and immortalized. The difference in his and the Hawks' playing between Europe '66 and Woodstock '67 is stunning.

A thick, shaggy carpet covered the concrete floor in the basement of Big Pink. The walls, draped with various cloths, were porous collectors of sound. Scattered around the room, a conglomeration of microphones, tape, cables, and stands collected from the Dylan tour and Grossman office helped make their recordings a reality. When weather permitted, the guys opened the garage door and played to the trees. Dylan's dog Hamlet, who became Rick's dog Hamlet, roamed the basement and acted as quality control. Dylan told *Rolling Stone* in 1969, "That's really the way to do a recording, in a peaceful, relaxed setting. In somebody's basement. With the windows open . . . and a dog lying on the floor."

Before working on his own songs, though, Dylan took the Hawks to school. The basement sessions moved through a songbook of Dylan's choosing, spanning a folk landscape previously alien to the Hawks. Dylan played traditional music for the band, country classics, folk songs, and blues, Ian and Sylvia, Johnny Cash, and Curtis Mayfield. The guys played funky readings of forgotten traditional melodies or honest tributes to the rock 'n' roll songs that inspired Dylan.

The Hawks were ready to follow the trail they had begun to blaze when they first left Ronnie Hawkins. Dylan needed to work because money wasn't coming in as he sat still. Grossman helped push the sessions into something cohesive because he needed Dylan to sell some songs. Eventually the loose basement sessions shifted in purpose to a focused workshop for Dylan's original music and publishing arm. But the original intent was no intent at all. Rick said on the British documentary series *Classic Albums*, "It was us getting together every day and applying ourselves when good things started to happen."

Beak in the Basement

As a result of Dylan and the Hawks' immersion in and recording of various musical forms in a number of Woodstock locales, a huge amount of music is available both officially and unofficially. Because Garth's tape machines were often running, music from the basement escaped to the public almost immediately after it was recorded via publisher demos and clandestine copies of the original reels. Now, most of the Dylan work has been officially sanctioned and released, and most of the music the Band recorded on their own at Big Pink remains in the vault.

From the audio that is available, Richard's musical contributions on Dylan's songs are numerous and worthy of discussion. Richard's piano pops vibrantly out of the Hawks' tapestry of sound for two takes of Dylan's unreleased original "I'm a Fool for You." The drumless sound swings, and Richard tip-taps the keys in the upper register. The same goes for the nineteenth-century sailor's song "Johnny Todd," for which Richard's piano sings the melody line.

Dylan's mysterious original "Lo and Behold!" finds Richard pacesetting on piano and running down the track along with Dylan's train car imagery. Richard breezily echoes the buoyant chorus throughout the verses and ends each line with a twist. For the changes, he settles into the warm bottom portion of a Manuel/Danko/Dylan vocal blend that results in a glorious three-part chorus.

"You Ain't Goin' Nowhere" and "Million Dollar Bash" find Richard serving the same musical purpose. He plays enthusiastic saloon-style piano support with a sensibility that never fails to pull the perfect melody out of the chord changes. "Million Dollar Bash" swings with a swampy urgency because of Richard's piano and Rick's bass, since the song includes no drums or lead guitar.

Garth told *Clash* magazine in 2014, "I think the catalyst was Richard Manuel's piano, and it was the accompaniment to that piano unamplified in that room—the cement block walls had a lot to do with it. So, the guitars played carefully, quietly, working together—and the bass as well. So, everything was . . . I think they say, 'living-room ready.'"

Not all was serious, regardless of the songs that were being played. The recordings are littered with camaraderie and hijinks, inside jokes and funny asides. Some days the looseness results in chaos and tomfoolery, with songs from the bottom of the bottle such as "Don't You Tell Henry," "Bourbon Street," "Get Your Rocks Off," and "I'm in the Mood." Those tunes are punctuated with Dylan giggles and goofy Richard and Rick voice-of-conscience backing vocals.

On Dylan's "Next Time on the Highway," the summer club Hawks come out and Richard bangs out heavy-handed licks. Dylan, who sounds like he's put away a couple, says good-humoredly during the instrumental break, "Let's listen to Richard play that piano. Oh, poor Richard, playing that piano shitfaced, just pounding the fucking piss out of that piano." The improvised high-tempo blues almost reaches a roiling boil before disappearing forever.

When things got serious, which was often, the songs touched upon the fat wings of the great angelic muse, with Dylan epics such as "Goin' to Acapulco," "Sign on the Cross," "Tears of Rage," and "I Shall Be Released." Dylan was writing prolifically, and the Hawks were forging their musical identity. The combination was mutually beneficial and musically magnificent.

On a song such as Dylan's "I'm Not There," in which the lyrics are an update of the talking-blues approach of his folk days, Dylan improvises his words and melody in real time over a repeated series of chord changes. Richard and his bandmates fall into place once they feel the song. They work in the moment and of the moment. And that's when the best things happened.

On Dylan's "Too Much of Nothing," the group experiments with their vocal harmonies, with Richard on top singing high harmony on the first take. On the next try, Richard moves to the bottom of the vocal stack. The same goes for the attempts at "I Shall Be Released," where Dylan, Richard, and Rick attempt several three-part approaches before Richard adds a sweet falsetto from someplace high above the wall. The inspired harmonies uncovered on the chorus were transferred to the later definitive version on *Music from Big Pink*. In the 1991 biography *Behind the Shades*, Dylan scholar Clinton Heylin refers to "I Shall Be Released" as the song Dylan wrote for Richard Manuel.

"Yea! Heavy and a Bottle of Bread" is the perfect song to express the spirit of the summer of 1967. The Dylan original combines all the best things that happened in the basement. Before the first take, Richard can be heard letting out a hearty sigh and an "All right!" before contributing the bounty that is the central melodic line of the song.

On both available takes, he plays a beautiful lick that is joyous and varied and contains a lightness of touch that adorns Dylan's strumming. The Manuel/Danko vocal duet lends cooler-than-cool backing vocals that chant in time with Dylan's verse-ending declarations, Richard moving just a bit out of time with Dylan and Rick. He closes the second take (which is the officially released version) with a humorous, deep-voiced groan.

These were heady times. Richard was full. Full of love for his bandmates, Woodstock, and, most importantly, his music. By this juncture, Dylan and the Hawks were well acquainted enough that the band could intuit his every move. Songs were created out of the air, from comments, jokes, or just divine inspiration, their execution of the moment and in real time. The instrumental lineups were as improvised as the music, with Richard acting as utility man of the basement. Whatever a song needed, Richard did what the musical circumstances required. He had the ability to give a song the exact detail it yearned for to push it over the top.

Once the decision was made to record the Dylan originals for demonstration purposes, a drummer was needed (Levon wouldn't return to the Hawks until the basement sessions had almost concluded). Richard slid into the drum seat, and with great success. Like everything else in his life, becoming a drummer just sort of happened.

Because Richard's piano playing was his rhythmic foundation, it naturally informed the drumming style that he had developed in the basement. For a novice, he played well, used a traditional grip, and hit the kit hard—so hard, he broke hi-hats and knocked over cymbal stands.

He had a knack for locking on the offbeat and landing on the one at the last possible second. His moves on the tom-toms were a full-out sprint toward a fast-closing elevator door, with the punctuating cymbal crashes Richard's sideways slip between the closing doors, right on time.

Levon wrote in his memoir:

> Richard was an incredible drummer. He played loosey-goosey, a little behind the beat, and it really swung. . . . I was amazed how good he'd become. Without any training, he'd do these hard left-handed moves and piano-wise licks, priceless shit, very unusual.

Garth said in a 2014 interview with *Something Else Reviews*:

> He did it playing backward. He moved the snare to the other side. He was like the main percussionist during the time when Levon was not there, and his rhythm and steadiness and natural flair for percussion carried over into piano.

It's easy to tell when Richard is playing because he's going for it with unorthodox rolls and accents that separated him from trained drummers. He had a flair for the dramatic, and his kick foot was active, constantly on the throttle, his playing expressing a percussive personality out of every accent. Levon said to *Gritz* magazine in 2002:

> Richard . . . oh, boy. Richard was just one of them self-taught people—it was almost like he was double left-handed. He wasn't, but he played like he was.

Richard might carry the backbeat with his right hand, or he might carry it with his left. It just came off fantastic.

Some examples of Richard banging on the skins in the basement are on the second try at Dylan's "Nothing Was Delivered," sticking to the ride cymbal and playing some loopy fills. He slaps the skins on the scattershot rocker "Odds and Ends," which is one of the songs that Levon loved when he first heard it. Richard also lends a honky-clippity-clop to the deliciously country funk of "Baby, Won't You Be My Baby." "Ain't No More Cain" also has Richard on drums, and he remained there when the Hawks later recorded their own version of the song. As Les Paul said, "You can't go to the store and buy a good ear and rhythm." Richard Manuel had both.

In September 1967, Grossman arranged a recording session for the Hawks in New York. No one remembers who played drums on the session, since Levon hadn't returned to the group yet. In the 2010s, a tape reel that appeared to have originated from that visit to the studio was put up for auction. The track list on the tape box reads as follows:

"Ferdinand the Imposter"
"Ruben Remus"
"Katie's Been Gone"
"Blues for Breakfast"
"Yazoo Street Scandal"

It's an impressive list of original music from Richard and Robbie, yet not one of the songs would make the cut for the group's debut, *Music from Big Pink*. This is a testament not only to the wealth of the group's material, but to their collective creativity.

But without a proper drummer, or a producer who was empathetic to their cause, the recording suffered. The group was not impressed with how they sounded in the studio, or the results, and the session was quickly forgotten.

Levon Comes Home

It's impossible to put definitive dates on the basement reels, but as harvest time returned to the Catskill Mountains, Levon Helm returned home. After a call from Rick explaining their inspired new direction, and a possible big payday from the record company, Levon flew to New York. Richard and Rick picked him up at the airport, and Levon immediately moved into Big Pink and joined the musical routine that the group had developed.

The Hawks were back to full flock. On one of the reels recorded after Levon's return and possibly in preparation for a performance with Dylan, the guys ran through rehearsal versions of several songs, which are essential listening for understanding both Dylan's and the Hawks' transitions from their previous incarnations into their new musical identities.

A segment features Levon's drumming that brought the swamp and the swing back to the Hawks. A refurbished "Blowin' in the Wind" and revisited "It Ain't Me Babe" capture Nashville Bob and the Hawks at their best. As with the fall 1965 versions of "It Ain't Me Babe," when the Hawks were last intact, Richard and Garth double-teamed the melody with alternating punctuations.

An important and stately revisit of "One Too Many Mornings" follows. The song, which had been such a focused element of the 1966 tour sets, forked into two divergent paths in 1967. One trail led to Nashville, Tennessee, and Bob Dylan's *John Wesley Harding* album, the other to the back roads of New York and *Music from Big Pink*.

What makes the song special is that Dylan and the Hawks rearranged it yet again. Richard had been given the opening verse of the song, and Dylan sang the verse that followed. Where Rick Danko sang the line *beeehind* on the 1966 tour, the knotted voices of Rick, Levon, and Richard now sang in spirited collaboration. The song epitomized all that Dylan and the Hawks had created in the basement . . . and what would follow.

The basement work also revealed Richard's previously clandestine and ghostly falsetto. Gone were the graveled primal howls of late nights at the Rockwood Club; in their place was smoothed-out and controlled singing. Richard used this discovery to create countermelodies, top-end harmony, and a diverse vocal approach that tightened up the basement vocals with a melodic twine. His ability to hit any note lent the Hawks a flexibility that no other group had at their disposal.

Richard's Stratford friend Chuck Kelly remembered in 2022 that Richard was very excited about discovering and mastering his ability to sing falsetto. In the same way that he had been laser-focused on improving his skills in the basement of the Rockwood Club back in the fall of 1961, Richard constantly practiced reaching his higher range. He applied it on top of harmonies and in improvised asides throughout the basement songs. Sometimes his ethereal quiver hung weightlessly in the room and sounded like some obscure instrument.

As the group turned down the volume on their instruments to accommodate the acoustics of the concrete basement, their naturally occurring three-part harmonies started to congeal. The nurturing of the Hawks' singing approach can be traced from the days of swapping vocals on Sam Cooke's "A Change Is Gonna Come" and "Go Go Liza Jane" to their studio performance of the Robbie Robertson–penned "Leave Me Alone."

Richard loved the gospel technique of call and response. He was a master at coming in late or blurring his vocal across measures. He tastefully applied his harmonies to enhance the other singers' voices. His place in the three-part wailing is spotlighted on Dylan's "Goin' to Acapulco" and "Minstrel Boy," perfect examples of Richard's and Rick's ongoing vocal development.

Garth remembered in a 2015 interview with *Something Else Reviews*:

> We started to develop this three-part harmony, to see which goes on top and which section they would add harmonies to—the whole arranging part of it. Singing the harmonies together, we had to pay attention. It had to be safe. We approached the whole experience with caution. I think everyone anticipated a chord, and they could move into it very quickly. You get to be very swift; a millisecond after you hear something, you can chime in or lay out. We knew how not to infringe on one personal endeavor, while living in the same structure.

Levon said in his memoir:

> One of the things we'd always loved was the way groups like the Staple Singers and the Impressions would stack those individual voices on top of one another, each voice coming in at a different time until you got this blend that was just magic.

A tantalizing fragment of the traditional song "Will the Circle Be Unbroken" appears on *A Musical History*, giving us a small window into the creativity taking place among Richard and his bandmates. Rick and Richard harmonize like brothers posting up on the porch after a hard day in the fields. For a fleeting fifty-eight seconds, we're transported to a hazy living-room session on Stoll Road. Richard's voice had never sounded so rich, content, and beautiful. Rick takes the high harmony, sitting on the edge of the porch steps, gazing over the tobacco fields, with only Robbie's acoustic guitar, Richard's electric piano, and the heartbeat of feet on the floorboards as accompaniment.

All good things must come to an end, and by the fall, both Dylan and the Hawks had business to take care of. The summer decayed, and the basement sessions came to a close. Richard was a different man because of the experience.

In October, Dylan headed to Nashville without the Hawks to record the songs that became the *John Wesley Harding* album. The Hawks continued with their own sessions at Wittenberg Road, and some of these recordings show up on the final reels of the basement recordings. It's not known how much music remains unreleased from those locations around Woodstock.

While Richard happily backed Dylan on his excursions through the Great American Songbook, the Hawks, and in particular Richard and Robbie, had their own songs to nurture. There are basement tapes that deal solely with the Hawks; unfortunately, many remain unreleased. The Hawks ran through in-progress originals, instrumentals, and some interesting moments of comedy. The ground in Saugerties was a fertile, muck-filled patch of creativity. The Band's debut album would soon break through the soil.

Richard as a Songwriter

The following songs were developed by Richard and his bandmates during their workshop days in New York City and Woodstock from fall 1966 through fall 1967 in preparation for their debut album. What follows is a closer look at Richard's compositions, works that he cowrote, and his instrumental contributions from the period leading up to the recording of the Band's *Music from Big Pink*.

Living at Big Pink with a ready-made studio in the basement was a gift from the muses. The house was saturated with song, music in every pore. There would be evening instrumental swap meets in the living room, with harmonicas, guitars, and accordions, which would inform the songwriting sessions that naturally took place any hour of the day.

Richard lounged in the coffee-scented and sun-speckled living room, blowing a Sonny Boy lick on the harp, with a guitar flat on his lap. Rick picked up an unamplified bass and began to play a loopy set of changes to the harmonica, tapping his boot on the hardwood. Richard looked excitedly at Rick and said, "Come play that line with me in the 'bass'ment," and let out a hearty chuckle.

"Orange Juice Blues (Blues for Breakfast)" (written by Richard Manuel): It's demeaning to classify "Orange Juice Blues" as a basement lark. It's an effortlessly cool tune, influenced by Dylan's philosophy that a song could be about anything. Richard took that approach to heart and composed a bounding early-morning blues that recalled his difficulties in waking with the rising sun. The song is one of Richard's first fully formed compositions, and the group attempted it on several occasions, both in the basement and the studio.

Available as a bonus track on the 2000 remaster of *Music from Big Pink*, Richard's original roly-poly basement demo, with Rick on bass, spotlights how playing the piano blues had become second nature to him. It's incredible how much rustic inertia the song gains with just Richard and Rick. Richard's lead vocal quivers like a daybreak aspen. The lyric "I'm tired of everything being beautiful, and I ain't coming back no more" is a sly commentary on his feelings about the happenings of the Summer of Love.

The band recorded the song in consideration for their debut, but for some reason it remained on the shelf. The full-band studio recording can be found on *A Musical History*. Richard plays a squishy electric piano and overdubbed acoustic piano. Highlighted by a slinky Helm shuffle and superior Hudson work on the Lowrey organ, the song brushes a little too close to the blues of the group's past stage show for Robbie.

Even though the Hawks couldn't find a home for the song, Cass Elliot could. She covered it on her 1968 *Dream a Little Dream* LP . . . with one John Simon playing piano. Richard received a nice royalty check for the cover version. The version of "Orange Juice Blues" released on the official 1975 *Basement Tapes* record is the original Manuel demo with later overdubbing.

"Words and Numbers" (written by Richard Manuel): This intriguing composition deserved a chance to have a slot on a record. The song combines the distressed melodic drama of Dylan's "Ballad of a Thin Man" and the unharnessed power of the Hawks. It's a moody and sturdily constructed track that allowed plenty of space for all the band members to strut their stuff. The version from the Big Pink basement, included on *A Musical History*, plays like a jagged mantra. The song creeps around the room, with an undulating rhythm and flashes of mystery theater organ from Garth.

An additional instrumental version from the basement of Big Pink is worth a listen. Also referred to on circulating tapes as "Don't Drink the Water," the tune, regardless of its genesis in R&B, didn't sound like anything else in the Hawks' arsenal. It captures Richard composing in his typically dynamic and observational style of the time, also reflected in songs such as "Orange Juice Blues" and "We Can Talk."

Robbie's midsong solo is a plethora of slippery riffing that sounds unlike anything else from the era. He bends the strings on his Telecaster to near their breaking point, as Garth's icy keys whistle across a groove that is in constant flux. A sinister Howlin' Wolf–influenced pulse finds Richard vocalizing over the top with a surreal litany of rhyming couplets:

> *Empty your pockets every night and save / You won't lose anything today*
> *If you look in the mirror and count the gray / Don't you wish you had more time to play?*
> *Go to bed / you're not quite dead*
> *Stick to your diet of fresh fruit juices / never indulge in self-abuses.*
> *Say that you try not to make excuses / you don't know what being loose is.*

"Words and Numbers" never appeared on an album or was worked out in the studio. It's somewhat strange that within three years, the group would struggle to come up with original material while songs such as "Words and Numbers" would sit in the vault for perpetuity.

"We Can Talk" (written by Richard Manuel): No basement takes have circulated, but the song title is legible on photos of the reel boxes. This Richard Manuel original would appear on *Music from Big Pink*.

"Lonesome Suzie" (written by Richard Manuel): While no basement versions seem to exist, a typewritten draft of the lyrics was born from the Big Pink typewriter.

"Ruben Remus" (written by J. R. Robertson and Richard Manuel): This basement collaboration contains all the hallmarks of an ambling Richard Manuel chord progression and what hits like a Robbie Robertson lyric. "Ruben Remus" sums up the basement aesthetic in lo-fi originality, and it gives us a sense of the Robertson/Manuel songwriting team's formative attempts.

An instrumental demo version from the Saugerties basement circulates unofficially, with Richard, Robbie, and Rick making up the instrumentation on piano, guitar, and bass. The loose, drum-free reading swings with quirky ambiance and a canonical feel. An additional version circulates from Big Pink with vocals and is notable for Rick's second-floor-high harmonies stacked onto Richard's foundational lead.

The melody is infectious, and Richard's voice is mysterious perfection. He adds his recently mastered basement falsetto at the conclusion of each chorus, decorating the melody with a tasty garnish. The official version from 1975's *The Basement Tapes* is a full-group rendition purported to be from their ill-fated test run in a studio on September 9, 1967.

"Katie's Been Gone" (written by J. R. Robertson and Richard Manuel): This cowritten song benefits from Richard's contemplative melodicism and Robbie's colorful narrative development. The song was in the running for inclusion on the Band's debut but was held back on the belief that the album had enough slow songs. That's silly, because with this song, Richard and Robbie had cornered the elusive muse. "Lonesome Suzie" got the nod on the album, and "Katie's Been Gone" languished in the vaults until 1975, when it was released officially on *The Basement Tapes*.

The unofficial basement version of "Katie's Been Gone" is majestic. Piano, bass, organ, and clean guitar compose the transparent backing track, and a sparkling jewel emerges. Richard's strong, confident vocals contain a longing that you can feel in your stomach. In contrast, Robbie harmonizes with Richard on the chorus in a creaky and strained voice that somehow works perfectly. The officially released version from *The Basement Tapes* offers up an empathetic vocal from Richard that reveals cracks in all the right places to let the light in. The song is an obscure blending of blues influence, yet totally original.

"Katie's Been Gone" and "Ruben Remus" create a musical bridge connecting both sides of a river, with the Hawks on one side of the torrent and the Band calling from the other.

"Beautiful Thing" (written by Richard Manuel): The song makes an appearance on the unofficial basement reels as witness to Richard's continued work on the song since New York. The versions on the basement reels sound as if they're the same as the one discussed from Feinstein's studio in '66. Rick's bread-and-butter bass coats Richard's melodic earworm inspired by the love songs of his Stratford youth. "Beautiful Thing," "Words and Numbers," and "We Can Talk" dispel any myth that Richard was incapable of writing songs without a collaborator. But, like many of the best songwriters, Richard's ideas blossomed when tended with another person.

"Tears of Rage" (written by Bob Dylan and Richard Manuel): "Tears of Rage" is one of the finest moments of Catskill Mountain sustenance to result from the Big Pink melting pot of influences. It's a fully developed song, signaling a new direction for the Hawks. A stately Richard Manuel melody and ambiguous Bob Dylan lyric conspire to deliver a sensitive soliloquy craving understanding and compassion.

Richard worked a series of chord changes at the piano with the same process that led to "We Can Talk," but he had no lyrics. He told the *Woodstock Times*:

> He [Dylan] came down to the basement with a piece of typewritten paper—and it was typed out—in line form—and he just said, "Have you got any music for this?" I had a couple of musical movements that fit, that seemed to fit, so I elaborated a little bit because I wasn't sure what the lyrics meant. I couldn't run upstairs and say, "What's this mean, Bob?"

Like his collaborations with Robbie, the song benefits from the perfect marriage of Richard's acute melodic acumen and Dylan's advanced lyrical expression. Dylan would later say on his *Theme Time Radio Hour* that Richard was a "distinctive voice with an unquiet heart." Both of those elements can be heard on any version of "Tears of Rage."

Levon remembered in his memoir, "Bob Dylan helped Richard with this number about a parent's heartbreak, and Richard sang one of the best performances of his life." The formative basement versions with Dylan on vocals, while sparse, exude a heavy aura. Dylan sings the takes with unusually great control, obviously inspired by the stellar vocalists in his midst.

Bob and Richard cracked a stone with one strike with this song. The accumulation of Richard's musical experiences culminated in the most important composition for the Hawks up to that point, and one that represented everything they stood for. Richard's desperate chord changes usher in Dylan's urgent lyric about honor, family, and faith.

The three basement takes of "Tears of Rage" are witness to the musical development of Richard and the Hawks. Dylan's honest poetics recited in

Richard's melodic construction reach an even-deeper realm of truth than his previous work. The music is so deeply righteous it becomes a crucible, as if it were able to get up and stroll around the basement, reveling in its divination. The Hawks' attempts at capturing a proper take of the song result in Richard conjuring a spectral voice that organically shadowed Dylan's lead yet remained an independent element of the song's movement.

Take 1 lurks like a folk song, but take 2 is spacious and with less guitar from Dylan. Richard and Rick have some trouble keeping up with Dylan's alternate phrasing on the changes. But take 3 gets everything right, with perfectly expressive playing by everyone. During take 3's verses, Richard contributes wordless snatches of melody that sound like a woodland specter. His improvised vocal asides inspire the entire group to greater heights. The recording is a witness to the ambient alchemy of the basement tapes in action.

Robbie recalled in *Testimony* that once he had heard "Tears of Rage," he knew that Richard's songwriting had taken the next step, and it drove him to improve his own work. Unlike many of the other Dylan basement originals, "Tears of Rage" wasn't going to Manfred Mann, the Byrds, or Fairport Convention. It was earmarked for the Hawks.

In the same way that Bob Dylan's songwriting abilities influenced the Hawks, Richard Manuel's and Rick Danko's singing prowess had an undeniable and understated effect on Dylan's vocal approach. He never used backing vocals on his studio recordings before he linked up with the Hawks. Throughout the Woodstock recording process in 1967, Dylan, Richard, and Rick engaged in harmonious interactions across a spectrum of genres. Richard was the steady tenor in their harmony gang, while Rick was tasked with harmonizing with the unpredictable Dylan by deftly moving up and down the scale.

Richard's and Rick's voices pressed together like a flower in a bible, a hippie angel choir that inspired Dylan to make a more concerted effort with his singing. Dylan's vocals in the basement and on his records in 1967 (*John Wesley Harding*) and 1969 (*Nashville Skyline*) were unlike any he had previously attempted. His compositions of that time contained attentive phrasings and were sung with an unusually clean timbre. There was a warmth and smoothness in his voice. His new vocal approach could obviously be attributed to his work with Richard and Rick.

Richard Manuel influenced and developed many of the nascent vocal arrangements that were coming into focus during the Hawks' musical soul-searching. Songs such as "We Can Talk" and "The Weight" reflected the influence of gospel and layered harmonies from his churchgoing days in Stratford. Levon remembered in a November 2000 interview with *Mojo* magazine:

> We had all the time we wanted to practice Staple Singers harmonies, take old standards, swap them around. Richard could sing all of them, from the highest

to the lowest, so he'd show us another one, and we'd swap them around and try that out.

The group continued to develop their music, and Richard and Robbie each had a substantial collection of songs they had written, both alone and together. The low-pressure, high-result workshop environment was successful for the Hawks.

Robbie recalled in the 2000 liner notes for *Music from Big Pink*:

> There's all this basement tape music going on. Some of it's a goof, some of it is serious. Some of it is "Ruben Remus" and some of it is "Caledonia Mission." There's a difference in these things. Some fall into the "Yea! Heavy and a Bottle of Bread" category and some fall into the "I Shall Be Released" category. "Tears of Rage" was not a goofy basement song. It was a beautiful song. At the same time, other things that we did were kind of funny like "Orange Juice Blues," "Ferdinand," "Ruben Remus," or "Long Distance Operator." Some of these outtakes are more basement tape lark.

While Robbie later categorized the music developed during the Hawks' first year in Woodstock into contrasts, the music is a cohesive body of work. The strengths of the songs are found in their distinct stylings and communal development. "Ruben Remus" is just as vital a song as "Caledonia Mission" when viewed as part of the entire workshop environment, and "Orange Juice Blues" and "Words and Numbers" are certainly as strong as "To Kingdom Come."

To minimize songs that were critical stepping-stones in the band's development is a cop-out. To separate their communal art into definable labels is contrary to the original vision.

Shortly before the album's release, Richard's brother Donald and Donald's wife, Kathryn, drove to Woodstock to visit. While they were sitting around the table, Richard excitedly played a tape of songs being considered for *Music from Big Pink* for his family, after which Donald complimented the music but then questioned its commercial viability. Richard said he and the guys knew they had something different, but he also wasn't completely confident about how others would respond.

Richard later said in the *Band Is Back*:

> During the conception of *Big Pink*, we discovered a whole vocal thing that we weren't aware that we even had before. I remember listening to playbacks after the sessions of songs and thinking, "I really like this stuff and I don't have anything to compare it to. I really like it and I hope everybody else does. I really think this is strong." But that was about all I had to go on.

Chapter 7 | Open the Door, Richard (1966–1967)

Richard at the house he shared with Garth on Spencer Road, Woodstock, 1968.
Elliott Landy

Chapter 8
BEAUTIFUL THING (1968)

Richard rose from his bed over the Big Pink basement garage, afternoon light illuminating the room. The Hawks had raised some serious Cain the night before. The house smelled of stale beer and smoke. He woke with blurred sight and frazzled hair yet was invigorated by the faint germ of a song. After a deep inspection of both eyes in the bathroom mirror, Richard stroked his cheeks, replaying a tune in his head.

He ambled out to the kitchen, where a summer snow of dust danced in the light of the room, and brewed up a pot of strong coffee. He sipped his drink and headed barefoot down the steep basement steps and across the cold floor to the corner piano. He sat down on the bench for a brief session of repetition and refinement, and a gospel-tinged series of changes coalesced out of the basement air. Richard continued his search and soon landed on the celebratory opening chords of what would become the song "We Can Talk."

After the holidays in the frosted hills, the Hawks reconvened with a cache of original music and an inspired focus for 1968. On January 10, the provisionally named Crackers entered A&R Studios in New York City for their first attempt at recording a full-length album. The group went in loaded for bear.

The Crackers recorded to four-track a substantial docket of impressive songs, including "We Can Talk," "Chest Fever," "This Wheel's on Fire," "Yazoo Street Scandal," "The Weight," and Richard and Dylan's basement masterpiece, "Tears of Rage." All in all, it was a solid collection of musical bricks stacked to build the foundation of the group's first musical statement.

The group recorded live with vocals on two of the tracks while saving the other two for horns, percussion, and overdubs. It was quite a prolific day of music for a group that had suffered several false starts in getting their music down in the studio.

Richard remained as engaged in New York City as he was in Woodstock. In addition to singing lead vocals on and composing "Tears of Rage" and "We Can Talk," he sang lead on "Chest Fever." He also contributed smoky piano and a cumulus falsetto that spilled over the edges of Rick's lead part in "This Wheel's on Fire."

While recording "The Weight," the song that would become most associated with the group, Richard contributed an organ part, while Garth played acoustic piano. Unfortunately, the organ line was left out of the final album mix, though it would be reinstated when the Band played the song live.

The final album version of "The Weight" was perfection in song, both lyrically and musically, a piece of art, expertly framed and hung to express the creative intent of its writer, Robbie Robertson. Just as important were Richard's improvised vocals decorating the song's periphery: wordless melodic sounds that appear in the moment and then disappear into the song's framework, an assortment of off-mic falsetto asides, a lacy shawl draped over the three-part-chorus harmonies.

Richard's voice plays the spectral mysterioso, the voice that sounds like everyone's in the band yet is completely his own. During the chorus buildup and the lyric "Take a load off, Fanny," Richard can be heard last and highest in the vocal queue. When the group reaches the word "and," his falsetto harmony part is distinct. He replies to the line "Put the load right on me" just a second late, with a fervent "meeee" more a soulful moan. His vocal addendum is a wax stamp finalizing the rough-hewn collection of distinct voices.

"We Can Talk" is a straight shot of Richard, no chaser, its piano chords pulled from a dog-eared hymnal tucked in the pew at Ontario Street Baptist. The song swings, a windblown wooden gate on one hinge. There is no other song like it in the Band canon. The three vocalists cajole, kid, and bicker in a melodic conversation, a call and response that contains both questions and answers.

"We Can Talk" is Richard's finest fully formed composition. Written during the basement sessions, the song encompasses all the elements that separated the Crackers' music from the usual. The officially released version spotlights pious chording lathered with resplendent splays of color by Garth. The song is effortlessly conversational, yet complex in its layered interpretations. Levon remembered in his autobiography that the group really talked that way: snatches of conversation nestled next to earnest proclamations.

The carefully crafted Manuel/Danko country wail nurtured in the basement with Dylan was now accentuated by Levon's distinct drawl. Nowhere was this more evident and effective than on "We Can Talk." Richard didn't compose the song for a single vocalist; as a result, we hear ebullience structured around whoever sounded right singing it. The verses are initiated by one voice and concluded by another. Cadences shift, melody lines are interwoven, and the vocalists' joy masks the undertones of guarded optimism.

Richard's innate ability to arrange vocals was drawn from those eyes-closed Sundays at Ontario Street Baptist and the after-hours sessions at the Rockwood. Just as bandmate Robbie had, Richard stockpiled memories from the road as a pool to pull characters from for his songs, recalling his vocal aesthetic from a similar subconscious place.

While the verses of "We Can Talk" got passed around among the vocalists, the core of the lyric was a blazing ember, and it revealed an eternal band dialogue composed of pithy asides and surreal images. Midway through the bounding verses, the song breaks meter into a taproom-style, half-time groove, and Richard's voice declares:

> *It seems to me we've been holding something*
> *Underneath our tongues*
> *I'm afraid if you ever got a pat on the back*
> *It would likely burst your lungs*
>
> *Whoa, stop me, if I should sound kinda*
> *Down in the mouth*
> *But I'd rather be burned in Canada*
> *Than to freeze here in the South!*

Flash paper images of Beak at the Rockwood emanate from his off-mic "Whoa," Richard's voice and its once-serrated edges now softened from a Woodstock summer.

"Tears of Rage" earned its place of honor as the opening track on *Music from Big Pink* through its development in the basement on Stoll Road. The subtle movements in the Band's version were harvested from the same patch as "In a Station" and "Katie's Been Gone." "Tears of Rage" is classical in its approach and stunning in its effect. It's serious and emotionally charged music, devoid of pretense.

Richard's emotional recital of Dylan's lyrics against the backdrop of his made-in-Saugerties chord progression reveals the small melodic threads to which the song is stitched: one pull and the entire tune threatens to unravel. The song moves like a breeze, held together with a rustic mixture of pine tar and twine. Dylan's lyrics contain images of misunderstanding, regret, and selfishness, capturing the disillusionment experienced by parents and their children as they grow apart.

Cut on the group's first day in the studio, "Tears of Rage" was adorned with liquid Robertson guitar achieved by running his signal through a rotating Leslie speaker. Robbie plays the stately opening salvo, with Richard echoing back on piano.

On the officially released version, Richard's voice is robust and confident, exploring every nuance of Dylan's intent. It provokes the emotion that Dylan explores, its tone ranging from pleading to resignation. Robbie said on the *Classic Albums* show, "There's a certain element of pain in there that you didn't know whether he was trying to reach for the note, or if he was just a guy with a heart that had been hurt."

The swampy rhythm of the song sways on Levon's moaning tom-tom work. The lack of a snare drum and cymbals puts the focus entirely on Richard's voice and the empty spaces surrounding it. The ghost ship moan of the Band's makeshift horn trio of Richard, Garth, and John Simon is a tasteful adornment.

Richard's voice had the ability to grab a listener and hold on with a powerful gravity. On the opening lyric of the song, "We carried you, in our *arrrmmms*, on Independence Day," Richard's voice intensifies a vibrant and stirring Dylan image, while stretching the word "arms" into a soulful wail.

THE BLUE NOTES

David Temperley, a professor of music theory at the Eastman School of Music at the University of Rochester, in Rochester, New York, has studied what makes a good singer great.

Temperley explained on the school's website: "As musicians, we're always taught there is an octave divided into twelve pitches. Now we're finding evidence that it's not so simple and that people sometimes deliberately fall between one pitch or another for expressive effect."

The space between pitches is what's called "blue notes." These are the accidental gaps between notes, the cracks in the sidewalk. A study by Temperley asked whether blue notes were a soulful accident, or an intentional tool used by a particular singer. In Richard's case, his immersion into the deep navy came on the *Big Pink* songs "Tears of Rage," "In a Station," and "Lonesome Suzie." Temperley said in 2022 that Richard often used notes from the minor scale in a major-key context. One specific example of this can be heard on "Tears of Rage," where the phrase "hand and foot" has Richard sliding down the scale and into the crevices of the melody.

An additional raw alternate take from the first day of recording was released posthumously. This version lacked the horn overdubs of the released version but featured a live-in-the-moment Manuel vocal that highlights the varied inflections in Richard's voice from the officially released version. On *Classic Albums*, John Simon called Richard "guileless, innocent, [and] in a sense the tacit soul of the Band." Listening to the opening day's work on "Tears of Rage," it's hard to disagree.

Simon, who had met the Hawks while working on the *You Are What You Eat* soundtrack, was now producing them. He was a sharp-eared translator of the sounds that the Hawks had discovered in the basement. Simon remembered in his biography, "They were there and there I was. In the right place at the right time."

Richard took to the drum kit for the first time on a session with Robbie's "Yazoo Street Scandal." Take 10 was included as a bonus track on the 2000 reissue of *Music from Big Pink*, and an alternate mix was included on 2005's *A Musical History*.

The song was in the running for *Big Pink* right up until the final hour. The dusty Southern tale is pushed by a loping Danko bass line and Richard's skipping-stone brushwork. Robbie's guitar shimmers with a bluesy attitude, and Levon lays down a tailor-made and sneering lead vocal over the group's shifty collaboration. A song other groups would have killed to have at their disposal, "Yazoo Street Scandal" would remain unreleased until it appeared on 1975's *The Basement Tapes*.

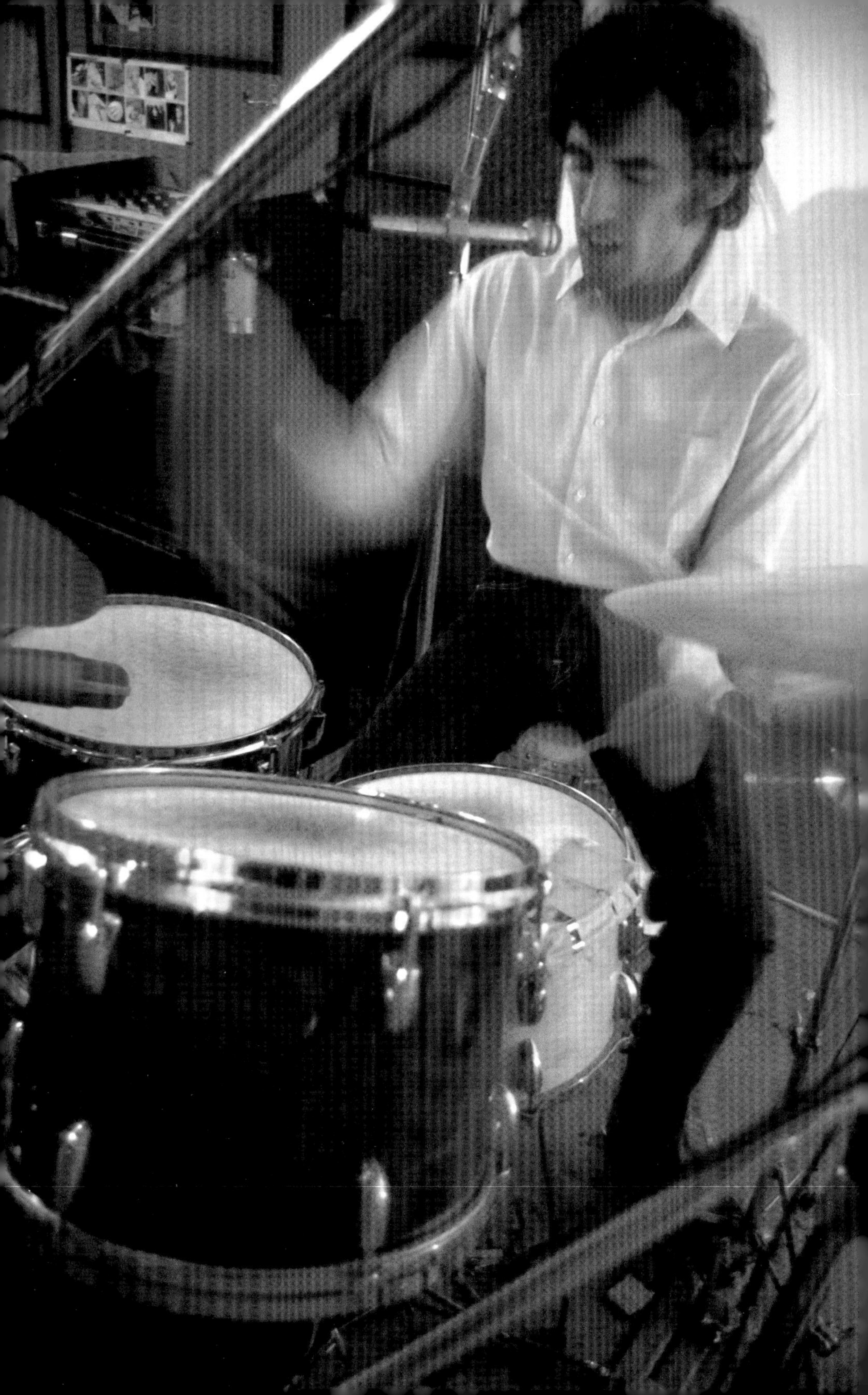

Tribute to Woody

The previous year's musical experiments and the new year's enthusiasm from the work on their own LP were transported to the Carnegie Hall stage on January 20, 1968. Just short of two weeks from their first studio visit, it was here that Dylan and the newly christened Crackers played a three-song set as a tribute to Bob Dylan's formative inspiration, Woody Guthrie.

Guthrie died in October 1967 at the age of fifty-five, and a host of fellow musicians gathered and collaborated in a musical tribute to his towering influence on folk music. A sense of intrigue surrounded the event: the performance would be Dylan's first concert appearance since May 27, 1966, in London. At this time, the Hawks/Crackers were still an unknown commodity to the public, even though they were backing Bob Dylan.

As a testament to the high regard that Dylan held for his Crackers comrades, there was no other thought to who would be playing with him at this legendary event. Dylan would not be performing acoustically, as many expected, in tribute to his mentor; he would be bringing his band of amplified basement noise. He reimagined Guthrie's songs, just as he did his own in 1965 and 1966, through attentive and fiery rearrangements with his trusted band of brothers.

The performance at the Guthrie concert sounds like a different group of men altogether from the band that spiked the tea in Europe. The Catskills water smoothed the edges off Dylan and the Hawks and accentuated the rustic curvature of their music. The dirty swing is back with Levon at the kit, and the music's previous silvery sheen has been replaced by the darkened patina of a copper kettle. Dylan's vocals are restrained, and the Hawks' talons have retracted. The entire collaborative has its respective fingers in each other's country pies, and a new mission has been established.

Richard on drums at Sammy Davis Jr.'s pool house, West Hollywood, California, 1969. *Elliott Landy*

TRIBUTE TO WOODY

Documentation of the event by rock photographer David Gahr captures the Crackers in their backcountry Woodstock aesthetic. Richard is dressed in black and nestled away at the upright piano stage left, behind assorted attendees who are seated on the stage. There was both a matinee and evening performance, and official audio circulates of the evening show. The concert expresses a tangible urgency and is the culmination of Dylan and the Hawks' musical relationship. The adventures that they had experienced together came forth in a stellar reimagining of songs from the Guthrie canon.

The show is one of Richard's finest documented concerts, and one of Dylan and the Hawks' most triumphant moments. Richard is up front in the audio mix, as can be heard on the official release *Woody Guthrie: The Tribute Concerts (Carnegie Hall 1968, Hollywood Bowl 1970)*, and his instrumental interplay with the group is joyous. January 1968 was a very good month for Richard Manuel.

Dylan and his Crackers open their set with a fearlessly funked-up rendition of Guthrie's "I Ain't Got No Home." Richard introduces the song with a sylvan boogie-woogie line and doesn't stop, playing endlessly inventive accents throughout. His piano is central in the sound, a capricious foundation on which lead players Garth and Robbie can build their auditory structures. Richard's jubilant chording is also the bedrock for Dylan's acoustic rhythm and melodic vocal dressings.

During the first instrumental break, Richard and Garth entwine, and Richard tosses out a neat left-handed lick that ruffles Garth's hair. He replies curtly, and Richard answers excitedly with a scurry across the keys. Robbie takes a solo, and Richard plays some quirky variations on the central theme with robust left-handed thumping and right-handed trilling. He answers Robbie's stringy statements in real time, mirroring him to the next verse.

As they did on basement efforts such as "Minstrel Boy" and "Goin' to Acapulco," all the Crackers get involved on the vocals. High and lonesome voices call from the stately pines of Overlook Mountain as Richard, Rick, and Levon pile their voices in a joyously haphazard chorus with Dylan. The resulting clarion call "I ain't got no home in the world anymooooore!" echoes around the rafters of the hall as an undeniable fact.

Guthrie's pensive "Dear Mrs. Roosevelt" is played with a gentle country lilt, Richard's shimmering tremolo answering Dylan's sweetly syncopated singing at the end of the verses. The Saugerties Country Choir joins in with the line "This world was lucky to see him born."

Dylan and the Crackers' reading of "Grand Coulee Dam" is their most jubilant example of music making, the misty summit of their collaborations. As the song begins, Richard's piano is a spinning top, wobbling around the arrangement, perfectly knocking into Rick's corners and Levon's bumpers. Robbie plays a jumpy Steve Cropper lick that renders Guthrie's original version respectfully outdated.

The song's first break has Garth, Robbie, and Richard leaning back, listening and responding, the sinuous meeting of their melodic statements expressing more than any solo could. The song breathes, each instrumentalist's contribution like diffused sunlight breaking through.

Multi-instrumentalist Larry Campbell, who would go on to tour with Dylan and eventually become music director of Levon's Midnight Rambles, attended the evening performance as a thirteen-year-old music fan. He recalled in 2023:

> I knew that Bob was going to close the show; I hadn't even thought about him playing with the Band. Here he comes out and he's playing these Woody Guthrie songs with a rock band. It worked, it worked so well. . . . A different kind of music than I had ever heard.

After a decade of preparation by Richard and his bandmates, something beautiful had been born. Joyous music poured from everyone on the Carnegie Hall stage. Jonathan Taplin, who would become the Band's road manager, remembered in his memoir *The Magic Years*, "The sense of joy that Bob and the Hawks were exuding kept bringing a smile to my face."

The Woody Guthrie benefit was a culmination of a three-year carnival, and a closing of the first chapter of Bob Dylan and the Hawks/Crackers. They created their own universe of music with a big bang of creativity and fearlessness. Their lives would be forever linked, and the Band was a port to which Dylan would return when caught in the most-hectic storms. The next time they played together on a concert stage, the Crackers would be the Band and Dylan would have recorded a country album.

In February, the Crackers headed to California to continue recording their debut album. Sessions at Capitol Studios in Los Angeles resulted in versions of both Richard's "Lonesome Suzie" and "In a Station" and Robbie's "Caledonia Mission" and "To Kingdom Come," as well as versions of the traditional "Long Black Veil" and Dylan's basement opus, "I Shall Be Released."

"Lonesome Suzie" was a song pulled from the typewriter at Big Pink. Sitting at the same desk where Dylan had peeled off reams of lyrics, Richard looked back in order to move forward and write his next song. "Lonesome Suzie" had its roots in reality and was inspired by one girl in a group of three female fans who frequented Revols performances in Stratford. Richard had the hots for Susan back then, but she rebuffed his advances since she was saving herself for marriage.

Richard opened himself up to Susan, as he later did Cathy Smith and Jane Kristiansen. Allowing himself to be available to others is what allowed him to be comfortable with his own deep-seated doubts.

Susan Howard held such a profound sadness that Richard's only choice was to immortalize it in song. His gentle understanding both of Susan's predicament and his own melancholy provide the song with a perceptive view of relationships and loneliness. Richard's desires waver between wanting to help Suzie yet wondering why he's been chosen to take on the emotional burden.

On the *Music from Big Pink* version, Richard conjures a wellspring of emotion. His delicate falsetto, as crazed as antique china, is symbolic of Suzie's fragile emotional state. Robbie channels Curtis Mayfield, and Garth performs as a phantom orchestra.

The song begins in the third person, then shifts to the first person by its conclusion, with the narrator speaking directly to Suzie. Richard's vibrato evokes the shaky uncertainty both he and Suzie have experienced. The narrator gives into the darkness and decides that rather than convince Suzie that everything will be all right, he will join her in distress. The song closes with "Why don't we get together, what else can we do?"

Richard said the following to Ruth Albert Spencer of the *Woodstock Times* about "Lonesome Suzie":

> That one was a definite attempt to write a hit record. It could have been a hit record; it's a good commercial song and everything, but I didn't realize at the time that I never sang it right. It wasn't for me. Somebody else should have sung it.

Lonesome Susie, never got the breaks.
She's always losing; so ~~she~~ sits, ~~and~~ cries, or ~~and~~ shakes,
It's hard just to watch her. ~~maybe~~ if I touch her?
Ahhh poor Susie; wonderin' what to do.

She just sits there, hoping for a freind.
I don't fit here;but I may have a friend to lend.
Maybe I mistook her,but I cant' over look her.
Must be someone who can pull her through

Anyone who's felt that bad could tell me what to say.
Even if she'd just get mad, she might be better off that way.
Where is all the understanding?
Her problems can't be that demanding.
Why is it she looks my way every time she starts to cry.

Lonesome Susie, can't watch you cry no longer.
If you can use me; untill you feel a little stronger,
I guess just watching you,
Has made me lonsome too.
Why don't we get together
        What else can we do?

Typewritten lyrics to "Lonesome Suzie." *Courtesy of anonymous donor*

Chapter 8 | Beautiful Thing (1968)   181

The group recorded two versions of Richard's song: the ballad version and one that swung. Producer Simon said he was responsible for the arrangement of the fast rendition and, years later, called it "inappropriate." While the alternate reading has promise, it doesn't wring out the emotion like the final version from the record does.

"In a Station" is an important and multifaceted song that resides in a realm outside the confines of waking, sleeping, and dreaming. The album version's delicate arrangement supported a spiritually anthemic melody by Richard. The song traces his journey from Stratford to Woodstock, and all stops in between, expressed through autobiographical dreamscapes.

Richard called "In a Station" his George Harrison–type song. The track is ethereal, an anomaly on *Big Pink*, its accompanying vocal harmonies sung through a veil of poignancy. The song came fully formed from the chrysalis, lyrics and music born together. It drifts through a verse/chorus format that seduces the ear. Richard explained to the *Woodstock Times*, "Yeah, I like to get out and wander around in nature sometimes. That song 'In a Station' was totally inspired by Overlook Mountain."

The song's narrative begins in a rattling Stratford railway station. Richard strides through Grand Trunk and wonders if his family and friends will ever truly know him, understand him. By the second verse, Richard is on a lush mountain slope in Saugerties, gazing up toward the summit of Overlook Mountain. He feels a woman next to him, and they sleep together on the alpine bed. Richard told Ruth Albert Spencer, "I always liked that line, 'I could taste your hair.' And also, to type it out, it looks so good on paper."

I could taste your hair

The central lyric of the song captures the very essence of Richard and his feelings about life:

> *Isn't everybody dreaming*
> *Then the voice I hear is real*
> *Out of all the idle scheming*
> *Can't we have something to feel?*

Verse 3 begins in a fictional world of "Once upon a time," which leaves the narrator feeling nothing in the present. He has reached an unknown destination, a place where not even love is sufficient to repay sacrifices and kindness. Garth plays a mystical melody on a Clavinet over Richard's introductory chording. His voice is as full and expressive as on "Tears of Rage."

A spectral slide guitar increases the sense of introspection. With "In a Station," Richard had successfully written a song independent of anything else, the music completely original yet still a distillation of everything he had absorbed.

Also recorded the same day was Robbie's "Caledonia Mission." According to Simon, he was the one who played the piano on the studio version. Richard did shadow Rick's lead vocal with a glistening falsetto harmony. The cover of Lefty Frizzell's "Long Black Veil" found Richard playing Fender Rhodes while he contributed chorus harmonies. Robbie's "To Kingdom Come" again found Richard as the phantom vocal doppelganger, doubling Robbie's rare vocal lead and shadowing Rick and Levon.

For what would be the closing song on *Music from Big Pink*, Dylan's "I Shall Be Released," Richard played piano and sang the lead. His vocal part featured the falsetto that he used to top the harmonies with Dylan in the basement. Peeled away from the song's roots, Richard's vocal became the light shining down and the voice of yearning and hope. The song is iconic, and Richard's interpretation is the reason why. Like everything he sang, the song became his.

While in California, the Crackers dropped by the famed Gold Star Studios on February 20, 1968. Curious to hear how their music would come across in a different room, the group recorded several tracks, three of which now circulate officially but were not included on their yet-to-be-released debut. The sessions were a continuation of the teamwork that occurred in Woodstock. Everyone in the band had a shared goal and a common vision. Both Richard and Robbie were eager and experimental with their work.

"Orange Juice Blues (Blues for Breakfast)" was cut in what sounds like a finished version. Originally released with later overdubs on the 1975 *Basement Tapes* album, the unadorned studio version was released in 1994 on the *Across the Great Divide* box set.

Played as a sugary shuffle, "Orange Juice Blues" is highlighted by Garth's swinging keyboard excursions. Richard's basement demo provided the blueprint, and then the band ran it through quality control as an infectious and breezy blues. The vocal melody is pure Richard: dynamic, cocksure, but with an underlying ambivalence. Robbie squeezes out a fuzzy Telecaster solo, and Richard uses his higher range to great effect.

The other song cut that day, Jimmy Drew's 1961 single "Baby Lou," sounds like a leftover Levon and the Hawks number, which it probably was. The band bangs out a last-call version of Drew's lament, and Richard's lead voice is typically expressive on the sexy stomp.

The band returned to the studio the next day and recorded a stunning reading of Dylan's "Long Distance Operator," as funky and fiery as anything the group would record. Last played onstage in December 1965, the Crackers' reading has an aggressive, sinewy beat and searing Robertson interjections. Ronnie Hawkins referred to his former protégés' recently discovered sound as country funk, and that is an apt label for the group's rendition of Dylan's song. Richard digs through all his vocal tools, the gritty and the smooth, to get the telephone operator to patch him through. He also overdubbed a harmonica part on the song. A masterful performance. It's a complete mystery why the track was left in the bin.

As the band finished up in the studio, its management hatched preparations for promotions and press. In the crowd at the Woody Guthrie benefit concert was another person who would go on to play a pivotal role in the lives of the Band as well as its individual members: Elliot Landy, who at the time was an unknown rock 'n' roll photographer. After Landy and Albert Grossman had an aggressive interaction regarding photographing the Woody Guthrie performance, Landy's name came up when Robbie was inquiring about a photographer to shoot the group.

Infiltrating a typically antifame group of guys, Landy slid into Big Pink and locations around Woodstock and captured the Hawks in several intimate settings. Richard was an ailurophile and bonded with Landy over cats as well as their shared interest in film. Richard had a cat named Phaedra that Landy took a liking to. He remembered Richard as "a very, very sweet person. That's the overall memory I have of him, that he was just always there with a chuckle and a little friendly grin whenever I saw him."

It was a sunny Easter Sunday 1968 when Richard and his bandmates gathered around the kitchen table at Big Pink. After a band meeting, the group donned their Sunday best, cracked some beers, and spent the day taking photos around the property. The iconic black-and-white photo that would grace the inside of the group's debut album was shot on this day.

Landy remembered in 2022, "Richard was gracious, always kind of concerned about how I was or if I felt comfortable." It's obvious by Landy's resulting images that Richard also felt at ease.

Asked about his impressions regarding the dynamics of the group when he was shooting, Landy said, "They were just a bunch of friends. They were like family with each other. They all totally respected each other. . . . I saw them as total collaborators."

He captured the guys in what are some of the most iconic rock 'n' roll photographs ever published.

Ten days later, on March 24, 1968, Robbie and Dominique were married in Woodstock, and the Band's debut album was in the chute. The guys had a little bit too much time on their hands and started to get a reputation around town. Because they were so well liked, they got away with more than your usual local would.

"Rick, Levon, and Richard tended toward drink and drugs as soon as the sun sank behind the mountains," said Jonathan Taplin, who had started working as the group's road manager. Richard's nervy driving excursions came back with a flourish in Woodstock. He and Levon would take their cars out to the fields that surrounded Big Pink and play rock 'n' roll chicken. Richard worked hard and played harder all throughout Woodstock, leaving a string of smoking heaps in his wake.

He'd jump behind the wheel of his 1947 Oldsmobile Custom Cruiser, swinging the back end out of the driveway with a dusty and resounding thump. He could cover the 6 miles between Big Pink and Woodstock proper in just minutes. He deftly navigated the tree-lined corners and hairpin turns, coming only fractions of an inch from kissing the cobblestone retaining walls . . . unless he had a few drinks in him. Richard tended to make his own roads and drove the death-defying sprint to Deanie's for music and drinks in little time and in varied levels of inebriation.

Deanie's was the local restaurant known from coast to coast that hosted weddings and housed impromptu concerts at the piano by Woodstock's resident musicians. As with Coaches Corner in Somers Point, Deanie's became Richard's favorite place to hang out and drink with the locals and his musician pals.

One early-spring evening after a night of revelry, Richard was at Big Pink with a group of after-hours partygoers. He begged Dominique Robertson for permission to drive her brand-new 1967 Mustang GT, a gift from Robbie.

After subtle pressure and persuasion, Dominique relented: she would let Richard drive the car, but she would join him. Richard settled into the driver's seat and reassured Dominique, saying, "I sober up behind the wheel." Racing off at unsafe speeds and into the ink black Woodstock night, Dominique asked Richard if could see the road, to which he replied, "I can see like a lynx."

Opening the car up wide open and only a short distance from Big Pink, Richard lost control on a tricky rise and pinballed the Mustang against every single concrete barrier along the side of the road before flipping into the ditch. After checking to make sure that they had all their bits and pieces, Richard thoughtlessly lit a match to check out the damage and was forced from the wreckage by Dominique, who feared he was going to blow them both up.

Word reached Big Pink that Richard had crashed the car, and Levon ran out the door at full speed and screamed off in his Corvette. As he approached Richard's accident scene at a high rate of speed, Levon was unable to negotiate the blind corner, clipped a police cruiser, and almost took out everyone in the road around the wreckage. After he got out of his car, a struggle ensued with police, and both Richard and Levon were taken to jail. Levon tells the tale in exciting detail in his memoir, *This Wheel's on Fire*.

The note line on a check signed by Albert Grossman dated March 31, 1968, reads "Bail for Mark Helm and Richard Manuel." In Robbie Robertson's film *Once Were Brothers*, he expresses his anger with Richard's carelessness, and rightfully so. It isn't known what effect the accident had on Richard and Robbie's friendship. The release of *Music from Big Pink* was still three months away.

Richard's drinking increased. He also started to take a liking to pills, usually downers. With the escalation of use comes isolation. With isolation comes alienation. With money comes freedom, and a willingness to go to the edge of how fucked up you could get. Richard Manuel liked to get fucked up, and he took it as far as it could go.

Richard crashed his Olds and a Pontiac Bonneville, and he was banned from Enterprise Rent-A-Car. The workers had gotten to the point that they would just lock the doors if they saw Richard coming. The phone rang at all hours of the night that one of the guys had crashed something. While Richard was king of the wrecks, Rick and Levon contributed accordingly.

As the group readied the release of the record, discussion continued about what to call the band. Listing each band member individually would work and reflected how the guys felt about the democracy of the group. They couldn't really go on as the Crackers. Richard voted for the Honkies, but that one wouldn't work either. Finally, a decision was made to just call the group the Band. Everyone called them that anyway. Dylan called them that, and Grossman, the locals, and the Woodstock cops all called them the Band, so why not go with it?

While the rest of the guys raised holy hell in the woods, the Robertsons and the Grossmans were growing closer. Dylan had moved on from Grossman's management and Robbie had moved in. It was in these key months of assimilating into the upper crust of Woodstock that Robertson started to steer the Band's ship into different waters. In Barney Hoskyns's book *Small Town Talk*, photographer Michael Friedman alludes to the lofty attitudes developing around the Band: "He [Grossman] hadn't cared a thing about the Hawks. When the Band started to become successful, all of a sudden, he started looking at the balance sheet and decided Robbie was the way to go. He was an opportunist."

Musically, things were amazing for the group. They were impermeable to outside forces and moved on their own inertia. While the ongoing development of the Band's songwriting direction was beginning to be curated by Robbie's collection of Southern and American imagery, just as important a contribution was Richard's quirky grasp of melody and special vocal approaches.

On *Music from Big Pink*, Richard composed three original songs and had a cowrite with Dylan, the same number of compositions that Robbie had. The record was a true collaboration in songwriting, instrumentation, and production. Its storytelling diversity enhanced its extraordinary and unselfish blend of writing. The music's mystery and drama increased because of the multifarious influence of its writers and players.

Richard composed his songs from the inside out. His songwriting reflected a private internal conflict. His songs are unabashed and real. Robbie created characters and told stories. He revealed bits of himself through symbolism and imagery. His writing was more narratively based than personal. He was adept at holding on to a snatch of conversation or an image and building around it for a bigger story.

Richard and Robbie's collaborations were natural. Their respective strengths negated the other's weaknesses. Their formative songwriting partnership in the basement was absolutely critical in the maturation of the Band's sound.

By late spring of 1968, it was high time to reap the results of years of hard work, both from the Rompin' Ronnie Hawkins boot camp and the trial-by-fire Dylan tours.

The Band traveled to Simcoe, Ontario, to Rick Danko's family farm for a photo session with Elliott Landy. Kiddo and Pierre drove down from Stratford to stand proudly with their musician son. The group posed in front of the Danko barn with family and friends in a photo called *Next of Kin*. Richard looks confident, strong, and proud to be representing the Manuel kinfolk. The sunny family portrait was featured on the inside of the record, a testament to what was important to the group and a thank-you to the support they had received from their families along the way.

This is how the Band really was. They enjoyed hanging out with their families and each other. They dressed the way they had always dressed; they acted the way that they were.

Music from Big Pink was released on July 1, 1968, a definitive statement of five men who together had traversed the musical landscape of Canada, the United States, and the world. It was a tangible testament to their shared belief in their music, their art, and their mission. For Richard, it represented a ten-year pursuit of musical satisfaction, of friendship, and of a never-ending party.

The album's release was shrouded in mystery and speculation. Was Dylan on the record? What was with that cover? Big Pink? Who are these people? The music was even more puzzling. The songs swam upstream against all trends. The music was homespun, honest, and strange. The voices hailed from another time and place; it sounded like the singers might have been related. *Music from Big Pink* was a diverse introduction to the musical mystery that was Bob Dylan's backing band.

The album simmered. It didn't roar up the charts, but it didn't need to. It did what it was naturally supposed to do: connect and influence. More importantly, it reached the Band's contemporaries. It touched the biggest players in popular music and pushed them to reconsider their musical decisions and directions. The record was a musician's record, a testament to how far Richard and his bandmates had come. Writer Jonathan Singer later said in *Hit Parader*, "In a world of flashy clothes and hallucinogenic over-production, *Big Pink* was a folksy knickknack." The Band looked odd, sounded different, and was a complete enigma to the mainstream rock media. Pilgrimages were made to Woodstock to find out what the hell was going on in those hills.

Robbie said to *Uncut* magazine in 2015, "It was just fun. We had lots of laughs. When I think about it now, it's really the way music-making should be." The Band released the record like a private joke among friends, and if you wanted to be an insider, you had to listen.

In his review for *Rolling Stone*, Al Kooper named *Music from Big Pink* album of the year and said, "There are people who will work their lives in vain, and never touch it."

The reverberations of the music crossed the pond, its influence so immediate that Eric Clapton made plans to disband the supergroup Cream, thinking they had it all wrong. Clapton had heard an acetate of *Music from Big Pink* at the house of Delaney & Bonnie's manager and was haunted by what he heard. He immediately thought his current musical station irrelevant.

The Beatles' "Get Back" sessions in January 1969 were a direct attempt to re-create the workshop environment that Dylan and the Hawks employed in Woodstock. The Rolling Stones got back in their own way with a no-frills return to their roots with *Beggars Banquet*. The Band's careful development and sharing of their music and image were a direct affront to the usual happenings in popular music. The Band's influence was widespread, the plaudits numerous and well deserved.

Guitarist George Harrison was among those who made the pilgrimage to Woodstock to suss out how these guys made their music. The Beatle was enchanted with the Band and told *Musician* magazine's Timothy White in 1987, "To this day, you can play *Stage Fright* and *Big Pink*, and although the technology's changed, those records come off as beautifully conceived and uniquely sophisticated. They had great tunes, played in a great spirit and with humor and versatility."

Roger Waters of Pink Floyd said definitively to the *Dallas Morning News* in 2008, "Sonically, the way the record's constructed, I think *Music from Big Pink* is fundamental to everything that happened after it."

The *Music from Big Pink* album is where all of Richard's talents coalesced into musical moments that would forever enshrine his legacy. His first thought was always "What can I contribute to the music?," quickly followed by "And how can I have the best time doing it?" His voice and his selfless musical contributions resulted in his irreplaceable membership in the Band.

Beak receded into the horizon silhouetted as a Hawk, while Richard Manuel emerged fully formed with the Band. Beak had been left behind in Stratford, Ontario, and Fayetteville, Arkansas, with the tattered remains of the Revols and feathers of the Hawks scattered on concert stages across the globe. Now stood Richard, songwriter, multi-instrumentalist, and singer, an equal member of a cadre of men who were on their way to becoming one of the most respected musical groups in the world.

Sadly, Richard's happiness could not be sustained by his abilities. French writer Anaïs Nin could have been speaking about Richard when she wrote in her diary, "I feel very small, I don't understand. I have so much courage, fire, energy, for many things, yet I get so hurt, so wounded by small things." Richard wasn't equipped as a human being to deal with the level of freedom that his talent afforded him. Setbacks floored him, and any slight, real or imagined, caused him to dwell on the motivation behind it.

Richard's drinking enabled him to play the fool and forget. His bandmates had grown accustomed to his antics, a roll-your-eyes and shrug-your-shoulders kind of deal. But Richard lived to see his friends and bandmates crack up. He'd chuckle so hard, his eyes would fix into a squint. He'd flash his big pearly teeth and get the room to quiver with laughter. Richard drank every tray of ale and roared with the punch line of every joke, but his lifestyle couldn't be sustained in a profession that welcomed excess and, in many ways, encouraged it.

The problem was, Richard Manuel wholeheartedly accepted the challenge.

Internally, as the Hawks matured into the Band, the group dynamics changed. When there was a front man in charge, such as Hawkins or Dylan, it was easy to be a cohesive unit. Levon was the foundation of the Hawks from the very beginning; he took care of business with Hawkins in the early days from the first kick drum strike. When Robbie joined Ronnie's Hawks, his street smarts placed him on an equal plane with Hawkins and Helm.

When Rick, Richard, and Garth joined the organization, Levon and Robbie were the big brothers. Robbie took care of the band's logistics and Levon the music, though the internal workings of the relationship was much more complex. Richard always felt like an outsider, no matter the circumstance.

Robbie said to *Billboard* in 2019:

> Levon and I were the first two together in the Hawks. We were the original brothers. For a long time, it was just Levon and me, and the other guys were catching up to that. He was like a brother to me, and then eventually everybody became part of this circle.

Levon's departure from the group in the fall of 1965 left a huge leadership void and a natural shift of band dynamics in Robbie's direction. Robbie made decisions and encouraged connections while he developed a keen understanding of the music business.

In the case of Richard, his talent naturally made him a force in the group. But as far as any sort of perceived leadership role, in the end he was just a rock 'n' roll singer.

Richard wanted to play music; Robbie wanted to cultivate a career. Richard was content to take the ride on his terms. He told the *Woodstock Times*, "We all just did our share. Robbie was our spokesman. He took care of that end. He had the best mind for business. Levon acted as musical leader . . . for the most part . . . although we traded. And I was always a sideman." Richard was a sensitive creative, the salve between two powerful frictions.

The Band was afforded a new freedom through the release of their debut album. The combination of songs by Richard, Robbie, and Dylan, played through the Band's practiced hands, expressed an alternative view of how popular music could be created. Richard had achieved his dream; now he had to work to keep the wheels on that road and away from the ditch.

His music had matured briskly. An ascendant chronology can be traced from "Beautiful Thing" to "In a Station," from "Katie's Been Gone" to "We Can Talk." The compositions he created during the development of *Music from Big Pink* come from a different place. Richard's music adheres to no genre. His songs are shaken out from experience and haunted with a vocal urgency that comes from a place of such sorrow that it hurts to listen.

Richard playing with Elliott Landy's Leica camera in the den of the house he shared with Garth on Spencer Road, Woodstock, 1968. *Elliott Landy*

Chapter 8 | Beautiful Thing (1968)

"I never assumed any authority and I just pitched in, wherever, since then people tell me that I'm responsible for the producing, engineering and mixing of our second album, our most important album, but I thought I was just doing my part. I thought everyone was doing as much as I was."

Chapter 9
RISING OF THE TIDE (1968-1969)

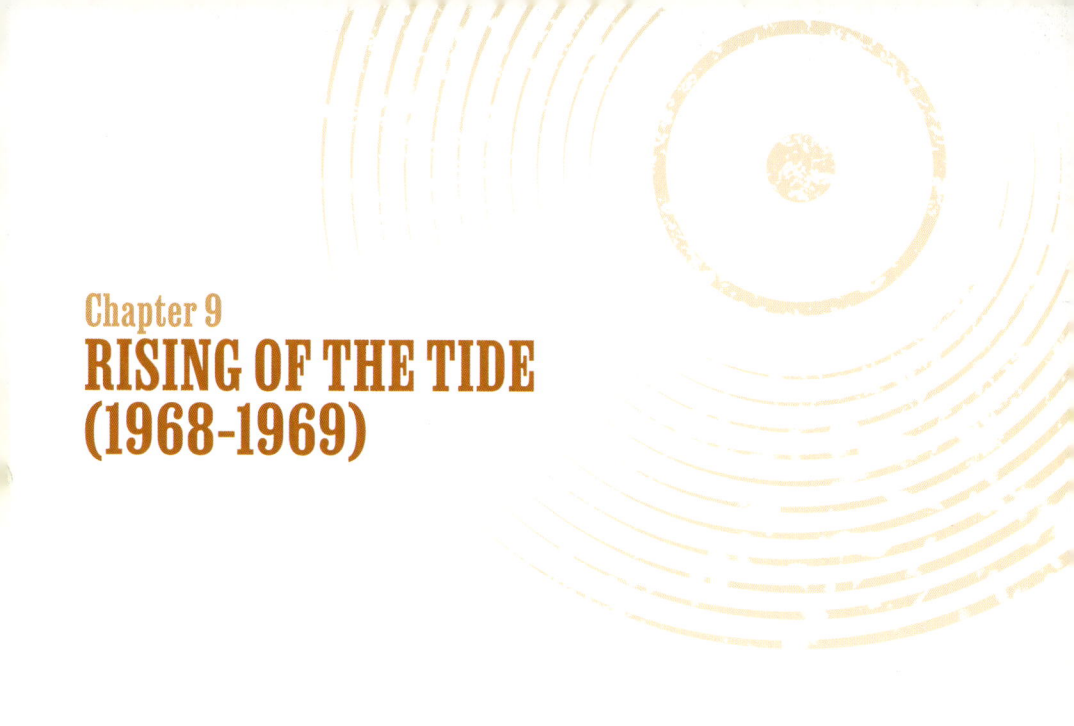

> Being famous is not great for the creative process.
> —Van Morrison

Music *from Big Pink* was the culmination of the Hawks' musical experiences together. It represented their ambition and hard work. The recording was the cumulative group vision made tangible, a definitive artistic statement.

The summer of 1968 saw the members of the Band reveling in their newly found artistic and personal freedom. The Big Pink gang moved to different locations around Woodstock. Rick and Levon took up residence together on Wittenberg Road, while Garth, Richard, and former Hawks manager Bill Avis moved to a home on Spencer Road.

Beginning as soon as the sun set over the mountains, most evenings saw Richard holding court at the Band's favorite eatery, Deanie's, or Woodstock's favorite watering hole, the Sled Hill Café. Richard could be found grinning like a crescent moon and laughing until he doubled over, or propped up against the jukebox looking to play some moody R&B. He was known to play bluesy piano into the wee hours at both locations if the spirit moved him.

The Sled Hill Café was a junky mixture of chintzy knickknacks, found wood, and thrift shop decor. If it rained too much, at some point you'd be standing in water. It was the perfect hangout for Richard and a host of other musicians around Woodstock.

Frank Spinelli, bartender at the Sled Hill Café, told the *Woodstock Times*:

> Around 2:45 a.m., members of the Band—Levon, Rick, and Richard—used to amble in and order ten or twelve Go Fasters. As these were lined up on the bar, the boys worked their way through them. Then, amply fortified, they turned their attention to the stage and performing.

Go Fasters were a high-octane concoction of two parts vodka, one part cherry brandy, and a lemon wedge, topped with 7 Up or club soda. The drink was a favorite of Richard and his bandmates.

On the small stage area at the end of the bar, the guys would play through standards from their rock 'n' roll education, with Woodstock night owl Paul Butterfield sometimes jumping in to blow harmonica. After an acceptable amount of music, chatter, and fun, Richard would rise slowly from his stool and smirk a toothy smile. Once steadied, he would offer a pithy reassurance to the assembled patrons that he'd have no problem navigating the twisted mountain roads home. Levon would agree from behind a cloud of cigarette smoke that Richard was a more than capable driver.

The moonlight miles home usually resulted in smoking heaps of rubble, with Richard surpassing limits in both sobriety and speed. Sometimes he'd pull off for a quick pit stop at Levon's for a nightcap and a joint before heading home. But Richard wouldn't learn his lesson, and over time the wrecks accumulated. He would sheepishly explain away his accidents with a most outlandish story: the barriers on the side of the road had been moved, or the road had been rerouted and he was tricked into turning too early.

The Woodstock constables fell victim to Richard's good-natured attitude and endearing stories. He sometimes ended up in the back of a cruiser after a crash, but only for a safe ride home, his wrecks abandoned, to be picked up by the rental car company at a later date.

During one particular close call, Richard was tearing along the back roads of Saugerties in one of his Rent-A-Wrecks when he roared past a local constable checking radar. Richard looked in the rearview and saw the cruiser pulling out to give chase, and immediately stomped the gas pedal to the floor. He weaved through the lanes and blew stop signs before he finally reached Spencer Road. Richard ripped up the road, parked, flung open the door of the car, and ran through the driveway dust cloud. He bounded into the house, where he tore off his clothes and jumped in the shower. After he quickly soaked himself, he wrapped himself with a towel just as he saw the flashing police lights pull into the driveway. Not soon after, he heard loud rapping on the front door.

He meekly opened the door, dripping with water and wearing his towel and a clueless grin. The officer looked at Richard and asked him where he'd been going in such a hurry and why he hadn't stopped when he saw the police lights. Richard looked him dead in the eye, raised an eyebrow, and said, "Officer, that wasn't me. I'm just getting out of the shower here. I've been home all day."

The officer looked at Richard quizzically and, having no ready reply, apologized for the inconvenience. He turned to walk back to his cruiser and, as he did, caught the scent of a burning cigarette wafting from the ashtray of the car parked in the driveway.

The hard-partying late evenings became pastel-pale early mornings and often left Richard out of commission until the afternoon. When a Band representative was required to meet with a journalist or make an appointment for studio time, it certainly was not going to be Richard. With the Band beginning to realize its full potential, a shift in priorities was required. The concept of priorities was somewhat foreign to Richard; nothing could be *that* important.

After the release of *Music from Big Pink*, a sixth element was introduced to the Band's mixture: fame. The group had long toiled in mysterious obscurity, but now the Band's contemporaries and admirers were enthralled by the group's debut record and enigmatic specter. More important was the effect the album had on popular music in general: the same mysterious aura that surrounded the group by virtue of its association with Dylan had attached itself to the Band's own music.

The widespread influence of the record allowed Richard and his bandmates to take stock of how far they had come, while starting families and realizing their personal ambitions. The group's increased visibility offered them exciting opportunities in several milieux previously unknown to them, including art and film. New relationships were being forged because of the group's music, and several of their contemporaries made their way to Woodstock to see what was going down in those upstate hills. Guitarists George Harrison and Eric Clapton became immediate converts to the Band's music.

In the weeks after *Big Pink* was released, Robbie and the Grossman management team brainstormed ways to take the group on the road. It was important to the Band that any performances were on their terms, after spending the last ten years touring. A support crew was assembled, venues were considered, and logistics were discussed.

Robbie brought Jonathan Taplin, who first met Richard and the guys at the January 1968 Woody Guthrie memorial show, on board as road manager for the group. As Taplin began preparations for the tour, in what would become an unfortunate recurring theme, there would be accidents. In one, Richard received third-degree burns on the top of his foot after a gasoline fire he built in the bottom of a grill turned into an inferno. That set any performance plans back at least a month or two.

Taplin remembered in 2022, "I could tell what role Richard played in the group, in the sense that he was kind of the joker. He was the party and fun guy, the guy who was playing pranks and doing stuff, you know?"

While Richard was ensconced as the group jester, his deeper feelings were obscured by his hijinks.

One feeling that had been stirring inside Richard was his attraction to Jane Kristiansen. As he made plans to attend his brother Donald's wedding in Canada in July, he reached out to her in Toronto to see if she would go with him, saying something about not having a license to drive. Their relationship had been on and off since Richard's return from the Dylan tour; Jane had an engagement that was called off when she and Richard rekindled their interest in each other.

Richard flew into Hamilton and arrived at Well Street for the rehearsal dinner the day before Donald and Kathryn's wedding. Jane drove down from Toronto the next day. Richard's oldest brother, Jim, officiated the wedding on July 27, and both Richard and his brother Alan were groomsmen.

The Manuel boys: Jim, Richard, Alan, and Donald at Donald and Kathryn's wedding in Stratford, Ontario, on July 27, 1968. *Courtesy of the Richard Manuel family*

Using the emotional scene to his obvious advantage, over the course of their week in Stratford, Richard extolled the virtues of marriage to Jane before finally popping the question. Jane accepted and they decided to get married on that Friday.

Jane was rightfully tentative about this major life decision, but she loved Richard deeply, with no thoughts about what might await her in the strange world of rock 'n' roll. Richard needed Jane not only as his wife but as his rock. Only five days later, on August 2, 1968, Richard Manuel and Jane Kristiansen were married in Hamilton, Ontario, in a very small wedding with Richard's brother Jim again officiating the proceedings. Jane recalled that both her parents, as well as Pierre and Kiddo, took part in the ceremony. Kathryn Manuel remembered Richard speaking to his brother while on their honeymoon and saying, "Hey, we got married too."

Richard and Jane's wedding in Hamilton, Ontario, on August 2, 1968. *Courtesy of the Richard Manuel family*

After the wedding, Jane and Richard took a small plane back to Woodstock, where they lived as newlyweds on Spencer Road with Garth. Jane remembered that the marriage was "tough from the get-go." Richard didn't let it stop his fun: not long after moving into Spencer Road, he came home after a late night turned icy early morning, sporting a gap where he had knocked out a tooth. Jane remembers his bloody face, the result of him missing a sharp turn on the way up the serpentine Ohayo Mountain Road and ending up in the ditch.

A month later, in yet another grim indication of the trouble and temptation lurking in the shadows of idyllic Woodstock, Rick Danko had a serious accident of his own. His neck was broken after the car he was driving hit a tree and landed in a ditch. He was placed in a neck halo, and any plans regarding live performance for the rest of 1968 were put on hold while he healed. The mystique surrounding the Band only increased with their lack of public visibility.

Meanwhile, Richard had received an influx of money from his songwriting efforts on *Music from Big Pink* and Cass Elliot's rollicking reading of "Orange Juice Blues (Blues for Breakfast)" on her 1968 *Dream a Little Dream* album. Elliott had asked Simon to produce her record after hearing his production work on *Music from Big Pink*.

Richard hung around Woodstock, dropping in on pals like Peter and Andy Yarrow or local folk artists Artie and Happy Traum. If there was a piano in the house, Richard was going to play it. Happy Traum remembers Richard stopping by their house, singing songs and playing the upright piano for him and his wife. With all the buildup around *Big Pink*, and then the letdown of no performances, Richard was getting restless, and his boredom was expressed in stereotypically crazy behavior.

He liked to stir the pot, and on one of those endless days, he had been knocking back a few and edging the rolling roads of Saugerties. By midafternoon, he ripped into the driveway of Wittenberg Road with a resounding sigh from the engine. One of the Band's roadies, Mark, was moving equipment for the group and had driven his brand-new Volkswagen Beetle convertible to Rick and Levon's house.

On the edge of the property, a safety-yellow front-loading tractor and some piles of dirt suggested some sort of landscaping job was going on. For reasons unknown, Richard jumped into the tractor and filled its wide bucket with a heaping scoop of sand.

When Mark came out of the house, he saw that his car had been filled to the brim with soil through the open top. Sand was spilling out of the doors and piled on the hood. It looked like a life-size hourglass had been emptied over the car.

Mark was furious. When he heard the tractor idling, Richard was smiling behind the wheel. Roadie Ed Anderson later recalled that everyone in the Band shared a "You did *what*?" reaction to Richard's decision. Needless to say,

Mark left his employment with the group not long after the incident.

In the fall, the group began to make tentative plans, firming up sessions for their follow-up record for Capitol. "The Weight" had received radio play, and the usual practice was to strike while the iron was hot and get the group back in the studio. The goal was to have twelve new songs. A brief September visit to New York City resulted only in a version of "Key to the Highway" that was played like a warm-up. While it didn't make it onto the second album, it was eventually released as a bonus track on the 2000 remaster of *Music from Big Pink*.

The band returned to New York for an October 24 session that found them recording a Richard Manuel original, "Working in the Canastas." The song had that recognizable Richard swing, balanced on a slowly descending piano figure. Levon's drumming was particularly snappy, with what sounds like a switch from a snare to a kitchen pot lending the song a strange clank. The basic track is complete, with bass, drums, and piano in place, and tentative organ and guitar parts overdubbed.

The Band laid down four takes of a rhythm track, which indicates a modicum of interest in using it for the next album. However, by the time the Band officially started recording sessions for their next LP, the song was nowhere to be found. There are no lyrics, perhaps explaining the song's disappearance.

Interestingly, the fourth and last take of the song was used as an instrumental bed on the *A Musical History* DVD, revealing another Richard original tune that had great promise. The text accompanying the track on the DVD reads "Although words did not come easy to Richard, between 1967 and 1970 he worked on a number of instrumental ideas similar to this."

This statement stands in strange contrast to the contention that Richard's creative output declined throughout that period. It's possible that he just got discouraged, with efforts such as "Working in the Canastas" shelved. Richard required constant encouragement in his craft; it couldn't have been easy on him to have toiled over several excellent pieces of music only to have them passed over or relegated to second-tier status.

Slowhand Meets the Band

Alan Pariser was a rock 'n' roll entrepreneur, promoter, and dear friend of Eric Clapton. He was what Clapton called "a friend of musicians" and was involved in several musical happenings in the mid-1960s, including helping stage the Monterey Pop Festival. In 1968 he was managing Delaney & Bonnie and invited Clapton to his Laurel Canyon home to listen to a demonstration record he had just come across by a group called the Crackers. The introduction to this music would change Clapton's life.

Clapton recalled in 2023 the first time he was exposed to the music of the Band, describing the setup Pariser had in his home:

> He had a McIntosh going into a Crown power amp, feeding two Voice of the Theatre speakers, Altec. . . . He also had some very special grass from Mexico, which only a select few were getting a taste of. And so I listened to *Music from Big Pink* with these things. These speakers were sort of hanging from the corners of the room. It was very loud, very big, a perfect way to hear it. I was stunned. I went into another dimension. It was quite a very profound experience. Both profound and depressing, as I felt like I had been missing something and suddenly here it was in my life.

The first thing Clapton heard on the tape was the quivering opening of "Tears of Rage" and Richard Manuel's resonant voice. Clapton said in *Classic Albums*, "He [Richard] was very shaky. He was very fragile and scared. And in some reverse way, that had a lot of power that drew you and attracted you."

Clapton immediately made a request to meet the musicians on the record he had just heard. Pariser arranged for Clapton to meet Robbie the next time he was in LA. After their meeting, Clapton decided to make the pilgrimage to Woodstock.

On his first evening in town, Clapton met the Band at their clubhouse. In 2023 he talked about the environment there: "It was really at home, domestic, and private." He continued:

> Richard and I connected instantly, in that we both liked to drink. I mean, everybody liked to drink then, but we liked to drink *more* than the others did. I think we kind of knew that about one another intuitively. When you get two breeds of a certain dog, when you get a couple of Airedales, they sort one another out. . . . That was my initial meeting. I was speechless because I didn't have any reference to anybody else like this, even the guys I had met with Delaney and Bonnie, or other people in American rock 'n' roll. This was as deep as I'd ever been.

The mountain scenery, work boots, and unpretentious attitudes—Clapton felt as though he had just become a member of an exclusive club. This was something completely different from anything he had encountered in music.

He came to Woodstock fully intent on becoming a member of the Band. In his 1994 speech inducting them into the Rock & Roll Hall of Fame, Clapton said, "I went to visit the Band in Woodstock, and I really sort of went there to ask if I could join the Band, only I didn't have the guts to say it. I didn't have the nerve." While he would never move into a second guitar chair for the group, he made a friend in Richard. Clapton said in the film *Once Were Brothers*, "I fell in love with Richard. He was the most mournful, soulful thing I'd ever heard."

Remembering Richard in 2023, he said:

> His vocal skills were really unusual, because he sang in a really kind of constricted way. Very, very controlled, and yet there was this incredible versatility. He could slide into falsetto very, very easily. He could merge falsetto with the natural voice. It just sounded seamless. . . . It felt like he drew upon the influence of everyone he probably listened to and came up with this thing that was unique and in the moment.

Clapton watched the group play together and develop songs. He was impressed by the musical abilities of each member and how they volleyed the leadership among them. He and Richard related not only as musical twins but as hard drinkers. Clapton said:

> At that point, it [alcoholism] was still quite undiscovered in me, and maybe it was for Richard too. But it was something in our characteristics and in the way we felt about ourselves. It was easy to identify. . . . With me and Richard, I knew that it was going to be a concrete situation. We were both fallible.

For Richard, that fallibility was a source of his soulfulness, what drove the very essence of his music . . . but it was also the root of his addictions. Richard's ability to receive and transmit through song was his gift; his inability to control his gifts, his downfall. Clapton continued:

> The thing about technique that I admired about Richard is that it was not about skill so much as feeling. He almost deliberately undermined his technique by being soulful, projecting the soulful aspect of it, in front of the technical aspect of it. I was drawn to people that sang like that, because it meant it was accessible to me.

Shortly after Clapton's visit to Woodstock, George and Pattie Harrison came to town to stay with the Dylans. On Thanksgiving, Dylan and his wife, Sara, hosted a dinner. The aroma of turkey and good pot hung in the air as friends and family relaxed in the natural light of the Byrdcliffe living room.

Happy Traum, who had struck up a friendship with the group, was at the dinner and remembered Richard sitting at Dylan's piano, playing an impromptu performance of "I Shall Be Released." Rick joined in harmony, and the holiday collective was witness to a jewel of a musical moment never to be repeated.

Shortly before the end of the year, Richard and Jane moved from Spencer Road into a house on Bellows Lane, built by famed painter George Bellows, who died at the young age of forty-two. The home was one of the artistic centers of Woodstock in the early twentieth century, and Richard found plentiful inspiration there during his short stay. Tucked away under the shadow of a deep-green Catskill mountain, Richard and Jane attempted some semblance of domestication. Richard told Jane that she no longer needed to work and that he wanted her home with him. When Jane explained that she liked modeling, Richard's reply was "It's my turn now."

Richard walked across the creaking cold hardwoods of the Bellows house and seated himself at the well-loved and slightly out-of-tune piano. Still fuzzy from sleep, he squinted through heavy-lidded eyes through the morning-bright windows across the side yard.

The house held a thick artistic vibe in its walls. Out of this organic inspiration, Richard tapped out a soft repetitive salvo on the piano. With one key slightly ajar, a fragile chord progression with broken lyrical fragments was born in the winter glare of the cold sun. He repeated the musical mantra and developed the imagery from it. Richard said to the *Woodstock Times*, "The songs that I wrote myself, I'd usually have a musical idea, then I'd give it a theme, an idea to go with it."

Richard paused, leaned on the keys, lit a cigarette, and watched a soft sprinkling of snow fall to rest on the branches outside the window. He chewed on the end of his thumb and sighed. He had the changes down for the verses but had lost the words. It was discouraging, but at least he had sequestered the melody. The cigarette burned down to a skeleton of ash as Richard ran through the entire movement humming and moaning the desperate melody.

At the Band's next rehearsal, Richard showed the tune to Robbie, who immediately helped flesh out a narrative around Richard's melody lines. This one was not going to slip through the cracks. Robbie took the song on vacation to Hawaii and wrote most of the lyrics there, successfully channeling Richard's inspiration and vibe into what would become known as "Whispering Pines."

Richard in a 1966 Chevrolet Super Sport convertible, California, 1969. *Courtesy of the Richard Manuel family*

California

After the holidays and with Rick's neck on the mend, the Band decided to escape Woodstock's winter doldrums and head for the West Coast in early 1969. Musically, Richard was on the same kind of roll he was when the Band was developing and recording *Music from Big Pink*. After they failed to capture the appropriate groove at the studio in New York, a group decision was reached to pull up stakes and move the entire Band family to California.

In February, the Band rented Sammy Davis Jr.'s house at 8850 Evanview Drive in the Hollywood Hills and converted it into a studio, in an update of the clubhouse vibe. The sprawling property worked perfectly for the Band's intent. The group and their wives, along with John Simon, and Robbie's mom as the cook, all stayed together at the house, with Richard and Jane taking over a second-floor bedroom. Jane remembers it as a surprisingly low-key time, with the guys driving around in a Chevrolet El Camino for errands and operating as a self-contained unit.

A studio was created in the 1,100-square-foot pool house with Simon's assistance. Garth and Richard procured an upright piano for the space, and the group began recording sessions for the follow-up to *Music from Big Pink*. The entire album was recorded in the makeshift studio with the exception of "Whispering Pines," "Jemimah Surrender," and "Up on Cripple Creek," which were taken back to New York to be recorded.

Having everyone in the same location was critical. The group thrived on the close-knit living conditions in the house, enjoying communal dinners, celebrating birthdays, and working late into the night. Playing checkers was a big part of hanging out, with Levon and Rick being the best players. Simon remembered in his memoir that Richard had invented "a new checker game called 'Gimmies,' the object of which was to lose, and he was the champ at that." Richard would also sprawl out on the couch playing solitaire, his mother's favorite game when he was growing up.

Plans evolved for the group's second LP, with a tentative working title of *Harvest*. This album differed from *Big Pink* in one major way: it had a preconceived thematic spread. Whereas *Music from Big Pink* was the culmination of a natural series of events, Robbie had curated a vision for the Band's next album. The Band recorded evenings, often into the wee hours, throughout March and April.

The group was peaking as artists, and the recording was the tightest they would ever be as friends and collaborators. As Robbie said on *The Big Interview with Dan Rather* in 2020, "This place became a sanctuary where we could cut off the world. We were all together, and the music that we were able to make, while being in that zone, was so together. . . . This is when the brotherhood was at its peak for me."

The complete immersion in the recording and in each other's lives was perhaps the most important element of the album's eventual success.

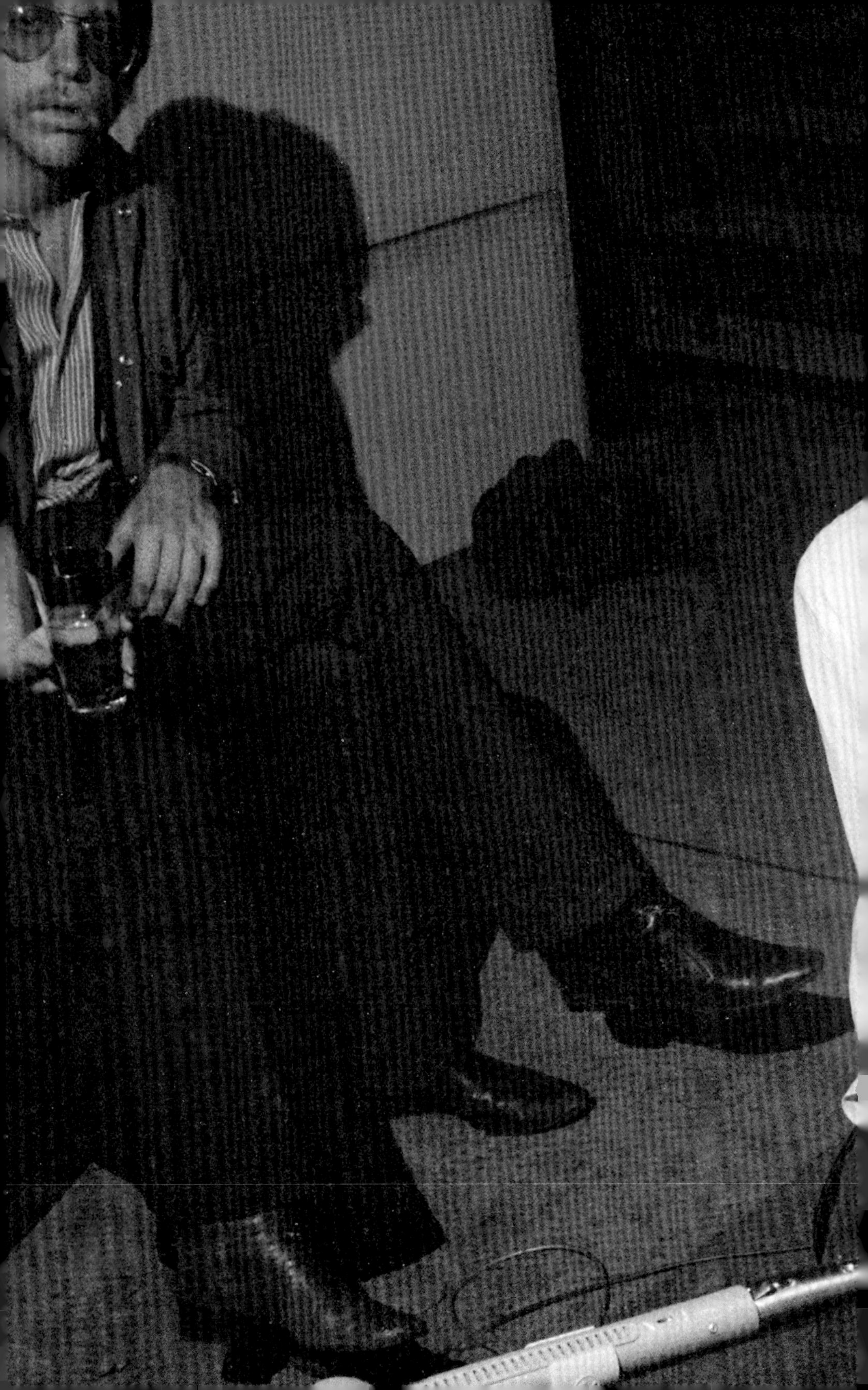

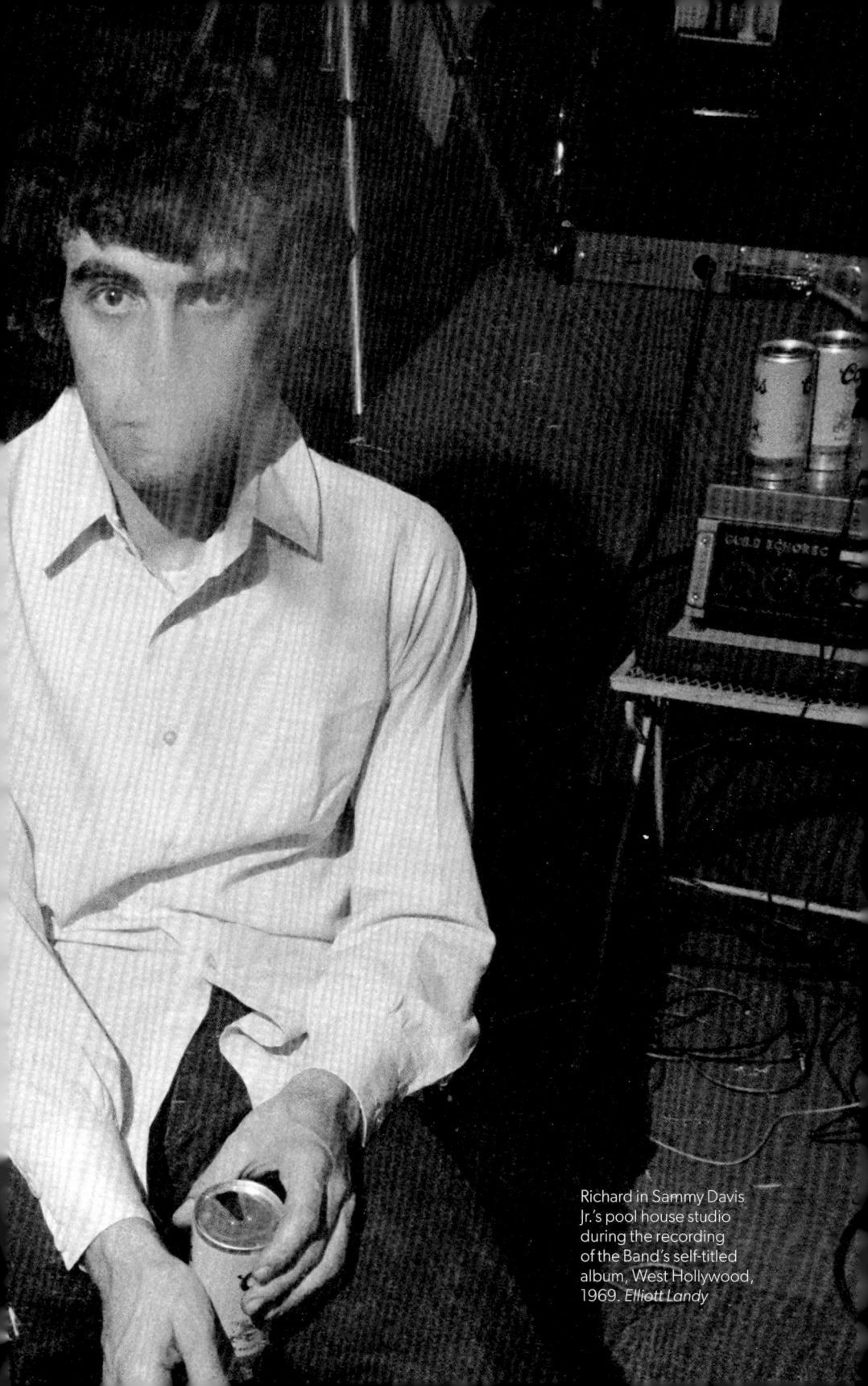

Richard in Sammy Davis Jr.'s pool house studio during the recording of the Band's self-titled album, West Hollywood, 1969. *Elliott Landy*

The level of collaboration is undeniable—and in some cases, debated and uncredited. Richard played piano, drums, harmonica, and baritone sax on the record. His natural musicality and collegial attitude are defining factors in the shape of the music. That his imprint is conspicuously absent from the Band's next two records makes his contributions to *The Band* even more poignant. You don't notice how much he did until it's gone.

The idyllic sessions were not without conflict. The recognizable curvature of a Grand Marnier bottle can be seen balanced on a corner of Richard's piano in photos from the sessions. He would mumble something about needing a drink to calm his nerves . . . before singing the shit out of "Across the Great Divide."

The Band was well aware of Richard's drinking at this point and tried to keep him on task, or at least drinking beer instead of booze. But Richard was so nonconfrontational that there was no way to be firm with him and still keep your wits about you. He could lull you into a sorry state with his doe eyes and slow drawl.

Jonathan Taplin recalled in his memoir, "The evening I returned to Princeton to finish college, Robbie was all over him [Richard] about his inability to get the lyrics and harmony right to accompany Levon on 'Up on Cripple Creek.'" An argument is barely noteworthy in a rock band dynamic; disagreements are as normal as a sunrise. But because Richard so often internalized things, a conflict often left a burn that lasted for a few days.

According to John Simon's memoir, other songs attempted during the sessions were two basement cuts, Dylan's "Tiny Montgomery" and "Yea, Heavy and a Bottle of Bread." "Orange Juice Blues" was attempted . . . yet again failed to make the cut. Robbie's "Get Up Jake" was also recorded, though it was not released until 1972's live *Rock of Ages* album.

On April 3, a beaming Richard was illuminated by candlelight as he celebrated his twenty-sixth birthday with a cake thoughtfully prepared by Jane. Two weeks later, in the midst of recording, the Band made its debut performance at Bill Graham's Winterland.

Richard's twenty-sixth birthday in the living room of Sammy Davis Jr.'s main house, West Hollywood, 1969. *Elliott Landy*

Chapter 9 | Rising of the Tide (1968–1969)

THE BAND LIVE

Finally, after almost a year since the release of *Music from Big Pink,* the Band was ready to take the stage to perform their own original music. The Band headlined Bill Graham's venue on April 17, 18, and 19, 1969, and all three nights were sold out. San Francisco was the axis around which popular live music was orbiting, and the Band was on its most popular stage. They had released their debut and disappeared—no shows, no interviews, nothing. The anticipation had reached its breaking point, and now it was time to pay the piper: their fans.

Immediately, on the very first night, there was panic as Robbie came down with an acute case of stage fright. His symptoms were diagnosed as the flu, but in a move of desperation, a hypnotist was brought in to assist in getting Robbie out of his incapacitated state. While he was barely able to perform, Robbie made it to the stage. The show was shortened and below average for the Band's standards. The crowd wasn't quite sure what to think, and neither was the Band. The concert was an underwhelming beginning to the group's live career.

By the final night of the run, they were in fine form, as documented on a tape that allows a historic listen into their first concerts as the Band. The group

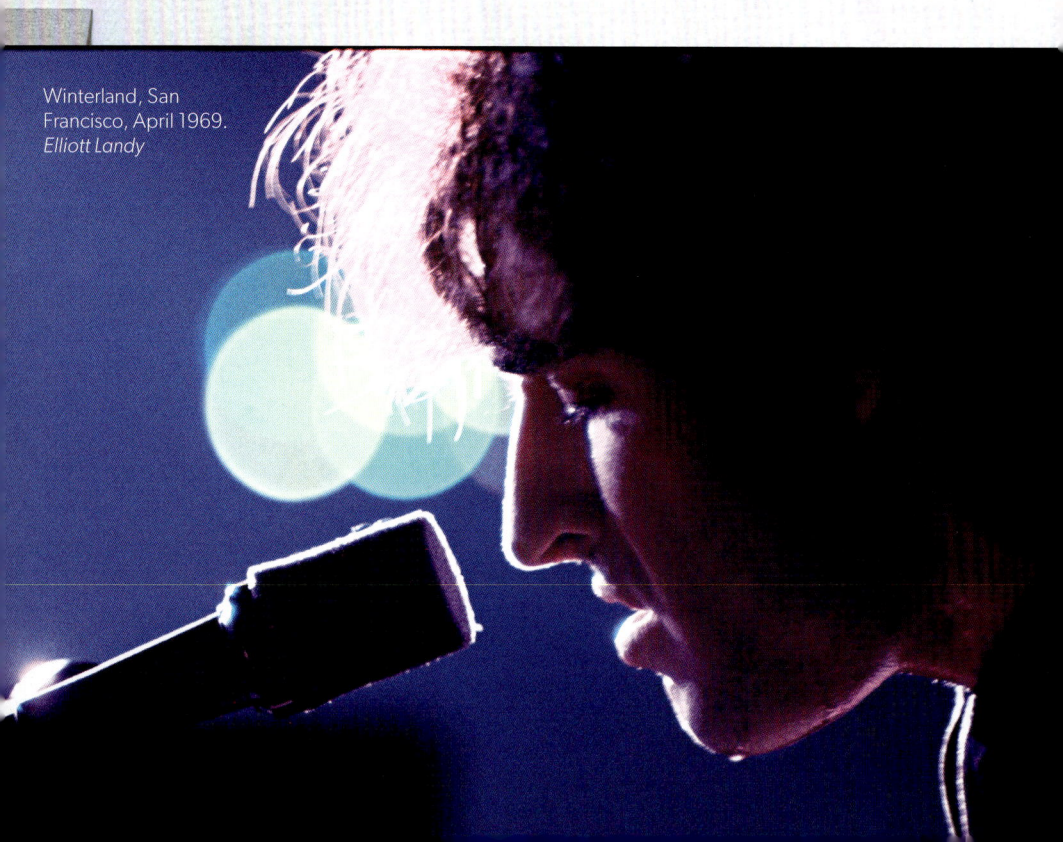

Winterland, San Francisco, April 1969.
Elliott Landy

was relaxed but deadly serious. Richard sipped beers in the small dressing room before the performance as friends and press lingered.

Even on a technically challenged tape such as this field recording from April 19, 1969, the group's practiced perfection shines through. The concert consisted of songs from *Big Pink* and a traditional song Levon had taught the group, "Little Birds."

The Winterland crowd was attentive enough. Though on one of the nights, in reference to the group's limited repertoire, an audience member yelled from the crowd, "Play the second side!"

For the debut concerts, Richard played a grand piano and jumped over to Levon's kit when the group shifted into their alternate rhythm section for "Little Birds." Richard sang both "Tears of Rage" and "In a Station" to great effect. The power of his voice is notable as it knifes through the muffled recording.

Greil Marcus, writing for *Good Times*, said, "Richard Manuel's vocal on 'Tears of Rage' was probably the finest singing that has ever been heard at Winterland; so dramatic that one could almost see the story taking place onstage." This is not hyperbole: Richard put on a show more in line with a classical performance.

Richard also sang lead on "Chest Fever" and shadowed Robbie's voice on a rare and rough reading of "To Kingdom Come." Richard's effortless emotion and versatile technique allowed him to shadow, harmonize with, or echo each of the Band's vocalists, even Robbie. John Simon said in 2023, "Robbie knew what a treasure he had in Richard's vocal ability. It was common for him to sing the part he imagined Richard would sing, and then Richard would repeat it almost exactly, but better."

In fact, the only time you can hear Robbie singing alone on the *Big Pink* album is on the second verse of "To Kingdom Come": "I've been sittin' in here for so darn long, waiting for the end to come along. Holy Roaster on the brink. You take your choice, swim or sink." On the next line, "False witness cast an evil eye," Richard joins him in unison. Simon said, "He was a really fine singer, with a lot of emotion in his voice. And he could sing both in full voice and falsetto."

The cavernous expanse of the hallowed hall enhances every nuance of his vocals. Instrumentally, the Band sounds every bit of their increasing legend, regardless of Robbie's somewhat precarious health.

Richard plays drums on "Little Birds," while Levon moves to mandolin. A tender and poignant traditional song, it was played only a handful of times before being replaced in the set with "Ain't No More Cane on the Brazos." This rendition finds Richard playing the drums with a hearty thump while singing a winging high harmony for the choruses.

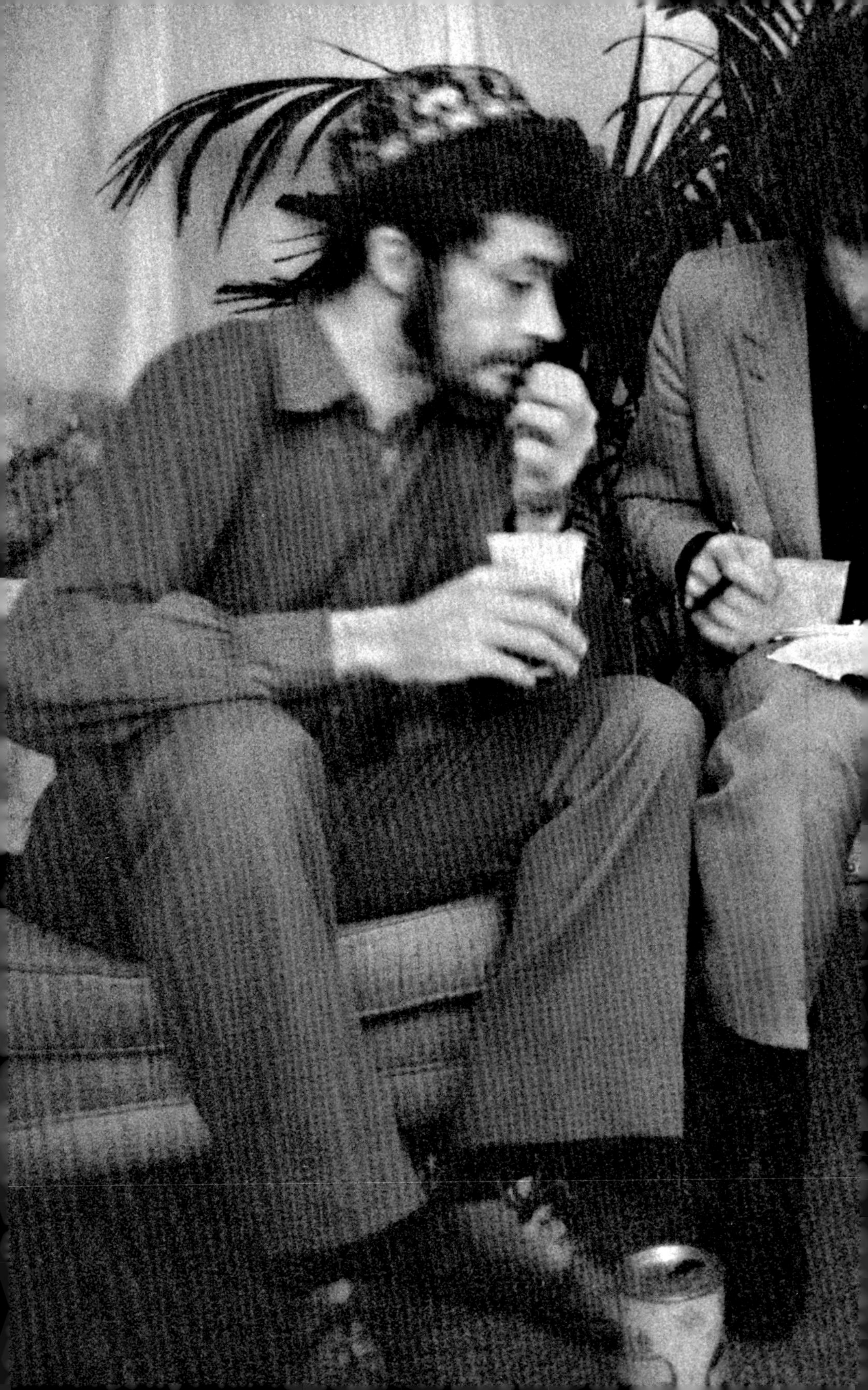

Robbie, Richard, Levon, and Jonathan Taplin. Backstage, unknown location, 1969. *Elliott Landy*

Concluding their California work on the album, and completing their debut live performances, the Band returned to the East Coast for additional dates and to finish the recording. On May 9 and 10, they headlined another set of highly anticipated dates at Fillmore East. The Band received an ecstatic response, and the shows were as close to perfection as a rock group could get. Taplin said in 2022, "Every show worked. Brilliantly. They were all ultimate professionals. I think the Fillmore East early on was pretty remarkable."

A critical element of the Band's extrasensory perception was the intimacy of its stage configuration. Levon liked to be able to see Richard clearly across the stage. He later told road manager Bruce Dener that it kept him centered. In a departure from their stage configuration with Dylan, Garth was placed on a riser center stage, with Richard and Levon on either side of Garth. Rick stood in front of Richard, and Robbie in front of Levon, at the front of the stage. The arrangement formed a semicircle in front of Garth and allowed all the singers clear sight lines.

Because there were three vocalists in the Band, the stage setup allowed them to see each other's mouths and cues. Bill Scheele, who was the Band's stage manager from 1969 to 1976, said in 2022, "It was a very visual setup, so everybody could see, because they did react to each other. . . . They were so damn tight as a group."

Levon would nail his drum accents on the basis of Richard's head movements, as would Rick, who would turn toward Richard when singing "This Wheel's on Fire," so their harmonies would be a matched pair visually and aurally. Robbie used his guitar neck as a conductor's baton, marking changes with well-timed dips and dives.

The Band was playing in a newly acquired nuanced fashion, yet the previously sharpened talons of the Hawks occasionally revealed themselves onstage. Scheele remembered that "the Band was loud. They screamed. It was chilling at times." Garth alone ran his keyboard rig through three Leslie speakers. Once the Band throttled into "Slippin' and Slidin'" or "Don't Do It," they would lock the door, tear their shirts, and let their rivers flow. The renditions of classic cover songs, just as in the Hawks days, were a true flex of their musical muscles.

Playing Bill Graham's famed East and West Coast venues was just the beginning, since in June and July the group would headline two festival dates. Richard and Jane moved into a temporary house on Dutchtown Road in Woodstock, where they became loving parents to a herd of cats. Jane remembers that things were already getting strange at this juncture, with heroin and cocaine entering Richard's life via some of his neighbors and bandmates. One night, a well-connected Woodstock resident stopped over for a house visit that lasted into the witching hours. When Jane was woken by the revelry, she went downstairs and voiced her concerns. Richard turned from his guest, annoyed by her interruption, and admonished her to return upstairs.

Richard at the Toronto Pop Festival, June 21, 1969.
Photograph by John Scheele; all rights reserved

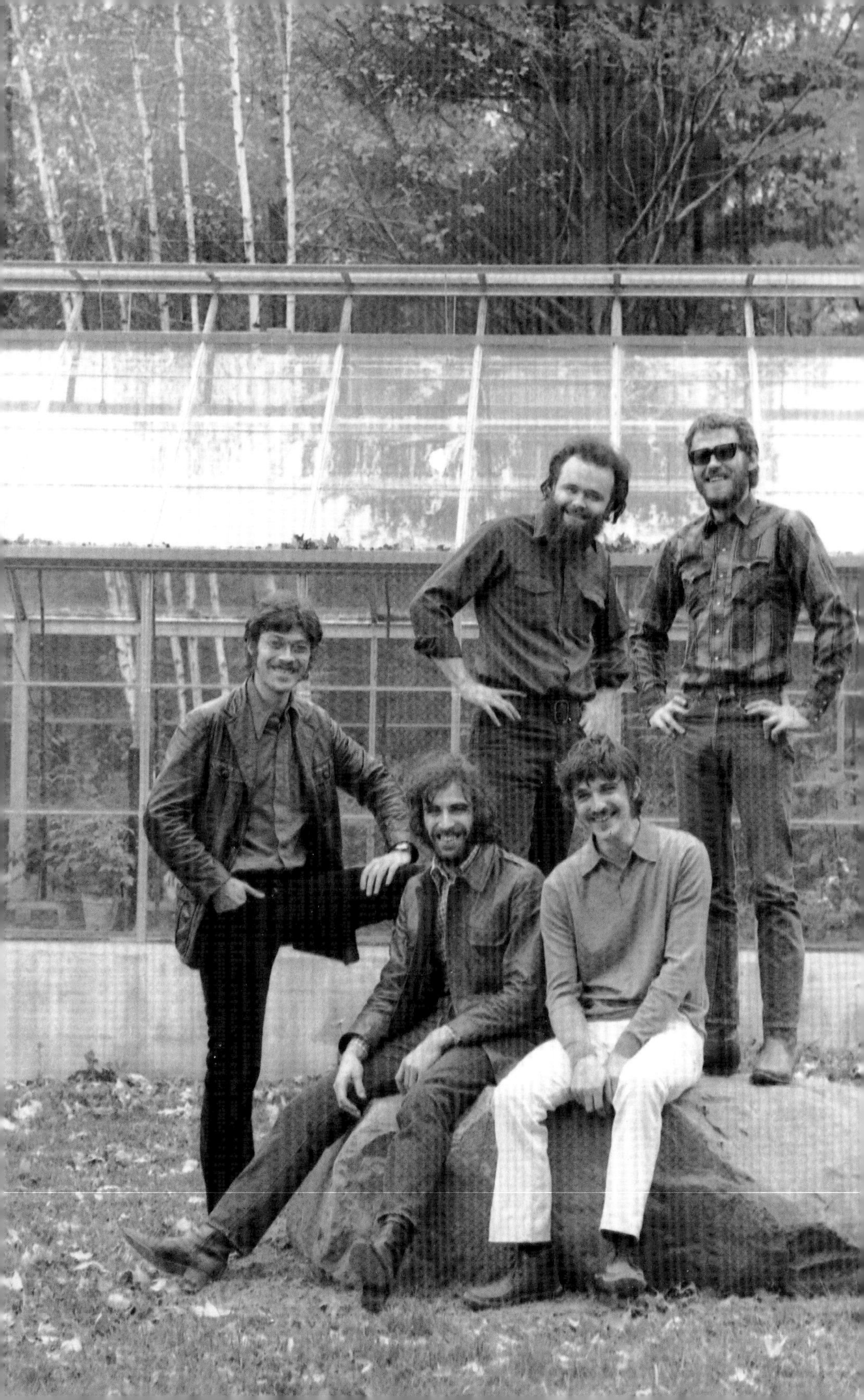

On June 21, the Band returned home for a performance in front of 27,000 at the Toronto Pop Festival. A few weeks later, on July 14, they played the Mississippi River Festival in Edwardsville, Illinois. The former included a visit from Bob Dylan, who sat in with the Band for the encores "Slippin' and Slidin'," "I Ain't Got No Home," and the traditional song "In the Pines."

The summer of 1969 had become something special for Richard and his bandmates. Still riding high from the release of *Music from Big Pink*, the Band was booked as a headliner at two of the biggest musical mass meetings to ever take place: the Woodstock festival on August 17, and the Isle of Wight on August 31.

On July 20, road manager Jonathan Taplin notified the Band that he had received a medical deferment and was no longer eligible for the draft. Richard heard this great news and was always game for any cause to celebrate. He screamed over to Taplin's in a rental car with some fresh Owsley LSD he had picked up for the occasion. While the members of the Band weren't exactly psychedelic rangers, they had their share of trips. Taplin said:

> I was not prepared for Richard Manuel's idea of an acid trip. Two hours into the experience, just as the Owsley was really kicking in, Richard suggested we go for cocktails at Deanie's. It also happened to be the local police hangout, but that didn't bother Richard a bit.

After a white-knuckle yet surprisingly tuned-in drive to the bar, Richard introduced Taplin to his pals in blue. Richard had become well acquainted with the town cops and local justices through some of his late-night mishaps. Those odd yet honest relationships are a testament to Richard's congenial attitude. Usually, any acquaintances of Richard's easily became longtime friendships of note. It didn't matter your profession, orientation, or direction; you were a friend of Richard Manuel's and always greeted as such.

The Band at Albert Grossman's estate, October 1969. *Courtesy of the David Gahr estate*

Woodstock Festival

On August 17, the Woodstock festival was held in Bethel, New York, a stone's throw from Dylan and the Band's backyard. The legendary three-day event's music was provided by the most gifted and influential rock 'n' roll musicians of the era. Woodstock cemented the Band's legacy and introduced them to a magnitude of live performance previously unknown to musicians.

Having the Band play at Woodstock was a big get. While the group's aesthetic wasn't developed for open-air gatherings, the Band shrunk the stage and played a low-key living-room set. They took the stage after a raucous Ten Years After performance. Scheele said the Band that night reminded him of angels in contrast to what preceded them.

Audio of the Band's entire performance was officially released in 2019 on *The Band 50th Anniversary* deluxe edition, albeit with an altered track order.

The Band arrived late afternoon via helicopter and made their way across the strange landscape. They'd always been up for some weird shit . . . but they'd never seen anything like this. Richard spotted John Till on the side of the rickety handbuilt stage and made his way across the backstage area to greet his friend. In a perfect moment of muddy rock 'n' roll coincidence, Richard and John Till would play the same stage. A decade removed from rowdy Revols gigs at the Pavilion in Stratford, Till—playing lead guitar with Janis Joplin's Kozmic Blues Band—had also made it to the summit of his profession.

At ten o'clock that Sunday night, the Band takes to the creaky Woodstock stage in immense darkness, opening with a sweaty "Chest Fever." Garth's alien etudes confound the mud hippies before the rest of the group drops into the pulsating backing. Richard and Levon holler for all they're worth. Next, a woody and rambling version of "Don't Do It" keeps the celebratory vibe going.

Perhaps the finest live version of "Tears of Rage" ever played is immortalized by cloudy pro-shot footage, though it wasn't included in the original *Woodstock* film. The spotlight catches Richard, silhouetted in a confident glow of heliotrope purple, his favorite color, his soft profile and sharp nose framed stoically by the camera. The thick air of history and the buzzing aura of an assembled crowd of 400,000 people surround him. Richard projects his song into the darkened hills, singing his soul into the formless void.

Richard moves his hands dexterously across the keys while his wrists hang low on the downbeats. The old Beak Manuel roar, honed over beer-soaked practice sessions in Arkansas, gloriously breaks through the cooled evening air to call out the lament he wrote with Dylan. Richard has a glowing halo of hair, looks like a divine messenger, and sounds like a rocker, the best singer onstage at Woodstock that weekend. The stunning performance is a high-water mark for the Band, and for Richard Manuel.

The Richard twofer concludes with a freshly baked version of "We Can Talk," the sonic clarity of which reveals the stratified layers of interplay by the group.

He plays drums and sings a joyous high harmony with Levon's lead on "Don't Ya Tell Henry," a basement cut the guys take for a burnout around the block. The jubilance in Richard's vocals and his exclamations on the kit sum up his musicality. "Henry" is an instant good time; just add Richard on drums and it's a song that could be placed in a Band time capsule. Richard also stays in the drum seat for a laid-back reading of the traditional "Ain't No More Cane on the Brazos."

He takes one more lead vocal with a crystalline and note-perfect version of "I Shall Be Released," one of the very best. Then, after the appropriate closing of their set with "The Weight," the Band headed home, just up the road, to await word of Dylan's next move. They had immortalized their names in rock 'n' roll granite, and their second album hadn't even been released.

Isle of Wight

Just two weeks after Woodstock, the Band jumped the pond with Dylan to headline England's version of a superfestival, the Isle of Wight, on August 30 and 31. Dylan and the Band arrived on Thursday, the 28th, and holed up and rehearsed at Forelands Farm in Bembridge. The entire Band family stayed on-site except for Robbie. Jane, who was very pregnant, had traveled to England with Richard. She had stayed away from the Woodstock festival since she was already growing tired of the rock 'n' roll lifestyle. While in preparations for the concert, the Beatles stopped in for some tennis and hanging out with Dylan and the guys.

When the day of the show arrived, the Band members and their families were taken to the island via hovercraft. The Band pulled double duty on Sunday, a testament to their popularity. They played their own early-evening set and then backed Dylan, who took the stage well after 11:00 p.m. in front of a crowd of at least 150,000.

Richard, in fine fettle, offers up a tight performance for both sets. Opening with a peppy version of "We Can Talk" signals that the Band had come to play.

ISLE OF WIGHT

Richard plays confidently, clean-shaven for the last time, and settles in at a grand piano stage right, wearing a crisply creased gray suit coat and purple shirt, sporting some impressive sideburns.

The piano is loud and clear on "To Kingdom Come," where Richard sings in support of one of Robbie's rare lead vocals. The Band's famed instrument shuffle follows in a campfire version of "Ain't No More Cane," with Levon on mandolin and Richard taking over the drum kit. The group keeps the same acoustic lineup, bouncing like bedsprings for "Don't Ya Tell Henry."

"Chest Fever" is given a careful reading, with Richard taking his usual lead vocal duties and pounding frisky sixteenth notes over the introduction. His right hand propels the groove while allowing Rick to move air with his bass.

The introductory notes of "I Shall Be Released" get a respectful round of applause from the crowd, to which Richard responds with another flawless rendition. Afterward, the Band plays "The Weight," notable for being one of the final versions with Robbie on acoustic guitar.

The Band's set concludes with a groovy version of the Four Tops hit "Lovin' You Is Sweeter Than Ever." The audience recording picks up the midsong Robertson/Manuel riff exchange to great effect. Boisterous and layered vocals conclude the Band's portion and set the table for the festival's main course. By the time Dylan and the Band hit the stage, the anticipation was thick.

Opening the set, gently rising from the ashes, is a tentative reading of "She Belongs to Me." Reminiscent of the previous year's Guthrie benefit, Richard's rustic piano chording takes a central role in the sonic spread, his viscous chording holding together Rick's and Levon's rhythmic interplay. The high and lonesome rendition concludes confident and swinging.

"I Threw It All Away," from Dylan's *Nashville Skyline*, is given the basement treatment. Richard's playing is delicate and attentive, and Dylan's vocals are reassuring. "Maggie's Farm" is defiantly funky and finds Levon and Rick adding some well-timed backing vocals. "I Dreamed I Saw St. Augustine" is played as a dramatic dirge, with Richard's piano in the forefront. "Lay Lady Lay" is also stellar, hammered into place by Levon's swampy tom-toms and Richard's woody left-handed trills. The guys blast off on a hot-to-the-touch version of "Highway 61" and a suave "I'll Be Your Baby Tonight," with Richard again lending some whimsical trickling to the former.

A rare performance of "Minstrel Boy" gets exhumed from the basement vault and retains the same vibe as its previous incarnation. "Rainy Day Women #12 & 35" also gets a *Big Pink* treatment with last-call vocals and Richard reciting the song's recognizable descending lick saloon style. The entire Dylan and the Band portion of the concert was officially released as part of Bob Dylan's *The Bootleg Series Vol. 10: Another Self-Portrait (1969–1971)*.

THE BAND

After Woodstock and the Isle of Wight, Richard and the group returned home to the Catskills. He and Jane were expecting their first child in just a couple of months, so Richard moved them into a family-style cinder block house on Hill 99. Amid all these pressures, the Band's long-awaited self-titled second record hit the shelves on September 22, 1969. The album was received rapturously. Its homespun storytelling, diverse instrumentation, and superior musicianship set a high standard that even the greatest of the Band's contemporaries aspired to.

This recording was an even-tighter representation of the group's collaboration than on *Music from Big Pink*. The arrangements were spacious and textured, offering up a sonic color wheel of influences. While the songwriting balance of the album had shifted to Robbie on paper, the music was even more of a group effort. The album sounded effortless, the vocals soulful.

Just as on *Music from Big Pink*, Richard's voice introduces the record. Robbie's "Across the Great Divide" begins the proceedings, but with a different sort of dramatism than "Tears of Rage." The prelude of "Across the Great Divide" is reminiscent of Levon and the Hawks' histrionic performances of Etta James's "Something's Got a Hold on Me" and James Brown's "Please, Please, Please." Richard sings the opening, the horns blowing as he draws out the syllables with thoughtful pauses between the anticipatory lines:

Standing by your window in pain. A pistol in your hand.
And I beg you, dear Molly girl. Try and understand your man the best you can.

Suddenly the Band drops into the verse, like a coin into a bucket, heading full pull for the edge of the world. Richard pounds out excitable triplets in support of the Rick-and-Levon thump. The song bounds forward and pauses to look over its shoulder at precisely the right moments. Levon said in his memoir, "Richard sang on 'Across the Great Divide' and came up with all those chord progressions and tempo changes in the song."

Hallmarks of Richard's stylistic choices and compositional acumen decorate the album. Similar to the time signature shift in the middle of "We Can Talk" or the hazy production values of "In a Station" on the debut, Richard

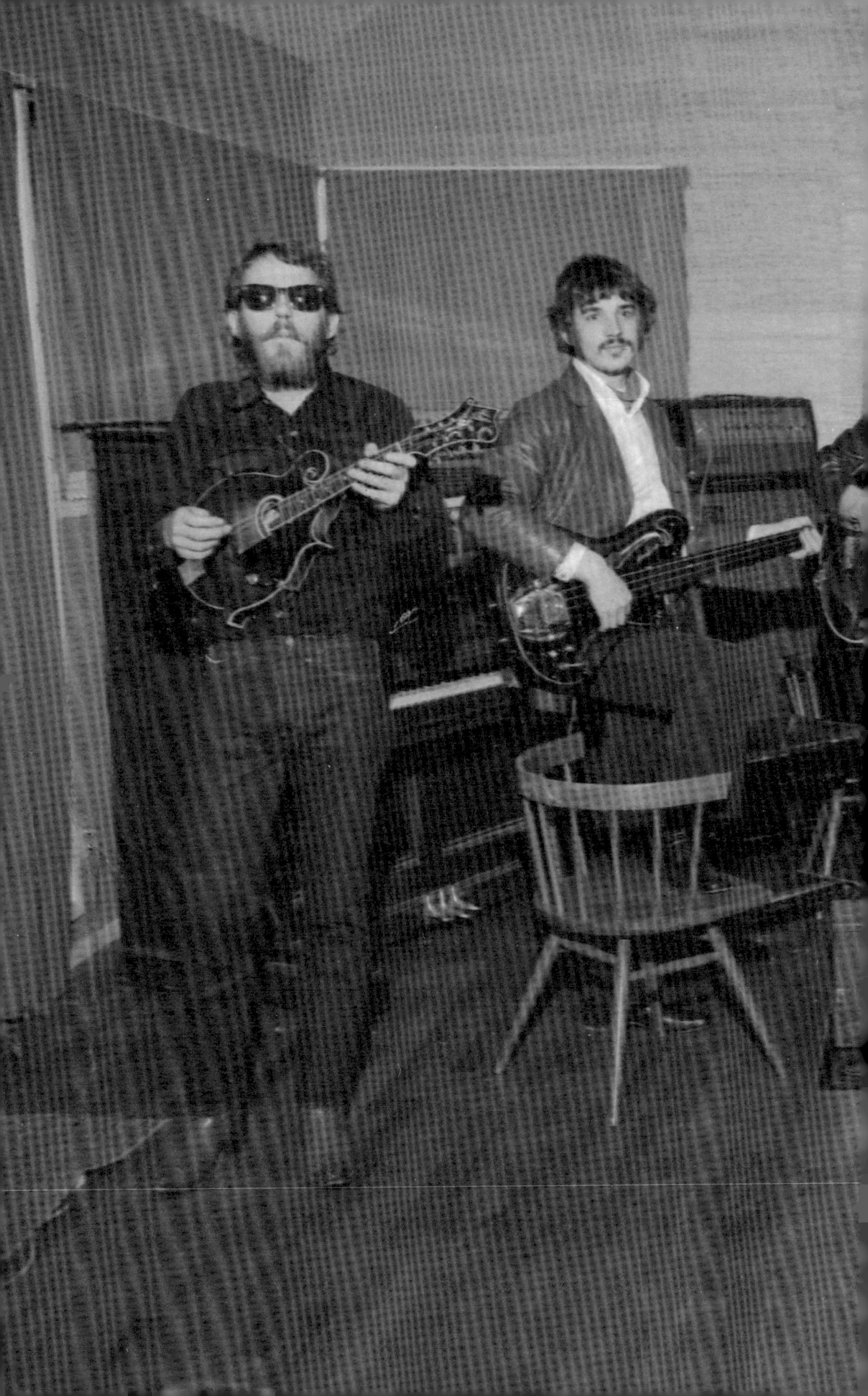

The Band at Wittenberg Road, Woodstock, October 1969. *Courtesy of the David Gahr estate*

experimented with rhythmic rope-a-dope on "Jawbone" and created a rising spectral steam on "Whispering Pines."

Larry Campbell, guitarist and musical arranger for musicians including Bob Dylan and Levon Helm, said in 2023:

> His [Richard's] sense of melody and chord structure was totally unique at that time. It's hard to know where that was coming from. . . . He loved to throw in these odd time measures. Levon said he'd always try to get him to straighten them out . . . Richard was adamant about keeping them in.

Richard took to the drum kit for "Rag Mama Rag," a jambalaya of musical influence and a game of musical chairs by the group. Rick played fiddle, Levon mandolin, and Richard the jumpy drums that John Simon called "galumphy." Banging like sneakers in a dryer, Richard slammed around the kit to Simon's tuba bass lines.

Robbie's Southern opus, "The Night They Drove Old Dixie Down," is augmented by Richard's ascendant piano chords separating the verses. He also blows a mournful harp that emanates from the song's ghostly Confederate procession.

"When You Awake" is a quirky, underrated Robertson/Manuel gem that finds Richard playing distinctive drums on the track. A galloping groove punctuated by light rim shots, stick clicks, and tom-tom hits moves with the gentle gait of a happy horse. Richard didn't play piano on the track since the song's melody was conveyed by Robbie's guitar line.

The ebb and flow of Richard's gurgling piano and Garth's rolling keyboards on "Up on Cripple Creek" is one of the finest moments on the album. Just like during the Hawks days, Richard churns up a foaming rhythm that works in conjunction with Rick's swooping lines. Hear Richard answer Levon's "when I come rollin' in" with a perfectly appropriate lick. Garth paints his masterpiece across this Canadian canvas, playing a Clavinet passed through a wah-wah pedal on the verses. He then segues back to a funky Lowrey line in the chorus. Robbie recalled in his memoir that Richard inspired the "drunkard's dream" line.

Of course, Richard lends the falsetto vocal scribbles that top off the mountain yodeling. Part of the reason that "Cripple Creek" is one of the group's most renowned and beloved songs is because everything is working perfectly, and all the members are at their most creative and collaborative.

Richard told the *Woodstock Times*:

> I never assumed any authority and I just pitched in . . . wherever. . . . Since then, people tell me that I'm responsible for the producing, engineering, and mixing of

our second album, our most important album, but I thought I was just doing my part. I thought everyone was doing as much as I was.

"Whispering Pines," the song Richard wrote at Bellows Lane, had the curious working title of "Cranberry Sauce." The song is a true representation of the Band's cumulative powers. The song was a dizzying peak of the short-lived Robertson/Manuel songwriting partnership. While Richard worked on getting the song together in California, the Band recorded it at the Hit Factory when they returned to New York City.

The resulting song isn't Americana, R&B, or rock, just as it isn't thematically consistent with the rest of the record. It's an entire world unto itself, a hazy soul ballad just like Beak had always loved, but with his introspective view and unique melodicism. The gauzy landscape of the song was one that Richard worked well in and had previously explored on "In a Station." This approach reached its pinnacle with Robbie's tender backward string strokes and Garth's ghostly undertow.

"Whispering Pines" closed the first side of the record. It's nestled on the edge of the treeline, outside the sepia tones and muted hues of *The Band* record. Robbie wrote in his memoir, "This mood, this performance was different from everything else we'd cut." The song is tall and stately, otherworldly, and obscured by fog. It coalesced in the space between chimera and reality. It arrives and then leaves the same way . . . on Richard's plaintive repeated chord.

Richard sings in a poignant falsetto, a hesitant vibrato, and a syrupy tenor, sometimes all in the same verse. The lyrics stretch to touch a sonic pastel horizon that sounds like watercolor. Midway through the song, Richard and Levon crack a vine-covered door, revealing a yearning call-and-response segment. Levon sings out

Richard in Woodstock, October 1969.
Courtesy of the David Gahr estate

from a distance; Richard answers in soft melancholy. Their voices embrace each other's lines, caressing the words. The intimate musical moment between Richard and Levon is the most beautiful piece of music the Band ever recorded.

Featured as a bonus track on *The Band 50th Anniversary* deluxe box set is take 14 of "Whispering Pines," recorded on June 16, 1969. A humorous exchange occurred between Richard and Simon regarding a squeaking in the studio. Richard stumbled slightly over the first verse and then recovered for a stunning recitation different from the eventual finished product.

He contributes flip-floppy drums with a heavy right foot on "Jemima Surrender," allowing Levon to play rhythm guitar and Garth to move to piano. The Band's alternate rhythm section turns the song into a mischievous romp. Levon said of Richard's drumming in *Classic Albums*, "He's doin' his licks half time to 'Jemima' and doubling up on the back beat." Richard's unhinged backing vocals are also draped all over "Jemima." Especially fantastic are his giddy high harmonies sung with Levon.

On "Rockin' Chair," one of Robbie's most nostalgic lyrics, Richard slides into the clothes of a senior sailor whose best days are behind him. In the finest example of Richard inhabiting a Robbie Robertson character, he becomes the song. With Ragtime Willie by his side, Richard speaks in a voice that sounds mature beyond his own years. Larry Campbell agreed: "There was no distance between who he was and what was coming out of his mouth. . . . When he sang these soulful tunes, you were getting the same authenticity that you got out of these old blues guys."

Robbie's lyrics and their sympathetic look at old age illustrated the Band's deep respect for their elders. Richard sang the main body of the song and then on the chorus moved to the top of the vocal log pile. Robbie said in *Classic Albums*, "The hurt in his voice . . . there's a certain element of pain in there, that you didn't know if he was trying to reach the note or if he was just a guy with a heart that had been hurt."

"Look Out Cleveland" rocks as hard as anything the Band ever created, with Richard's excitable opening piano reminiscent of his Jerry Lee Lewis impersonations from the Revols days. His excellent playing continues throughout the song's stormy construct. The song is built backward: the chorus opens the song as the rhythm section pulses; it then shifts into a rickety double time for the verses. Richard's piano breaks up the segments, offering a safe harbor full of melodic quotes.

"Jawbone," which Robbie and Richard cowrote, recalled the sketchy "Ruben Remus" character study. "Jawbone" experimented with multiple time signatures—7/4, 6/8, and 2/4—and navigated the transitions between them. Levon and Richard worked hard at perfecting the shifting arrangement and locking into the loopy licks. Musically the song is spectacular, spotlighting Richard's playing of multiple diverse segments all the while singing his ass off.

Lyrically, Richard inhabits the lead part of the main character hand in glove and lets loose with some of his best rock 'n' roll singing since "He Don't Love You (and He'll Break Your Heart)." The song also features one of Robbie's finest guitar solos cut to disc. Underneath it all, Richard pumps out an aggressive left-handed thump through the changes.

"The Unfaithful Servant" is Rick Danko's spotlight, and Richard plays it straight and keeps the delicate construct of the song taut with feathered keystrokes. The wavering Salvation Army Band horns make another welcome appearance.

"King Harvest (Has Surely Come)" is the song that encapsulated what the Band was all about, a true synergy of their talents. Similarly to *Music from Big Pink*, it was a statement, a stake in the ground marking their turf. For Robbie to lyrically tie into the essence of a life he never knew, and for Richard to express it so truthfully, is a testament to what made the Band special: Levon's and Rick's earthy groove, Garth's multifarious orchestration, Robbie's songwriting . . . and Richard Manuel's voice.

In the words of Levon Helm, "It was like, *there, that's* the Band." He recalled that the genesis of the song came from a group discussion about the things they had seen and shared together. The line "A scarecrow and a yellow moon, pretty soon, a carnival on the edge of town" could easily evoke Beak's Stratford, the fairgrounds on the outskirts of town, across the tracks and the black Avon River, the spicy smell of fallen leaves and crackling fires.

The song is about a broken spirit, a struggling farmer whose life hangs precariously on the changing attitudes of the winds and rains and the businessman. Richard slides into the broken landowner's overalls and translates the tale like a medium in trance, his voice expressing as much of the story as the lyric. When Richard implores the rainmaker to "*pleeeaaase*, let these crops grow tall," his voice strains under the weight of moral responsibility, life and death.

Right after the release of *The Band*, the group traveled to New York City to see the Staple Singers at the Fillmore East, where the Staples encored with "The Weight."

In late September and again in October, the group took a series of pictures with photographer David Gahr at Albert Grossman's estate in Woodstock. The group looks happy and healthy, and Richard looks stylish in leather and jeans. About that time, he started growing a coal-black beard that would not leave his face for the rest of his days.

Once *The Band* record was sprung, Richard's partying increased exponentially. There are a multitude of reasons for this, most speculative. Woodstock had become a hotspot for wayward dropouts and was packed with psychic vampires—or in other words, hangers-on and wannabes who increased their self-worth by attaching themselves to artists and musicians. Richard couldn't say no, had no one to tell him no, and wouldn't listen if they did. If you wanted to raise your glass, Richard would clink your cup. Because he was Richard Manuel of the Band, *everything* was available. There was somebody pushing something on him almost everywhere he went. Richard did everything, to excess. His inability to deal with the pressures of his newfound fame was another reason for his retreat into drink and drugs. In order to deal with the responsibilities of studio work, performance, songwriting, and appearances, Richard would drink.

There was also the feeling of the Band becoming an increasingly separatist camp. Its members all had solitary interests in different things, including women, drugs, and artistic pursuits. It was all part of growing up; it was part of life. Business intervened and something true and beautiful became a commodity. Levon said the group was surprised at the lack of shared credits on the back of *The Band* record. Richard told Jane that he felt the group was drifting apart. No matter the cause, the effect on Richard was one he was ill equipped to handle unless fully medicated. Heroin, despite its already well-publicized dangers, was used by more than one member of the group.

Later that fall, the group cut seasonal promotional footage at Grossman's estate, performing "Up on Cripple Creek" and "King Harvest (Has Surely Come)."

Richard looks loose, smiling and seated at the piano in purple pants and brown leather jacket, with his dog Mitzi milling around. He's smiling brightly at Levon as the Band gets ready to count off the song.

On "King Harvest," the camera shoots from above and films Richard in fall light as he dances into the downbeats. It moves in close for Richard's singing, which while tentative is working its way into character. The group gets a good take, to which Levon responds, "That was slow, John," speaking to producer Simon. "I think we're warmed up now." "Cripple Creek" is autumnally funky and is a glimpse behind the curtain into the workings of the Band. Garth's mischievous grin as he hits on the wah-wah'd Clavinet is worth the watch.

Not long after shooting the film, the group hit the road in support of *The Band*, beginning October 11 at the Brooklyn Academy of Music for both a matinee and evening performance. At the conclusion of the stellar evening concert, one attendee screamed out, "Play all night!" To which Richard joked from the stage, "Someone send out for sandwiches."

The Band played mostly weekends through the end of the year, inviting their Woodstock friend Van Morrison for an insane double bill in Boston. Morrison, who was in rare form, sang lying down on the floor of the stage, to the consternation of the promoters. Richard thought it was hip and said, "I think we should all lie down and sing tonight. It's different!"

Morrison had recently moved to Woodstock and had taken up residence in Richard and Garth's vacated house on Ohayo Mountain. He fit right in with the Band and hung out with Robbie and Richard the most. Morrison recalled his first impressions of Richard in 2024, saying, "I was struck by his sense of humor; he could sum up a situation with a one-liner," and that Richard "was fun to be around and didn't take the whole Woodstock 'mythology' seriously."

PHILADELPHIA 1969

Capturing the high that the group was on after the release of *The Band* is the concert in Philadelphia on October 26. The performance is an airy-sounding audience recording with all instruments audible, and the group has never sounded better. They are confident in their presentation, flawless in their dissemination, and impenetrable in their collaboration.

The crowd is respectful and responds appropriately to the musicianship on display. Opening under red stage lights with a burning "This Wheel's on Fire," the tape's clarity reveals Richard's top-shelf falsetto mirroring Rick's lead vocal.

"Don't Ya Tell Henry" was an onstage favorite for the group despite never having been recorded for a release. Richard hops on drums for a quick bang, some harmony howls, and then heads back to his place at the piano.

Besides a reading of "Rockin' Chair," the Band moved through a mixture of covers and songs from *Music from Big Pink*. The band's confidence is palpable. "Chest Fever" struts flush-faced across the stage, just like the tracker it references in the lyrics. It's intense without being over the top, the sound powerful yet clean.

"Tears of Rage" is given a stellar reading with subtle and nuanced playing by the entire group. "Loving You Is Sweeter Than Ever" features the triad of vocalists and a midsong Robbie and Richard call-and-response segment.

The latter part of the show featured songs from the recently released *The Band* record. Richard slams around the skins on a big "Jemimah Surrender," and the entire venue sings along to "The Night They Drove Old Dixie Down."

The music was dead serious. The Band was so tight onstage that it became a criticism. Keith Richards said at the Isle of Wight concert that the Band was just "too strict." As if the Band were too perfect. The tapes reveal a prideful group of perfectionists, error-free in their presentation.

The group successfully transported the vibe of their clubhouse environments to the stage for their concerts. They wanted to be close; they needed the contact, the subtle signals, the real-time charge of creating music. They didn't posture; they didn't pretend; they just played. Timothy Crouse of the *Boston Herald Traveler* said after the group's Halloween performance, "The Band has played together for 10 years, and their togetherness is nearly telepathic."

Stage manager Bill Scheele said in 2022 that the concerts in late 1969 and early 1970 were some of the best the group played. The group was able to "tune the room" and played a series of fine concerts in midsized and ornate theaters.

For Richard on the tour, the Band's rider required a 7-foot semiconcert grand piano, tuned for every performance. The crew outfitted the piano with three microphones that fed into a mixer and then through a Fender Twin amplifier, which connected across the stage to a monitor that was set up behind Levon. After the spring 1970 tour, Richard also used a Hohner Pianet when a song required electric piano.

In the middle of the tour, on November 2, the Band appeared on *The Ed Sullivan Show* dolled up in television makeup and staged on a corny barnyard set. The group played "Up on Cripple Creek" flawlessly if not a bit sterile. In spite of the large number of headshots, the performance was a solid representation of the Band's music for a large audience and was a proud moment for the group and their families.

Richard's friends back home at the Woodstock police department snapped a photo of Richard on the television when he met Ed Sullivan. The photo was laminated and presented to Richard, and he carried it in his wallet for the remainder of his days. When he didn't have or couldn't present a license, he pulled out his picture of him with Ed Sullivan and dodged several driving violations.

At this moment in the Band's rising popularity, Paula Ann Manuel was born to Richard and Jane on November 7, 1969. Jane Manuel said that they were both excited by the prospect of being parents. But a new wave of responsibility washed over Richard. He was barely able to take care of himself, and the realization of taking care of a child scared him. In the middle of this major life change, the Band played a series of dates through November and into December, concluding the year with shows at the Felt Forum in New York and the Miami Rock Festival in Florida. As the expectations surrounding his job in the Band increased, his ability to handle them diminished. The more Richard was intimidated by his new responsibilities, the more it stifled his creativity.

Richard took refuge in the bottle because it was comforting, and because he was afraid. He was fearful of comparisons to his contemporaries and to other singers. He was touchy about his piano playing and started to slip into the background. He also succumbed easily to peer pressure. Whether to make others feel at ease or to deflect his own uneasiness, Richard would often use the shock factor of something to keep the laughs coming and cover for his discomfort.

He was becoming unreliable, and the group suffered because of it. Drugs and alcohol became a crutch. It became uncomfortable for everyone in the group, so to combat it they each got more wasted. When the bottle didn't work, Richard looked for alternative ways of numbing his emotions. Everybody wanted to hang out with the Band, and by the end of 1969 they were arguably the most influential group in popular music. Richard was accessible, too accessible: people wanted to be with him, get high with him, and he was more than happy to oblige.

The Band at Felt Forum, New York City, December 26, 1969. *Courtesy of the David Gahr estate*

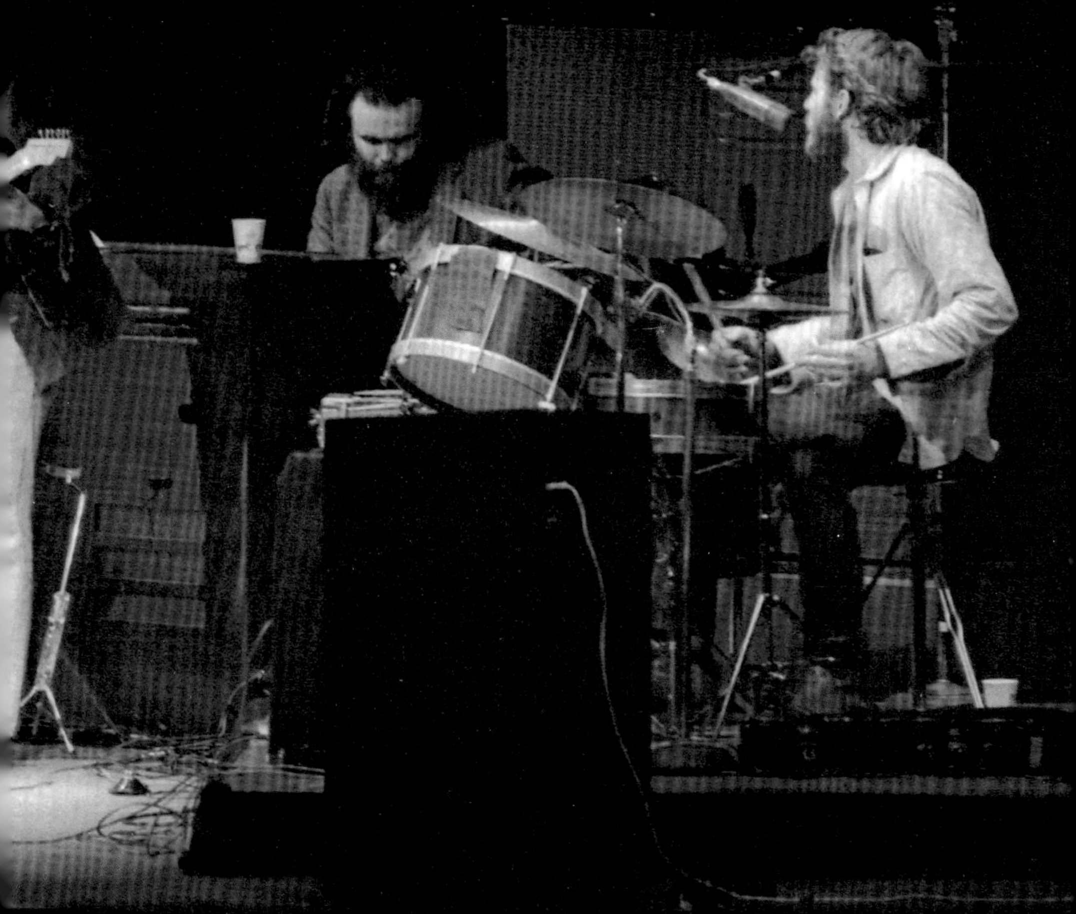

October 1969. *Courtesy of the David Gahr estate*

Chapter 10
ODD MAN (1970-1971)

On January 12, 1970, the Band was featured on the cover of *Time* magazine, their individual portraits melded into one large inky portrayal. Richard's likeness is imposing, with a raised eyebrow, a large black hat, and haphazard beard. A yellow banner across the top of the page proclaims "The New Sound of Country Rock." *Time*'s was a simplistic view of the group's music, but also one that conveyed the magnitude of its impact on popular culture.

In this era, the significance of a rock band being featured on the cover of an iconic newsweekly was monumental. The article put the group on a lofty level with its most-popular contemporaries: "The Band has now emerged as the one group whose sheer fascination and musical skill may match the excellence—though not the international impact—of the Beatles."

This newly found recognition drove their popularity to a new and different place. The Band was respected by its peers and acted as a cultural compass directing a widespread shift in the aesthetic of rock music. The Beatles and the Rolling Stones, in *Get Back* and *Beggars Banquet*, emulated the Band's recording methods and approach. An entire movement of music was coagulating around its albums, influencing bands such as Fairport Convention and Pink Floyd. Mainstream rock music that had recently been drenched in sitars, electric jugs, and backward tapes now faded into verdant pastures of stripped-down and homegrown instrumentation . . . just like *The Band* album.

Richard was smack-dab in the middle of this magical chaos. He faced more responsibility rooted in these new expectations. In addition to the mounting musical pressures, Richard was a new father and was faced with providing for a wife and a baby girl.

While Robbie seemed to meet the challenges and increased pressure with eagerness and creativity, Richard appeared to wilt under the scrutiny. Years of hard work had sharpened his musical skills, but a different level of determination was required to keep his abilities from dulling. Rick Danko told Nick DeRiso of *SomethingElse Reviews*:

> I think we shipped a million copies of that second album, and that changed a lot of people's lives—in particular, the Band's. After that, we were only getting together once a year, for a couple of months to record. It was like we were too decadent to play.

Richard combated his anxiety in other ways—namely, hell-raising. Jon Taplin remembered in 2022:

> Richard had a Hertz car at the clubhouse where I lived up there in Bearsville. It had a very long, curving road off to the top where the house was, and a huge field that this road curved around; it was open. There was a huge snow and then like in a classic Woodstock thing, it started, and then it froze. And so, Richard somehow got his car all the way up to the top and everybody was hanging out in my house.
>
> Garth had a Mercedes diesel and somehow managed to get it stuck in the middle of the driveway. So when the party was over, like around 11 o'clock at night, Richard was totally drunk out of his gourd and he saw that he couldn't get out of the driveway because Garth's car was blocking.

Richard walked gingerly across the frozen field, showing everyone that it would hold his weight. He analyzed the possibilities, arms outstretched for balance as he slid his feet across the ground. Richard made the connection that if the ice could support his weight, it surely could hold the vehicle's.

He skated over to his rental and jumped in. He revved the engine in preparation for his big move. He began to carefully pull around Garth's car and, as Taplin said, drove about 10 feet before the car sank all the way up to the door handles. The car was submerged in the deep snow, and Richard was stuck inside.

After managing to get the window down, he crawled out, and after coming to the realization that the car wasn't going to move, Richard sheepishly threw up his hands and went inside. Hertz was notified the next morning by Band roadie Ed Anderson that the car was stuck, and they sent some adjusters up to look at it. Once they approached the field and saw the vehicle encased in ice, they told Ed, "Call us when the snow melts."

With new money coming in, Richard moved on from the rentals and bought a new 1969 Pontiac Grand Prix. Jane Manuel recalled in 2022 that Richard

October 1969. *Courtesy of the David Gahr estate*

called it the "Grand Pricks." Excited to see what it had under the hood, Richard took it out for a spin. Bill Avis remembered in 2023 that when Richard got the car, he immediately got it stuck in a local farmer's cornfield. The only reason Richard was caught was that he had to leave the car behind, buried in muck.

The farmer called the police and reported that the brand-new vehicle had been left embedded in his crops. Richard was summoned by the officials to pay restitution for the corn destroyed by his joyride. By this point, Richard had had so many accidents that the car rental agencies placed him on their "do not rent" list.

For Richard, the transition from freewheeling, road-running rocker to a musician under contract was complex. What should have resulted in complete artistic freedom slowly became an anxiety-inducing burden. Rick Danko was once asked if he thought that success got in the way of the group's creativity. His answer: "Absolutely."

When the Band did get together, finding inspiration and true spirit was a difficult proposition.

Richard compared himself with his contemporaries and constantly sold himself short. While he liked to get inebriated and crazy, he certainly wasn't stupid. He was aware that the Band's biggest hits were being sung by Levon and written by Robbie. He told Jane that he didn't think his songs were being taken seriously. When asked in 2023 whether Richard was confident in his contributions to the Band, John Simon said, "Absolutely not."

The Band
Live 1970

The group took to the road in January, February, and March 1970 with well-spaced shows in midsized venues and concert halls on the East Coast before moving into Canada and then out west. They tried to play on weekends and for only a few nights out at most. While their popularity was soaring, the Band remained insular: they did their work and went home.

An ambient and well-recorded audience tape exists from one of the Band's two January 9 performances at Colden Auditorium in Queens, New York. It's a perfect audio document of the group in early support of *The Band* record. The tape begins with the concert in progress and Richard playing slapdash drums for "Jemima Surrender" and not letting up for the duration.

The simmering country funk of "Caledonia Mission" is perfect. The playing is airy, detailed, and patient, with Rick playing acoustic guitar instead of bass. Richard's high harmony and wordless falsetto act as a poignant refrain. His first lead vocal of the evening comes on "Rockin' Chair," which would become a concert highlight by the summer. His voice reverberates in the hall, as rich as a maple syrup harvest.

After the tour's opening shows, the group headed to Canada for a series of five homecoming concerts in Guelph, Toronto, and Hamilton. The two performances at Massey Hall were a proper return home, since the group had been roundly criticized after their 1965 concert there with Dylan. Friends, fans, and family made for an invested and appreciative audience for both full houses.

Richard strode to the stage in a groovy purple shirt and a full beard. The Band opened with "This Wheel's on Fire" and proceeded to burn the house down. The group's sound was spacious and light, and they played a resonant rendition of the set that would carry them through the month.

THE BAND **LIVE 1970**

Jack Batten of the *Toronto Daily Star* wrote, "You can at least recall some of the glories of the night. . . . The deep, visceral cry that was never out of Richard Manuel's voice . . . the beautiful weaving together of Manuel's voice and Levon Helm's in half a dozen different songs."

In February, the Band continued to tour behind the record, staying on the East Coast for concerts in Massachusetts and Pennsylvania. No tapes circulate from these shows, however.

In March, the group headed to the Midwest. A soundboard recording of the Band at the 3,400-seat Kiel Auditorium in St. Louis on March 19 finds the group running through songs from the first two LPs with rustic aplomb. A Tilt-A-Whirl reading of "We Can Talk" is a highlight of the concert, as the group whips off a rendition decorated with tangled voices and bounding instrumentation.

"Look Out Cleveland" is another musical highlight of the show—and probably of the tour. Richard and Garth pop, their piano and keyboard a stormy bacchanal. Peter Vaughn of the *Minneapolis Star* confirmed with his review: "The Band's distinguishing quality is its reliance on Manuel's piano and Garth Hudson's organ for much of its rhythm." This rhythm was in a constant state of flux, with Richard's drag and Garth's pull. Richard always played just a shade behind the beat, like rounding up the back end of a street parade.

The Band concluded the month of March with concerts in Ann Arbor and Minneapolis before retiring to Woodstock in preparation for their next studio recording. Things had worked well on the road, and the group was in a good place musically. But when the Band reconvened in May 1970 to record what would become *Stage Fright*, something was amiss. From an outsider's view, the group seemed secure in its stature. But internally, they were entering a period of uncertainty.

Richard and Jane had moved from the Dutchtown Road house to a place on Hill 99, and then to Maverick Road after the tour. They were constantly on the move around Woodstock. Richard was in charge of the housing, and Jane, who longed for a traditional life, followed wherever they ended up. As far as she was concerned, he could have been an accountant. It didn't matter to her. She was focused on her husband, not his lifestyle. She said, "I wasn't a groupie. He was my husband, and that's how I related to him. He was Richard."

The Band's leveling up in popularity gave the group a gravitas that didn't suit Richard at all. Albert Grossman, Robbie, and Taplin often spoke in their own special language and made grandiose plans. Photographer Michael Friedman said in the book *Small Town Talk*:

> Everybody kind of sounded a bit the same, except for Levon, Rick, and Richard. There was this kind of whispering wisdom, the way Robbie spoke, and the way Jon Taplin spoke. They all got into this kind of Band-speak.

Richard was on the receiving end of this attitude by Band management on more than one occasion. Jane recalls being very upset at the way some people talked down to her husband, and those simmering frustrations resulted in Richard putting his fist through a wall at the house on Hill 99.

Expectations were heavy, and the Band hoped to produce a piece of musical art that was light, something loose and funky. They came up with the idea of performing a live concert of new material at the intimate Woodstock Playhouse. When local officials soured on the idea, thinking they would have another Woodstock festival on their hands, the group decided to record there anyway, without an audience.

The Woodstock Playhouse

As the Band's notoriety had ratcheted up over the past twenty-four months, fans and critics discussed, dissected, and disseminated their first two albums to the point of boredom. The group wanted to have fun again, and the Playhouse gave them an opportunity to create an intimate and positive working environment.

The Woodstock Playhouse was a rustic building, planted along the agrarian Mill Hill Road in Woodstock. The venue was host to summer theater performances, and its intimacy and location held promise. The Band set up a tape machine in the back and recorded on the stage. Sometimes they would open the curtains to the theater, and sometimes they would leave them closed. A tape box from the sessions reads "The Band Hack It at the Playhouse."

A bit of rot had started to set into the Band's camp. The sessions were strained and unnatural, the environment was tense, and the attitudes were chilly. Richard was stoned, and he wasn't the only one. Simon was out as producer, and Robbie brought in Todd Rundgren to engineer the record; they had just worked together on songwriter Jesse Winchester's debut. Simon was still a friend of the group and was only a phone call away, but the Band was taking over their own production of the LP. Simon said in 2023, "I got along with the guys. Todd did not. Different species from a different planet."

The separatist vibes in the room had an effect on the group's productivity. Robbie told Paul Myers on the *Pullmyears* blog:

> It wasn't really a great time for the guys in the Band, right then. There was just a lot of, you know, distraction and a lot of drug experimenting, a lot of things going on. The other guys in the band didn't exactly like Todd. They just. . . . One thing was, we'd all go in there and you'd be kind of waiting until the mood struck you. Until someone might say, "Okay, let's go in and cut something." [I'm sure] Todd thought, "What are we doing? How come we don't just show up and start recording?" He was impatient; he didn't know what we were waiting for. I didn't even know what we were waiting for either! But you could just tell, when it was getting harder just to round everybody up and get them all sitting down in front of their instruments, learning the songs, and doing all those things.

During the sessions, Richard sang well and played some of his best piano on record, but his songwriting contributions dwindled for a third time in three records. Debate is fruitless: Richard was shaky, and copious amounts of drugs and alcohol were not helping.

Robbie, Richard, and Levon, Woodstock Playhouse, 1970. *Photograph by John Scheele; all rights reserved*

The Band sat in a circle in the middle of the stage and talked about the shape of the verses of Robbie's new song. Richard sat slumped in his chair in front of the line of amplifiers, his head resting in the palm of his hand. Cigarette dangling from his other hand, he stared at the lines of the lyric sheet for "Daniel and the Sacred Harp" and wondered to himself if he'd ever write such a song. Robbie sat just over his shoulder and offered subtle encouragement as Richard prepared to lay down his vocal overdub.

Richard flicked the edge of the paper with his slender fingers as Levon's boots echoed hollow steps across the cold floor of the stage. Robbie asked Richard, "Do you have any songs you're working on?" Richard chewed on the side of his thumb and shook his head "no" as he averted Robbie's exasperated gaze and turned his eyes back down to the lyrics.

No matter the purported level of brotherhood in the group, these weren't outwardly expressive guys. They took care of their own business and didn't get overly emotional. They were musicians in a band together, doing a job. If Richard didn't have songs, he didn't have them, end of story. Or maybe he had the songs and chose not to share them with his bandmates.

Simon said in 2023, "Writing was an effort for him, I think. And he was a perfectionist about that, reluctant to call anything complete. Like 'Whispering Pines,' for which he never completed the lyrics, but his musical compositions were good."

The Band tried in vain to re-create an environment that had been critical to its success, and in doing so made the situation something forced. Richard received cowriting credits on just two songs on *Stage Fright*, "Sleeping" and "Just Another Whistle Stop." It's easy to say that Richard had lost interest in songwriting because of his addictions, but more importantly, he had lost his confidence.

The same sensitivity that gave his music such incredible power and depth is also what made him so vulnerable. As the Band's popularity grew, Richard's insecurities increased at the same rate. The soulful emotions that he poured into his songs were born of the same demons that haunted him during his downtime.

Robbie said to David Browne of *Rolling Stone* in 2021:

> I was really trying to get everybody to show up and participate. I was trying to stir things up. I was thinking, "Come on, you're being *lazy*. We're all going to write and co-write and we're all going to participate. It's a new day now." And trying to write with some people who *don't* write was really frustrating.

By the time of the *Stage Fright* sessions, Richard had developed an impressive cache of compositions. He knew how to write songs. His natural knack for arranging and for developing melody was one of many elements that helped elevate the Band above its contemporaries.

As it became clear to Richard that a singular vision was being cultivated for the group both internally and externally, he slid his compositional gearbox into neutral. He would never say a bad word about his bandmates, regardless of how he felt about the situation. He would just raise his glass for a toast and sing his ass off.

Levon said in his memoir, "Robbie took most of the credits, played a lot of guitar, and generally tried to assume full control of that part of the whole process."

The truth, as it usually does, lies somewhere down the middle. Levon wasn't a songwriter and didn't have patience for the process. He was a master musical mind, arranger, and creator of feel but did not write songs. Richard wrote songs, good ones. He developed chord progressions, created melodies, and composed lyrics. Simon said of Robbie's and Richard's songwriting approaches that "Robbie was prolific, ambitious. Richard was self-effacing, underconfident."

Robbie said he begged Richard to write. Richard said he was writing. For whatever reason, Richard couldn't deal with his work being vetted, resulting in feelings of inadequacy that couldn't be deflected by drugs and alcohol.

In thinking about the Band's situation, Jane said,

> If you take a group of people—and I don't care who it would be—and you give them fame, you give them money, and you have people who will give them anything and do anything they want—it would be interesting to watch each individual to see what road they go down or what course they take . . . because those things have an effect on you.

The effect it had on Richard was that it smothered his spirit.

In a May 1971 interview, Barend Toet, the founder of *Oor* magazine, asked Richard what he did with his free time in Woodstock. Richard replied, "I'm writing something. We [the Band] often play together. My family."

When Toet pressed him about working in the studio, Richard's view changed:

> I don't call that free time. That's more difficult work than giving concerts. It's hard work. It takes a lot of patience. Concerts are often accompanied by more tension, but they're soon over. In the studio, it's often difficult to see that you're making progress. Some days, you go home feeling like you didn't give a shit. Then you have to forget everything and start again the next day.
>
> I want to get into it [studio work]. But before you can do that job, you need to develop a sense of communication so you can understand the guy making the record.

Richard wasn't built for the restrictions or pressures of studio work. It was like being back at school. He didn't like being put on the spot. He just let it

Richard, Jane, Paula, and John Simon, Woodstock, 1970. *Photograph by John Scheele; all rights reserved.*

Chapter 10 | Odd Man (1970–1971) 243

rip. Eric Clapton said in 2023, "Richard was one of the characters who would be in the moment. He would sing a song the way it felt *that night*." Cutting take after take and listening to playbacks of songs he wasn't involved in creating was a grind, and working at the Woodstock Playhouse was a struggle. There was a lot of waiting around for decisions to be made that didn't involve his input. That the spirit of the Band was crumbling made the situation worse.

It was too much work. For Richard, composition required inspiration and perfection. He had the melodies, licks, and riffs. But in that same *Time* cover story, he told writer William Bender:

> I lean more into chord changes and melodic stuff. I can write music very easily, but when it comes to words, I cringe. It's hard to get those words in the right slot, to just get going.

The pressure was mounting, and Richard couldn't keep up. Simon remembered:

> Robbie had some compassion for Richard's nonproductivity. He bought him a typewriter. In preparation for the second album, there had to be twelve new songs in a hurry. Richard was just too slow in doing that.

It wasn't so much that Richard was unproductive at this time, it's that he didn't think of his writing as a commodity, and he couldn't force it. It was as if he were being interrogated under the hot light of the Band's fame. Van Morrison said the following to the *Irish Times* in 2015:

> The thing about being famous, the problem is, you become objectified, and when you're writing, if you're talking about the creative process and being able to stand back, that's no good, because you need to freely look at what's going on and observe people: what they're doing, what they're saying. And it's very difficult to do that when people are focusing on you.

While Richard pumped the brakes creatively, he was throttling his leisure experimentation to a most precarious edge. Everything he did was taken to its absolute limit, whether it was driving or drinking. But Richard's musical blade had dulled. The delicate balance within the group had been disrupted by fame. When working at its optimal level, the group was built for fostering creativity. When one element was misaligned, the functioning of the entire unit was put at risk.

In a 1989 interview with Timothy White, Eric Clapton said this of his friendship with Richard:

> We were going through a lot of the same difficulties . . . screwing around with drugs and drink . . . getting crazy down deep. He was finding it difficult to cope with his talent.

Self-deprecating to the point of no return, Richard held himself to unrealistic expectations and more and more frequently came up short.

Therein lies the essential tragedy of Richard and the Band: while Robbie Robertson was peaking creatively and immersing himself in film, books, and social circles that would help him realize his greater ambitions, Richard had reached the nexus of his profession and then sunk himself deep into self-pity and the plush comforts of narcotic sleep.

With Richard's diminishing contributions, Robbie's own relationship with the group changed, because he was now the solitary narrator. There was less intimacy and a limited perspective. Songs were composed almost exclusively from guitar, and the endearing interweaving of vocal lines and off-mic asides was gone. When Richard lost his joy, it went out of the Band's music too.

Without a doubt, the close relationship between Grossman and Robbie created tensions within the group. Levon was suspicious of deals being made on his and the group's behalf, Rick absorbed Levon's observations and rebroadcast them as the voice of reason, and Richard was generally incommunicado. Grossman pushed Robbie to the front of the line after he had lost Dylan as his bell cow.

In a strange way, Robbie's ambitions started to erode the unity he had with the other guys. Robbie became the Band company man. He said in the 2000 *Stage Fright* liner notes,

> The musical unit was no longer connected in the way it had been before. We were starting to move apart. . . . Nobody wanted to be there that long, so we made *Stage Fright* very quickly, and it wasn't the same experience as before.

Levon said in his memoir, "That's when that great sense of teamwork stopped. Who wanted to pour out their souls and not get credit? Richard stopped writing completely after a while." In total opposition to a sensitive artist, the Band was now about contracts, percentages, royalties, and excess. Richard was already a goner.

To his wife, Richard expressed regret about the way that the Band's collaboration had seemed to run its course. He felt guilty because of the part he played in its demise. No matter the circumstance, Richard never made the Band's issues anyone's fault but his own and took the brunt of all the guilt he was feeling. That guilt was glossed over with Grand Marnier and pills, and when they didn't work, then cocaine and heroin. If he was going to be marginalized anyway, why not just get wasted?

Jon Taplin, who as the group's road manager had a front-row seat to the internal changes happening in the group, said in 2022,

> What happened was people in the Band all of a sudden started making real money. They bought nice cars and got nice houses. But Richard would drink every night. I mean, drink a lot. He wouldn't get up till late in the morning. And Robbie developed the habit of getting up early and writing songs.

Taplin said he believed that even though they had collaborated, and that Richard had written some of his own songs, the reason their partnership ended abruptly was pure laziness.

When Richard returned home from work in the studio, the party immediately accelerated. One day, Jane returned from an afternoon out with Paula and walked into their house with an immediate sense of foreboding. She heard muffled voices and smelled the aroma of smoke and stale beer. As she stepped lightly into the living room, she saw Richard's form sunk into the chair, staring at a television with the sound off while holding court with a group of young dropouts, all of them replete with bulging eyeballs and seated in a dirty circle at his feet. Jane turned on her heel, walked out of the house, and took Paula with her.

Robbie looked back on this period with *Rolling Stone* in December 1976:

> We made a couple of albums and then we went on the road as the Band. Not long after that something snapped. All of a sudden, we were in the outer limits and didn't know what was going on. Things were happening right and left, and we all went off on different kinds of dangerous adventures in life.

What cannot be denied is that Richard Manuel did not contribute another original song to the group after 1970's *Stage Fright*.

And the Band was never the same.

THE TRANS-CONTINENTAL POP FESTIVAL

Midway through the year, and shortly after work on *Stage Fright* concluded, the Band prepared to take their show back on the road. They played a series of successful shows in June on the East Coast, with a review from the *Evening Star* in Washington, DC, that took note of Richard's "wiggling straw-man shoulders," and one from the *Boston Herald Traveler* noting his hip fashion sense: "Rick Manuel, in striped hip-huggers and a flowery shirt, could have felt at home in any bar on Madison Avenue," while also noticing his "banging out a magnificent boogie on the piano."

At the end of the month, the Band joined the Trans-Continental Pop Festival tour with the Grateful Dead, Janis Joplin, Ian and Sylvia, Buddy Guy, and others. The silver bullet was loaded to the brim with rockers, drugs, and booze. In typical fashion for the Band, Richard missed the train, Rick took the train, Robbie and Levon were on their way to New York with the *Stage Fright* tapes, and Garth did Garth.

Richard and John Till met again on the festival tour and shared the same stage. The Stratford connection was a circle never to be broken.

In 2000, a documentary film titled *Festival Express* was released, featuring sharp color footage of the Band performing three songs. Shortly after its release, other clips appeared online in varying states of quality. The footage captures the group at its performing summit. The Band's enthusiasm for performance had not yet been dampened by the road. Sharing a stage with their peers only increased the quality of all their performances, each driving the other to musical peaks of ecstasy.

The crazy cross-country concert caravan began with two shows in Toronto on June 27 and concluded with two shows in Calgary on July 4 and 5 after a midway stop in Winnipeg.

The clips included in the official documentary were shot in Calgary. During a stirring version of "I Shall Be Released," Richard gazes toward the darkened horizon line of the crowd, his eyes cracking under the spotlights. He retrieves a distressed and delicate falsetto that rings out from the Calgary stage and crosses Canada to a Stratford Baptist church.

The performance of "The Weight" is conclusive, a capture of the Band as the quintessential quintet. Richard and Garth switch seats, and Richard plays the chorus line on Garth's keyboard.

Robbie introduces "Slippin' and Slidin'" as a rock 'n' roll song they had played ten years ago. Richard can be heard saying "teenagers" off-screen as he initiates the song's pumping piano introduction, and the Band shakes out some of its old Hawks feathers. Richard does his best Jerry Lee Manuel and pounds the keys to dust as the crowd explodes. The music pours off the celluloid, and the Band pulses to the rhythm. It's mythical and critical footage in the Band's story.

Additional clips of officially sanctioned footage were included in the box set *A Musical History*, which features two more songs from one of the Calgary sets, "Long Black Veil" and "Rockin' Chair."

The footage of "Rockin' Chair" is special and shows Richard unfiltered and immersed in his element. His hair is mussed, his movements shaky, his singing intense. One story is that Richard had tapped into the display-sized bottle of Canadian Club that had been procured by the musicians on the train during a stop. What Richard didn't expect was the adult-sized dose of LSD that had been added to the bottle by the Grateful Dead.

He *leans* into "Rockin' Chair" with a heavy-lidded urgency, hanging on the lip of the Steinway as if his grip were dependent on hitting the note. Richard draws in a deep breath and, with a succinct head cock, intensely pushes it back out, emptying his soulful vessel in the name of music. When Rick and Levon join in on the chorus, the sweet Canadian breeze caresses the stage and takes Richard's song to the masses.

A wealth of raw watermarked footage is available for those who search, revealing stellar versions of "Across the Great Divide," "The Night They Drove Old Dixie Down," and "Time to Kill" from the Toronto shows. There is additional music from Calgary, including reelin' and rockin' versions of "Strawberry Wine," "Chest Fever," "Don't Do It," and "Jemimah Surrender."

The unofficial clip of "Strawberry Wine" has the cameraman filming from behind Garth on accordion and next to Richard on drums. Watching Richard and Levon lock eyes while Levon shakes it on guitar in time with Richard's drumming makes any technical shortcomings with the footage forgivable. It's a crime that more of this footage hasn't made its way to an official release.

The Calgary segment of "Jemimah Surrender," like all the stellar versions played on the spring tour, is infectious. Richard pounds the drum kit until it gives up the ghost, and just as the group lands on the middle eight, he joins in with closed-eye high harmony with Levon. The cameraman zooms in on Richard at precisely the right moment, just as he is getting completely lost in the creation of the music. It is a stunning and inspired moment.

In typical fashion, after the concerts were over, a low-key hang is when the authentic magic happened. That's fully evidenced by a recording included in the *Stage Fright* fiftieth-anniversary box set. Taped by photographer and friend John Scheele, the hotel room renditions of "Get Up Jake" (a leftover from *The Band* sessions), "Rockin' Pneumonia and Boogie Woogie Flu," and "Before

You Accuse Me" feature the lineup of Robbie, folk singer Eric Andersen, Rick, and Richard.

Perched on the edge of the rigid hotel bed, Richard blows hardy blues harp while lending handclaps and improv harmony to the intimate jam. The version of "Mojo Hannah" is a revelation. Originally recorded by Henry Lupkin as a single and released in 1962, this is the same kind of deep cut that Richard and the Hawks liked to get their talons into. This hotel room performance has a feel similar to the intimate basement recording of "Will the Circle Be Unbroken." Richard takes the vocal first, with support from Eric Andersen and Rick, spreading the melody to the song's edges, then moves to harmonica. The effect is inspired and beautiful.

After the conclusion of the train tour, the Band played the Hollywood Bowl with Miles Davis. The audience recording, one of the first bootleg recordings of the Band to make the rounds, offers stellar sonics. While the performance is solid, both Robbie and Levon had memories of the show not going as planned, with Levon admitting to having some issues keeping the tempo straight.

The show opens with a fresh version of "The Shape I'm In" that offers a glimpse of Garth's and Richard's second-sight interplay. Richard's voice is authoritative and limber, allowing all nuance of his tenor to be heard. His piano playing is also fantastic on a typically strong summer tour version of "Look Out Cleveland." He stays in fine form throughout the performance, culminating in a sparkling version of "I Shall Be Released."

Once again, the version of "Rockin' Chair" is worthy of deep inspection. You can feel the warm Southern California evening air and sense the audience's rapt attention. Every pluck of mandolin and puff of accordion is detectable.

Stage Fright

Stage Fright was released on August 17, 1970, and quickly became the Band's bestselling record. The album had a cleaner sound than its predecessors as a result of a multitude of production factors, including the absence of John Simon and two engineers making separate mixes of the record. Levon wanted famed British engineer Glyn Johns to mix the record; Robbie wanted Todd Rundgren. In the end, the record featured mixes from both.

The LP features a vibrant sunrise-themed cover by artist Bob Cato, wrapped by a moody black-and-white poster of the Band. Richard is cocredited with two compositions on the record.

In 2021, the fiftieth-anniversary deluxe edition of *Stage Fright* was remixed and reorganized with a new running order. Robbie said that before the album's original release, he changed the intended track list. Robbie told *Rolling Stone* in 2021:

> The guys were like, "Man, you know, some of the songs, you were really pushing us for our part, they're buried in the sequence." So, I thought, "Fuck it, I'm going to push all of that way up front." And it was a mistake. We weren't falling apart, but we were wrangling, and we never had to wrangle before.

So Robbie front-loaded the album with the songs that contained shared songwriting credits, to appease any sore feelings among his bandmates.

Going with the record's original running order, the opening groover "Strawberry Wine" finds Levon on guitar, so Richard went to drums. In typical fashion, he bangs out a beautifully syncopated beat that falls perfectly on the punctuation of Levon's vocal lines.

"Sleeping" is a chord progression pulled from the same lush garden patch as compositions such as "In a Station" or "When You Awake," using the metaphor of sleep as a liberation from reality. The song radiates a wistfulness and a longing for a permanent dream state. It's an insightful composition and glimpse into Richard's state of mind during this period. The song also illustrates his penchant for quirky time signatures when the song moves through a buoyant waltz theme through the chorus.

Robbie later alluded to the song being about heroin seeping into the seams of the group, while others contend it could be a blissful analysis of sleep. Richard's vocals are some of the finest he ever committed to tape. He caresses the lyrics forever associated with him—"To be called by noon, is to be called too soon, today"—with a lazy resignation.

Richard contributed electric piano and shared lead vocals with Rick on the cedar-scented "Time to Kill," a clandestine jewel of the group's catalog and a good-time live stage highlight. The duo's singing consisted of the highest-quality blend, with Richard rolling his harmony over Rick's lead.

Richard's second cowritten song on the album was "Just Another Whistle Stop," originally called "Odd Man," and was the last song to come together for the record. The melody is Richard's, and the song chugs along on a celebratory series of strident piano changes. The buoyant introduction was a racing locomotive, smoking down the track toward Stratford's Grand Trunk station.

> *And it's odd man out, and you know that's the rule, you can scream, and you can shout, but they'll only call you a crazy fool.*

Lyrically, the song leans toward Richard's introspective style but expresses a rowdy attitude. Understanding Richard's tendency to leave songs unfinished, there's a good chance that Robbie completed Richard's fragmented attempts.

The muffled sounds of young people out in the street, first heard in a station, were now emanating from outside the whistle stop, with the flashing lights of the police not far behind. The song develops a natural tension as it careens through the changes, slowing only for the descending introduction to each verse highlighted by Rick Danko's fretless Ampeg bass.

The Robbie Robertson composition "The Shape I'm In" was purportedly a statement on Richard's condition. Over the course of time and countless performances, it would become the song most associated with him. It's a perfect rock song, containing a dramatic prelude and a relentless beat through the verses. The groove drives by steam and passes by Buddy Holly's "Not Fade Away" and Diddley's "Hey Bo Diddley" on the way to water. The imagery about going down to the shoreline evokes Richard's renditions of Ray Charles's "I'm Going Down to the River" from the Hawks days. Except this time, he isn't going to jump into the water . . . not yet. The squishy keyboard line that was played in the studio on a Hohner Pianet and later onstage on a Clavinet became a signature sound for Richard.

Richard also contributed some clown-car piano and high harmony to the chorus of "The W. S. Walcott Medicine Show," a funky showstopper. On "Daniel and the Sacred Harp," Richard inhabits Robbie's lyric of the soul seller and plays the part perfectly. All three Band vocalists contribute to the narrative.

Strange Vibes

While critics focused on comparisons to the group's first two records, *Stage Fright* is an album that any of the Band's contemporaries would love to have recorded. One tremendously insightful review by Ed Ochs in the September 12, 1970, edition of *Billboard* reads:

> This is the Band today. The relationship of music to message is noticeably off-center, cool, perhaps, or just naggingly overworked. Still, I keep on, despite the super manipulation of their material and Robbie Robertson's slow, greedy, grudging growth from record to record, they are too creative and public to stunt their own group or individual growth.

By late 1970, both the Band and Woodstock were full of strange vibes. The town had become a safe haven for all sorts of dropouts, drop-ins, and drop-deads, all in varying states of sanity. The musicians were just as lost as everyone else, and the unifying factor was that everyone was wasted.

Richard was an easy target for the star fuckers and drug dealers. His personality was not conducive to turning people away, regardless of their intentions. It's well documented in the annals of rock 'n' roll history: alcohol and heroin had amazing abilities to stifle creativity by chemically working their alluring ways on the most-creative members of a group . . . who were also usually the most susceptible to suggestion.

Despite the chaos surrounding the Band, Richard was still staying relatively active both in film and music. At the end of summer, he tested his abilities on the big screen. An October 30 article in the *Ottawa Journal* notes that Richard was on set filming a movie titled *Eliza's Horoscope*, in which he plays Quine, an eccentric composer, and makes several on-screen appearances. He was trying his hand at other things and was developing outside interests, as was everyone in the group. Robbie said in his memoir that Richard had a few offers for films but was too focused on the Band and his music. At some point in the year, Richard was asked to play some thumping drums to "Motorcycle Man" on John Simon's solo record, *John Simon's Album*.

FALL 1970

The fall tour brought more excellent performances. Beginning in Tuscaloosa, Alabama, on October 30, the tour ran through mid-December and concluded in Florida. Two field recordings, one from Tufts University in Boston and the other from Worcester, Massachusetts, on November 5 and 7, represent the tour in varying degrees of audio quality. Two *Stage Fright* tracks, "Just Another Whistle Stop" and the rarely played "All La Glory," were added to the set.

A crisp soundboard recording of the group's performance at the Syria Mosque in Pittsburgh on November 15 spotlights a well-played concert that is kind to Richard in the mix. This aural focus of the tape allows us to fully appreciate his contributions. While Levon Helm is the fulcrum from which the Band's groove swings, its tottering soul comes from Richard.

Every song is a crystalline capture of a night where the entire band is on. In addition to the soundboard audio, professionally shot color film of four songs also circulates. Richard's hair has reached shoulder length, and his beard has grown to match.

Onstage at the University of Alabama homecoming, October 30, 1970. *Courtesy of the University of Alabama Libraries Special Collections*

He is captured on organ for "Time to Kill" and "The Weight," and then back to the piano for "This Wheel's on Fire" and "Up on Cripple Creek." The camera circles behind Richard's piano for "This Wheel's on Fire," allowing for an intimate glimpse of his cross-stage view.

Young Brothers Join in *Cahoots*

In what can be considered the start of the *Cahoots* sessions, the Band convened at the newly built Bearsville Studios on February 8, 1971, as a test run for the new recording space. Bearsville Studios was state of the art, created by Albert Grossman so that his stable of artists would have a creative home base.

The backcountry barn off Speare Road would be a clubhouse for the Band, one where they would never have to pack up their instruments, a place where they could drop in whenever their creative juices were flowing. The only issue was that when the Band arrived to work, the studio itself was still under construction.

The Band in unfinished Bearsville Studios, 1971. *Courtesy of the Barry Feinstein estate*

The Band attempted Robbie's "Endless Highway" during the first session in a piano-heavy version that featured both Garth and Richard on keys. Richard takes the lead vocals on this early rendition. The song moves along like a highway ride with the windows down. He sings free and easy over Robbie's acoustic guitar and Garth's piano acrobatics. By the time the Band played it live onstage, the lead vocal job would be Rick's and the song would intensify.

Over the next few months, the Band would meet at Bearsville to work. The same internal issues that cropped up during the recording of *Stage Fright* reared their ugly heads again. Individual parts were overdubbed, which meant that songs weren't given the opportunity to develop in the usual, close-knit, organic way.

Robbie was going through a period of writer's block and admittedly was having issues coming up with material for the group, as was Richard. His drinking escalated, and he was starting to bottom out. Robbie said in *Across the Great Divide*, "He had the disease of alcoholism, even though none of us realized that it was anything more than that he liked to drink too many beers." Simon confirmed that he was going overboard, and that Richard had "three levels: drunk, real drunk, and too drunk. But he was also a very sweet man. He was never an angry, hostile drunk."

Additionally, the complete absence of Richard Manuel songwriting contributions was glaring and left the Band a musical body with no bones. Once Richard disconnected from the songwriting aspect of the group, no matter how well he was playing, all the vocal camaraderie, improvised tricks, and playful collaboration ceased. The members of the group were so wrapped up in their own individual worlds that the bond that had developed through years of hard work and shared dreams had started to fracture.

Simon said in his memoir that by 1971, "Robbie didn't . . . consciously intimidate him [Richard] . . . but when you met Robbie, he was so smooth and urbane and witty, whereas Richard was such a gee-golly-gosh kind of guy." Combine this with Richard's overthinking and heavy drinking, and the ground was fertile for the seeds of doubt.

As evidenced by Robbie's decision to have Bob Clearmountain remix the entire *Cahoots* record for its fiftieth anniversary, even he wasn't happy with how the original record turned out. The album emits a whiff of inauthenticity from its hollow sheen. It's a well-intentioned rock album, just not one recorded to the Band's previously established high standard. Whereas *Stage Fright* was the dusk settling in on the Band, *Cahoots* was immersed in that darkness.

In spite of the album's inconsistencies, Richard's contributions illuminated much of it, though it's notable that Garth played more piano on the record than usual, given Richard's unpredictability.

"Life Is a Carnival" is a driving opener to the record and notable for Richard's lyrical addition of the line "two bits a shot." "When I Paint My Masterpiece" was Dylan's contribution to the record. Levon moved to mandolin, so Richard slid into the drum seat. "Last of the Blacksmiths" is a differently built Robertson song that expresses a yearning for days gone by, and nowhere is that more evident than in Richard's desperate lead vocal. His voice sounds like a lone refrain from an empty white room, solitary and stark. The Bearsville echo chamber was not fully ready for use, so the vocal is unadorned. His piano is up front and crisp, and when Garth comes in midsong with a filthy saxophone solo, Richard lays down some funky rhythm piano underneath.

"Where Do We Go from Here" contains all the elements of a classic Band song but lacks the spirit of previous efforts that would have taken it over the top. Robbie later expressed his dissatisfaction with the song, wishing that the group could have gotten more out of it.

THE BELFAST COWBOY AND BEAK

In a December 1970 interview with *Jazz & Pop* magazine, Van Morrison said he and Richard were thinking of recording an album of Ray Charles covers. When the interviewer mentioned that he thought Richard seemed reluctant to take on such a project, Morrison said, "No, no. He was up for it. Maybe if we could just get the studio to come here. Sixteen-track. We could sit around here and work it out." When asked in 2024 about this prospective project, he said, "Ray Charles songs were always talked about but never made it off the ground."

Three months later, a bit of the old Woodstock alchemy reappeared when Morrison visited Bearsville Studios on a brisk evening during the recording of *Cahoots*. Robbie had written "4% Pantomime" (a reference to the difference in alcohol content between Johnny Walker Red and Black) earlier in the day when Morrison stopped by Robbie's house. While searching for lyrics to match the chord changes, Morrison was inspired to start singing about his musical mate, Richard Manuel.

Mary Martin recalled in rejected liner notes for the Band 2000 reissues that "Richard and Van were close pals. . . . For Van, Richard was the real *soul* of the Band." Morrison was asked to describe a moment that illustrated Mary Martin's comment, and he said, "He had his own interpretation of the Ray Charles sound when he did the Bobby Bland song 'Share Your Love with Me,'" adding, "As a singer, he didn't sound like anyone else. As a songwriter, I cite 'Tears of Rage' as a great song."

Exhumed from the vaults for the *Cahoots* fiftieth-anniversary box set, the first two takes of "4% Pantomime," originally known as "Belfast Cowboy," begin tentatively with everyone contributing except Garth, who's in the control room. Morrison sings the opening verses before the take comes to a halt. Then he is heard saying, "That was better live. It was closer to the wire."

Take 2 is a liquid take, with Richard now singing the opening verses. The song begins with Robbie's finger-popping fretwork and Richard's soft trilling. Morrison and Richard are set feet apart from each other in Bearsville Studio B, red faced and sweaty. Two hard-drinking troubadours, poured out musically in pub-soaked friendship; a line of smoke swirls around the room with each of their inspired breaths. The musical charge touched off a jolt between two of rock 'n' roll's best soul singers.

Robbie said in the liner notes for the *Cahoots* fiftieth-anniversary box set that "the physical performance that Van was giving, and Richard with the veins in his neck sticking out, he's just pulling the trigger and Van is all over the place." That second take has a charm all its own, especially after we've had the album version soaking into our ears for so many years.

When Richard comes in with the "Belfast Cowboy" lyric, he ignites a besotted and spectacular call and response that becomes a giddy melodic exchange. Richard and Morrison could be at the local pub, arms pretzeled over shoulders in a teeter-totter sing-along. The take concludes, and Garth can be heard saying from the control room, "That was spectacular."

The official version released on *Cahoots* has Garth's organ added to the instrumental mix. Richard and Morrison duet, duel, and cajole their way through a shared bottle of spirits. The intensity of their exchange rises as the level of liquid in the bottle decreases. The conclusion of the song encapsulates everything about the collaborative environment, with them entering into a wordless sing-along that swirls into the fade-out.

After the session concluded, Richard insisted on driving Morrison back to his home at the top of Ohayo Mountain. As everyone in the studio was in questionable driving condition, roadie Ed Anderson joined Morrison and Richard for the drive home. They left Bearsville Studio together in Richard's Grand Prix but first decided to take a detour to Deanie's for some grub and a quick nightcap.

After a few tall glasses of Go Fasters, the guys staggered out the door and piled into Richard's car. Ed crawled through the window and into the back seat and Morrison took over shotgun. The guys tore through the crisp night toward Spencer Road, and Richard wheeled into the icy driveway.

Morrison bid Ed and Richard farewell and slid out of the passenger side door while Ed crawled into the front seat. Stepping into the oil-black Woodstock night, Morrison took a wrong step and slipped hard on the ice, falling to the ground beside the car. As soon as the passenger door had clicked shut, Richard, oblivious to Morrison's plight, threw the car into reverse and ripped out of the driveway, headed back down the mountain.

The next morning, Ed and Richard were notified of Morrison's fall. It became clear that in the confusion, the tires of Richard's car missed Morrison's head by mere inches. The incident was traumatic enough that Morrison immediately switched from drinking booze to Tab diet soda.

Morrison said in 2024, "I remember the time he almost ran me over. I got out of the vehicle and fell in the snow, and he almost reversed over me!"

"Thinkin' Out Loud"

Richard tore into the puddled driveway of Bearsville Studio, almost sending his car into a 360-degree swing into the pine-dotted yard. It had been a few days since he'd been to a session, and he was already late. He turned off the ignition and walked across the brown muddy gravel and entered the studio. He had overslept; he didn't even hear Jane and Paula leave the house that morning. Hell, they could have been gone for a few days.

The Band was working on a Robbie song, "Thinkin' Out Loud"; by this point, they were all Robbie songs. The mood in the studio was chilly but soon became cordial when everyone showed up and was ready to work.

The guys switched instruments for this folky number, and Richard took to the drum stool so Garth could play piano, and Levon could move to stand-up bass. The guys laid down a fun rhythm track with that lineup. Afterward, Robbie and the guys discussed options for potential overdubs on the song.

During a break in recording, Richard moseyed up from the drum stool and walked over to the acoustic guitar propped up in the corner, and placed it in his lap, Dobro style. With Robbie's slide on his finger, he began to pick out a wobbly recitation of the melody line for "Thinkin' Out Loud." Robbie and the rest of his bandmates looked on in shared amusement, since no one knew that Richard could play slide guitar.

Richard recorded the slippery opening line and midsong solo that graced the *Cahoots* LP, a testament to his only formal musical training: his days of Hawaiian guitar practice at the mobile Western Ontario Conservatory of Music.

The second side of *Cahoots* opens with "Shootout in Chinatown," a cinematic song that harkens back to the collaborative vocals of the first two records. Richard sang lead during the verses with support from Rick, while Levon's voice moved to the forefront on the chorus. The wordless vocal fade-out, with Rick and Richard entering a slippery "Cripple Creek"-like yodel, recalls past glories.

"Moon Struck One," where Richard illuminates the circular arrangement with a silvery lead vocal, follows "Chinatown." The song spotlights one of his finest Band leads. Jon Landau, in his review of the album for *Rolling Stone*, remarked that Richard's vocals on "Moon Struck One" were superb.

Richard's Melobar lap steel. *Thanks to Levon Helm Studios*

"Smoke Signal" burns with big descending chords and a stomping rhythm. The song would become a live standard for the group in the fall of 1971 and never failed to ignite the Band. On the sly-eyed sexy funk of "Volcano," Richard offers the highest harmony vocal and does the same for the closing beauty of "The River Hymn."

After the conclusion of the *Cahoots* sessions in April, the Band members went their separate ways, with plans to reconvene before their scheduled European tour.

Richard Manuel

The Band in Europe

In complete contrast to the chilly and clinical feel of the *Cahoots* sessions, the Band's tour of Europe was a high point of their career. It would be the first time the Band had visited the continent on their own. Their previous trip to Europe had been in 1966 as the Hawks, when they were booed constantly. This time, retribution was a nightly ritual on the same stages they had graced five years before. When they were free to simply perform, the encumbering vibe of the studio would fall away, and the Band again found its center.

The afternoon of May 17, 1971, the Band was introduced at a press conference at the Inn on the Park's Hamilton Suite in London. The group first went to the stone-covered roof for a series of surprisingly happy-looking group photographs before retiring to the suite for interviews with the British press.

Richard, dressed in a blue shirt and a favorite orange suit jacket, giggled and stroked his beard as the reporters milled around and met the group. In contrast to the posh surroundings, the Band appeared to have been plucked from a Catskill Mountain camp and dropped into the plush confines of British hospitality.

The tour officially kicked off in Hamburg on May 18; critically and internally, it was a success, and the Band's playing was accurate and enthusiastic. The circulating audience tapes bear this out, with field recordings available from May 20 in Frankfurt, May 27 in Denmark, both the June 2 and 3 shows at Royal Albert Hall, and the concluding June 6 performance in Rotterdam. Officially, a partial soundboard of the Paris show from May 25 was released as part of the *Cahoots* fiftieth-anniversary box set.

Three songs from the first night at Royal Albert Hall were released on *A Musical History*. A soundboard compilation of the two nights at the Royal Albert Hall was later officially released as part of the *Stage Fright* fiftieth-anniversary box set. A wonderful overview of the European tour can be gained through all the audio captures, both official and unofficial. The Band's performances at the Royal Albert Hall were the crowning achievement of the trip. Robbie said he thought they were some of the best shows the Band ever played.

Richard's piano playing on the tour was some of the finest of his career, and his voice the perfect combination of age and control. The Band's musical highlights were numerous, and the European crowds were respectful and hungry for their music.

Musical moments of note include the version of "Across the Great Divide" from Paris, as the Band rolls across rutted roads toward the edge of the world. It's a large, lumbering rendition, with Richard's voice spiced up with the perfect amount of ethos. Levon replied to the lyric "Now tell me, hon, what ya done with the gun?" with an enthusiastic "Give me some chicken too!"

The crowd was going crazy, and Richard can be heard replying to the multitude of song requests coming in from the audience with "We'll play all of 'em." Color footage of a chunky "Slippin' and Slidin'" is also available; while Richard isn't shown during most of the song, it allows for a cool cross-stage view of Levon's perspective of the group. Geoffrey Cannon, writing about the Paris show for *Melody Maker*, said, "They ended with the perfect number for the Hawks: Little Richard's 'Slippin' and Slidin'.' Richard Manuel played stride piano, as every singer in the band roared the words into his mike."

"The W. S. Walcott's Medicine Show" from Denmark on May 27 is a Technicolor carnival. Richard's playing on the soundboard recalls Ray Charles's piano on the 1955 single "I'm a Fool for You"—rickety, tasteful, and beautifully emotive. One of the last-ever performances of "We Can Talk" teeters gloriously, with Richard's vocals hitting all the right notes in perfect time.

The Albert Hall performances are Band perfection, capturing them at the peak of their craft. Music journalist Richard Williams talked about the shows on his web page thebluemoment.com:

> Those of us present at the Albert Hall still talk about the pin-sharp but very warm quality of the sound, and how they were the first rock band to master the acoustics of a venue that had been notoriously unfriendly to amplified music. . . . The sound was just like the records, allowing us to appreciate the astonishing quality of their playing. It was one of the great gigs.

Everything the Band plays at the Royal Albert Hall sparkles. "Stage Fright" is as big as the room; "We Can Talk" is so damn good, it could have been played twice; "Chest Fever" and "Rag Mama Rag" almost bring the house down.

"I Shall Be Released" is heavenly. It's Richard's craft at its apex. The Band conjures a drift through its back pages, playing as one instrument, thinking as one mind, and emitting one musical breath. When Richard sings the timeless Dylan lyric "Every man must fall," Robbie and Rick slide their hands down their guitar necks in perfect unison, illustrating the line, fret by fret.

Jon Taplin remembered this as a good time for the Band on the road:

> We went all through Europe, never had any problem other than one incident: Rick Danko snorted some heroin in the south of France, and I had to take him to the hospital. But other than that, we had no problems whatsoever, in terms of abuse or being stupid. You know, the girls were beautiful, and Richard was funny. He was always able to kind of keep everybody laughing.

Life Is a Carnival

After the Band's return from Europe, they played three large shows over the course of a week, culminating with two incendiary shows at New York City's Central Park on June 30. Well-recorded audience tapes capture both steamy summer sets, and the Gotham crowd is treated to the finest version ever played of "King Harvest (Has Surely Come)" during the early show. Surrounded by the skyscrapers of a concrete jungle, the Band pulled everything out of its bag for the rowdy New York crowd.

Their sound on the tape is much closer to the Hawks of old, with screaming guitar solos and popping snare hits. Richard's "King Harvest" vocals are full of pastoral angst, and the Band reflects his investment. He lets out a hearty "Thank you" at the song's conclusion, as he always did. "Stage Fright" is also a concert highlight with dramatic transitions, solos, and typically wonderful Rick Danko vocals.

The Band took July off and started to brainstorm a way to document their recent live performances. A decision was made to record the last week of concerts of their fall tour in New York City at the Academy of Music. Robbie told Robert Hilburn of the *Los Angeles Times*, "The reason we are thinking of a live album is it will help us end this era in our music properly."

On August 1, Rick and Richard traveled back to New York City for George Harrison's Concert for Bangladesh. Word is that Bob Dylan had warned the Madison Square Garden staff about keeping Richard and Rick away from the backstage area. Dylan didn't want them causing any trouble with the performers, "trouble" meaning the chemical kind.

A one-off festival in Toronto on August 21 found the Band as the headliner in their old stomping grounds. Richard met with family and friends backstage before the show and put on a fine performance for his people, highlighted by an anthemic "I Shall Be Released." A clear-sounding recording of most of the Band's set circulates. A big, fat, "Up on Cripple Creek" showcased extra-exuberant vocals by Rick, Levon, and Richard.

After two large outdoor performances at racetracks in Trenton, New Jersey, and Monticello, New York, of which no tapes exist, the Band retired to Woodstock to prepare for a fall tour. They updated their set list and added songs from *Cahoots*, which was released on September 15, 1971. "Life Is a Carnival" was installed as the set opener, and "Shootout in Chinatown," "Smoke Signal," and "Where Do We Go from Here?" debuted on the tour.

The fall run began on November 27, 1971, on the West Coast at Civic Auditorium in San Francisco. On December 1, at Arie Crown Theater in Chicago, Richard had cut his hair and appears silhouetted in the amateur Super 8 footage that has made the rounds online. An audience recording of the show is also available and contains a few rare performances.

The Band in a greenhouse on Albert Grossman's property, date unknown. *Courtesy of the Barry Feinstein estate*

"Shootout in Chinatown" is a treat to hear live. The groovy backing vocals and Robbie's guitar make the recording worth hunting down. The same goes for "Where Do We Go from Here?" Onstage it gains a plethora of emotion, which is lacking in its studio counterpart. Of the new songs, only "Life Is a Carnival" and "Smoke Signal" would stay in the set though the end of the month.

Concerts in Baltimore, Boston, and Philadelphia would lead up to shows at the Academy of Music in New York City. A tape exists from Boston on December 6, but you need a high-end pair of bootleg ears to enjoy it. After the Philadelphia performance, the Band headed back to Woodstock. They had invited New Orleans legend Allen Toussaint, who had arranged the horns on the studio version of "Life Is a Carnival," up to town.

Toussaint had been called back to compose horn charts for the Academy of Music concerts from a cabin on Robbie's property. The Band planned on having a five-piece horn section of New York's best players to back them for the second set of each of the four nights. Just two days before Christmas, the Band headed down the salt-stained New York State Thruway to Ultrasonic Studios in Hempstead, New York, with Toussaint and the horns in tow to rehearse the set.

During the rehearsals, there was no attempt at "In a Station," "We Can Talk," or "Tears of Rage." It appears that Richard had given up on getting any of his songs in the live program or having them adorned with horns.

ROCK OF AGES

The Academy of Music was on East 14th Street between Irving Place and Third Avenue in Manhattan. The 3,400-seat former movie theater was the site of several stellar rock 'n' roll performances, with the Band's concerts highlighting the list. The Band played there for four nights in December and rang in the new year on the final evening. Nerves were frayed in the group as they prepared for their opening night on the 28th. By the time they reached the last song on the final evening, no one could touch them. In what would become a theme for the group, the Band neatly tied up a musical era with a meaningful event.

After a concert opening of "Up on Cripple Creek," the throbbing introduction to "The Shape I'm In" gets the crowd stomping their feet. "Shape" is played as close to perfection as it could be, with Richard changing the lyric from "Come downtown, have to rumble in the alley" to "Come to New York . . ." Richard testifies from the pulpit of his Clavinet, the Band in full gallop. While the opening sets remain static, the playing is deadly, and Richard soars on versions of "Time to Kill," "Rockin' Chair," and "I Shall Be Released." "Smoke Signal" is also a highlight of the first set, with Richard moving over to play some disorienting organ and Garth to piano for a hazy bit of jamming with Robbie.

On *Stage Fright*'s "The Rumor," Richard takes the chorus break that begins with "Close your eyes" and holds it up for inspection in the stage lights, allowing the crowd to bask in its warm glow. As the song moves through the verses, Richard's vocal intensity increases with each pass. His piano playing, like a soft tire rolling across a warm stone road, adheres to the shape of the song. The final chorus is a cathartic vocal release, Richard ringing a glorious bell, sliding into falsetto, and wordlessly singing the song to a spectacular conclusion.

When the horn section joins the group for the second half of the show, any nervousness by the group disappears into the percolating groove and pumping horns of "Life Is a Carnival." The music swirls around the room, and the Band is beaming. Richard and Levon lock eyes across the top of Richard's grand piano, with Richard throwing Levon a sideways grin and a nod, which Levon answers with a cymbal crash and a flourish of sticks.

The horns ornately decorate the walls of "King Harvest," "Caledonia Mission," "The Night They Drove Old Dixie Down," and "Across the Great Divide," nailing the songs down and hanging new artwork from their familiar studs. All the second-set songs receive definitive readings over the course of the four nights, with the horn players a part of the Band, trading melody lines and adorning the arrangements with intricate playing.

Richard on stage at the Academy of Music, New York City, December 1971.
Courtesy of Ernst Hass / Iconoclast

Richard at the Academy of Music, New York City, December 1971. *Photograph by John Scheele; all rights reserved*

In footage officially released in 2003 from the December 30 concert, Richard is dressed in stylish floral threads and is shown singing "King Harvest," throwing his body into the downbeats. During "Don't Do It," he undulates in time with the music while the long fingers of his left hand tap out the individual bass notes of the song. In the classic clip of "The W. S. Walcott's Medicine Show" from the same night, Richard's bounding piano is a Slinky, as if sent down a staircase fast and wobbling its way toward the end of the song. He is all shoulders, lunging in place to the beat.

Between songs, he sips from a series of cups he had set along his piano. But he was touching the alcohol to his lips only for the taste and not swallowing the booze. He brings his best efforts to the performances at the Academy of Music.

Taplin said in his memoir, "The last truly great moment with the Band for me was a week of performances at New York's Academy of Music at the end of December. Because every night was being recorded, Richard, Levon, and Rick stayed on their best behavior."

In addition to the resulting Rock of Ages live album, there is an expanded look at the entire run. Released in 2013, *Live at the Academy of Music 1971 (The Rock of Ages Concerts)* includes an updated look at the original release and an entire raw soundboard mix of the show from New Year's Eve.

The full New Year's Eve show is a special collection of the Band's salvo of albums and performances since 1968. Six songs from the evening ended up on the *Rock of Ages* album. After a prophetic and slamming version of "(I Don't Want to) Hang Up My Rock and Roll Shoes," a familiar figure emerges from the shadows dressed in dungarees and wearing mirrored aviator sunglasses. Once the crowd picks up on what was going down, they detonate. Bob Dylan who hadn't been onstage with the Band since his appearance at the Isle of Wight in 1969 joins the group. Richard lights a smoke and saunters to the drums, while Levon picks up his mandolin, and the six men do their best to conjure up some basement alchemy.

Opening with the Saugerties outtake "Down in the Flood," Dylan and the Band play a rough-and-ready—yet rocking and poignant—twenty-minute set. Richard keeps the groove knee-deep during "Down in the Flood," combining well-timed rim shots with hollow tom-tom hits.

Just like during the summer of '67 sessions at 2188 Stoll Road, Richard stays on drums for a rare version of "When I Paint My Masterpiece" and a raucous slam dance through "Don't Ya Tell Henry." The latter is a good-time stomp, with Levon and Dylan sharing vocal duties. Richard kicks out triplets on the bass drum and accessorizes with splashes on the hi-hat, his drumrolls spectacularly quirky and well timed.

For the final song, Levon returns to his place at the drum kit, and Dylan and his Hawks launch into a tune that Dylan said they hadn't played in sixteen years. The group starts the rock rolling downhill and blasts into an appropriate version of "Like a Rolling Stone." Richard falls in like a gentle rain and nails the recognizable opening piano lick.

The crowd joins in to create an epic sing-along that puts a wax stamp on the Academy of Music performances. The Band feels good, and Richard walks off the stage with a look of exhausted satisfaction.

The Band's sense of their place in the rock pantheon was solid, Taplin said in 2022:

> They were very aware that people thought the Band was the most amazing thing in the world. . . . I don't think anybody doubted that they were making great music. The problem is, as everyone knows, ultimately the road is a hard mistress. You have to get up and keep doing it again. And again. And again. And maybe it's not quite as inspiring as the first time. It becomes more like a job.

Music was never a job for Richard. It was life. He told the *Woodstock Times*:

> We were drifting farther apart. We weren't putting our hearts into it. That's what I claim has been missing in music for all this last stretch. . . . Soul. What they used to call soul music. Whatever color they paint it, soul has been missing. And I know about it because it's the only kind of music I can play. I can't do hack stuff unless it's for humor.

In a series of career-defining concerts designed to embody a cross section of the Band's career, it's unfathomable that not one Richard Manuel composition was performed over the four nights.

The shows were wildly successful, and there was more than enough material to compile a live album. The Band felt confident about the tapes and planned to reconvene sometime in the new year. Still, everybody looked forward to a break. A decade had passed since Beak Manuel had left Stratford to join the Ronnie Hawkins traveling circus. Richard's musical course had traversed an incredible creative landscape. He changed from musical interpreter and sideman to songwriter and rock star, and then back to musical interpreter and sideman.

Winter in Woodstock, 1971. *Courtesy of the Barry Feinstein estate*

Chapter 11
THE GREAT PRETENDER (1972-1976)

> I could feel them wondering why I wasn't dead yet, and it made me uncomfortable. They probably weren't thinking any such thing, but a man gets paranoid when he has 300 hangovers a year.
>
> —Charles Bukowski, *Women*

Richard walked off the Academy of Music stage feeling like he had just been a part of a major event. The ambient heat of the audience and the reverberations of "Like a Rolling Stone" were still rippling around the hall, and everybody was high. He had experienced a similar kind of feeling at the conclusion of the 1966 Dylan tour: it was a strange mixture of giddy anticipation and existential dread. Or maybe he just needed a drink.

The backstage area was a cornucopia of carnival scents and sounds, teeming with action. An assortment of New York City's artistic elite and endearingly seedy slinked around, waiting for an opportune moment to secure their musical prey. Robbie and Jon Taplin were discussing business at a small table in a far corner of the greenroom. Levon was sucking on a smoke at the catering table, throwing together a heaping plate of grub. Rick was bouncing kinetically from group to girls in the backstage area, gesticulating excitedly as he told a group of friends the details about the Band's concluding set with Bob Dylan.

Both Dylan and Garth had already made hasty clandestine exits from the venue. Richard took a hearty swig from his sweating bottle of Grand Marnier and winked hard with an off-balance grin at Bob Cato, who had done the artwork on *Stage Fright*, as he sauntered by. He took a seat on the couch, lit his smoke, and leaned back into the soft corner cushions. Letting out a heavy guffaw, he stretched his arms up to the ceiling with long fingers laced and yelled across the room, "Looks like we fooled 'em again, huh Rick?"

Levon said in his memoir that after the Academy of Music concerts, "for all intents and purposes, Richard had retired." Extenuating circumstances contributed to his withdrawal from the Band. Richard simply no longer enjoyed the labors of creating music. He had fallen victim to the stereotypical trappings of fame. What was once inspiration had become an obligation, and that in turn killed his enthusiasm for the music. His disappointment only drove him deeper into the ditch of addiction.

John Simon recalled to *Rolling Stone* in 1986: "There was a lot of pain in his personal life, too. I've seen him so messed up sometimes, he'd be so shaken, that I couldn't imagine he could muster any strength to perform."

The fall was swift; only six months earlier, Richard had said to Caroline Boucher of *Disc and Music Echo*:

> We spend a lot of time writing and arranging, which works better. We'd rather put out fewer things that we are satisfied with than pouring out a lot of hot discs we'd be sorry for later. . . . Robbie and I write together or separately. Our music has come from a variety of influences, really. I think it's just the most comfortable type of music for our collection of people. We're not trying to out-rock anybody, or to outdo them. We let it be as natural as we can.

It appeared that the spirit of collaboration was still something the Band strived for; yet, in a short period of time, it had deteriorated completely. Instead of playing the disgruntled bandmate, Richard was the agreeable sideman. He had no grasp on the internal workings of the music business, nor did he care to have one. His affairs were messy, and he spent his royalty checks frivolously on parties for himself and a host of others. He celebrated the Band's 1972 break by immediately drinking himself into a place where he was in no condition to work. He couldn't cope with his responsibilities, and he couldn't be bothered with fulfilling his obligations. While he had gotten it together for the Academy of Music performances, it didn't take long for him to fall down the well. The year 1972 would not be a good one for Richard Manuel.

As the Band had changed, so had Woodstock. The town boiled over with unsavory remnants of the counterculture. The once personable and artistic community had turned suspicious and paranoid. In the wake of the Woodstock festival, spooky seekers in search of enlightenment now draped themselves over the area. Richard was the perfect pushover and conspirator for these cosmic dropouts. He was charitable and loved to hear everybody's story. Especially if you were down on your luck. He saw the good in everybody: dealers, groupies, artists, musicians, or wayward cretins, Richard let everybody in.

Robbie had separated himself from the pack. He was traveling in and out of Woodstock while attending high-society mixers and educating himself on the details of art and film. Richard, on the other hand, was losing traction on the icy slopes of the musical mountain he had worked so hard to conquer. Soon, he would be covered in the remnants of its resulting avalanche.

In the early months of the new year, Richard sat insentient on his couch, with shades drawn tight, and he was hummed into sleep by the electronic murmur of the television. Jane fought a losing battle to keep the house in any semblance of order. Richard thumbed through the channels, often in a boozy, narcotic haze, landing on random television shows, where he would work himself into laughing fits with whoever would sit among the squalor with him. He wasn't upset; he was complacent.

All the responsibility for the home and for young Paula fell to Jane. She and Richard were constantly moving around Woodstock, with brief stops in multiple locations around the area. Jane tried to hold the marriage together but couldn't do it by herself. If Richard did leave the house, it was to visit Bobby Charles and Michael Pollard, who had a party place over on Tinker Street.

Richard was paranoid and always thought that something was amiss. If he dwelled on something long enough, he felt like it would eventually manifest, and that frightened him. He woefully underrepresented his own importance in a band that he was an essential element of. He hated himself for his condition but was too far gone to change it.

After the Band's final concerts and conclusion of their recording obligations in 1972, there was nothing on the horizon for Richard except self-imposed quarantine. The real or imagined psychological squeeze that he felt as a result of management or group pressures absolutely hindered his ability to remain creative. John Simon said in a 2012 article in California's *Anderson Valley Advertiser*, "Richard used to write beautiful songs in the early days. I wouldn't say he was intimidated out of writing, but there was a dynamic to their personalities that resulted in Robbie writing more and more of the Band's material."

Concerns about songwriting attribution or money management were out of Richard's grasp. In his mind, he and his bandmates were always contributing to a greater whole. It wasn't until Levon started to outwardly verbalize his issues about Albert Grossman and the group's songwriting credits that Richard looked up from the bottle. He still wouldn't complain.

In early 1972, Richard and Jane moved from their house on Maverick Road to one on Plochmann Lane, right across the street from where Levon Helm's studio would later be built. Plochmann Lane quickly became a house of horrors for the Manuels. Jane remembered one shady Woodstock character who would show up early every morning to visit with Richard with a bottle of Grand Marnier in tow. From that moment forward, the day would be chalked up as a complete loss. Richard would let the friend in the house, and the duo would spend the day drinking and playing darts.

The parties would continue into the early-morning hours, with Richard completely oblivious to his wife and daughter sleeping upstairs. Jane said that during this period, things were simply bad. Richard was not only drinking heavily but troubled by something unknown.

Drugs and alcohol anesthetized Richard's guilt and numbed his self-esteem and, eventually, his musical ambition. In 2023, Eric Clapton offered an insightful view of the struggles Richard faced:

> I think, with someone that is that proficient, it's the in-between times that's dangerous, if you're not actually busy with your craft. Say you're on your own with your instrument. It doesn't necessarily mean you're going to be compelled to play it. You can sit in a room with your instrument and do nothing and get depressed. Taking that first step toward the instrument, picking it up and not really knowing what you're going to do, is really dangerous ground, and it can go either way. And when you pick it up, it can be a real disappointment. Or it can be inspiring. It's like rolling the dice.
>
> With Richard, that would have been the daily dilemma, the in-between times. Then, when you've got something that will change that feeling, if you lay your hands on a substance or a drink that will delay that process, or just put it back a few hours, then you're really in the clutches of something else.

By mid-1972, Richard found himself more interested in feeling good than putting in work on musical ideas that may or may not ever come to fruition. The Band had dried up, and much of the reason fell on Richard, but not all of it. He wasn't hurting for cash, or recognition. Jane said, "Richard was not a self-promoting kind of guy." If he had any lingering issues, it was getting his work to be considered seriously.

Having other artists perform his songs brought him some success. In addition to Cass Elliot singing "Orange Juice Blues," Gene Clark recorded a version of "Tears of Rage," and Karen Dalton covered "In a Station" on her 1971 record, *In My Own Time*. A few chubby royalty checks and no one checking up on Richard fueled his freedom and creeping apathy.

He didn't stop composing; he just stopped collaborating on songs with Robbie and offering his music to the Band. It's an odd juxtaposition that as Robbie was struggling to wake his slumbering muse, Richard was holding his underwater. No matter the narrative that has developed in the intervening years, Robbie and Richard needed each other. The Band required both to be present in order to fully function as a collaborative, just as it needed each individual member operating at his peak level to be the best group it could be.

In what would become an endless cycle for the next four years of the group's existence, Richard felt guilty for letting his bandmates down, which in turn led him to get wasted. He would recover, only to get discouraged again, rinse and repeat. Robbie said to *Rolling Stone* in 1986, after Richard's death:

> He was an extremely creative person and was almost a victim of his creative ability. It controlled him somehow, which made him real good at what he did, but sometimes you didn't know if the horse was pulling the cart or how it was really working.

Regardless of what was expected from Richard at work, one thing that hadn't changed for him in the years since he left Stratford was his love of classic R&B singles. Stage manager Bill Scheele's brother John was a photographer and had become a close friend of the group. He and Richard hung out often, spun records, and got loose, giving John witness to the eccentric approach Richard took with his records.

Richard would put the 45s on his turntable, set the speed to 33⅓, and let the songs play in a decelerated fashion. Eager to share his insight with John, he'd say, "Listen to this," and start to sing along to the slowed-down versions. Two songs that Richard mined for inspiration were Smokey Robinson's 1960 single "Who's Lovin' You" and Johnny Nash's then-current chart offering "I Can See Clearly Now." Through the slowed-down music, he was able to immerse himself in the nuance and approaches of the singer. The melodies were stretched and every detail was available for inspection. Richard discovered particular intonations and hidden complexities in the songs he thought appropriate to study. He could then incorporate his findings into his own vocal approaches.

Sometime that spring, Robbie called a band meeting at Turtle Creek, a smaller studio space on the pastoral Bearsville Studio property. The first two meetings were postponed; Richard didn't even show up for the third one. According to Robbie's memoir, after Rick and Levon admitted that one of the issues facing the group was that they had scored some heroin, Levon said, "I believe ol' Beak's done bit off a bit more than he can chew already."

To straighten him out, Grossman sent Mason Hoffenberg, who had just completed a successful stint in rehab, to stay with Richard and provide him with some companionship. Hoffenberg was a semifamous counterculture author who had written the popular book *Candy* with Terry Southern in 1958. Through his art, Hoffenberg fell in with Dylan and his crew in the 1960s and by 1972 had taken up with the Band in Woodstock.

Richard was hanging with a motley crew of Woodstock's underworld. He was living a cloistered existence. Admittedly, everyone else around the Band was too self-involved to notice. Richard held the group and his family hostage and sank lower into self-pity and self-loathing.

A November 1973 *Playboy* article documented Hoffenberg's time in Woodstock and, perhaps unintentionally, his peripheral view of the situation conveyed the precarious state Richard was in. Hoffenberg said:

> I'm supposed to head off all the juvenile dope dealers up here who hang around rock stars. So I answer the phone and say Richard's not here. He's not allowed to answer the phone. And I go around privately and tell them to leave him alone because he's really going to kill himself. But if they actually come over to the house, he can't say no. He's brilliant, that guy. An incredible composer.
>
> But we just sit around watching *The Dating Game*, slurping down the juice, laughing our asses off, then having insomnia, waking up at dawn with every weird terror and anxiety you can imagine. The four other guys in the Band are serious about working, and he's really hanging them up. They can't work without him and there's no way to get him off his ass. He feels bad about it. He's just strung out.

Grossman didn't have a good track record with addicted rock stars, and the Hoffenberg connection did nothing but connect two artists with addiction problems. Jane said in 2023 that Hoffenberg circled in Richard's orbit but that he never lived in the Manuels' home.

Regardless, Richard was shackled. He would wake up in the middle of the night, soaked in cold sweat and prisoner of his night terrors. He was going through withdrawals, hard. Hoffenberg said to *Playboy*:

> He's really fucked up. I was in better shape before I moved in with him, and the idea was that I was supposed to help pull him out of the thing he's in. . . . He can't do anything. He's drinking like I never saw anybody drink. And now I'm drinking a lot.

Hoffenberg confirmed that Richard had kicked heroin, but according to Robbie's memoir, Richard had started shooting cocaine to combat the withdrawals. Jane told Barney Hoskyns in 1993, "Everyone thought it was amusing to watch this guy drowning." Even she, the only one who truly understood what was happening to Richard, was powerless to help him.

Richard was *so* out of control that it became a joke. He became a joke.

He was still a member of the Band, but even that was being called into question. Robbie said in *Testimony*, "We called him daily. We pleaded with him. We yelled at him. . . . We even discussed having to replace Richard in the group and went over to his house for an ultimatum." Everybody in the Band knew they couldn't replace Richard, but what else could they do?

The Works

Creem writer Jim Brodey went to Woodstock during the Band's downtime, with the goal of compiling a book of tall tales and road stories from the Band. While the work never came to fruition, a few excerpts escaped in some counterculture rags, with the main subjects of the tales given aliases. To call Brodey's views of the Band's Woodstock a debauchery would be an understatement. There were a lot of ideas in the air, but no firm direction or group vision.

The constant badgering and threats finally worked, and according to Robbie's memoir, Richard rejoined the land of the living. The guys started to meet up at Turtle Creek, and Robbie said in *Testimony*:

> The idea was to work on new material and try to get everybody involved. For a few weeks we tried all kinds of different approaches to discovering new songs. It made Richard feel discouraged, not being able to write, and he stopped coming.

Robbie was composing an ambitious musical project titled *Works*, which seemed to have been lost on some members of the group. It was a departure from the Band's usual approach, with only instrumental pieces and movements. While the music continued to roll around Robbie's consciousness for the next few years, the Band could never get a firm enough grasp on it to keep the project from slipping through their fingers.

"Two Piano Song," with Garth and Robbie on the pianos, would eventually be the only piece from the sessions to be released, appearing on *A Musical History*.

In August 1972, the Band released *Rock of Ages*, the resulting live album from the December 1971 Academy of Music shows. The record is a definitive live appraisal of the Band at its best. Richard's vocal timbre on the album was the perfect combination of youthful power and seasoned grace, his piano playing the ideal canvas for Garth to color.

Across the Borderline

In the early 1970s, the Woodstock community was a beautifully incestuous musical hive of cross-pollination. Everybody knew the Band, and there was no degree of separation among friends, neighbors, and bandmates in the town.

Jon Gershen was a singer-songwriter-guitarist who was part of the late '60s / early '70s Woodstock music scene. He and his brother Dave, along with bassist Tony Brown (of *Blood on the Tracks* fame), played the local clubs with their band, the Montgomeries. Jon and Dave would later go on to form the group Borderline with well-known musician Jim Rooney.

Gershen first met Richard in the fall of 1969 through Van Morrison. Morrison had taken a liking to the music of the Montgomeries and one day took Jon up to Richard's house to meet his friend. Gershen's first impressions were that of a guy who lived and loved music. In 2023 he said, "After some preliminary exchanges, he went right to the upright piano. He was working on some stuff, and I just felt like this guy was all music. Music was in his veins. He was riffing on some interesting ideas."

In the close-knit Woodstock community, it wasn't a stretch for musicians to cross currents. A couple of years after their initial meeting, when the time came for Gershen and his brother to document their own musical statement at Bearsville Studios, it was the natural thing to get assistance from the local talent.

In September 1972, Richard came out of hibernation to play some funky piano under the alias Dick Handle for Borderline's 1973 LP, *Sweet Dreams and Quiet Desires*. Grossman insisted on the alias for contractual reasons. Garth Hudson also played on the record under the name Campo Malaqua. The record also featured contributions from Ben Keith, Vassar Clements, Billy Mundi, and a host of other gifted musicians. The album is a wonderfully rendered Woodstock moment.

Gershen said in 2023 that Richard fit in seamlessly and that what he brought to the table was exactly what he had hoped for. Richard spent the entire day with the group and was fully invested in the vision they had for their music. Gershen continued, "There was not an ego anywhere in sight. This was not a person on any sort of a trip."

The first song of the day was Dave Gershen's "Don't Know Where I'm Going," a song with heavy Band overtones in part because of Richard's piano part. Gershen remembered:

> [That song] was right up his street. . . . He played his heart out. It makes that song his song. His playing is a big part of why that song works. I remember him getting that shoulder thing going and realizing it was like watching some kind of whole-body soul engine churning out the funky licks. He really nailed it.

Attention then turned to Jon Gershen's "Dragonfly," a song with a complex arrangement and a departure from Richard's usual parts in the Band. Gershen said:

> By the second run-through, he was already off and running. He wasn't hanging back. He was in the thick of it, and he was very creative with the parts he was playing. . . . He wasn't just playing the padding chords; he was doing interesting stuff with his right hand and coming up with these cool licks. . . . We ran through it a few times until he zeroed in on the emotional center of the song. He was able to add a unique gravity to the track that moved it to a whole other level. Even so, he would ask me after listening to the playback if I wanted him to do another take . . . he thought maybe he could do better. I was like, "Are you kidding?" It was perfect! This guy was giving us everything we could ever ask for, and he wanted to be sure we were happy. His was a generous spirit.

After Richard set his piano parts into place on "Dragonfly," the group worked on another of Jon Gershen's songs, "As Long as It's You and Me." They listened to the work that Borderline had already done on the track in the control room, and Richard said he heard something in it that called for Clavinet. Gershen said:

> He came up with the idea of using the Clavinet on this one. It never had occurred to me to use it, but as soon as he started playing, I realized what a good call it was. It had that strange otherworldly sound that right away telegraphed that something unusual was happening with this piece of music. Because the chorus was quite rhythmic, we decided Richard should switch to acoustic piano to give it the percussive drive it needed, which he did to great effect. So much so that we had him record a second track, and we ended up using both blended together. It was pure joy working with him, and he made an enormous contribution to the magic of that album.

After checking out a playback of his part, in his typically self-deprecating style, Richard said, "Well, if you want, I can do it again." There was no need for that. The contrast between Richard's confident contributions and his quick dismissal of them was memorable to Gershen.

Gershen told *BigO* magazine in 2000, "Really, Richard was an unbelievably intuitive and talented player in his own right. He would find the soul of a song instantly and enhance it with his unique style."

With the session winding down for the day, the group retired to the Bearsville control room to listen to the results. Richard saw a guitar in the corner, sauntered over to the instrument, smoke dangling from his lips, picked it up in his large hands, and placed it strings-up on his lap.

Gershen recalled, "Richard just started playing it." The melody line that Richard pulled out of the instrument was the squiggly slide part from the Band's "Thinking Out Loud," recorded in the very same studio fourteen months earlier.

Around this same time, Richard also contributed to Bobby Charles's self-titled record, which was recorded at Bearsville Studio and produced by Rick Danko and John Simon. He played piano on the swinging "Long Face," which also featured his bandmates Levon, Rick, and Garth. He also played on the song "Grow Too Old," which he would later go on to cover in his 1985 solo shows.

Interestingly, instrumentalist and friend Marty Grebb recalled in a 2014 letter to Richard's estate that Richard had expressed to him an interest in recording a solo record during this period of Band downtime. A strange comment, considering the belief that Richard wasn't composing music during this period.

By the dawning of 1973, after additional failed attempts at recording Robbie's ambitious *Works* project, the group reconvened at Bearsville Studios in an attempt to get something useful on tape. The group's only option at this dire point was to revert to simpler times by delving into the backlog of their favorite songs for inspiration. New songs were few, if any; Robbie's muse was napping, and Richard was discouraged with the sessions. What better way to touch off a creative fire than to get back to being the hippest cover group with the coolest musical taste.

THE MOONDOG MATINEE WITH THE BEAK

In order to prime the pump and heat the hearth, the guys worked out a variety of songs at Bearsville Studios in late winter. By March 1973, the Band had recorded enough songs for a proper covers album. The sessions were made up of old favorites and songs from the not-so-recent past that the group could really get into while still respecting the originals. When they were on the road doing sound checks, the Band would play similar songs and tributes to their favorite artists. Bill Scheele remembers the Band really getting down during these private preshow rituals. The end goal of the Bearsville sessions was to release an album that would seem like the group's favorite jukebox.

Richard threw himself into the sessions wholeheartedly. He loved to sing his favorite songs, and the low-pressure sessions allowed him to remove himself from the anxiety of instant creativity. He sang well and drummed on a couple of songs. He even got down on his knees and squawked Robbie's wah-wah pedal by hand on "Holy Cow."

There was no real plan, just a "shout out some song titles and see what happens" kind of vibe. This was as close as the Band had gotten to the spirit of collaboration that had been missing since Sammy Davis Jr.'s house. Sometimes you must move back in order to move forward, and by revisiting his influences, Richard was able to ignite the fuse of the ambition he had lost.

Richard's lead vocals on the record reveal a deeper insight. He had come full circle with the Band, and now he was back to where he began, singing Bobby Bland. The Band recorded his "Share Your Love," just like when Richard crooned it with the Revols at the Blue Water Lounge, but now with better gear.

The music of Bland was imprinted on Richard's being, and it felt good to sing one of his favorite numbers. He had grown into the song's substantial shoes and effortlessly outlined Bland's dramaticism with the colors of his own voice. Richard was proud of the way his version of the song turned out. Tantalizingly, two other Bobby Bland cuts were considered for the album: 1959's "I'll Take Care of You" and 1962's "Yield Not to Temptation." The mind sweats at the thought of Richard singing these cuts, with the Band lending their sympathetic instrumentation.

The Leiber-Stoller rocker "Saved" is a high-tempo boogie and flippant song of repentance. The tale is about a hard-partying sinner who has finally seen the light of the Lord and celebrates his redemption in song. The Band celebrates in a joyous double-time groove while Richard sings with a grit he hadn't dug up since 1965. Garth fills the room with a plethora of praise, and

Robbie tosses a weighted solo into the donation plate. The irony of the lyrics was not lost on Richard, who got a kick out of singing it.

If one cut on the album epitomized the shape that Richard Manuel was in, it was the Band's cover of the Platters' hit "The Great Pretender," a classic song that Richard had loved since his Revols days. He immortalized the song on *Moondog Matinee* with one of his most confident vocals ever captured on magnetic tape. Richard begins the song playing majestic chords while Garth spreads the theme across the progression. Richard's voice caresses the grooves of the original 1955 single and explores every nuance. He pushes for the note, his resonant voice breaking in all the right places, until reaching and touching the cloudiest falsetto during the lyric "too real when I feel what my heart can't conceal." As Richard sang "The Great Pretender," he poured out all the pent-up musicality of his hiatus.

The finished album, *Moondog Matinee*, was released in November 1973. The Band wasn't alone in revisiting their past; rock 'n' roll seemed to be lacking inspiration across the board that year. Several artists, including John Lennon, who also recorded a covers record, returned to the music that had originally turned them into musicians.

The Band had its own reasons for the direction it was going. Levon Helm told *Gritz* magazine the following in 2002:

> You know, nobody gave us credit for it—the critics certainly didn't, and the record company, they didn't know what was going on, anyway. That was all we could do at the time. We couldn't get along—we all knew that fairness was a bunch of shit. We all knew we were getting screwed, so we couldn't sit down and create no more music.

Summer Jams

After completing *Moondog Matinee* in June, the Band came out of a sixteen-month performing deep freeze and thawed out in the 1973 summer heat for the concert event of the decade, Summer Jam. The brainchild of rock impresario Bill Graham, a dream lineup for the ages gathered at the Watkins Glen racetrack: the Grateful Dead, the Band, and the Allman Brothers Band. Leon Russell was originally tagged for the show, but Jerry Garcia pushed for the Band to join in on the festivities. By the opening day of the festival, an estimated 600,000 people clogged up the New York State Thruway, blocked back roads, and generally disrupted central New York, all in the name of rock.

By July 27, the night before the concert, the Band arrived at the 95-acre festival site with their entourage and all their gear. With already 150,000 people on hand, the Allman Brothers Band asked Graham if they could do a sound check. Since all the bands would be playing through the Grateful Dead's massive PA system, it made sense to give it a test run.

Graham told the assembled musicians that all they had to do was get onstage and play, so the impromptu sound checks slowly became a full-on concert event. The Band played for a half hour, highlighted by a fully fleshed-out, piano-driven instrumental jam.

After a run through "The Night They Drove Old Dixie Down," Rick Danko starts a springy ascending bass line, which Richard immediately jumps on with a heavy left hand on the keys. A cool groove coagulates, and Garth and Robbie start to solo over the top of the established changes as a high-pressure jam unfolds. A soundboard source of the jam is sonically acceptable, and Richard is documented trilling his keys and even taking a folky piano solo midway through the instrumental. After a reading of "Raining in My Heart," the Band pulls it together for practice runs of "Don't Do It" and "W. S. Walcott." The Allman Brothers and Grateful Dead follow, both playing excellent sets of impromptu music.

Bill Scheele told Alison Liscoe Nottingham of Cleveland.com in 2010, "When the Band was doing sound checks, they would play some of the funkiest music around. There is nothing like rhythm-and-blues music to make you want to move. They had such flair and were tight as a band." What was usually a private case of the Band "tuning the room" became a full-blown preparty at the Glen.

As the day of the concert dawned, Richard wasn't handling the pressure of the moment well. He arrived at the venue with midnight-dark shades and got properly hammered in the backstage RV. A valiant effort was made to sober him up with strong cups of coffee before the Band took the stage. Levon said in his memoir:

> Richard was in a period, as Rick would say, which meant that he was drinking pretty hard, but once he got started, man: drums, piano, play it all, sing, do the

lead in one of them high, hard-assed keys to sing in. Richard just knew how a song was supposed to go. Structure, melody, he understood it.

The coffee must have been strong because Richard recovered quickly, and the Band played a rough but ripping set for the assembled 600,000 crazies who had just witnessed a three-hour-plus jam extravaganza by the Grateful Dead. While the Band's set had some rough spots, every song at the Summer Jam had a little something extra. Whether it was an extended spin through a verse, a unique flourish during a solo, or just a bit more oomph in the singing, the Band rose to the occasion. The circulating audience recording is well balanced, with Richard heavy in the mix.

After an introduction by Grateful Dead manager Sam Cutler and Bill Graham, the Band absolutely tears into Chuck Berry's "Back to Memphis." The entire group explodes, and Richard prefaces the opening verse with a rattling rock 'n' roll flourish up and down the keys. The audience tape perfectly captures the group's enthusiasm throughout their extended set.

A door-slamming "The Shape I'm In" erupts from the stage. Richard plays with the lyrics and sings, "Here *we* are back on the street" and "Two young kids might start a ruckus, you know they feel they're trying to *fuck* us." The Band's shared enthusiasm results in an explosive one-two opening punch.

Right after the rowdy debut of a powerful version of "Endless Highway," a rumbling summer storm settles over the city-sized crowd. The Band bails from the stage, and their equipment is covered with plastic sheeting. A bottle of Glenfiddich is passed around in the rain, and Garth takes a hearty swig and returns to the stage. He soothes the mud army with a prolific keyboard extravaganza, later named "Too Wet to Work," which precipitates its way to "Chest Fever."

An up-tempo instrumental jam develops after a high-stepping reading of "Across the Great Divide." All the Band members contribute to the improv, and the crowd responds to the large swells of sound coming from the stage. Both Robbie and Garth take confident solo breaks, and Richard plays a piano solo as a surprising diversion from the darker understated grooves. The instrumental sounds like a solid foundation to build a killer Band cut.

"Saved," freshly baked in the *Moondog Matinee* oven, blows off steam and gets the crowd swinging in the fields. Richard digs into both his piano and vocals ferociously. Rick, Richard, and Levon all holler in celebration during the choruses.

The Band takes it home with crushing versions of "Up on Cripple Creek," "This Wheel's on Fire," and a proper closer of "Rag Mama Rag." Inspired by the whole event, the Band looked forward to playing again. They'd get the chance soon enough.

After Summer Jam, the Band played two additional concerts with the Grateful Dead. Soundboard recordings of both nights at Roosevelt Stadium in New Jersey circulate unofficially. The show on July 31 is a bit sloppy but an energetic affair. The group is not very accurate, but they put forth a valiant effort. Toward the end of the performance, they lock it in and finish in fine form.

Richard rallies for another redemptive version of *Moondog Matinee*'s "Saved," where he sings a raucous reading replete with Robertson and Hudson overtures. The performance peaks with a heavy stepping "Life Is a Carnival" before the Band—er, the Hawks—drops into a sure thing with an earnest version of Bobby Bland's "Share Your Love." Richard's voice wavers expressively, and he wrings out everything he has for a rare performance of the song.

The August 1 performance was a much-stronger affair, and the group extends their songs beyond the normal boundaries and even throws in an additional improvised instrumental for good measure. "The Shape I'm In," similar to the version at the Glen, explodes as an aggressive urban stomp. Richard breathlessly thanks the crowd at its conclusion.

"The Weight" has extra pep in its step and moves with a quicker gait than usual. Obviously inspired by the Grateful Dead's jamming skills, the Band premieres another shifty instrumental (named "Jersey Jam" on recordings) centered on a fuzzy Robertson lick and accompanying Danko bass line. This cool set of changes would have made a strong starting point for a track on a Band record . . . and it makes one wonder why they weren't.

A chunky reading of "Life Is a Carnival" is steadied by Levon's extraordinary tom-tom work. Richard steps forward for the final and best rendition of "Share Your Love" of the summer. His voice is emotionally dynamic, and the group frames his efforts perfectly. The show concludes with fresh, enthusiastic versions of "Cripple Creek" and "W. S. Wolcott," wrapping up a week of concerts that not only reinvented the Band but encouraged Richard's frayed sensibilities.

The Band steadied itself and got a desperately needed shot of inspiration. Ideas were bantered around about what to do next, and nobody wanted to lose the momentum. By the end of the summer, Bob Dylan called from Malibu after hearing about the massive Watkins Glen festival. Not long after the call, he invited Robbie out to talk about doing something together again.

Malibu

In the Band's constant search for the perfect recording environment, the group moved to Malibu. A second, more secretive reason for the defection was to remove Richard and his bandmates from the temptations and leeches of Woodstock. By the end of the summer, Robbie and Dylan were hatching plans for a tour, and soon the rest of the group traced the gold-flecked trail out west.

Similarly to the Hawks' relocation to Woodstock after the 1966 Dylan tour, Richard, Jane, and Paula moved to the glistening sands of Broad Beach, Malibu, where the same polarizing issues they had encountered in Woodstock came back with a vengeance.

But there was work to do. Rehearsals for the prospective tour took place at a Boy Scout camp in the mountains just north of Malibu. Bill Scheele recalled Richard setting up a pair of congas so he could also jam along on percussion. Increasingly unkempt, and while he always tried to give his best effort musically, physically he was spent.

During the early tour rehearsals, the idea for a record came into focus. Rob Fraboni, the engineer and producer who had worked with the likes of the Beach Boys, the Rolling Stones, and Joe Cocker, was not only one of the best studio cats in rock music at the time, but he was a huge admirer of the Band and jumped at the chance to work with the guys.

He was brought in as producer of the record, and on November 2, 1973, Dylan and the Band arrived at Village Recorders in Los Angeles, a former Masonic Temple turned recording studio. Richard took up his usual position at the piano and contributed drums on the fast version of "Forever Young" and "Never Say Goodbye." Fraboni recalled in 2023 that there was no thought put into Richard moving to the drum stool and that it just happened naturally: "I loved the way Richard played drums. It just had so much personality."

Dylan and the Band recorded the album in four days.

Fraboni was witness to the mysterious magic that took place when Dylan and the Band plugged in together:

> Dylan would go home after the session and write the songs that were going to be recorded the next day. That night. So, nobody ever saw the chord changes or anything—they were just watching his hands. Nothing was ever written on a piece of paper.

PLANET WAVES

Unbelievably, *Planet Waves* was the first official studio album by Bob Dylan and the Band. Highly underrated, it was a reinvention for both Dylan and the Band. There is a notable excitement in the playing and a looseness to the songs. Dylan's "Going, Going, Gone" sounds like a distant relative of "I'm Not There," from the Big Pink basement. Richard's piano playing is rich and blends perfectly with Garth's melodic superimpositions. His piano drifts in during the first verse and then comes on strong the rest of the way with free and beautiful additions. It's a high point of his playing on the record.

"Tough Mama" brings a backwoods beat and simmering swing that can come only from the country funk of the Band. "Hazel" is a delicate torch ballad and features the classic Band lineup in all their normal spots. Richard plays bell-like chord accompaniment throughout the verses.

While the Band's own compositional prowess had waned, its instrumental backing was better than ever. "Hazel," considered an underrated love song in Dylan's canon, is a perfect example of the Band's sympathetic backing and Richard and Garth's special synthesis.

On "Something There Is about You," the updated Dylan and the Band sonic aesthetic works in perfect harmony: Dylan's wiry acoustic scrubbing, Robbie's watery lead lines, and the masterful colors of Richard and Garth's two-for-one playing.

Dylan's "Forever Young" spotlights sympathetic and poignant playing by the Band. It's a dramatic reading of the song, a summation of their respective strengths. (Dylan and the Band also recorded a second version of it that opens the second side of the record. The clattering of Richard's rough-and-tumble drumming drives this honky-tonk version along cheerfully.)

Richard, whose name is somehow misspelled as "Manual" on the finished record sleeve, played fantastically and added something exclusive to each song. While *Planet Waves* sank beneath the surface foam of the eventual Tour '74, its aural gifts continue to reveal themselves after all these years.

Richard and Bob's dynamic hadn't changed since the 1966 tour, and their affection for each other was obvious to those involved in the sessions. Fraboni recalled that "Bob and Richard were very close. . . . Bob has a really dry sense of humor and Richard had a great sense of humor. . . . Bob and Richard would joke with each other quite a bit."

He recalled a time when Bob tried to overdub a vocal onto a track (which he never did successfully until 1979) and afterward walked into the control room, where Richard was listening on the couch. Without missing a beat, Richard looked at Bob with a huge smile and asked, "Why do you always sing sharp?" Bob looked Richard in the eye and said, "Because I want to!"

In what was becoming a recurring theme, Richard passed out under the piano at least once during the sessions but recovered admirably when duty called. Fraboni immediately knew something was a bit off in the dynamic of the Band, and later said, "Witnessing this deterioration was a big drag." Part of the issue, he said, was that "Robbie was doing what Richard should have been doing, what Richard used to be doing, and Robbie just pushed his way into that position. Nobody liked it, but of course Richard especially was upset by it."

Regardless of his condition, Richard never lost the knack to put the perfect voicing of a chord into the right position in a song. His innate ability to channel the muse was never in doubt. Fraboni, who had worked in the studio with another damaged genius, made an apt comparison in 2023:

> They [the Band] were so in awe of him. I know from working with them just even in those sessions on *Northern Lights*, even on *Planet Waves*, Richard's the one who would make the comments. There would be a take or something, and Richard would say something, and it would be spot on the money, like Brian Wilson. . . . Whatever he would say, musically it was just perfect. There wasn't a duff thing out of his mouth.
>
> He would come up with a lot of the parts too. When they were doing harmonies, Richard would find the notes. They could sing them, but Richard would find the harmonies and intervals. It was very evident that he was the musical leader of the group. Everybody contributed a certain amount, but he was the one, like the Brian Wilson of the situation, who came up with the real zingers. When he said something, it was like, "Yeah, that's a great idea."

When sessions for the album concluded, the focus for Richard was going back on the road with Dylan. Everyone held their breath in preparation for what adventures awaited them. Just before the tour began in January 1974, Jane and Paula returned to Woodstock before the chaos leveled up. Jane had no interest in staying in Malibu, especially without Richard.

Bob Dylan and the Band on Tour '74. *Courtesy of © Bob Gruen.com/www.bobgruen.com*

Tour '74

The Dylan and the Band 1974 tour was almost the end of Richard Manuel. It certainly signaled the conclusion of something. The insane excess and blatant disregard for his own well-being resulted in a downward slide that no one could stop. What's notable is that even as the Band—and Richard—emerged from a dark valley among the mountains of their careers, they played with a ferocity and focus that was noted by attendees and critics of the shows.

Richard came to play but was fighting demons whose battles are audible on tapes of the concerts, his talents and his condition in a constant tug-of-war in front of 15,000 people. There are some uneven performances and the unfortunate deterioration of his voice. Some of these factors can also be attributed to the fact the tour was long and grueling, and Richard wasn't in the best shape physically or mentally.

But Richard soldiered on, made the gig, and raised hell. Perhaps the thing that most aptly sums up the tour is a Barry Feinstein photo. Richard and Robbie face opposite points in a men's restroom in Somewhere, USA. Robbie primps in the mirror, sharp, ready for war. Richard pisses in the urinal, disheveled, hunched over, and ready to burst out laughing.

Nat Hentoff wrote for the *New York Times* on February 10, 1974:

> The Band, on the other hand, while uneven in the past, is now perhaps the most exhilaratingly "together" group in all of country rock. The rural church-like vocal

harmonies thrusting out into space like spears; the hard but loose percussion; the joyously unabashed honky-tonk piano; the careening interstitching instrumental skills of all these raffish minstrels; and above all, the Band's beat, are true phenomena. They stretch time, curve it around corners, lash it and caress it, all the while keeping up a whirlpool-like pulsation that almost had me up and dancing, and I don't dance no steps of any era.

The shows were powerful. There were moments of transcendence. Like old war buddies revisiting past battlefields, Dylan and the Band were satisfied with the success but were not inspired by any artistic revelations. They had done this before in '66 and were abused. It amused Dylan and the Band that the fans who tore them apart had finally caught up.

Dylan and the Band played forty shows in forty-three days from January 3 through February 14. The final shows were to be recorded for a live album. The decadence of the tour was matched only by the Crosby, Stills, Nash & Young megatour later in the year, which stole the Dylan and the Band blueprint. Dylan chartered the famed luxury hotel of the skies, "Starship," to fly the band across the country.

Richard was still Richard, and once the tour started, the hijinks on the private plane and in various backstage areas reached astronomical levels. He drank from his flagon of Grand Marnier like a gunslinger and often laughed so hard he'd pitch over and pass out. Rick was a key player in Richard's guileless excursions into fun and laughter. Richard and tour photographer Barry Feinstein, whom he'd known for almost a decade, would act out comedy routines in greenrooms throughout the tour, concluding a nightly laugh riot.

Robbie, Rick, and Richard, on Tour 74. *Photograph by John Scheele, all rights reserved*

On one tour stop, Richard wrapped himself up in telephone cords while making calls on several handsets, using both ears. He ran around the catering table tossing food at Feinstein before winding up with a huge bowl of fruit ready to launch. There were hangers-on, press, friends, management, security, and girls. Richard would put himself in the middle of everything.

Before shows he lounged around, snoozing backstage in his Toronto Maple Leafs jersey, which he loved so much it became a second skin. When the spirit moved him, Richard challenged many unsuspecting friends and visitors to arm-wrestling matches. He was deceptively strong and had huge hands; his forearms were well-defined trunks conditioned by years of piano workouts. He was virtually impossible to beat. He cast a frumpy visage, dressed like a wino tourist who was up to no good, with his old-man loafers, mismatched socks, and sleepy demeanor only a cover for his wrist-slamming winnings.

Onstage, the Band stuck to a static set throughout the tour, with few exceptions. The only Richard Manuel–composed song they played, "When You Awake," was a cowrite with Robbie Robertson from the second album. Richard sang lead on "King Harvest," "The Shape I'm In," and "I Shall Be Released." While the sets settled into predictability, the Band played with reckless abandon for their old boss, taking his songs around the bend on two wheels and blowing smoke.

After spending the last decade carefully developing their volume and interplay, the Band reverted to its "cut you up in the back alley" style of playing. Robbie said to author Michael Gray, "There was a thing that happened between Bob and the Band that, when we played together, we would just go into a certain gear automatically. It was instinctual, like you smelled something in the air, you know, and it made you hungry."

This Band is a totally different animal from the one that backed Dylan at Carnegie Hall in 1968, or even at the Academy of Music in 1971. Instrumental and technological changes discernible during the summer 1973 performances added a harder edge to the Band's updated sound. Levon's drumming was relentless, and Robbie returned to his Hawks style of pinched and aggressive soloing. Richard played more electric piano and Clavinet onstage and added a Moog synthesizer to his rig. Garth's keyboard spread had become a self-contained spacecraft of sound, comprising his Lowrey, electric pianos, and a plethora of synthesizers.

Most of the 1974 tour was documented by audience field recordings of varying quality. Soundboard tapes from Boston, New York, Oakland, and Los Angeles are also available in unofficial channels. In 2024, a complete collection of the available 1974 tour soundboards was released by Sony Music.

The tour began with two shows in Chicago on January 3 and 4, 1974. Versions of "Share Your Love," with Dylan on harmonica, and "Holy Cow" were featured. Both songs disappeared by the time the Band left town. Highlights of the Dylan set are a rare electric opening of "Hero Blues" and

Richard, Levon, Robbie, Bob, and Rick having a laugh backstage, 1974. *Courtesy of the Barry Feinstein estate*

rollicking versions of "Leopard-Skin Pill-Box Hat" and the new "Something There Is about You." A stadium-sized "Maggie's Farm" on the third finds Richard digging into his treasure chest of Jerry Lee Lewis licks.

Captured via an excellent audience recording, the concert in Philadelphia on the 6th began with both Richard and Levon playing drums for a driving "Ballad of Hollis Brown."

Spectacular performances by Dylan and the Band took place in Toronto on January 9 and 10, with Richard's family and friends in attendance. Both shows were recorded from the audience, and his piano pours dark and rich off the tape. Every piano lick ends in a curl. A rare and welcome reading of "It Takes a Lot to Laugh, It Takes a Train to Cry" during the first show is a highlight. Both "Rainy Day Women #12 & 35" and "Just Like Tom Thumb's Blues" feature a latticework of piano by Richard.

A major feature of the second night is the patient reading of Dylan's "As I Went Out One Morning," played for the only time on the tour. Additionally, Richard's piano graces a beautiful version of "Forever Young."

After the show, Richard reconnected with Hawks groupie Cathy Smith, who had a knack of popping up at the right . . . or wrong time (in 1986, she pleaded no contest in the overdose death of actor and comedian John Belushi). She was in a relationship with Gordon Lightfoot but had run into Rick and made her way to the Inn on the Park, where Dylan and the Band had reserved several floors.

Manuel's Law

Richard and Smith retired to his opulent room, where they reminisced about the Hawks days: the reefer, the girl swapping, the band babies. Smith discovered that Richard was taking Placidyl, a sleep aid, in addition to his alcohol intake. She struggled to understand Richard's depression, saying in her memoir, "There was only one thing wrong with him and that was his unhappiness."

Smith wrote that she spent the night with Richard, and he told her that he loved her and would be there for her. Smith chalked it up to the drugs and alcohol. She then remembered what she called "Manuel's Law" in her memoir, "which is, Richard Manuel can get drunk but never impaired."

After Toronto, the Band headed to Montreal and then down to Boston. The soundboard tapes from Boston on the 14th have Richard loud in the mix, and his playing is up for the challenge. He can be heard warming up the keys as the Band lights up the opening "Rainy Day Women #12 & 35." He also plays ambidextrous rolls in another stellar version of "Forever Young," a highlight of the set.

From the evening Boston show is an ascendant reading of "I Don't Believe You (She Acts Like We Never Have Met)," where the Band reached multiple and glorious climaxes. With the Band hitting its stride, the January 15 set from Landover was dominant and found Richard singing a powerful version of "King Harvest" that rates as one of the best performances of the tour. The rendition of "I Shall Be Released" is also sung with a delicate fragility, as are Richard's vocal contributions for the entire show.

The January 19 matinee show in Hollywood, Florida, is played with attitude. A monumental "Just Like Tom Thumb's Blues" peaks with a threatening Robbie solo, and Richard is right there responding to every single lick. The Band swings like a saloon door, and Richard shines on a honky "It Ain't Me Babe."

The Fort Worth concert on January 25 roars out of the gate with a thrashing version of "Most Likely You'll Go Your Way (and I'll Go Mine)," finding Richard and Robbie dueling it out in a flourish of licks. The audience recording perfectly captured the excitable ambiance of the event as well as Richard's muscular piano. Dylan and the Band had a storied history in Texas and appreciated the crowd's response. Later in the show, a strong version of the *Planet Waves* song "Something There Is about You" also finds Richard searching for new ways to express his part. The culmination of the show came

Richard and Robbie on the road, 1974. *Courtesy of the Barry Feinstein estate*

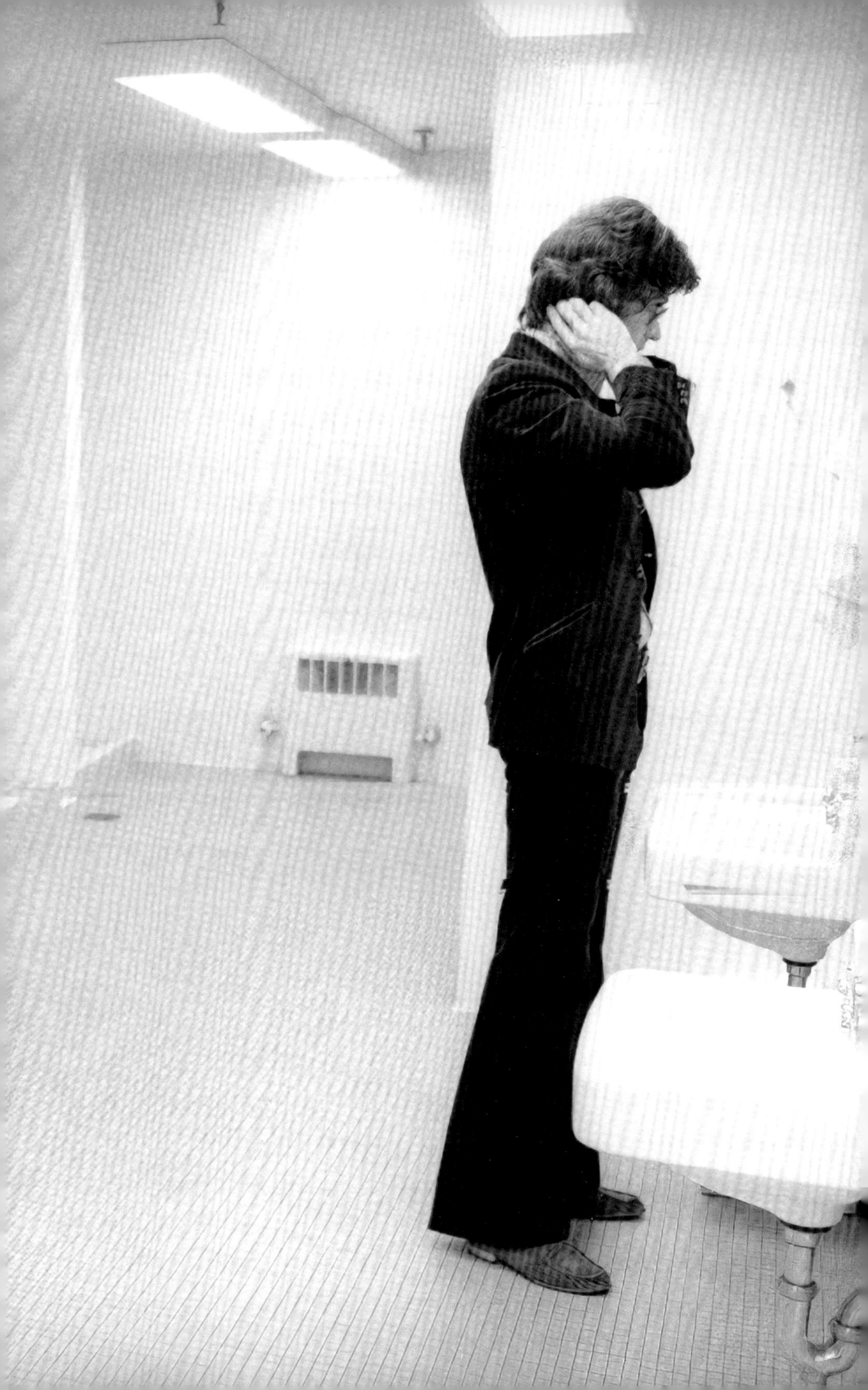

with Richard tumbling around the keys for a massive "Like a Rolling Stone." The performance was explosive and one of the best of the tour.

The January shows settled into a comfortable groove. An audience tape of the Band's set at Nassau Coliseum on January 28 is stunning in its clarity and captures the group in superior form. The month peaked with the Madison Square Garden performances on January 31. The New York City crowd was amped for Dylan's return to town, and the group reflected the same kind of energy. The soundboard tapes are stunning, revealing a wealth of interplay. Richard and Garth volley licks around the stage throughout the shows, turning Dylan's sets into dizzying strobes of sound.

"Rainy Day Women #12 & 35" from the evening show in New York is notable for Richard's fantastic playing as well as being one of the best versions of the tour. He continues the trend with sharp staccato chording on "Just Like Tom Thumb's Blues." As a testament to the strength of the New York performances, the high-octane version of "Highway 61" from the same show was officially released on the Band's *A Musical History* box set.

By the start of February, the shows ascended to another level of controlled chaos. Promoter Bill Graham remembered the evening show in Denver on February 6 as being especially majestic. Richard got everybody laughing backstage as they passed a bottle of high-test Tennessee grape wine around the room. The music's edges became frayed, and the energy unhinged. Dylan's vocals increased in intensity, becoming a loopy wail by the end of the tour. In Richard's case, he was reaching his limit, if he had any. Cocaine use gave his vocals a disconcerting gargle, which forced him to reassess his approaches to some songs. He carried around a bottle of nasal spray and used it constantly to keep his passages clear.

In February some of the shows were professionally recorded for a prospective live record. In Oakland on February 11, while Richard's voice was spent from the long tour, he played piano aggressively. Dylan and the Band are charged, and the highlights are many. A soundboard recording of the early show is marked by a vibrant flamenco-style "Just Like Tom Thumb's Blues" and a fairground version of "It Ain't Me Babe" that is the best of the tour. The Band rattles like a rollercoaster through the song's changes while Garth plays an endless calliope of sound.

The final two nights of the tour in Los Angeles on the 13th and 14th made up most of the resulting live record from the tour, *Before the Flood*. The concluding concerts were bombastic. It was *the* ticket to get, and *the* place to be seen. Celebrities, fans, and fellow musicians gathered in anticipation of the event. The press was relentless, with Dylan and the Band impervious to it all.

The highlights were endless and the concerts the perfect culmination of the tour. The Band then steamrolled Dylan's catalog, leaving only a strip of smoking rubble behind.

Reviews for the tour were excellent, while both Dylan and the Band reportedly felt that they were only playing parts. Levon said in his autobiography, "The tour was damn good for our pocketbooks, but it just wasn't a very passionate trip for any of us."

Forbidden Fruit

When the tour concluded, Richard was ready to cash out. With his marriage to Jane on the rocks, he needed a guilt-free companion to join him in his immersion of post-tour decadence. Sally Mann was a rock 'n' roll fox. Once married to Jefferson Airplane drummer Spencer Dryden, she was a fixture on the West Coast rock 'n' roll scene.

She met Richard backstage after the February 11, 1974, concert. In her memoir, *The Band's With Me*, she wrote:

> I was inexplicably transfixed by a disheveled wraith of a man sitting with one leg crossed over the other at the knee, folded over onto himself with a goofy grin on his black-bearded face, caressing an amber bottle of Grand Marnier with more fervor than Bogey ever felt for Bacall.

Richard had reached the end of the line and was hanging on for dear life; Mann's fate was sealed with that "goofy-ass grin" that put her, as she wrote, "down—and out—for the count." On their first evening together, Richard confessed his undying love and affection for Mann and invited her to the tour conclusion in Los Angeles on Valentine's Day. They spent a passionate night together with the sound of Richard's dehumidifier the only accompaniment. Sally Mann Romano said in 2022, "Truly, he just bowled me over, telling me we were going to live together the first night I met him!"

Richard wasn't kidding, and he filled the void left by his family with Mann. She remembered:

> In the weeks after I first moved to Malibu, it took an act of God to get Richard dressed—he didn't have any clothes to speak of! His birthday was in April (I had moved down there in February), and in addition to his Pulsar (watch), I bought him a decent bathrobe so he wouldn't look quite so ratty. Ambition was not a factor in his life at the time, but the whole band had worked really hard for the months prior, so he had earned some time off—just not forever.

While Richard and Rick often got together when they could, members of the Band weren't social with each other. Romano said in 2022:

> The first few months after the Dylan tour were sort of a vacation, and he truly laid [*sic*] around a lot. We both loved to watch goofy shows on TV, but it's impossible to overstate the effects of [first] alcohol on everything he did at the time, and [later] heroin, which absolutely, 100 percent saps any vestige of creativity, energy, or ambition. I didn't really see it was a lack of interest in the Band so much as a lack of interest in anything that wasn't Grand Marnier, Mumm's pink-label champagne, or heroin.

Referring to herself in her memoir as Richard's "deeply cherished something-or-other," Mann became known as an enabler in the Band camp, and her relationship with Richard was always looked at with a suspicious side-eye. Richard posted up in a posh new Malibu rental that belonged to Goldie Hawn and, while his family was back in Woodstock, moved Mann in.

Richard didn't have a car or a license. Whatever Mann wanted to get into, Richard was more than willing to join in on. The first order of business was getting Richard a new ride. Completely unaware of Richard's checkered past with automobiles, Mann couldn't have known that Richard's car situation, or lack of, was almost encouraged by the group to keep him out of trouble and jail.

In the spring of 1974, Richard got a California license and both bought a classic Cadillac and leased a brand-new 1974 Citroën SM Maserati. The Citroen was a luxury vehicle that could easily cruise in comfort at 125 miles per hour. Robbie had one as well. Almost immediately after procuring the car, Richard was escorted to his home on Broad Beach by a CHP officer who had witnessed him switching between lanes recklessly. After he had deduced that Mr. Manuel had been drinking, he kindly offered him a chauffeured ride back to the house. It's almost a certainty that Richard had flashed the officer the photo of him and Ed Sullivan from his wallet.

Around the same time, guitarist Michael DeTemple, who would later become part of the house band at the Band's studio, encountered Richard broken down on the Pacific Coast Highway near Trancas. Richard was grinning maniacally from ear to ear behind a veil of smoke pouring out from under the hood. DeTemple recalled that Richard was probably the only guy in the world who could break an axle on a Maserati.

While Richard was sinking into the sparkling quicksand of Malibu, Robbie was networking with David Geffen and other Hollywood bigwigs while making plans for a post-Band career.

Richard was a wreck physically, and mentally he was lost. Why? Jane revealed to Richard that she was pregnant with their second child. While Jane and Richard's marriage had been on slippery slopes for a while, they were still a couple. But Richard had changed for the worse, and she had changed as well. They were finding out that their paths diverted at harsh 90-degree angles. But she loved him, and they both had responsibilities to their children.

Richard spent the Malibu summer lounging around the house in an unproductive druggy bubble. The only musical activity was when Libby Titus would visit, and she and Richard would duet on "Miss Otis Regrets" and other favorites. Richard's house was equipped with a harpsichord, and Romano wrote in her memoir, "Drunk or sober, he coaxed such an exquisite tone out of that borrowed, barely tuned harpsichord, he could have easily given Scarlatti a run for his florins."

The only other hope for musical magic in mid-1974 was extinguished by Richard's hard drinking. He had reached a point where it was getting the better of him. What could have been a legendary studio session with Joe Cocker turned into an embarrassing scene when Richard fell off the piano stool and ended up on the floor with a pile of ashtray sand on his head.

The Band hit the road for a summer tour, coheadlining shows with Eric Clapton and Crosby, Stills, Nash & Young while they were still riding the momentum gained from the Dylan tour. Romano said in 2022, "When rehearsals for the next tour started up, it was almost impossible to even get him dressed and headed into town. Things were a bit better when he was on heroin, as opposed to alcohol, because he wasn't as sloppy and falling down drunk all the time, but in short, he was a mess."

The Band with Eric Clapton, Rich Stadium, Buffalo, New York, July 6, 1974. *Courtesy of wattcasey.com*

Chapter 11 | The Great Pretender (1972–1976)

The two-week tour started on the Fourth of July in Wentzville, Missouri, for a bill with Leon Russell and ended with two shows in Oakland on July 13 and 14. The Band revamped their set in the interim, adding an instrumental called "The Slop" with Garth on saxophone that recalled the Hawks days, Richard's "Just Another Whistle Stop," and *Cahoots'* "Smoke Signal." After the opening show, there were two fun shows on a double bill with Clapton in Pittsburgh on the 5th and Buffalo on the 6th, of which a nice-sounding recording circulates. Richard has major issues remembering the lyrics but makes up for it with impassioned singing. Clapton joins the Band at the end of their set for an extended "Chest Fever," which concludes a beautiful disaster of a performance.

Richard was living hard, and only Joshua Christian Manuel's birth on August 5, 1974, generated any sort of response from his anesthetized state. Shortly after Josh was born, Jane and the kids returned to Malibu and were subjected to Richard's revolving door of girlfriends, nurses, and dealers. He showed a glimmer of the youthful spirit he had when he and Jane first got together, but it seemed pointless to Jane at this point. He made all sorts of overtures and promises he couldn't possibly keep to Jane, who was convinced to go back to Malibu in the hopes of reconciling their marriage. The one thing that was never in doubt was that Richard loved his kids. He just couldn't love himself, and for that they suffered.

The Band with Eric Clapton, Rich Stadium, July 6, 1974.
Courtesy of wattcasey.com

The second half of the summer tour, beginning at the end of August, had its moments, but even the Band's supporters were aware that something was up. Jim Stephen wrote in the September 14, 1974, issue of *Billboard*:

> It's puzzling, however, why the group, one of the tightest extant, chooses to play safe when in concert and dedicate an entire evening of songs they performed in the early seventies. Basically, they are as sound as ever. All excellent musicians, strong vocalists with all the attributes of stardom, but their concert was almost boring.

With his family back in Malibu, Richard once again valiantly tried to detach himself from the debauchery of his profession and the guilt in his own head. Jane didn't want to know what had gone on in her absence; she just wanted her husband back.

Richard playing organ for "The Weight" at Rich Stadium, July 6, 1974. *Courtesy of wattcasey.com*

Richard tucked himself into the plush corner of the couch in his living room and laid his newborn son, Joshua, on his chest. Paula snuggled in the crease between the cushion and her dad. It was soft private moments like this that Jane valued, and so did Richard.

Paula recalls her dad's deep voice and hearty laughter. She said in 2023, "He walked like a dad and talked like a dad. I was his princess; his love was true." She remembers him teaching her about the important things in life, such as riding a bike, wiggling your ears, and rolling your tongue.

Paula remembers that much of the time with her father was spent watching the tube. Paula laughed along with her dad at the jokes even if she didn't always understand what they were laughing about. Richard taught her dance moves from *The Gong Show*, but most of all the time was spent bonding together. Sometimes they would laugh so hard that Richard would lean back and fall out of his chair, once almost landing in the litter box.

But before the clock would strike midnight, Richard would hit the road and delve back into an array of temptations.

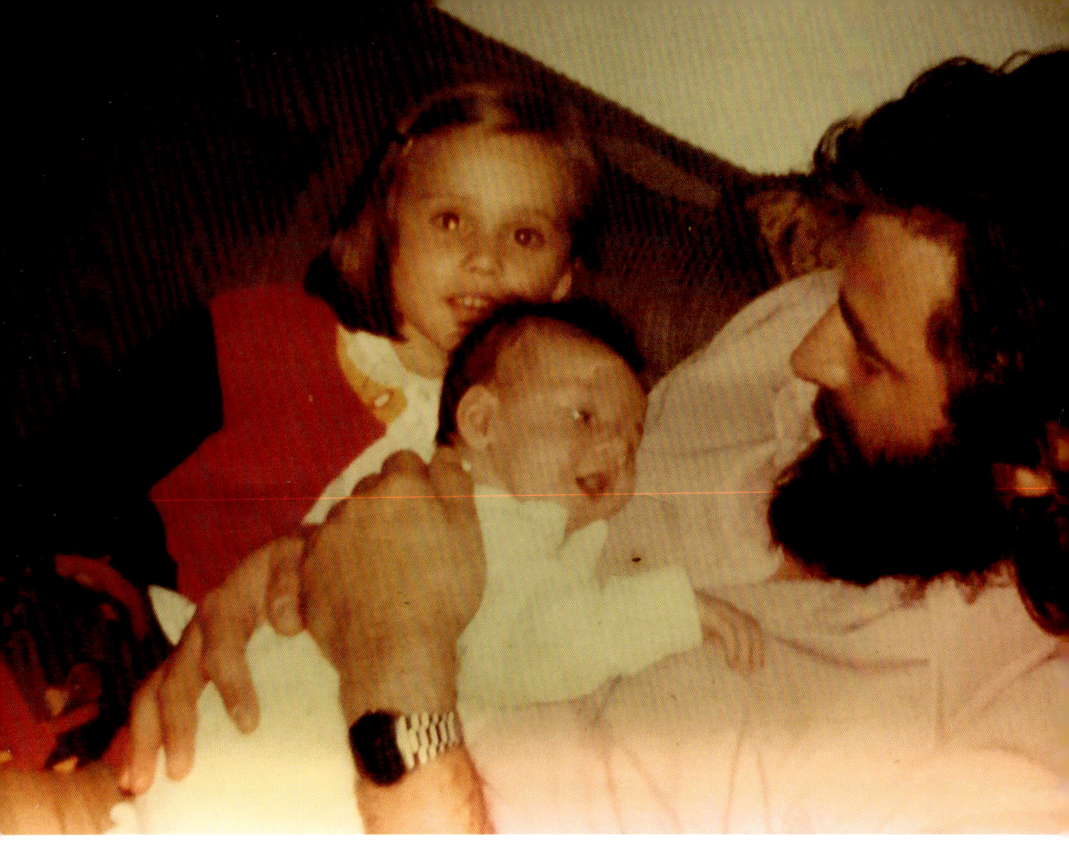

Richard, Paula, and Josh, fall 1974. *Courtesy of the Richard Manuel family*

The Band had a weeklong tour planned at the end of August, culminating in a major performance at Wembley Arena in London, and it didn't take long for Richard to slip right back into bad habits. The night after the opening show in New York on the thirtieth, it finally all came to a head. On August 31 in Cleveland, for the first time, Richard couldn't make the gig. The word was that he missed the show because of illness, but everyone in the Band knew what the real issue was: he was desperately strung out. In the September 4, 1974, edition of the *Plain Dealer*, critic Jane Scott noted his absence, writing, "There was a definite hole in some of their songs." The Band played an admirable set for the crowd, but it was like driving a car with three wheels.

After the Cleveland debacle, the Band played to a crowd of seven thousand in St. Paul, Minnesota, on September 1, before heading home to perform in front of a crowd of 40,000 at Toronto's Varsity Stadium on the 2nd. On a well-recorded audience tape made at the show, one attendee can be heard yelling at the stage, "Play some new songs!" Richard wasn't the only member of the Band struggling, and it translated to the stage and some stale performances.

Wembley Stadium

The summer tour concluded with a huge show on September 14 at Wembley Stadium featuring Joni Mitchell and CSNY. In what had become the usual practice for big events, Richard somehow pulled through. Looking a bit worse for wear, Richard was jittery, but he did his job, and the Band did theirs and got Wembley up and dancing. Rick had a cast on his hand after Mountain guitarist Leslie West sat on it during a party, and the entire crew looked scrambled.

Professionally shot color footage exists of the Band's set, with two of the songs ("Just Another Whistle Stop" and "Chest Fever") officially released on *A Musical History*. The Band, inspired by sharing the bill with their Canadian mates Joni Mitchell and Neil Young, plays a focused show. Sticking to their recently reconfigured set list, the Band opens the show with "The Slop" and segues into a galloping version of "Just Another Whistle Stop," where Richard nails his cues and Rick is all over the choruses.

"Endless Highway" continues its run as a concert highlight. "Smoke Signal" burns at a furious pace and concludes in a Garth-and-Robbie-led jam that threatens to combust. A clear-eyed Richard magnificently sings a mighty "I Shall Be Released," and at its conclusion the group looks his way with smiles on their faces.

A dangerous version of "Mystery Train" follows and has both Levon and Richard on the drums. Richard wails on the kit pendulously, his shoulders limber, his drumrolls loose. As "Mystery Train" slows, it morphs into a steamy "Chest Fever," where the entire Band lets loose in a hard-hitting, show-closing rendition. The Band then returns to the stage for an encore, concluding their fun and funky set with a raucous "Up on Cripple Creek."

The Wembley performance was a good one and a solid bounce-back for Richard, who'd had a precarious August on the road.

At the conclusion of the summer tour, the Band returned to Malibu and started to look for a new clubhouse. Just as he had back in Woodstock with Big Pink, Rick found a new place for the Band. This time it was a former bordello near Zuma Beach that he thought would make a fine studio location. The Band got a lease option on the property and paid $175,000 for the building and 4 acres of beachfront property. Engineer Rob Fraboni was put in charge of developing the space, which would become known as Shangri-La, and turning it into a functioning studio.

Through the rest of 1974 as work on the studio began, Richard waited for his bandmates and tried to keep his head above water. Levon and Garth worked studio sessions; Robbie began to dig through the reels that Dylan and the Band had made in Woodstock back in 1967. A plan was made with Dylan to compile the music from that fertile period into a proper package. It was a long time coming for Richard to finally see "Orange Juice Blues," "Katie's Been Gone," and "Ruben Remus" officially released. In the interim, his ambitions flickered intermittently like his television as he wallowed in inactivity.

Northern Lights–Southern Cross

By the spring of 1975, the Band convened at their new studio and started to formulate a plan for the songs Robbie had written for their next album. It had taken Robbie almost four years to compose 1975's *Northern Lights–Southern Cross*'s eight songs. He was now the sole songwriter for the group, and it was ultimately his vision on the record. Robbie had even started writing and playing on piano more often than usual, lending Richard additional feelings of inadequacy.

Fraboni was brought in to engineer and mix the record, since he had developed a friendship and rapport with the Band after working on *Planet Waves* and assisting Robbie in compiling Garth's basement reels into a cohesive official release. Fraboni witnessed firsthand the group's dynamics and Richard's confidence issues, as well as Richard's incredibly insightful contributions to the production of the record.

Fraboni said in 2023, "He was one of the most sensitive people I had ever known." Richard never expressed verbally what he was feeling, and Fraboni continued:

> Richard never really talked about it, because he *was* it. He wasn't in an encouraging atmosphere at the end of the day. Or, let's say it was encouraging, but at the same time, the element that was encouraging was also having difficulties of its own.
> ... That's where the drugs messed everything up. It screws up the communication between people.

Richard felt too much too often, and the only way for him to combat the dysfunction and disillusion he felt was to get numb. While the Band was holding on for dear life, trying to get it together in the studio before it fell apart, Richard and Jane were in the same state. Jane longed for normalcy and was looking for stability. Richard wanted the same but didn't know how to get it.

Jane, Paula, Richard, and Josh in Malibu, California, 1975. *Courtesy of the Richard Manuel family*

The Band took advantage of its new studio digs and prepared to record its first album of original music since 1971's *Cahoots*. *Northern Lights–Southern Cross* was a return to form and a wonderful musical recovery for the group. It took a year to finish, longer than any other Band album. But over that time, they regained a touch of the collaborative alchemy that had been the essential element of the first two albums.

Recording to twenty-four tracks at Shangri-La offered the songs a cinematic spread of sonics but also gave the songs a feeling of space that didn't suit the group. The separation was also physical, as Fraboni remembered: "It was impossible to get them in the studio at the same time."

The record and sessions began with Robbie's "Forbidden Fruit," an obvious statement on the temptations and addictions that were hanging over Richard and the entire band. Fraboni remembered that it took the Band forever to get a track that suited Robbie's wishes: "We took two weeks to get a take of 'Forbidden Fruit,' and Levon was ready to kill Robbie." After recording take after take of the song, the group ended up using a version from the first day of sessions.

There was a lot of eye-rolling and exasperated looks while Robbie searched for perfection. The Band had recorded *Planet Waves* in four days and now couldn't decide on a take for two weeks. Sessions were uptight but started to loosen by the time the Band tuned the signal into "Ophelia" and "Acadian Driftwood," both conjuring a bit of the Band's usual collaborative quality.

While the record didn't have any songs written by Richard, according to Fraboni "the songs that he sang on the record he had a lot of input on." It's hard to imagine that hearing lyrics like "Don't you shoot the whole works away" and "Little brother got caught in the web; he ran off to join the living dead" fell on Richard's deaf ears. But they did.

Working kept Richard on an even keel. He did his usual thing, singing a comforting vocal on "Hobo Jungle," a song he would have never written but sang perfectly. Robbie obviously had Richard's voice in mind when he composed the song's gentle changes and illustrated the implied resignation of a lonely train jumper.

On the Band classic "Ophelia," Richard played a ragtime electric piano part and offered husky vocal support to Levon on the New Orleans–style chorus. "Acadian Driftwood" was the crown jewel of the album and a perfectly constructed Robbie Robertson composition, one of his best. Richard, Rick, and Levon passed around the lead vocal like a peace pipe. Robbie's story of a people forced from their lands was convincingly told by the return of the Band's three-way vocal blend.

"Ring Your Bell' was a well-intentioned but forced bit of camaraderie with Richard, Rick, and Levon again alternating verses: it seemed as though they were reading from a script more than letting it ride naturally. This feeling can also be attributed to the fact that the vocals on the record were often overdubbed instead of being sung live. Regardless, it's a classic slab of the chunky funk of the Band's rhythm section.

Richard contributed piano to Rick Danko's emotional singing on "It Makes No Difference" and reached back into the furthest reaches of the closet to retrieve his highest falsetto on the choruses.

"Jupiter Hollow" was a leftover from the unsuccessful Turtle Creek sessions in 1972–73 and is a typically particular Band-like stew of influence and experimental originality. Both Levon and Richard play drums on the song in time with the click of a drum machine. The vibe feels inspired. The song is a natural blend of Richard's, Rick's, and Levon's voices, together, more or less in line. Celestial keyboards and Garth's glorious electronic experiments streak across the sonic solar system.

"Rags and Bones" is a song written by Robbie, again tailored to fit Richard. He croons a breathy and patient vocal over a rolling set of lounging changes. Garth is once again the one responsible for coaxing a multitude of emotions from the song, while Richard's vocals put flesh on the song's skeleton.

Sessions for the album concluded in the summer, and the group unanimously felt as though they had done good work. *Northern Lights—Southern Cross* was released on November 1, 1975, and was received as a welcome comeback for the Band and set the stage for their eventual finale.

At the end of the sessions, Richard went back to his bottle. At some point, he moved out of Broad Beach completely and into a bungalow on Shangri-La's property. Oddly enough, in a bit of humorous coincidence that Richard loved, the converted bungalow had originally been used to stable the famous television horse Mr. Ed.

Richard, Josh, and Paula in Malibu, 1975. *Courtesy of the Richard Manuel family*

According to *Testimony*, around this same time Richard apologized to Robbie for not holding up his end of the musical bargain. They were supposed to have been a songwriting partnership, a team, and Richard felt guilty about his part in it never coming to its full fruition. They were both at fault for not nurturing the collaboration but still had an opportunity to right past wrongs.

Richard was honest in his words and intent; he was just unable to follow through with his promises.

Robbie lent some insight into the group's dynamic at this point in a March 1976 interview with Harvey Kubernik for *Crawdaddy!*:

> It's no different than it's always been. It's just a particular time when one of the guys has more songs written than other times. It just fell that way this time and will probably change again. Sometimes people get so lazy that when you have to do something, you don't do it. A few years ago, I *had* to do it—I had to come up with it—and now maybe I don't have to do as much, so I don't push myself as hard.

While Robbie was referencing himself, he was also obviously speaking about Richard.

Chapter 11 | The Great Pretender (1972–1976)　　　　307

NO REASON TO CRY

Richard was in the beginning of what he called his "beige period." Typical of Richard, nothing was black and white anymore; his color wheel was made up of bland. Misery welcomes company, and Richard found a perfect foil in Eric Clapton. Over the years, Clapton had built a relationship with Richard and the Band, and their time together at Shangri-La cemented it. In December 1975, Clapton started his own recording sessions in the Band's studio. Ron Wood stopped in, Bobby Charles was there, and Bob Dylan showed up and posted up in a tent in the flower garden.

While holed up in the confines of Shangri-La, Richard and Clapton commiserated through their shared love of alcohol and rhythm-and-blues music. They were kindred spirits whose life situations ran concurrently. Clapton recalled that *No Reason to Cry* wasn't really meant to happen. "It was fueled by the collaboration of working with all these guys." He recalled in 2023:

> I had the time of my life. I do have regrets about being so smashed all the time. It seemed to be the thing; that was the flavor of the day.... Most of the day was spent playing pool, then we would go and make music, but it was very haphazard, and it went on for quite a long time, and I think that's when our relationship flowered. We would sit and play and talk and hang. I understood him, I was drawn to him. I felt very similar about myself: I was shy, inarticulate, and I liked to drink.

A parade of rockers used Shangri-La as a place to hang out, jam, or just get loaded. Clapton and Richard would often take getting smashed to the next level. Clapton said, "Then this other being would come out, and it was the same, I think for Richard. And we would probably leave everyone behind, or they would leave us behind, I don't know which."

He and Richard talked into the small hours about their favorite cuts and then played songs from Bobby Bland, Ray Charles, and Muddy Waters. Clapton said in 2023, "We could go on all day about who we liked to listen to.... We tried hard to cut a version of 'Mean Old World,' because we both loved Little Walter too."

Tucked away as the last track on the remaster of *No Reason to Cry* is the core musical essence of the Manuel-Clapton friendship captured in the sway of a Little Walter song. Included as a bonus track, "Last Night" is a boozy duet with Richard and Clapton swapping verses of one of their favorite songs.

Richard kicks things off on piano, and the band initiates a slow inebriated jaunt punctuated by his rippling piano work. Rick is playing bass with an unknown drummer and acoustic guitar player. Both Clapton and Richard take a ring around a verse, their voices sticky from their special beverages. Richard's voice is taut with desperation, the despair in Clapton's vocal just as real. Clapton said:

> Because of all the different things that melded into his voice, I'd never heard anyone sing like that. And to be in a room with someone that can sing like that, or even try to do a duet with someone that can sing with that kind of voice, was earth-shattering.

Clapton takes a slippery clean-toned solo, and Richard skips across eighty-eight black-and-white steps reaching for a bluesy roll. The Little Walter blues is liquid, impromptu, and real, the way it's meant to be played.

Clapton and Richard join for the final recitation of lyrics. Richard's singing colors outside Clapton's lines, blurring the harmony in precarious perfection. Clapton said that Richard's strength was "never doing the same thing twice, singing a song in a way that you have never heard it before." That assessment is on full display with the ragged but right reading of "Last Night."

In addition to the improvisational musical fun, Richard retrieved and contributed "Beautiful Thing," first recorded in Barry Feinstein's photography studio in 1966, to Clapton's sessions. With Clapton's and Rick Danko's willing assistance, they tightened up the lyrics and brought "Beautiful Thing" back to life. All it took was a modicum of care and a multitude of patience for the song to end up opening Clapton's album.

Clapton also cowrote "All Our Past Times" with Rick while Richard played piano on the cut. Clapton was finally able to fulfill his dreams of playing with the Band at Shangri-La. Good music, better times, and lifelong friendships were the result.

Separation

Richard laid his head on the pillow, his stomach sticking out from the edges of his floral button-down shirt. A wad of cash and cigarettes crested the top of his chest pocket. He was a gloomy figure, his usual toothy smile covered by his black beard and shadow. He laced his long fingers behind his head and focused on Jane's mouth with a steely look. Jane told Richard that she was leaving Malibu and taking the kids with her. She bluntly stated to him that he was an alcoholic and that it was over.

Richard looked up at his wife and said, "It's tough on the top of the pile." Jane glared back and said, "Yeah, a pile of shit." Richard was held together tenuously with packing tape and twine, and now it had deteriorated beyond repair. He had packed on the pounds, and his liver could be seen pushing out from his stomach even under his shirt. His skin had a spooky pale hue, and his hair was greasy and pasted to his sweaty brow. He hadn't called home to Stratford in six months. When he finally did, he told his father, Pierre, he couldn't even pull up his pants because his liver was so swollen.

When not playing pool or singing the blues at Shangri-La, Richard had built the modern marvel of a 6-foot tree of spent Grand Marnier bottles as the centerpiece of his solo bungalow. When he was hungry, he was cooking minute steaks on a clothes iron. He was alone, then Cathy Smith showed up.

Summer 1976

The Band was hitting the road again. Every single night would be a game of cutthroat. Richard, just before the tour departed, insisted that Smith join him for the six-week tour as a "medical necessity." No one thought it was a good idea except Richard, who sternly told his bandmates that he would not go on the tour without Smith as his nurse.

The Band's 1976 summer tour kicked off June 26 at the Frost Amphitheater in Palo Alto, California. Richard cut his hair and looked far removed from the pathetic aesthetic he had cultivated in Malibu. A strong-sounding audience recording exists of the stellar opening show at the beautiful venue.

Richard kicks off the tour in spectacular fashion. He sings three of his songs from *Music from Big Pink* on the opening night: "Tears of Rage," "In a Station," and "I Shall Be Released." Of note is the ultrarare version of "In a Station," last performed in 1969 and played at the Frost for the final time.

Richard's investment in the performance is tangible. He sounds confident, singing one of the first songs he wrote in Woodstock. Pushing the verses and pulling the chorus, he sounds at ease and in complete control. It's a mystery why the song was a one-off performance, since Richard hit every single note and explored every detail.

Richard onstage with the Band. Frost Amphitheatre, Stanford University, June 26, 1976. *Photos courtesy of Chris Bradford*

The next afternoon the Band played the resplendent Santa Barbara Bowl. Protected from the midday sun by tasseled umbrellas, the Band illustrated that there was no one better on a live stage when the five members played as the fingers of one musical hand.

The Band continued their summer road trip with a series of shows at the beginning of July, of which no audio tapes circulate. A widely available and crystal-clear soundboard recording from the Carter Barron Amphitheatre in Washington, DC, on July 17 captures the Band in masterful musical form. Every song is of official release quality. Unfortunately, on this night, Richard's greatest gift was but a shadow of its past glories. The constant abuse had taken its toll. The effort was there but his throat was giving out. Charlie McCollum from the *Washington Star* commented, "Only Richard Manuel, whose voice is now almost totally gone, struggled with the music."

In the same review, McCollum stated what was painfully obvious:

> It is disturbing that this set has remained the same for over five full years. . . . It smacks of a group holding onto past artistic achievements and past glories, as if to let go and stretch out would somehow destabilize its musical existence.

Chapter 11 | The Great Pretender (1972–1976)

Richard sang "Tears of Rage" at concerts throughout July, but it was an eyes-closed toss at a dart board on how it would turn out. He pushed valiantly but sometimes sounded like he was out of breath . . . at thirty-three years old. On some of the verses, he hit the lines perfectly; on others, he struggled to hit the notes that used to arrive effortlessly.

There is a powerful audience pull of the Lenox, Massachusetts, show on July 18, and a rowdy crowd responds well to a shaky but soulfully performed "Tears of Rage." Richard's battle with his voice played out dramatically on stages throughout the tour. Sometimes the wear of a couple of songs forced him into a croak by midset. Ken Marks of the *Berkshire Eagle* wrote, "A rather severe hoarseness on the part of Manuel became evident as he sang 'King Harvest.'"

Richard at Sunday Break II, Austin, Texas, September 5, 1976. *Courtesy of wattcasey.com.*

Black-and-white video footage from an in-house camera of the Band's performance at Casino Hall in New Jersey on July 20, 1976, circulates. While the performance has several moments of note, it was not one of Richard's better nights. He looks like he's hanging on for dear life. His voice is desperately choked out from the abuse of five shows in seven days. His eyes are inky-black saucers shivering under the glare of the stage lights. He plays piano admirably and shares steely glances with his bandmates, but it's obvious that he's on shaky ground. In comparison with previous nights, the version of "Tears of Rage" is difficult to take in.

The Band returned to Malibu for a month before picking up the second leg of the tour in August with an opening show on the twentieth at the Civic

Auditorium in Santa Cruz, before a three-night stand at the Greek Theatre in Los Angeles. The rest obviously helped Richard's voice, since his singing was fantastic at the Greek. Decent-sounding audience tapes of the second and third nights circulate. Additionally, for this run of the shows the Band brought along a four-piece horn section playing the *Rock of Ages* charts. The Greek shows were a success and proof that the Band could still deliver. They played two sets a night and stacked up a series of their best late-era concerts.

The group then flew back to the East Coast for another show in Lenox, followed by a hometown festival in Toronto on the 31st, and then Boston on September 2.

On September 5 the Band played a large music festival in Austin, Texas, called Sunday Break II. It was the scene of an incident that effectively ended the Band. A powerboat was used to ferry the performers across the choppy Colorado River to and from the venue. Richard and his bandmates basked in the wind on the water as they made their way across the channel.

Midway through the journey, Richard stood up to get a seat at the front of the boat. He was hot and wanted the breeze in his face. The boat glided at full speed across the choppy river, cresting one wave, then another, and whipping around aggressively. It rose, nose in the air on one wave, and then crashed back into the water. Richard was thrown back into his seat, with a force so extreme that it cracked his neck.

The performance was a success in spite of the oppressive heat and Richard's severe injury. While he powered through the immediate discomfort, after the

Sunday Break II, Austin, Texas, September 5, 1976. *Courtesy of wattcasey.com*

show he was in bad shape. A doctor was brought to the hotel and told Richard that he had broken bones in his neck and would need six weeks in traction to heal. During a tour, that wasn't an option. The Band and acting manager Rock Brenner decided to hire a team of Tibetan healers from the area to help cure Richard of his ailment. Brenner's father had undergone a similar treatment for pain with success from the healers.

Just as Robbie was hypnotized out of his sickness in order to make the show at Winterland in 1969, the Tibetans were dispatched to Richard's room to perform a miracle.

Richard lay uncomfortably on a table and was left to the mysterious men and their alternative medicine. The healers surrounded Richard and used frequency and sonic pressure to work on him. At one point, he thought his

Sunday Break II, Austin, Texas, September 5, 1976. *Courtesy of wattcasey.com*

eardrums were going to explode during the intense tonal procedure. Something happened to him that could not be denied; while he was not healed, he was at least feeling better.

    Cathy Smith said in her biography, *Chasing the Dragon*, that Richard had never looked better after the procedure. He wore a neck brace for the next week but had recovered enough to finish the tour. Despite ten canceled shows, there were still performances to play. Richard put forth an admirable effort, but the writing was on the wall. Robbie later told Barney Hoskyns, "It was particularly hard on Richard, whose health was not great. We felt we were kinda dragging him along on this thing. We couldn't go out and give it our best shot, working without our full force." He said in his memoir, "We always wanted to help Richard, but we didn't know how to help ourselves."

Chapter 11 | The Great Pretender (1972–1976)

With Richard's accident the excuse, but Robbie's growing impatience the impetus, Robbie began to think about shuttering the doors of the Band's musical shop. His increasing ambitions outside the group, coupled with the dread of the road, made the decision simple. By the time the tour reached its conclusion, so had the Band.

At a September 25 show in Nashville, the Band was billed second to ZZ Top. The crowd of 25,000 was surprisingly indifferent to the group, despite a fantastic performance. In response to the crowd's reaction, the Band left the stage without an encore. Jon Marlowe of the *Miami News* wrote, "It was one of the best rock concerts I'd ever seen, but all the Band got for the supreme effort was mild applause."

The Band was being passed by in the mainstream, and they didn't have a choice in the matter. Not that they cared, but they were risking their lives to do it. Robbie couldn't and wouldn't handle the rejection. He didn't want one of his bandmates to die in a random hotel room either. He was going to get off the road . . . and do it quickly. Robbie told the Band his plans. Rick said to *Rolling Stone*, "We first started talking about it when we canceled the ten shows. I knew we were gonna put it away, but I wasn't planning on announcing it."

An idea, hatched by Rick, was that if the Band was going to park the musical cruiser in the garage for a while, why not have their friends on hand and really go out big? Thus began the genesis of "The Last Waltz," a name that conjures sounds and visions of the most-legendary performances in rock 'n' roll history.

On Thanksgiving Day, the Band would be the backing group for a roster of their all-star musical pals, from Hawkins to Dylan, and Morrison and Muddy. The best backup group in the world would be the house band for music's most legendary players.

The location for the Last Waltz would be Bill Graham's Winterland in San Francisco, in a case of the Band going back to where it all began. The concert was promoted as the Band's farewell performance.

After the Band's concert obligations had been settled, their full focus shifted to finishing their final album due to Capitol and planning the Last Waltz. Richard responded to the pressure in his typically inebriated way. He took it all in stride and promised his bandmates that he would hold up his end of the show as long as they played. The Band was his life. What else was he going to do, go back to Stratford and fix cars?

The Band on Late-Night TV

One month before the Last Waltz, the Band was scheduled to perform on *Saturday Night Live* on October 30, and Richard was holed up in a New York City hotel with Cathy Smith. This was to be the last performance before the Band retired from the road with the Winterland show on Thanksgiving.

Two days before their *Saturday Night Live* appearance, Richard had a visitor to his room with a sinister delivery. The shady stranger knocked on the door and told Smith that he was an old friend from back in Woodstock. After an uncomfortable silence, he revealed to Smith what he had brought for Richard, and pulled some packets of powder from his jacket. Richard was in the shower, and Smith, never one to say no, partook of what the stranger had procured. Thinking it was cocaine, she did a couple of lines and went about her evening.

It was not cocaine. As soon as Smith left Richard's room, she grew very ill. She started to sweat and was fading fast. She puddled in the hallway and clawed and crawled her way to Band manager Larry Samuels's room to alert him to what was happening in Richard's room upstairs.

Samuels took off out the door, and when he arrived at Richard's room, he found him sprawled out in a chair, eyes rolled back in his head. Samuels acted quickly and called a doctor; otherwise Richard may not have made it. The attending physician administered a shot to counteract the heroin. Richard spent most of the next forty-eight hours in his hotel room over the toilet, vomiting from underneath sweat-plastered hair. It was a close call, too close. He was advised to stay in bed, which he had no problem doing.

After two days of convalescence in his room, Richard was still in rough shape. He made it to rehearsals and was slated to sing "Georgia on My Mind" on national television.

SATURDAY NIGHT LIVE, OCTOBER 30, 1976

The Band plays a funky four-song set with a horn section. After stellar versions of "Life Is a Carnival," "The Night They Drove Old Dixie Down," and "Stage Fright," the group closes their set with "Georgia." Richard, buzzing with bruised soul, sits sideways on his piano bench facing the studio audience. Elegantly frazzled, he holds on to the microphone tightly with one hand as if he were holding on to a rope over a precipice (Smith said in her memoir that "his bones seemed to be vibrating").

Whether a tribute to the state or an imaginary woman, Richard squeezes every bit of juice from Ray's Georgia peach and deep-breathes every single note. Caught in the spotlight, his skin shines like transparent porcelain. The gaze of the unforgiving television eye fixes on Richard's vulnerability while illuminating his effortless stage presence.

The cathartic peak of "Georgia" lays bare the pure, undistilled musicality of Richard Manuel. It's the same sweet song that shocked Stratford and the Hawk in 1961 at Rock-A-Rama. Richard dives deep into a heartbreaking growl and then ascends with the collected shards of his splintered falsetto. He caresses the melodic curves of Brother Ray's classic and takes it home.

"That's why I'm irked to the point of just saying, 'Fellas, this is it, I'm going on with my own career.' So I've been planning how to catapult this whole thing with myself into a position where I can remain occupied all the time and have some work at all times, because it's the down time that drives me crazy."

Chapter 12
SLEEPING (1976–1986)

> All of all of it.
> —Richard Manuel

The Last Waltz was a historic musical event that Richard likened to the Warren Commission and was, in essence, a funeral procession for the Band. Famous rock friends and neighbors gathered at San Francisco's Winterland to pay their respects to the group on Thanksgiving night 1976. A typically well-planned and over-the-top Bill Graham production served Thanksgiving dinner to attendees and featured choreographed ballroom dancers before the concert. Robbie, who had been introduced to filmmaker Martin Scorsese, asked him to film the concert for posterity. Scorsese, a huge fan of the Band, leapt at the chance, and his resulting film secured the concert's status in the annals of American cultural history.

Feelings about the event within the group were mixed. Levon didn't want to get off the road but really had no choice in the matter. Rick was looking forward to a solo career and was typically excited about the possibilities afforded to him. Garth did everything that was required of him to make the Last Waltz successful but also had several opportunities for work waiting in the wings.

Richard was apathetic, though his spirits were lifted when he received a telegram from Ray Charles, saying how much he enjoyed the Band's cover of "Georgia on My Mind."

Robbie told *Mojo* in 2017 that part of the reason the Last Waltz was conceived was that Richard was in such bad shape that they had a sense he wouldn't make it through another tour. Richard allowed himself to be dragged along by the energy of Robbie's enthusiasm and the Band's grandiose plans for the performance. He had not a thought of what would happen when it all came to an end. The members of the Band agreed on one thing wholeheartedly: to put on the best show that they possibly could.

When establishing the framework of the production and the set list, Robbie kept things easy for Richard. Richard would sing "The Shape I'm In," a song he'd been playing every night since 1970; "Georgia on My Mind," which he'd been performing for over fifteen years; and "King Harvest," a Band concert standard. None of Richard's original songs would be played at the show, intended to immortalize the Band's career. One bonus would be a duet with Van Morrison that he and Richard worked up during rehearsals.

The Band worked diligently to learn their songs and their guests' songs. There were also new compositions specific to the concert, as well as logistics for the film crew, camera cues, and concert schedules. And of course they were also finishing up their last studio album. Richard responded in typical fashion. His disappointment in the Band's conclusion and the pressure of the show were assuaged with an abundance of alcohol. Though he was drinking hard, the way he cracked wise and inspired comradery was critical in keeping the Band laughing and their workload manageable.

The Last Waltz

As with many of the Band's concerts from the summer tour, Richard put forth an admirable but inconsistent effort over the course of the Last Waltz. Before the show, he slunk around backstage, sipping from a cup and commiserating with longtime friends. There was a steady supply of cocaine for everyone, with a backstage room set up for the artists with the walls ornately decorated with rubber noses.

Richard donned a ghastly but groovy plaid getup he christened the Pizza Suit. He found the one-of-a-kind piece in a San Francisco thrift shop when the Band went to pick out stage clothing for the concert. Robbie found an elegant scarf to dangle from his neck at the performance.

Winterland was awash in a regal rock 'n' roll elegance, complete with glittering chandeliers and glowing candelabras sending diffused light around the venue. The Band took to the stage in a punky stateliness, their instruments set up in front of the decorative lighting and thick red theater curtains. They opened the show with the gritty flow of "Up on Cripple Creek," their playing inspired and at times positively giddy. Both Rick and Robbie naturally looked the part of rock stars, sharply dressed and the focus of the cameras. Levon didn't have to do anything special; the music poured forth from him and the film crew naturally gravitated to him. Garth was tucked away behind his cathedral of keyboards, his thinning hair billowing with his every move.

Richard was posted at his usual spot upstage right at his grand piano and Clavinet. He smiled with surprised eyebrows and acknowledged assorted friends seated just off the corner of the stage. Early in the set, he moved to the Clavinet and performed a typically admirable version of "The Shape I'm In." Later, Richard sang another fantastic rendition of "Georgia on My Mind." He unfortunately stumbled on the lyrics to "King Harvest," in effect removing it from consideration for the film or soundtrack.

The Band's opening set reached its nexus with the finest version of "The Night They Drove Old Dixie Down" ever played. The Band played their hearts out, swaying in eyes-closed ecstasy. This version was followed by a definitive version of "Stage Fright" and a rolling and tumbling version of "Rag Mama Rag," minus mandolin but with both Levon and Richard playing drums.

As the first guest of the evening was introduced, the Band was humming. Richard shared a sip of his drink with his longtime mentor Ronnie Hawkins as he walked onto the stage. Just like the old days, the Band banged out the Bo Diddley beat for a pointed "Who Do You Love?"

Dr. John took to Richard's piano stool for a mini set with the Band, so Richard moved over to drums. He also played the kit on Bobby Charles's "Down South in New Orleans" and on "Mystery Train" with Paul Butterfield, as well as for a fiery set by the king of the blues, Muddy Waters.

Richard and Van Morrison teamed up for a reverential rendition of "Tura, Lura, Lura (That's an Irish Lullaby)," which was easily a highlight of the night but was unfortunately left out of the film. It's a tantalizing segment of music, with Morrison and Richard rekindling a Woodstock fire through the soulful sparks of their duet. Richard's voice is dark espresso, rich and strong; Morrison soars in Celtic contrast.

Both Joni Mitchell and Neil Young played memorable sets with their Canadian brethren and collaborated on a breezy North Country tribute, performing "Acadian Driftwood."

Eric Clapton appeared onstage and finally got to be an official member of the Band, playing a crushing reading of Bobby Bland's "Further on Up the Road," where he and Robbie exchanged six-stringed blows. At the song's conclusion, he gave Richard a smile and a wave of acknowledgment from across the stage.

The evening steadily increased in intensity, and anticipation was high for Bob Dylan's appearance with the Band. Their performance revealed the stunning strata of their musical relationship. The four-song set was sandwiched by two halves of a start-and-stop "Baby, Let Me Follow You Down," a version perhaps even more unhinged than even the most raucous 1966 readings. In the middle were rowdy recitations of two *Planet Waves* ballads, "Hazel" and "Forever Young." The set was explosive and emotional—everything the crowd had hoped for.

Tucked away behind the front line of artists, Richard sang the second verse of the concluding song, "I Shall Be Released," sans falsetto and left the rest of the verses to Dylan. As he left the stage, he gave Neil Young a kiss, smiling as he sauntered off.

After an unplanned and improvised all-star instrumental jam, the Band returned to the stage for the last time to play "Don't Do It." The group was wrung out, physically and mentally. Richard looked across the stage at Levon as he had for fifteen years and cocked his head with a grin, as if to say, "Well, this is it, old friend."

A quick thank-you, and the concert and the Band were over.

Let the Night Fall

Scorsese and his crew gathered at Shangri-La for post-production interviews, inserts, and additional footage. The Band was called to an MGM soundstage to film concert addenda with the Staple Singers and Emmylou Harris. The Band's country and gospel influences were somehow underrepresented in the film and were included in the movie in postproduction.

The studio work was tedious, and the days dragged. Richard rubbed his eyes and cut up constantly, trying to make the session work move at a better pace. He told jokes, some distasteful, and had to be told to tame his comments around the Staple Singers.

The resulting film *The Last Waltz* is a vibrant, historic Technicolor tribute to the Band. It is unequivocally one of the best rock films ever made. The performances are stunning and catch several of the era's greatest rockers in their prime. It deserves all the plaudits it has earned over the years. But like the best films, it's sometimes hard to separate the truth from fiction. The Last Waltz concert and film further minimized Richard's contributions to the Band's overall legacy.

At times, both Richard and Garth are reduced to sideman status, both by the editorial choices and the musical mix. From Richard's perspective, the movie is just a glimpse through a crack in the Band's fence. But this resulting view created a narrative that would define him for the rest of his days.

Jane Manuel said Richard never got to a point where he had healthful self-esteem or self-confidence. Something had been lost in translation on his way into becoming a secure, mature adult. She alluded to the dissonance between Richard's deep-seated insecurities and the constant musical adulation that he encountered as a rock star. A sharpened pendulum swung between the two extremes of self-loathing and self-assurance every single day.

Everyone around Richard told him he needed to get help, and the constant badgering got him down. He was trying, but he was failing. Rick Danko said to *Rolling Stone* in 1976, "Richard's coming out of a period, and it's nice. Now he's going to have some real choices to make."

In the interviews filmed for *The Last Waltz*, Richard appeared spongy and is captured lounging around looking happily sloshed. His eyes are murky pools, his speech measured, his demeanor distant. Richard reminisces about women on the road and gets a pat on the shoulder like an embarrassed relative from Robbie. In one of the segments, Richard quips, "I just want to break even," and his laughter almost squeezes out tears.

Eric Clapton said this in 2023 about the finality of the Band:

> The personalities involved had probably just about had enough of one another. . . . They tried so hard. Every one of them seemed to have their own demons. They were just fighting to survive, and then at some point, it all just imploded, with barely any survivors.

Without his family, and now his band, Richard had more time to devote to Arlie Litvak, whom he had met at a party at Bob Dylan's house.

Arlie was a young woman who had been living in Malibu and working in a restaurant there. The famous clientele at the restaurant enabled her to navigate the periphery of rock 'n' roll. One famous musician in the mix was the Who's Keith Moon, who was friendly and tipped well.

By mid-1977, Arlie was staying in a local guesthouse; when the owner sold the place, she needed to find somewhere to live fast. Moon offered Arlie a place to stay with him and his fiancée, Annette. Through a mutual friend, Richard and Arlie had connected again. Soon after, Richard started to come to the "Moon" to visit. Eventually Moon headed back to England to work with the Who and offered Arlie a substantial salary to stay in his Malibu home and be its caretaker.

Richard had been living in a bungalow at Shangri-La but was being evicted. The phone and gas had been cut, and Richard ended up briefly living a hermit's existence in the stable.

After his exile from Shangri-La, Richard lived with a woman named Suzie . . . who was also interested in the Band's acting manager at the time, Larry Samuels. It made for a strange rock 'n' roll triangle that Richard played for all it was worth. He had been getting serious with Arlie and had to orchestrate a plan to get out of his relationship with Suzie.

Richard invited Arlie and one of her friends over to hang out at the apartment where he was staying with Suzie. When they arrived, Richard was in full swing and jamming with drummer Jim Keltner and sax player extraordinaire Bobby Keys, and the group had a splendid time partying together.

That is, until Suzie arrived home and exploded at the assembled crowd. Pointing in Arlie's direction, she screamed red-faced at Richard, "Get her out of here!"

Richard often joked that Suzie's discolored teeth were a result of her considerable guacamole consumption. He looked at Suzie and said, "Pack your guacamole bags and get out of my house!" The screaming match intensified and escalated to the point that Richard pulled out a BB rifle and threatened to shoot himself if Suzie wouldn't leave the house. He raised the barrel to his head, contending that he was going to do it. Suzie yelled, "Pull it, pull it!"

Richard pulled the trigger and promptly lodged a BB in the side of his head. Suzie summoned the police, and Richard rode in the squad car to the hospital, first to get the BB removed and then for a seventy-two-hour observation.

After the police loaded him into the cruiser for transport, they got as far as Santa Monica and made a stop for coffee. Richard offered from the back seat, "I'll be right here waiting, guys." As soon as the police entered the store, he popped open the door and made a run for it.

In jeans, T-shirt, and leather jacket, Richard ran through the streets of Santa Monica, moving swiftly through the shadows. A police helicopter was summoned and soon he was being tracked from the sky.

Richard ducked into an open door and discovered a laundry room, where he pulled a warm blanket from the dryer, laid it on the floor, and fell asleep. He was woken not long after by the unsuspecting owner of the blanket, who walked into the room and screamed, "Fire, fire!" Richard, startled and dazed, sat up with a shot, blood dripping from his bandaged temple, and said, "Hey lady, I don't even smoke!" . . . with a pack of cigarettes poking out of his shirt pocket.

He stumbled for the door and escaped into the church-lined Sunday morning streets of Santa Monica, ragged and dirty, running from the law. He eventually clawed his way through brambles and bushes down to the Pacific Coast Highway, desperate for a drink and exhausted. He popped out of the brush and spilled out onto the shoulder of the road.

Just then, a local Hell's Angel and his girlfriend drove by as he thrashed through the highway privets, causing the Angel to say to his rider, "That looks like Richard Manuel crawling through the bushes." They turned around and picked him up. Richard said, "I need a drink," so the Hell's Angel took him to a liquor store and then to Shangri-La. Once Richard arrived safely at the studio, he called Arlie and asked if he could come over. She said she'd be over to pick him up. She took him home with her, and he never left.

Arlie met Richard at his lowest. Fully immersed in his beige period, which could have easily been called the blackout, Richard was running on empty. The West Coast had the same effect on Richard that it had on John Lennon during his famous "lost weekend," where Lennon turned to drink and drugs to pacify his family issues. Richard would say to Arlie, "They want to put me in a mental institution, but I'm not crazy, I'm an alcoholic." Arlie later said, "He terrified me, he was so fucked up."

On an Island

The Band's final album, *Islands*, was released in March 1977 as postproduction work continued on *The Last Waltz*. It was a contractual-obligation record, a collection of leftovers and reheats, an admirable but ultimately forgettable hodgepodge of songs.

Richard, typically, regardless of his physical or mental state, turned in stellar vocal performances. Robert Hilburn of the *Los Angeles Times* said about *Islands*, "The usual high quality of the performances (particularly Richard Manuel's vocals) gave the Band a viable album." As with *Moondog Matinee*, Richard's voice made all the difference. The opening track on the album, the light jazzy drizzle of Robbie's "Right as Rain," is successful because of the soulful undertow of Richard's vocals.

Richard also sang lead on Robbie's middle-of-the-road "Let the Night Fall" and on a studio take of "Georgia on My Mind," the same version the group had released as a single at the end of 1976.

The album collected a couple of the Turtle Creek cuts from 1972 and 1973, including the instrumental title track "Islands," a Robertson-Hudson-Danko composition. The collection of songs, while still a Band record in name, was an unassuming end to their recording career. Of note is an alternate take of "Georgia," later included on the 2000 remaster of *Islands*, which spotlights different phrasing by Richard in addition to some belly laughs.

In 1977, both Rick and Levon released solo records and toured in support of their recordings. Garth was in demand for studio work, and Robbie was completely enveloped in *The Last Waltz* postproduction. Richard said to *Oor* in 1971, "I believe that musically, at least, I couldn't do anything without the rest. Or I would become a pair of extra ears to the head of another."

The Band wasn't supposed to be breaking up; they were just taking a breather. The intent was to get back into the studio and keep creating music. They had signed a deal with Warner Bros. after the release of *Islands* and were paid a hefty advance toward another studio album. Later in the year, Richard cashed out his publishing share of the Band's music for $10,000. A rash decision, but one he made without regret. Instant gratification outweighed any thought for tomorrow. Richard was paying high rent, was spending freely, and had a lifestyle he wanted to keep. In the end, everybody sold out their shares to Robbie, except for Levon.

Watching his bandmates keep busy, Richard tried to take advantage of the rowdy collection of musicians hanging out at Shangri-La and attempted to get something musical started. He hooked up with Rick's brother Terry, who played in a band with songwriter Marty Grebb, for a short-lived musical diversion sometimes called the Pencils. Richard had told Grebb way back in Woodstock that he wanted to record an album, and now was their chance. A few clandestine live performances and some unfinished studio recordings resulted from the short-lived collaboration. Grebb later said that everybody involved was too far gone for their own good because of booze and cocaine, and the music suffered.

While Richard put considerable effort into composing songs for the group, the songs weren't up to his previously set high standard. Grebb recalled that Richard's intentions for the sessions also weren't clear, but he *needed* to get a record out. Richard had mentioned possibly recording a Pencils album as well as offering some of his songs to other artists.

One Richard Manuel composition in particular, "Saving Grace," name-checked Stratford in the lyrics and showed melodic potential. With some more-appropriate production decisions and clear-headed encouragement, the song could have been something special. Unfortunately, many of Richard's post-Band attempts to get music recorded just didn't happen.

On March 1, 1978, the Band unintentionally reunited at a Rick Danko Band concert at the Roxy in Los Angeles, where they performed for the last time together onstage. The elements of the Band were there to see Rick perform and were lovingly persuaded to pick up their instruments. Musically, nothing earth-shattering took place, but the circulating tape sure sounds like a good time. Richard jumped behind a Fender Rhodes for a set made up of edgy renditions of "Stage Fright," "The Shape I'm In," and "The Weight."

Not long after, Arlie woke one morning to see Richard, frazzle-haired, wild-eyed, and propped up cross-legged at the foot of their bed, as naked as the day he was born. He had a bottle of Grand Marnier with a napkin tuft puffed out of the top like a backwoods Molotov cocktail, with a sticky trail of booze leading to the fireplace.

Another frantic morning, Arlie woke up to find Richard missing and was concerned enough to call Rick and Elizabeth Danko over to help find him. After an extended time searching, they couldn't find him anywhere. Eventually their search led them to the sauna that was off the bedroom. It had glass on the door that you could see out of but not into. They opened the door to the sauna and turned on the light, and there was Richard, dressed in a black-and-white kimono, bandanna tied around his head, a necklace of loose wires, and a kitchen knife with a pink eraser on the end poked into his stomach. He said to his rescuers, "If you call somebody, I'm going to plug myself in!"

By mid-1978, Richard was, in Arlie's words, "out of control." She constantly monitored him and wondered if he was going to make it. Richard was begging for someone to intervene, but everyone was too fucked up to see it. He would drive 100 miles an hour through the Malibu Canyon tunnel, laying on the horn and passing cars at the last minute. When Richard got crazy, his flair for the dramatic was unleashed. He humorously recognized that the influence of his hometown of Stratford may have colored this part of his personality. From Arlie's perspective, regardless of any mayhem, Richard remained a gentleman, and whenever they would reach their destination, he would jump out and open the car door for her.

Amid the madness, some clarity was gained when Richard realized he needed to do something about his health. He and Arlie made a concerted effort to get straight and moved in with Garth and Maud Hudson. This attempt at reconciling his affairs was also truncated as Garth and Maud and in turn Richard and Arlie lost everything in a devastating house fire at the Hudsons' home.

Back to Bearsville

Soon after the fire, Richard moved back to Woodstock with Arlie. On the way back home, the airline lost what few belongings they had, and they returned to New York in rough shape. They bounced around a bit before landing in a Grossman property, a duplex near the Bearsville complex. Arlie recalled that it took hours to get Richard to do anything during this period of their lives. They lay around in a state of suspended animation.

Looking back at this time, Richard said in 1984 to the *Woodstock Times* that "I had to take care of my health. I was drinking two-fifths of Grand Marnier a day, trying to avoid the inevitable hangover by staying drunk forever." Removing himself from the temptations of Malibu at least gave him a chance. Richard knew his current reality wasn't sustainable, and shortly after returning to Bearsville on August 28, 1978, he stopped drinking.

Within twenty-four hours of going cold turkey, Richard's body went into shock. He collapsed at the duplex and had a seizure. Arlie got him in the car and rushed him to Kingston Hospital, where he was admitted into the intensive-care unit. A doctor told Arlie, "It's fifty-fifty. He could be here today and gone tomorrow."

Richard said that while he was in the hospital, he "became a walnut." The shock to his system was devastating. He was there for over a week and had a fear-based realization that something in his life had to change. The near-death experience had a profound effect on Richard, like it would anyone. He had pushed his body to its absolute limits with drugs and alcohol, and his body fought back for the first time.

Near the end of his stay in the hospital, members of Alcoholics Anonymous visited and encouraged him to come to a meeting once he was released. The AA sponsors implored to him that he would not be able to get and stay sober without attending meetings. Unable to run from his hospital bed and with some sober clarity, Richard agreed to attend a meeting once he was able to go home.

Arlie picked Richard up at the hospital on September 7, 1978, the same day that Keith Moon died. Richard had a new determination to stay sober and went to AA meetings for three months. He received his ninety-day sobriety chip for his hard work. The day he got it, he came home to Arlie, elated and proud of himself. Of course, he wanted to celebrate, and he told her to score them some coke. She said in 2023, "I got him some coke and his Porsche Carrera sunglasses, and he was off."

He made tenuous plans to get his music together but didn't know where to begin. He went to Albert Grossman for advice. Grossman had distanced himself from the world of rock music, while concentrating on building his Bearsville real estate empire. But Grossman loved Richard: he had helped get him into rehab and went as far as having movers relocate one of Bearsville's studio pianos to Richard's place so he could compose music at home.

Grossman also connected Richard with a personal assistant named Anthony Millington. Richard liked Millington's no-bullshit attitude and sharp style, and the two became close friends. Richard explained to Millington that he was trying to get his music career up and running and that he couldn't pay him yet but could offer him the benefit of hooking up with beautiful women. Millington moved in with Richard, Arlie, and Mitzi the German shepherd at their duplex behind the Bearsville studio office. He could tell that Richard was in a healing place and that Arlie was his attentive nurse as well as lover.

Richard and Millington would visit the juice bar every day and bowl in the evenings. Richard was a very good bowler. They had also started to enjoy the social aspect of teatime together. Richard and Arlie even got Millington a teacup as a gift to celebrate their newfound enjoyment of the beverage. Millington recalled that Arlie and Richard's relationship was supportive and that they often shared cute asides, since Richard was constantly playing with words. Richard referred to spontaneity as "spontnitty," and when Arlie would ask what kind of tea he wanted, instead of saying Darjeeling, Richard would say "Gee Darling," or "English Brecky."

From Millington's viewpoint, Richard was putting in the effort needed to get himself straight. He played his piano every night, stayed clean, and was trying to spend time with his kids. He felt tremendous guilt over his situation and was acutely aware of how it affected his children.

It didn't take much of a setback to discourage him though. He didn't have a car, so Millington let him use his truck to cart Josh and Paula around town. Millington felt that Richard was embarrassed about his location in life, and this affected his relationship with his children. To go from fabulously wealthy and popular to broke with an alcohol problem was a tough thing to handle for Richard. Millington recalled in 2023, "Richard felt bad that he didn't have what he should have had [for the kids] and that he blew it." Richard was clear to Millington that he was healing and getting stronger, and that Millington would have to be patient.

Richard in California, 1978. *Courtesy of Arlie Manuel*

Arlie, Richard, Rick, Elizabeth Danko, and friend, California, 1978. *Courtesy of Arlie Manuel*

Chapter 12 | Sleeping (1976–1986)

In 1979, Millington, who also worked in real estate, invited Arlie and Richard to stay at one of his homes on Mount Desert Island in Maine's Acadia National Park. Richard was immediately sold on the trip because he recognized the connection to the Band song "Acadian Driftwood." The lush green solitude appealed to Richard, and the trio headed north.

The Last Waltz had come out the previous year, and some of Millington's friends had heard that Richard, an actual rock star, was staying at Millington's house. These were just regular working guys who wanted to meet a celebrity, and one day they came knocking at the door.

Richard smiled big and regaled the unexpected visitors with a few stories while being patient and accommodating. Millington said:

> Richard was so gracious and wonderful and humble to these guys who asked questions. You had a picture of who this guy Richard was. He wasn't this asshole rock star, getting drunk, who had done too much dope and blown too much money. He was a good human being who was struggling to come out of a tunnel he had built himself into.

Removed from both the music industry and temptations, Richard was just Richard, and Millington said, "Every day there was something where you would say, 'This guy is a pretty interesting cat.'" He described a vision of Richard slinking around the woods of the island, identifying mushrooms and wild plants, crouched on the ground, squinting to investigate the details of his findings.

As their time together involved fewer and fewer musical activities, Millington began to wonder what Richard's actual plans were. He loved to hang out with Richard, but the intent was to get something going for him musically. One positive development was a prospective collaboration with Memphis producer Willie Mitchell, who had recently become part of the Bearsville production family and would go on to produce Paul Butterfield's 1980 album *North South*. Grossman was hoping to set up a songwriting session for Richard with Mitchell.

Richard and Arlie drove down to Memphis and stayed at Mitchell's home for a few days. While the meeting was positive, it is unlikely that any musical recordings resulted from the visit.

Millington was disappointed that nothing ever came of this idea. He believes that Richard was holding on to the hope that the Band would work together again. This idealistic dream was like grasping a fistful of sand for Richard: every time he held on tighter, it would slip away. Millington said, "Richard wanted to do it with Robbie. I think he felt connected and that he could write with him."

Richard was under the mistaken impression that the Band would reconvene and record. That was the plan: to get off the road but continue operating as a recording group. He didn't think they were going to pull the cruiser into the garage, shut the gate, and throw away the keys. Richard struggled with the thought of the Band becoming a museum piece.

His musical ambitions in the late '70s and early '80s continued to stay simple: be the helpful sideman, and when someone needed a groovy Clavinet or a soulful backing vocal, he'd be there. He practiced constantly at home and put a real effort into getting his piano playing to a place where he was confident in his skills again.

Back in Woodstock, Richard was the same cat who walked the streets of Stratford. He was starting from scratch again. Always on the prowl for someplace with a piano and good conversation, he liked to frequent the homes of photographer Barry Feinstein and singer and songwriter John Sebastian. Richard and John had met years earlier playing gigs and connected through both music and humor.

A usual day would consist of Richard tearing up the steep graveled climb to the Sebastian home for a wake and bake, and maybe some easy music making on the hill. Sebastian and Richard's meet-ups were something they both looked forward to, a welcome escape from the worlds of music and commerce that both had spent their lives in. Their relationship wasn't entirely based on their shared musical experiences; it was based in friendship. In 2023, Sebastian remembered their time together: "It was one of my favorite exchanges with another person."

One of Sebastian's musical projects was contributing music and voice to animated features, and he thought it would be the perfect opportunity for Richard. He traveled to Toronto to help Sebastian's session and happily offered his deep voice as the cartoon Junkman. Sebastian enjoyed Richard's rendering of the junk monster so much that he hired him for other parts, including assistance on the Strawberry Shortcake cartoon series.

Sebastian remembered one moment when he was working on a song that had derived its influence from the Staple Singers. He loved their ability not only to harmonize in tune, but to harmonize moving into tune. Sebastian had been a fan of the Staple Singers since he was eighteen, and Richard just as long. The Band had tapped the same syrup tree of influence when arranging the vocal parts on *Music from Big Pink*.

When Sebastian played the song he was working on for Richard, he was "right on top of it." Richard said to John, "Hey man, you used that note!" John replied, "What note?" Richard continued, "You know, that note like what Mavis sings! When she sings a scale, it's like you're sharp of the major third, but it sounds really good because you're moving."

Chapter 12 | Sleeping (1976–1986)

Sebastian thought to himself, "I'm busted." Later, he said:

> It was exactly what I was doing. That was one of the delicious moments where I said, "Who else would not only think this, but say it out loud to me and give me the thrill of somebody having recognized that I was working in the cracks a little bit?"

Richard would also go over to Happy Traum's studio to visit. Naturally, he would make his way over to the piano to mess around. Guitarist Larry Campbell remembers Richard stopping by Traum's house to "just make music . . . easy and natural."

When Traum recorded his 1980 album, *Bright Morning Stars*, he added a version of "I Shall Be Released." He remembered in 2022 that he sheepishly called Richard to see if he would contribute to the song, and Richard responded without hesitation that he'd help. Traum said, "When it came to the music, he was totally all in." He said Richard always emanated a sincerity and a warmth whenever they were together.

When Richard arrived to record, he asked Traum what instrument he wanted him to play, and Traum suggested some sort of keyboard. Richard excitedly offered to find a Clavinet for the song. Traum said, "He went out and borrowed or rented a Clavinet . . . and spent the whole day in the studio." It's safe to say that Richard probably absconded with the same Bearsville Studio Clavinet that he used on the Borderline session in 1972. Traum couldn't recall whether he had been able to compensate Richard for the session. "He came in completely committed and the result is pretty good. . . . He did it for friendship, and I feel kind of blessed by his trust and generosity."

Richard was at his best when helping his friends make music. It's a silvery thread that weaves its way through Richard's tapestry as a working musician. He added the perfect tinge of emotional connection to anything he touched. Sebastian said, "Richard could bring the pain and sweetness with equal veracity. He was always real, always doing something precarious."

Richard's contribution to Traum's album is a spacious addition to a song Richard had already made his own. His lo-fi Clavinet part sounds like fallen bright leaves of scattered melody across the autumnal floor of the track.

Since he had stopped drinking, Richard's reinvestment in his music was clear and inspired him to perform. It also encouraged him to visit home. Richard and Arlie traveled to Stratford during this time to stay with Richard's family and to see Richard's brother Donald and Donald's wife, Kathryn. While at Well Street, Richard's parents insisted on Richard and Arlie staying in separate rooms.

Back in Woodstock, Rick and Richard started to play together again. They often sat around the house and sang, the headiest vocal blend of high and lonesome, and as particular as a fingerprint. The duo easily put together a "living-room set" of collected songs from their loose home sessions that they could play as a two-piece or by fronting a small band. Millington was excited as well, since it finally appeared that there was a shift out of neutral from Richard.

Rick and Richard played a series of one-nighters in April and May 1980. An article in the *Baltimore Sun* from April 21, 1980, said, "Mr. Manuel is singing better than he has since the late 1960s when the Band enjoyed its heyday. Employing everything he has learned by listening to Sam Cooke and Ray Charles, he renders a soulful version of 'Share Your Love.'" Reviewers and fans alike lauded Richard's return to performing but noted the lack of new original material.

A show booked at the Bijou Café in Philadelphia featured a full band backing Rick and Richard. But before the performance, Richard got cold feet. Millington recalled, "Richard didn't want to go because of the lack of preparation. Richard was a person who really wanted things to be perfect and right. He didn't just want to go to make money." Richard wouldn't be made a fool onstage and held firm in his decision to not play the show.

To encourage Richard to play the gig, Millington rented a limousine and booked a suite at the Bellevue-Stratford Hotel in Philadelphia. He thought that taking Richard to the show in style might lift his spirits, and he was right. On their way to the show, Richard gazed out the window and stroked his beard. He smiled at Millington and said, "This is great. This is what we used to do."

After a few Rick and Richard concerts in mid-1980 and not much else, Millington decided to move on from his job as Richard's assistant. He wanted to be successful, he wanted Richard to be successful, but he saw no discernible movement on either front.

The Best of Everything

Richard's creative spirit was stirring, but it woke only when gazes were averted. When feeling inspired, Richard visited Bearsville Studios after-hours to play the beautiful Bösendorfer piano in Studio B. He would meekly inquire if anyone was using the studio before sneaking in to cultivate some of his own musical ideas.

On June 4, 1980, Richard stopped by Bearsville Studio to record a moody instrumental piano piece that had been spinning around his head. It spanned two distinct movements and showed a bluestone load of promise. Arlie recalled him working on perfecting the parts of the song back at the house. He didn't have any lyrics quite yet. He wanted to get the fragments down on tape; he hoped that the lyrics would come later.

In the small pine-paneled studio, Richard laced his fingers together and stretched his arms palms out. He let his fingers rest on the keys and caressed out a regal set of changes. His trademark rolls informed an internal melody that longed to break free of the progression. The formative attempt at this

Richard Manuel

Richard and his father, Pierre, at Donald and Kathryn Manuel's house, outside London, Ontario, 1981. *Courtesy of the Richard Manuel family*

unnamed song (which would later become "Breaking New Ground") was a tune that Richard wouldn't let get away. He played through the changes for a minute before letting the final chord decay to silence. Richard took a recording of the song home for continued work.

By 1981, with Richard putting considerable effort into staying sober, he was for all intents and purposes out of the music industry. Richard and Arlie found their way back to Malibu, and he still held a dim hope that the Band would do something together again.

Richard tried to stay busy and played piano on the title track of Willie Nelson and Webb Pierce's *In the Jailhouse Now*. A straight boogie-woogie line wiggles under the boot-kicking groove—you know that's Richard. He also helped friends such as Rob Fraboni, who was producing Bonnie Raitt's 1982 record, *Green Light*. Richard sang gritty backing vocals on the song "River of Tears."

Richard's voice comes in on the chorus, and immediately the melody's resonance is multiplied, the unsurprising and expected result to any song that Richard contributed to. Raitt's and Richard's voices collaborate in a smoky hybrid. His vocals are the soulful shadow, the final garnish.

His proximity to the industry through that work pried open old, rusted doors, and he finally reconnected with Robbie (Richard did play drums on a couple of songs for Robbie's 1980 *Raging Bull* soundtrack).

Robbie was working on a new soundtrack and asked Richard to lay down vocals on a song that he had written. Their get-together resulted in some good work: the song "Between Trains" was featured on the soundtrack for *The Color of Money*.

Richard sang harmony on the chorus, doubling Robbie's lead and stepping in his footprints just as he had back on *Music from Big Pink*'s "To Kingdom Come." "Between Trains" emitted the faint scent of a Band tune, like the fleeting aroma of a woman's perfume as she passes on the street. Both Richard and Garth contributed to the track, with Garth playing his recognizable flourishes. At the song's conclusion, Robbie and Richard sing a falsetto note as a matched pair that sonically signaled fresh hope for the future.

The chemical reaction between Robbie and Richard had been reactivated: Richard was asked to lend vocals to a Tom Petty song, "The Best of Everything," which also featured Garth. Robbie had been producing the cut for *The Color of Money* soundtrack, but record company red tape kept it from being released until Petty's 1985 album, *Southern Accents*.

"The Best of Everything" was a beautiful Tom Petty composition that he called a favorite. Robbie produced it—adding sturdy horns, along with Garth and Richard—and executed the most Band-like version of a non-Band song recorded. Richard's harmony vocals are intensely passionate and embrace Petty's lead, like a flowering vine wrapping around the sturdy slats of a fence.

Richard joins Petty on the chorus:

> *Wherever you are tonight.*
> *I wish you the best of everything in the world*
> *And honey, I hope you found*
> *Whatever you were looking for.*

Richard comforts the edges of the notes, and at the end of the second line he sings "in the world" and elevates the song to a new place of exposed honesty, cracking open the melody, revealing its true intent. It's a poignant musical moment that defies explanation and, in a way, is as significant as Richard's debut vocals on *Music from Big Pink*. Very few singers in the world could offer a song what Richard gave freely and effortlessly.

When asked about singing with Richard, Petty said to author Paul Zollo in 2005, "Oh, it was a dream come true. I really looked up to him as a singer."

Richard stayed relatively low key for the rest of 1982 and into 1983 while living in Malibu. He moved on the fringes of the industry, just keeping his head above water. He still received great joy when he was recognized in public. If caught in the wild, Richard would split a grin and quip, "I'm a legend in my spare time."

Richard had also recently gone to the dentist and replaced his banged-up teeth with a set of gleaming white choppers. Remarkably, this oral update made his smile even more radiant.

Bonnie Raitt said to *Blues Access* in 1997:

> You know, the '80s were a very rough decade for a lot of us. Our kind of music was completely off the air; disco was in, and then power pop and new wave. We felt really disenfranchised on a lot of levels. For a lot of people, what had been habits became serious vices. That everybody was suffering was obvious.

One night during a terrible storm, bad enough that the Pacific Coast Highway was closed by fallen branches and random debris, Cathy Smith appeared at Shangri-La. Arlie admitted that while she was naive at the time, she had no idea how Smith made it to the studio. She materialized at the door like an angel dust apparition with a suitcase full of dope, accompanied by a strange man named "Lefty."

Richard later said "Lefty" got the name because once he went into a bathroom, he never left. In a scene straight out of a Frankenstein film, lightning and thunder lit the room with a raindrop-diffused darkness. Smith opened her traveling case and revealed a Just Say No suitcase containing a bottle of Grand Marnier, a large amount of cocaine, heroin, and needles.

Smith knew that Richard was clean, which made her overture even more sinister. Since the last time they had seen each other, Smith had upped her game and was now dealing drugs full time, and to many high-end clients such as Ron Wood and Keith Richards. Falling victim to temptation, it didn't take long for Richard to regress. Arlie, who was no saint but would not put a needle in her arm, left Richard shortly after Smith's visit.

It didn't take long before Richard was in deep again, and, with Arlie's departure, he drifted into another relationship, this time with a woman named Hannah, whom he had known for a few years and referred to as his "charity case." He lived at her home for a brief time and tapped his relocated friend Anthony Millington for rides to any musical jobs he picked up.

The scattered and random jobs helped pay the bills but did nothing to satisfy Richard's soul. What was coming over the horizon would. He had been waiting for the moment since 1977 . . . and he was ready.

The Band Is Back

In a February 1983 interview with the *Los Angeles Times*, Richard spoke with Stuart Goldman about his recent lack of productivity: "It's been slim, but I'm getting into gear again. . . . I've been writing a lot too. I love my music more than ever. When I think about playing now, it's a privilege not an obligation." He continued, "I'm having labor pains and anxiety attacks, and I love every minute of it."

Richard was all in when the idea of touring as the Band was broached. The plan was born from the response to Levon and Rick's duo shows together.

It took no convincing to get Richard and Garth on board. Richard said in another interview with the *Los Angeles Times*, in March 1984, that "I had so much faith that it was gonna happen, I just sat at home and waited for six years."

As the Band reunion was set in motion, Richard's father, Pierre, passed away on June 14, 1983. Richard returned to Stratford for services to be with his family and to comfort his mother. Kiddo was moved to a care facility not long after Pierre's death, and her well-being was constantly on Richard's mind. Pierre's funeral would be the last time all four Manuel brothers were together.

Robbie Robertson would not be a part of the upcoming reunion concerts. He was finished with live performances and was immersing himself in soundtrack work. He had moved on and wasn't looking back. The Last Waltz was exactly that for Robbie.

Just two weeks after Pierre's passing, the reunited Band played a show at the Joyous Lake in Woodstock as a warm-up and kickoff for their tour. From July through December, the Band hit the road and performed until the tour concluded with a New Year's Eve show with the Grateful Dead at the San Francisco Civic Auditorium. This wasn't the Band that everyone remembered; a more apt description would have been to call the group the Hawks. Without Robbie, Levon added his friends the Cate Brothers: Earl Cate on guitar, his brother Ernie Cate on keyboards, Ron Eoff on bass, and Levon's cousin Terry Cagle on drums.

The opening shows were exciting, fresh, and enthusiastic. As the Band moved through Canada, friendships were rekindled, and the crowds were hungry. Richard was clean, looked fantastic, and was playing well.

While the music was good, the additional instruments were excessive. With an extra four musicians onstage, the sound was cluttered. In a way, it was the antithesis of the Band's original vision. The decision to double up all the instruments was an odd one, especially since it also meant paying four additional musicians to tour.

The Band's show at Queen Elizabeth Theatre in Vancouver, Canada, on July 18, 1983, was filmed for broadcast and finds Richard dressed in jeans and collared shirt and in complete control. The performance was broadcast interspersed with interview segments, and Richard's pieces are vital and well-informed documents. In a plaid suit coat, Richard is cordial, conversational, and a far cry from his besotted guise in *The Last Waltz*.

In August the Band went to Japan, and, surprisingly, Richard took his girlfriend, Hannah, instead of Arlie. It turned out that Richard loved Japan and didn't want to come home. He found Japanese elevator music fascinating and enjoyed the culture. Richard said to the *Woodstock Times*, "I think they've got so much class. I was actually ashamed to be Western. I had moments of being ashamed because they have so much respect. They are so gracious, that's the word." Though Richard was feeling strong and performing well, in the evenings he would make his way down to the lobby and call Arlie back in the States and express his loneliness.

One of three performances in Tokyo was filmed for broadcast and is notable for the stellar footage of Richard singing "You Don't Know Me." With a trimmed beard and clear eyes, his breathy rendition of the Ray Charles classic was a high point of the performances. It continued to be a highlight when the Band returned to the States for their fall swing, as Geoffrey Himes of the *Washington Post* wrote in October 1983: "Manuel proved he's lost none of his richly expressive tone as he milked the heartbreak blues ballad 'You Don't Know Me.'"

In Syracuse, New York, on October 22, Richard reunited with Arlie. Garth had called Arlie and told her that Richard missed her and that the band would send her a ticket to the concert. Arlie accepted Garth's invitation, and later that evening Arlie and Richard reconciled. Not long after their reconnection, they moved back in together.

The next weekend the Band had a gig in Buffalo, New York. The plan was for Richard to ride from Woodstock with Levon to the show. Levon avoided air travel whenever possible, so he wanted to drive his station wagon to that evening's performance. When their agreed-upon departure time had passed, Richard called Levon's house, and no one picked up.

Richard eventually decided it was time to head over to Levon's house. He knocked but there was no answer. Running out of options, Richard picked up some pebbles and threw them at the windows. A second-floor door opened to empty space, and when Richard made a direct hit to the door with a stone, it swung open. Levon stood at the precipice with a shotgun raised to fire.

"Goddamn it, Richard. Do you realize I could have shot you?"

Richard said, "Levon, we got to go. We have a show!" Levon unzipped his pants and started to urinate from the second-floor landing onto the yard. He assured Richard that he would be leaving soon and would pick him up on the way out of town.

Richard and Arlie returned home and waited and waited. Levon never showed up. After furious scrambling and countless phone calls, a private jet was procured to get Richard to the gig, because if he didn't make it, the Band wouldn't get paid.

Most of the fall tour was a success, and the Band put together a series of consistent performances. The November 1983 issue of *Rolling Stone* reviewed the Band's concert at the Capitol Theatre in Passaic, New Jersey, saying, "Perhaps the most thrilling was the performance of the enigmatic, heartbreak-voiced Richard Manuel. A dark, handsome, and healthy-looking Manuel romped through 'The Shape I'm In' and delivered the concert's high point: a tender rendition of 'You Don't Know Me.'"

When the tour stopped in New Orleans, Richard hit the streets with Mike Neel, a friend from the area who showed him around town. Neel remembers that Richard was sipping from a plastic cup he was carrying around, but later found out that he was just touching the drink to his lips. He wasn't drinking; he just needed that taste.

They stopped at a club where Allen Toussaint just happened to be performing. The pair caught the legendary pianist's eye as they entered the room. After finishing one song, Toussaint called Richard's friend over and asked if his mate was Richard Manuel of the Band. Neel said it was, and Toussaint responded that he'd like to play a song with Richard.

Richard had disappeared. When Neel found him later that night, Richard explained that he knew Toussaint would want him to come up onstage; he just couldn't possibly do that unprepared.

Professionally shot color footage of the Band's celebratory 1983 New Year's Eve show in San Francisco circulates and is a high-energy capture of the big band version of the Band. Richard starts out the set on drums for the first two songs, "Rag Mama Rag" and "Long Black Veil," before his first vocal of the evening on the obligatory "The Shape I'm In." Both the Band and the Grateful Dead look as though they were feeling no pain.

The first days of the reunion were successful, but after the initial enthusiasm of playing together again dissipated, the same problems began to bleed through. No new original music was being written, the shows were static, and sometimes the performances were rickety.

Around this time, Richard and Jane's divorce became final. He was as active as he could be with the kids but was still having issues facing up to his responsibilities.

Richard and Arlie rented a quaint house on the corner of Glasco Turnpike and Patricia Lane just outside Woodstock. The owner of the centrally located house also had the last name Manuel, which gave Richard a great chuckle when he saw it on the mailbox. The modest home had a large pile of *Car and Driver* and other auto magazines on the living-room table, with Richard's Kawai electric piano set up on a stand and darts and a dartboard at the ready in the basement.

Richard doted on Mitzi, his German shepherd, whom Arlie said he loved like a child. Mitzi loved to howl, and when Richard blew harmonica, he could get her to sing along. He also got great joy out of sharing toffee with Mitzi and watching her chew the sticky confection.

On June 17, 1984, Richard and Arlie were married in a small ceremony on Maverick Road. Rick Danko played accordion, and a small group of close friends were on hand.

Richard and Arlie's wedding day, Woodstock, June 17, 1984. *Courtesy of Arlie Manuel*

Richard and Arlie's wedding day, Woodstock, June 17, 1984. *Courtesy of Arlie Manuel*

Richard and Arlie's wedding day, Woodstock, June 17, 1984. *Courtesy of Arlie Manuel*

Richard retained his penchant for tinkering, and he was constantly keeping his hands busy by dismantling things around the house, including the telephones. But he had also slipped back into some nasty habits. Even though he wasn't drinking, he was engaging in other behaviors that would drain him of the momentum he was starting to gain. Josh and Paula would come over to visit their dad but often would end up watching television as Richard took to napping for the afternoon.

Richard and Arlie, 1984. *Courtesy of Arlie Manuel*

Richard and Arlie in silly hats, date unknown. *Courtesy of Arlie Manuel*

By the time the 1984 spring tour started, Richard was haunted by some of the same old issues. There was no new music, and he felt like an employee in his own band. In his 2008 book, *The Riot Act*, poet Geoffrey Young delicately outlines a random moment during the tour when he encounters Richard in a Williams College restroom. As Richard intently washes his hands, Young asks him if he will play "Georgia on My Mind" that night, to which Richard

Chapter 12 | Sleeping (1976–1986) 343

replies, "None of the guys seem to know it anymore." Young says to Richard over the running water and bubbles, "I'd love to hear you sing 'Lonesome Suzie' tonight." Richard looks up, flashes a quick smile, and says back to Young, "So would I."

Richard was discouraged again. He had remarked to a friend at a recent Band show that he thought they were turning into a country group. He was back to singing the same songs, for the same crowds, at the same venues. According to Levon Helm's memoir, after one concert Richard said, "Do you realize that we have become these songs?"

A brief respite from his doldrums came in mid-1984, when Richard and Arlie went to see Eric Clapton in New York City, where Clapton was on tour with Roger Waters. Clapton and Richard had stayed in touch since the Shangri-La days. Clapton said this of their connection:

> That's what made it [the friendship] really valuable, for me, anyway. I had a kind of peculiar inroad that nobody else could really interfere with. It was an exclusive relationship that really had nothing to do with the Band itself.... What was great about it was what was great about him. His humility was very attractive. To me, it was very attractive because he was so humble. Actually, self-critical to the point of being really, really shy and reticent. To be introduced to him, and for him to make a fuss about meeting me, was really extraordinary, because I held him in real high esteem.

Richard and Clapton compared calendars and made plans for a 1986 collaboration. Clapton remembered in the liner notes for *Whispering Pines* in 2001, "We had plans to do something together, but time and events came between us."

Richard still held on to the hope that Robbie would produce a solo record for him, but was finding it difficult to connect. When *Woodstock Times* reporter Ruth Albert Spencer asked him about the status of their relationship, Richard said:

> Robbie... he avoids the answers, evasive, illusive.... Not that I don't like surprises or anything. I've tried a number of times to get together with him and bounce some song ideas off—for my use, for the Band's use, whatever. It went on for about a year, trying to get appointments together. It would end up being fifteen minutes long in his living room. Finally, I said, I'll be in a motel room and we can just meet there, and I won't tell anybody.

Ronnie Hawkins thought that Richard should have had multiple albums out on his own. Surprisingly enough, Richard was the *only* member of the Band not to release a solo album in his lifetime.

Richard was like a cold engine in the dead of a Woodstock winter. He was trying to turn over, but it was hard work and at times almost impossible. He couldn't connect with anyone for anything permanent. He longed for a collaborator, and he hoped for a new opportunity for an aging rock singer. He had burned bridges to ash by his sometimes poor behavior and needed to rebuild them to move forward.

Joe Forno Jr. was a friend and confidant of the Band and worked as a pharmacist in the Woodstock area. His father, Joe Sr., was the Woodstock town judge back when the Hawks rented Big Pink. He had grown close with the guys in the Band, and they could count on him to get things done. Forno Jr. had helped Levon straighten out his business affairs and in turn had gained everyone's trust. When Forno's other obligations prevented him from managing the Band full time, Bob Illjes was brought in.

Forno did make time to take on the task of managing Richard personally. They had become good friends, and Richard liked to keep things in the family. Forno even let him drive his 1957 Thunderbird when Richard needed to use a vehicle. More importantly, Forno helped Richard get his affairs in order. Richard was getting statements from Capitol Records . . . but no cash, because he owed money to the IRS and his wages were being garnished.

Toward the end of 1984, while trying to do quick-draws on a movie set, Levon accidentally shot himself when a gun went off and lodged a bullet in his kneecap. This put a crimp in the Band's plans, and the first half of 1985 was spent in suspended animation. Richard was starting to get antsy, as he said to the *Woodstock Times*:

> In just this last year and a half, I've seen millions of dollars go by . . . doors open, but we haven't taken advantage of it. That's why I'm irked to the point of just saying, "Fellas, this is it, I'm going on with my own career." So, I've been planning how to catapult this whole thing with myself into a position where I can remain occupied all of the time . . . and have some work at all times, because it's the downtime that drives me crazy. I get nuts when I'm not working, when there's nothing to look forward to, when there's no work.

There were whispers around Woodstock that Dylan wanted to reunite with his old bandmates, but when it didn't materialize, he started looking for other musical options.

At the beginning of 1985, any Band project was put on hold while Levon's leg healed. In February, Richard contributed to a Canadian charity single, "Tears Are Not Enough," and can be seen on the record sleeve photo with a fresh haircut and dark sunglasses.

Richard beating the skins with the reunited Band, 1983.
Courtesy of David Seelig

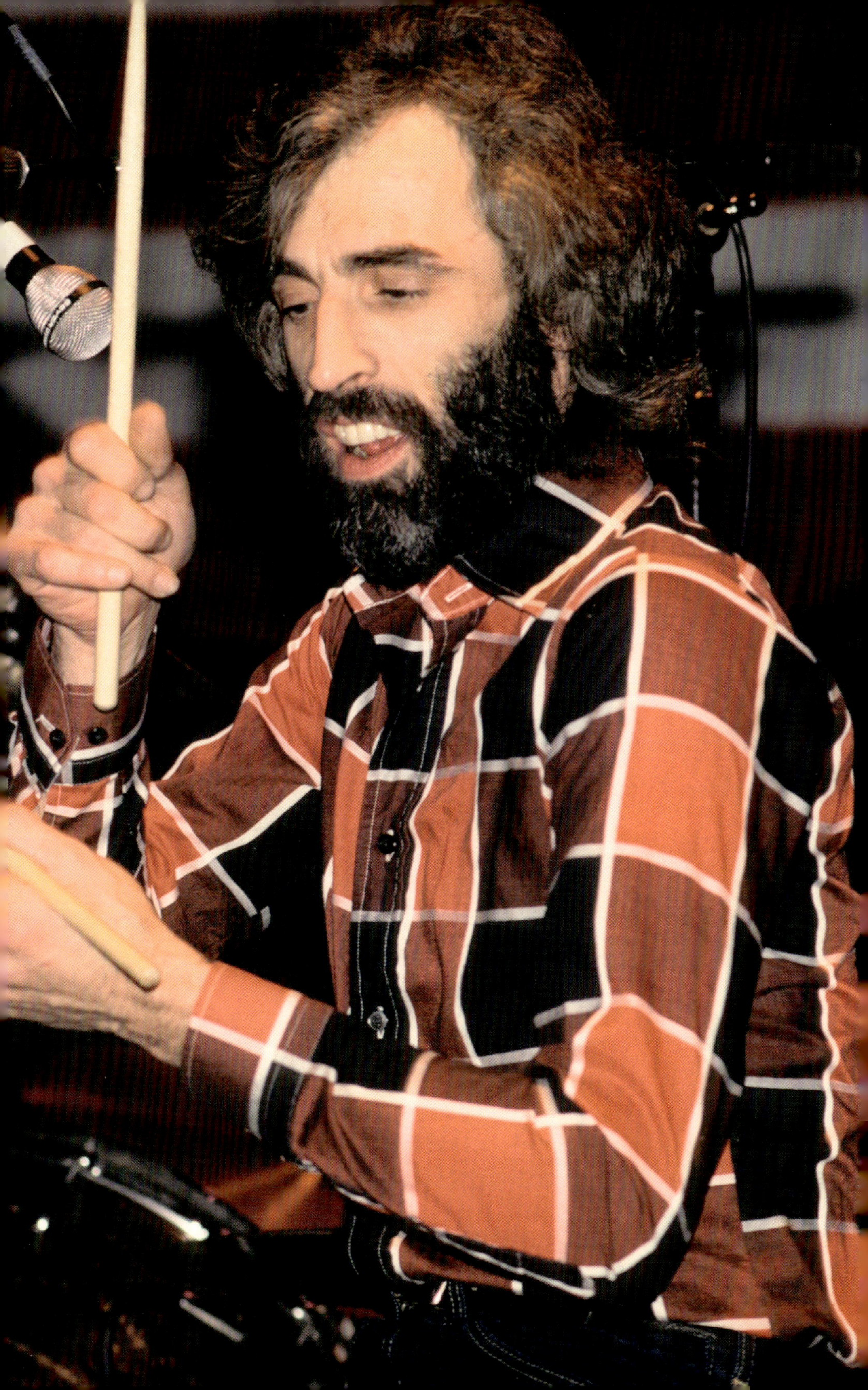

On a chilly March evening, Levon Helm and Friends played a gig at the Getaway Club, just off Route 212 heading into Woodstock. Richard attended the show with Joe Forno but was feeling inadequate because the great Stan Szelest was playing piano in Levon's group. Forno remembered Richard being wishy-washy about going to the show.

Late in that evening's performance, Levon called Richard to the stage, followed by a "only if you want to." Richard got up the gumption to sit in and directed the band through a full-throttle version of "The Shape I'm In." After Richard's performance, Levon said from the stage, "There are guys that can bullshit and there's guys that can deliver. Richard is the head of the delivery service."

Richard, Rick, and Garth still had bills to pay, so they played a series of dates as a trio. Richard then jumped on the Byrds reunion tour with Rick and former Byrds Gene Clark, Michael Clarke, Rick Roberts of the Flying Burrito Brothers, and Blondie Chaplin. While the shows had some special moments, they often bordered on self-parody. Richard was playing well enough, but there was a distinct void in the creativity department.

Arlie remembered that Richard fell off the wagon for the first time in a very long time on this tour. She spoke with him on the phone on May 7 and could tell that he had been drinking. He slurred his words, and she demanded that he put Rick on the phone. Rick confirmed her suspicions, so she immediately flew out to Indianapolis and confronted Richard at the venue, where they argued about his condition. Richard angered her so much that she left the show that night with Clarke, drummer for the Byrds.

For Father's Day that year, Forno gave Richard a copy of Greil Marcus's *Mystery Train*. Richard floated inches above the ground when he read the piece about his cover of Bobby Bland's "Share Your Love" and how Marcus thought it improved on the original. It left Richard brimming with confidence, albeit briefly.

Later that month, Richard and Forno drove to Saratoga Springs, New York, to see Eric Clapton on his *Behind the Sun* tour. Before the gig, Clapton invited Richard to join him onstage, but Richard declined, saying there was no way he was going to follow Clapton's keyboardist, Chris Stainton. After the show, Forno took Richard to visit Clapton at his hotel, where he and Richard caught up and Forno was treated to an unplugged Clapton/Manuel performance of the Band's "The Moon Struck One."

As summer rolled in, Levon's leg was mostly healed and the Band reconvened for a summer tour with Crosby, Stills, and Nash. Not exactly the best double bill to keep Richard on the straight and narrow, but it was honest work. The Band would be the opening act and play a shorter set to allow Levon's leg to get back into full touring shape. The group had stripped back down to a five-piece lineup and let the Cate Brothers go and brought in hotshot Woodstock guitar ace Jim Weider.

In what had now become a theme when returning to the road, Richard had fallen off the wagon with a heavy thud. Weider remembers him being poured onto his piano stool by three roadies at one of Weider's first gigs with the Band.

Richard donned dark shades, looked gaunt with sunken cheeks, and subconsciously alternated between high and low emotion. He would sit in the back of the tour bus, cracking dark jokes and ruminating about technological advances such as virtual reality. When not perusing *Popular Science* and car magazines with Levon, he was in constant need of reassurance, requiring almost daily affirmation from friends and bandmates. Since the Byrds tour, he had been struggling but once again had started to crawl his way out of the darkness and into the light.

Returning to the group's base in Woodstock after the tour, Richard again tried desperately to get his affairs together. Since the original Band ended its career in 1976 with the Last Waltz, Richard had been straddling the fence between sobriety and inebriation. He had logged a divorce, thought he was a marginal parent, and constantly felt like he had let someone down.

As he approached the anniversary of his sobriety date and the CSN tour reached its conclusion, he made a decision. In a slow climb out of the warm nest of addiction, Richard, with the help of his brother Donald and Joe Forno, began the process of organizing his affairs. They created an LLC called Rarley Inc. (a portmanteau of Richard and Arlie), with Forno developing a logo, printing business cards, and putting together an updated biography noting Richard's musical accomplishments. With the scent of fading leaves and a discernible nip in the air, King Harvest had surely come, and things were looking up for Richard.

During this time, Richard compiled a collection of his work on cassette and went to Grossman's office to meet with him and the Bearsville director of A&R, Ian Kimmet. Richard expressed hopes that Robbie would help him get a solo record together. But it turned out that no one wanted to take on the huge responsibility of getting something together for Richard. He would have to do it on his own.

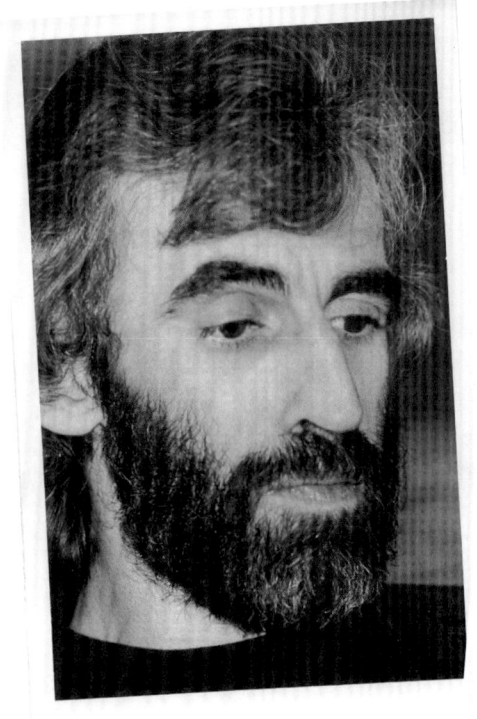

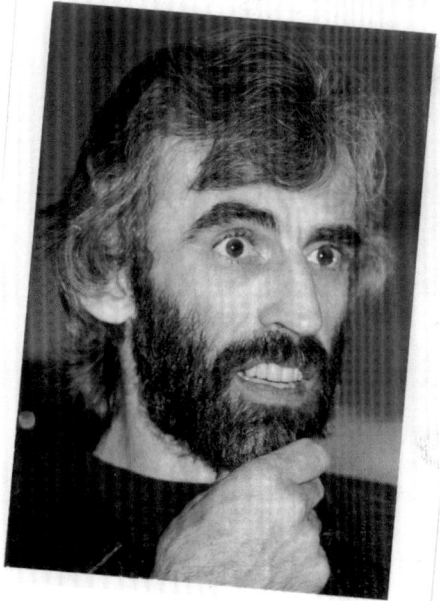

Richard in Stratford, September 1985. Both images *Courtesy of the Stratford Beacon Herald*

Across the Great Divide

"Stratford's my hometown. It's been good to me," Richard said in a September 1985 article in the *Kitchener-Waterloo Record*. The world-renowned Stratford Festival had been operating in the red for several years. A group of volunteers called Friends of the Festival had come together to develop a plan to reduce the festival's $2.8 million deficit. Meetings were called, discussions were had, and options were considered throughout the summer of 1985. One idea that quickly gained traction with the friends was to have Stratford hold a rock concert at the Festival Theatre.

The obvious choice was to invite hometown hero Richard Manuel and the Band to headline the proceedings. The idea was broached to invite Ronnie Hawkins and to also have Stratford's Rockin' Revols reunite for the cause.

After the Band's return from concerts in Portugal, Richard headed to Stratford for a press conference outlining the plans for the show. Richard said to the *Stratford Beacon Herald*, "I've always loved Stratford, always bragged about it. It's a return to my roots, and I'm bringing my partners of twenty-five years with me."

Rumors, which Richard tried to diffuse, started to swirl about Bob Dylan, Robbie Robertson, and others possibly joining the festivities. When asked by the *Toronto Sun* about his relationship with Robbie, Richard said, "I haven't heard from him, and he hasn't replied to my telephone calls."

He looked forward to the challenge of playing rock music in the hallowed halls of the Festival Theatre: "It's going to be delicate playing our music in this type of theater, a chance to not just crank up the volume and hand out the earmuffs." November 2, 1985, would feature two shows with both the Revols and the Band performing in Richard's hometown.

In an interview with *Now Magazine*, Richard discussed the opportunity to contribute to the Stratford concert:

> I got behind this project because it is in my hometown, but also because I get the chance to reunite with my high-school group the Revols. And because I want to see the Festival do better—to upgrade their off-season programming—and I think a show like this will help them branch into a very interesting line of different kinds of entertainment, like rock concerts during the winter. Involving some younger people is important.

Jim Weider and Richard had become friends and flew up to Stratford together to suss out the plans for the concert. Weider remembered, "Richard was great, a down-home good guy. Very musical, and a really great guy." Richard and Weider spent the day taking care of business and then visiting Richard's haunts around town.

After Weider and Richard finished their obligations, Richard insisted on driving to Niagara Falls, where Weider had never been. Somehow, Richard procured a car for the trip. Weider remembers their small Pinto-like vehicle screaming at 100 miles an hour on the flats heading east out of Stratford. As they tore down the highway leaving town, Richard pointed out the window: "Over there in that field is where we drove my old car Dixie down." He motioned toward a barren southern Ontario cornfield where the spectral ghosts of vehicles past were laid to rest.

When they saw the mists of the Falls rising from the Niagara River gorge, Richard throttled around a corner and perfectly swung the car 180 degrees into the parking lot. He assured Weider he could make the car fit perfectly into the very tight spot. He did, but only after using the front and back bumpers to bang the cars parked on either side out of the way.

A Getaway

Richard's slumbering muse was stirring with one eye open. Gently encouraged by Forno, his brother, and Rick Danko, Richard had been convinced to get out and play some solo shows. Forno booked Richard for two performances at the local watering hole, the Getaway Club, on October 12, 1985, and another on December 7. The Getaway was owned by Band manager Bob Illjes . . . who had taken over the group's management and was not in Richard's good graces.

Illjes came on board with a heavy hand, wielding his own management rules—including wanting to drug-test the band members and not allowing girlfriends or spouses on the tour bus. Both requests were completely unacceptable to Richard. In fact, his reply to Illjes's drug testing was "At least we can know who has the best stuff!"

Forno knew it would take a lot to keep Richard on task to play the Getaway shows. He took him shopping and bought a white dress shirt and slacks in preparation for the recitals. He kept pumping Richard up with positivity. Richard had worked up a set list: his own favorites, a few Band classics, and a couple of the original instrumental pieces he had been working on.

Richard liked playing at the Getaway: it was close to home and felt right. The vibe was loose, and the building was worn like holes in the knees of a comfortable pair of jeans. The ceiling was just above head height and featured various coat hangers hanging from exposed pipes. The room was veiled with pot and cigarette smoke and vibrated with the buzz of conversation. There was no pressure, and Richard could sleep in his own bed after the show. Forno had the Band's soundman Andy Robinson tape both the October and December performances for posterity.

The night of the show, Richard was shivering with nervous energy and almost bailed. But once Forno got him to the venue, his confidence steadily increased. Rick helped by shouting encouragement from the crowd. Richard looked good, sounded strong, and played well. His voice was hardened by the years but aged to perfection, especially when singing his favorite songbook classics. He had finally achieved the voice he had been working to get since his bedroom pillow-screaming sessions and late-night visits to the Rockwood Club piano.

Richard sat behind his Kawai electric piano with his new white button-down and big smile. He opened the October 12 show with Bobby Charles's "Before I Grow Too Old," a song that had all the essential elements for Richard: relatable lyrics, a singable melody, and some rollicking piano. Richard had played on the song for Charles's solo Bearsville LP in 1972. It stuck, because lyrically the song was tailor-made for his sensibilities. The tune was also a favorite of Richard's preteen son, Josh, who ran around the club while his dad played and remembers the Getaway shows fondly.

Richard debuts two of the original instrumental tracks that he had been workshopping at home. The first piece begins with a jumpy minor-key prelude, with a feel similar to "Just Another Whistle Stop." The introduction drops into a buoyant double-time change that feels like a perfect place for lyrics. A second variation on the theme appears midway through the song, as Richard thumps out the bass line with his left hand and his right pulls out a delicious, syncopated melody.

Next, Richard welcomes his "main guitar man," Jimmy Weider, to the stage to help on a spacious version of "Across the Great Divide" and to add delicate filigrees to "You Don't Know Me" and "King Harvest." "I Shall Be Released" is played in the perfect spot, closing the first set of music. Rick Danko urges the crowd, "Let's hear it for Richard Manuel!"

Returning to the small stage, Richard begins the second set with a loose and easy version of "The Shape I'm In," after which he asks the crowd with a giggle, "Do you want to hear another instrumental? I knew you would."

His second new original is based around an ascending opening lick that immediately hits upon an energetic and funky change. The song is packed with Richard's penchant for odd time signatures and rhythmic shifts. While the song is short, the positive possibilities of Richard's new music pour off the recording. At the song's conclusion, he excitedly exclaims, "Jazz!"

Introduced as a novelty tune, Richard premieres "Miss Otis Regrets," a show tune he used to sing in Malibu with Libby Titus. Previously performed by Cole Porter and Ella Fitzgerald, Richard's version is heavy with pathos and gentle understanding. His piano playing is perfect and his voice in the room is intimate, ranging from a raspy whisper to a comforting falsetto.

Richard then says, "We're going to gang-rock here for a minute," as Rick Danko, Jim Weider, and harmonica player Sredni Vollmer join him onstage for a swinging version of J. J. Cale's "Crazy Mama." The song was a favorite both of Rick's and Richard's during live concert performances.

A Ray Charles twofer follows, first with "She Knows," a Charles deep cut from his 1978 album *Love and Peace* performed delicately and replete with falsetto garnishes. Richard trills the keys in place of Brother Ray's lush orchestration and pulls out the pulsating heart of the song. After the tune, Rick yells from

A GETAWAY

the audience, "We Can Talk about It Now!" Richard stroked his beard, closed one eye, and replied, "I didn't get that one on the drawing board."

"Hard Times" is gut-wrenching, especially in hindsight; it was far too easy for Richard to slip into the character of Ray's 1961 single. He then closes the set with a flush rendition of "Chest Fever," featuring his friends to help bring the performance to a fantastic finale. After a huge response from the crowd, Richard says, "This calls for something extreme."

Someone yells out, "Whispering Pines!" Unable to hide from or deny their loving requests in the intimate space, Richard replies, "I really don't know if I can hit that one," and asks the crowd to hum it if he misses it. Richard plays the opening salvo to the song he had written just up the road on Bellows Lane, when the world was his and his creativity reflected his ambitions. In the case of this performance, Richard's reaching for the note is as vital as his hitting it. It's all right there at the ends of his fingers and on the tip of his tongue. The talent, the fame, the guilt, the addictions. His humor and self-deprecating attitude about missing a line. His ability to turn a phrase like a key in a lock and then snap it off, immortalizing its soulful originality.

Woodstock musician and fiddler Larry Packer saw Richard after the performance and told him how much he enjoyed the show. Richard squirmed under the glare of his praise but was thankful for the company and the compliment.

Breaking New Ground

At his house on Glasco Turnpike, Richard had been refining the set of chord changes that he had recorded back at Bearsville in the summer of 1980. He was struggling to come up with lyrics but refused to quit on the song. One evening, with Joe Forno visiting, Richard called lyricist Gerry Goffin and played the changes of his song over the phone. A long-distance collaboration was underway. Richard repeated the changes and trilled the keys as a devil's tower of ash dangled off the end of his smoldering cigarette. He caressed the chords while scribbling notes on the papers spread across the top of his piano.

The back-and-forth between the two musicians sparked a set of lyrics for Richard's long-labored-over instrumental and resulted in the song "Breaking New Ground." Richard felt a deep sense of accomplishment after completing the song. He had been saving the changes for years. He knew it had potential; he couldn't waste the opportunity to make it count. He looked at Forno sitting on his couch and gave him a satisfied smirk.

The Band convened in October for an attempt at recording a new record. They tried a few cover tunes, including "The Battle Is Over (but the War Goes On)," and Richard laid down a few takes of "Country Boy," but no originals, according to the session reels. Richard said to *Now Magazine*:

> We're in the studio now and some of that new material has been included for these shows. We should have an album out early next year, which also includes some songs that have been submitted to us—and I have a couple of songs that we need to toss around and finish up.

A series of Richard's works in progress believed to be from the Band's visit to the studio in October were included as bonus tracks on the reissue of *Whispering Pines: Richard Manuel Live at the Getaway 1985*. The first instrumental featured is one that Richard would premiere in a live setting at the December Getaway show. The second instrumental is a previously unknown Richard composition that recalls the glory days of the Band with an excitable set of chord changes.

An instrumental run-through of "Georgia" follows and is probably a practice session for Richard's Getaway appearance. The last track, "Mitzi's Blues," is just that, a full-band jam that Richard's beloved dog takes the lead vocals on.

When asked by the *Woodstock Times* in 1984 if he submitted his work to the Band, Richard said, "Oh, yeah, I've got tapes of things. It's hard, it's especially hard for me to pick lyrics to songs, lyrical songs, because I just can't get on a 'na, na, na, na' song, you know. I have to have some sort of lyrical content."

In between scattered studio sessions, a theater tour continued through the fall and culminated in Stratford, Ontario, on November 2, 1985.

Richard Manuel

The Revols: Ken Kalmusky, Richard Manuel, John Till, 1985. *Stratford-Perth Archives image, #2012.12, Beacon Herald negative collection*

Stratford Festival

On November 1, the night before the concert, the Revols got together to rehearse and sound-check the Festival Theatre. It had been almost twenty-five years since the guys had played together, and they had a hard time remembering their repertoire. The Revols' updated lineup included Richard, John Till, Garth Picot, Ken Kalmusky, Doug Rhodes, and Danny Brubeck sitting in for Jimmy Winkler on drums. Till said it was a special experience in rehearsals, hearing Richard sing naturally in the empty room. The Revols reminisced, joked, and played part of their old set. After they finished rehearsals, Richard went to the Stratford hospital to visit his mom.

Saturday, November 2, 1985, dawned a brisk, blustery fall day. Two shows were scheduled that day at Festival Theatre: a matinee and an evening performance, and the Revols would open for both. The concert wasn't only a reunion for the Revols, but a remembering of an era for the entire town.

Richard in performance at the Stratford Theatre, November 2, 1985. *Courtesy of the Jane Edmonds estate and the Stratford Festival archives*

Richard was in fine fettle, and his former history teacher told Joe Forno that Richard never looked better.

He put on a stellar performance for his hometown people. The Revols sounded solid. While they didn't have the polish or practice of the Band, the energy and intent were palpable.

The Band opened its headlining portion of the show with "Chest Fever," with Richard pushing vocally for the hometown crowd. Cries of "Beak!" poured in from the audience. In video footage, Richard looks at ease. He was home and easily conjured the same joyous feelings that he'd had performing at the band shell in 1960.

The Band's set was incendiary, with the whole group aware of the concert's importance to Richard. It is definitely one of their best post-Robbie performances. They played a couple of songs in the running for a prospective studio record, "Battle Is Over (but the War Goes On)" and Ray Charles's "I Wish You Were Here Tonight," and Richard rolled and tumbled on the drums for a swinging performance of "Caledonia."

At the conclusion of the Band's set, the emcee stopped Richard as he made his way off the stage, giving him an opportunity to address the crowd. Richard declined and slinked offstage to be with his friends, family, and bandmates.

Richard walked around backstage after the concert, feeling better than he had in a long while. He was flush with the reception he'd received from his hometown crowd, and there were lots of hugs and lots of smiles. People were lining up for autographs. Richard loved Stratford and it loved him. Till remembered in 1986, "That concert at the festival was real magic. It was a big moment for me, and I know it was for Richard too."

Richard would never again return home.

GET BACK TO THE GETAWAY

After the success in Stratford, Richard and his bandmates headed to Arkansas to start filming the movie *Man Outside / Hidden Fear*. Richard gets a moment of screen time as a vigilante who throws a nice punch. He said to *Now*, "It's not a music movie, but a script that was submitted to us. Levon has a major role, and the rest of us have small or intermediate-sized parts. And we're doing the soundtrack for it. So, it's always been busy for us, and it looks like it's going to stay that way. I'm really happy about that."

Rick and Richard played a strong show at O'Tooles Tavern in Scranton, Pennsylvania, on December 1, which circulates as a high-quality soundboard. On December 7, Richard returned to the Getaway Club for another intimate solo show. The second performance is even better than the first one in October. Richard was fresh off his triumph in Stratford and was standing in high cotton. Richard took requests and was in complete control of his craft.

Richard opens the show with his longtime favorite, Bobby Bland's "Share Your Love with Me." His voice is strong and full of confidence. His piano playing had reached a level where he could easily sustain a solo performance with just his voice and instrument.

"Georgia on My Mind" follows and is perfect. Richard is relaxed and plays in an unhurried fashion. The recent performing success, the positive response in Stratford, and the spirit of writing new music had inspired him.

Richard premieres another work in progress at the second Getaway show. He quips, "I've got an instrumental . . . looking for lyrics. Send them to the bartender." The midtempo blues in C-sharp minor rolls along through a twilight-tinged progression. Richard plays through the main body of the tune a couple of times, landing on a delightful change that is pregnant with possibility.

Later in the show, Richard plays a rendition of the instrumental he had premiered at the Getaway in October, a bounding tune with a moody minor-key change. Richard says at its conclusion, "Need lyrics for that one too." Sharing new music is one of the most personal things an artist can do, and for Richard, playing these new songs was a tremendous step in the right direction.

"Country Boy" is played as a request from the crowd and is a definitive reading.

"Hard Times" is devastating, even better than the version from October. It's Richard's finest musical performance of the 1980s. Richard's rendition is swollen with uncomfortable truths and brimming with attitude. His voice is soaked with a pleading desperation not heard since "Tears of Rage." He even pulls out one of his deep-seated and long-hidden Hawks-era vocal "whoas" that helped him make his name. At the song's conclusion, Richard quips, "I'm gonna call it a night," as if he knew there would be no way to follow up such a definitive performance. Richard was back.

He returns for a rare solo encore of "The Weight." The sing-along version carries an added value, with Richard's show-worn voice taking all the verses. While Levon and Rick are missing from the mixture, something special is gained in this solo version.

By the end of the year, Richard had several instrumental compositions in his cache. He had also set aside "Breaking New Ground" and had planned for cover versions of "Country Boy" and "She Knows" for a prospective record project. Richard also knew he could count on Eric Clapton to contribute once their calendars were synced up. It was easy to make music with Clapton; now they just needed to get it down on tape—1986 would be the year.

While all of Richard's plans sounded amazing in concept, the stark reality was that he was going to have to make his album happen on his own. Richard's idol, Ray Charles, once said, "You must work at maintaining a musical standard. It's like a house; you've got to be constantly dusting and doing something to it every day; otherwise it'll go down."

It was cleanup time, and Richard was reinventing his standard. He practiced every day at home, sometimes for hours on end if he tugged on a musical thread. Richard said to the *Woodstock Times*:

> It took me a long time, but about three years ago all of a sudden, I realized that I really love what I'm doing. It took me that long . . . to actually really love it. Not that I just wanted to do it, but that I really love it. I've never considered myself more than just a good piano player. Now I think I'm a contender. No, I just improve, pay more attention. I know I play a lot better than I ever have and I'm singing better.

His nervous creative energy also came out in doodles. Richard was always scribbling and leaving notes. Proud examples of his artistic drawings were displayed throughout the house. He was discovering several outlets for his creativity and slowly gaining his confidence back.

December 1985 and January 1986 featured a few duet shows with Rick in frosty East Coast bars and clubs. This was their work: as in the early days, they carried their own gear and made their own way. Rick and Richard would pull into town, hauling their equipment through the snow and salt to play their assess off for a small conglomerate of locals, hard-core Band fans, and folks looking to party. The shows were fun and well played but also insulted Richard's sensibilities.

Richard continued to work on new songs but didn't play them in his and Rick's sets. They updated their set list with some deeper Band cuts such as "The Rumor" and "Just Another Whistle Stop." A nightly highlight of the duo shows was Richard digging into Ray Charles's "She Knows." The falsetto that he had worked so hard to perfect was still intact.

Oddly enough, Richard was content with letting Rick run the shows, even after his successful solo performances. Most of the songs were Rick leads, with a few Richard spots thrown in. What is instantly notable is Richard's piano playing. It's obvious that he had been rehearsing, and the smaller venues allowed for his instrumental work to be a focus of the duo shows.

The guys played valiantly, and while the concerts were rough and ready, the heart and soul were what mattered. If you were lucky enough to catch a Richard Manuel and Rick Danko show, you knew you would get the most authentic musical experience you could find anywhere. Rick's duo shows with Levon and then Richard were ahead of the curve in this sense, since performances like their intimate "living room" shows would soon become en vogue.

After the positive conclusion to 1985, the new year started painfully when Albert Grossman died of a heart attack on January 25. Richard was crushed by the news. Grossman was his advocate and had become, as he was to many, a father figure to Richard.

Robbie and Dominique came to Woodstock for Grossman's funeral, and afterward everyone was going to meet at the Manuels' house to visit. As they prepared for their guests, Arlie was at one end of the basement shooting darts and Richard was at the other end when the phone rang. It was Levon, inquiring about the funeral, and Richard told him that Robbie and Dominique were on their way over to visit. Levon exploded in such a rage that Richard had to hold the phone receiver away from his ear; Arlie could hear Levon's expletive-laden tirade from across the room. Richard looked at Arlie with raised eyebrows and clenched teeth, the phone in his outstretched hand.

Arlie said Richard "just wanted everyone to be OK." He wanted nothing more than for everyone to get along. He had no illusions about the Band reuniting with Robbie; he just wanted them to be friends again. The negativity stressed him out terribly, and he hated being caught in the middle. He loved Robbie and Levon and didn't have the energy or inclination to fight over what had happened in the past. He was firmly hoping for something in the future.

Less than two weeks later, the Band left on what was ironically referred to by the Band and the crew as "the death tour." The weather was miserable, everyone was sick, and Richard was feeling down. Beginning in New York City at the Lone Star Café on February 6, the group zigzagged between poorly planned gigs in the frigid late winter.

At the peak of the Band's popularity, part of their appeal was their mystery and their keeping the music industry at arm's length. In a 1971 interview with Barend Toet, Richard was asked about the Band's performance schedule. Richard said, "We do them so often that the people who like them keep coming, and we can't get enough of them. If you do it too much, all the fun is lost." Toet asked, "Is that danger great? That your fun would be lost?" To which Richard replied, "When it happens, it's disastrous."

After the Lone Star shows while still in New York, Richard headed to SIR Studios to help John Sebastian with his new television project, *Deja View*. The idea was to develop an MTV-like video show made for the 1960s generation that featured well-known artists in a modern format. Richard mimed drums in a band with Sebastian, Ronnie Spector, Roger McGuinn, Felix Cavaliere, and Al Anderson, playing Sebastian's "You and Me Go Way Back." Richard fooled around with corny dance steps for the video but let everyone else take the lead. He ironically didn't sing a note on-screen.

At the end of February, the Band headed to Florida for a series of four performances.

Richard quickly fell back into a rankdom he hadn't experienced in twenty years. The lethal combination of Grossman's passing and the Band heading back out for a series of shows playing the same songs didn't sit right with Richard. Just as there was a glimmer of hope at the end of the year, a return to the temptation and grind of the road dulled Richard's high hopes. He had said to the *Woodstock Times* in 1984, "I want to press ahead. I'm tired of dwelling in the past. We're well established in the history books, and I don't want to continue doing what we've been doing for the last year and a half because we've done it to the point where we're dragging ourselves down . . . unless we come up with a new product."

When the tour swung south, so did Richard's attitude. His feelings about the Band's manager, Illjes, hadn't changed, and he was even less enthusiastic about the way he ran the group's tour operations. Illjes and Richard had already had a physical altercation at the groups' hotel when they played Portugal. With their disparate personalities, a clash was inevitable.

One luxury that had been lost since the Band's glory days was Richard's piano setup. The Band couldn't afford to carry a grand piano between gigs.

Additionally, Illjes didn't want to pay for a vehicle to carry the Band's gear, so the promoters were left with the responsibility of providing Richard a piano. The venues where the Band played were lucky to have a functioning jukebox, let alone a real piano.

While it was a perceived convenience, Richard was left with gear that was usually well below his preferred and expected standard. Levon said in his memoir that one of their road jokes was to ask Richard what he thought of the piano provided for that evening's show, and Richard would usually respond by pantomiming hanging himself. For Richard, this was the ultimate insult to his musicianship and a slight that cut deep. He was a prideful man, and the painful realization that his role was being minimized was more than he could take.

No matter the profession, when you become accustomed to a certain standard and lifestyle, the fall from that place can be difficult. In Richard's case, his expectations for sound, instrumentation, and a certain modicum of respect were consistently being ignored. Every smart-ass snide remark and perceived knock by a club owner or promoter, Richard took to heart. Any disrespect, real or imagined, by the crowd or even his own bandmates was almost impossible to recover from. The slow positive steps he was making were constantly undermined.

Eric Clapton said in 2023:

> I'd been living for quite a while in a cell in my mind, and I think Richard was suffering in the same way, in a parallel kind of universe. We had both drunk ourselves into a corner. I had someone close by who knew exactly how to deal with that. I was lucky. . . . I had kind of used music up. I had to get help through a treatment center and then through a twelve-step program.

Richard was also struggling with his place as a father, not because of lack of love, but his inability to get his own life together. Usually, most rock star fathers are lacking something at some point along the line. It's impossible to be focused on your career and have the attention to provide as a caregiver. He tried, he failed. Richard could barely take care of himself, and he was constantly struggling with how to be a better father. If Josh had a problem at school, Richard tried to be available and attentive. He once said to Arlie, "I'm worried, honey. I just see too much of myself in Josh."

Richard was scared. He was wasted, again. Richard's friend Chuck Kelly said:

> I can imagine that one of the shittiest ways to make a living is to be on the road in a different hotel room every night and traveling all the time. He did the same things and had the same values and suffered from the same things that we all do, and yet he overcame a lot. You've got to admire a person like that for how hard

that would have been for him to maintain his life after the Band split up, because being on top of the mountain, I know the descent can't be that nice. It couldn't have been that comforting for him to have to start playing in these two-bit joints, one-night-stand places at the end there.

Cheek to Cheek

When asked by the *Woodstock Times* what caused his personal problems and heavy drinking, Richard replied:

> Well, kind of seeing what was happening, I can kind of see and read ahead a little.... I don't mean to brag, 'cause it's a curse, actually, to see things coming ... 'cause it's more based on a progression of logical events and the logical outcome of what they lead to.

The Band pulled into Winter Park, Florida, on March 2, 1986, for two shows at the art deco Cheek to Cheek Lounge. Arlie had flown into Florida with Rick's wife, Elizabeth, to meet the Band and was waiting at the Quality Inn when the tour bus pulled up. Everyone in the Band filed off the bus except for Richard. Arlie and Elizabeth looked at each other quizzically.

On their way to the venue, Richard had gotten off the bus at a truck stop to take care of business and look for some Grand Marnier. When the bus departed, no one had taken the time to do a roll call, and Richard was left behind. After some logistical maneuvering, Richard was retrieved by taxi and returned to the hotel room.

A $5,000 payday awaited the Band for these two shows. The day of the show, Richard was lounging around the hotel room and decided to walk to a car dealership up the street. There he saw a beautiful robin's-egg-blue 1957 Chevy and immediately fell in love with it. He returned to the hotel room and mentioned something to Arlie about calling Forno to see if he could afford it.

Soon after inquiring about the car, Richard headed to the venue to prepare for the matinee performance. He immediately had issues with the venue-issued piano and ripped into several people about it. In his memoir, Forno said he received a call the day of the show from one of the Band's crew that Richard had gone through three pianos at that afternoon's sound check. Not one of them worked properly, and Richard was angry and yelling at the club owner.

Richard later called Forno and explained the situation, saying that he wasn't mad with anyone from the Band's staff and that he kept winking at the crew to let them know he was on their side. He also told Forno that he wished that he wasn't in Winter Park that night. Forno then updated Richard on his mother's health; he had talked with Richard's brother Donald and passed along the news to Richard.

The afternoon show came and went without an obvious hitch, but when Richard returned to the room, he was bothered by something. Arlie remembers him being annoyed about the set list and grousing, "I never want to fucking play 'The Shape I'm In' again."

The late show on March 3 was a rowdy affair. The crowd was lubed up and screamed aggressive requests at the stage, drank gallons of ale, and yapped through the ballads. The Band's audience had become what John Simon called "the sawdust and vomit crowd." It was a carbon-copy gig, one that Richard had played a thousand times before, mostly when he was a youngster. Richard's first song at the evening show was a rickety "Chest Fever," not "The Shape I'm In," followed later by the usually stirring "You Don't Know Me."

The Band played a paint-by-numbers set, and Richard did his thing for three songs. As the show went on, Richard grew morose. He was fed well drinks from the crowd, who would pass them to the front of the stage and slide them with sweaty trails across the top of the shitty piano. One fan who attended the evening show said Richard looked "very tight and gaunt."

There was nothing unusual about the evening, nothing special either. That was the problem. The show was just another slash through a calendar square, just another night playing the same songs, for the same people, at the same bar. Richard graduated from the school of hard knocks back in 1965. No matter how his bandmates felt, he wasn't equipped to go back to school. He hated school.

After the show, Richard leaned hard on a road case, lit up a smoke, and thought about how he had given his daughter, Paula, a hard time about her own smoking. He didn't want his kids to end up like him. Midway through his thoughts, Rick walked up and said something to Richard about his drinking. Rick was Richard's closest friend in the group, and he was always looking out for his well-being.

Richard asked Rick to lay off and headed toward the backstage exit. On his way through the maze of gear, Richard stopped and thanked Garth for their last two-plus decades of music making together and headed out the door.

An article in the *Orlando Sentinel* on March 6, 1986, reported that two Central Florida students had seen Richard leave the venue at 1:20 a.m.: "He looked really tired, and his voice was strained. But that was more stress from singing two shows, I think. I asked him if we could expect an album from them and he said, 'Yeah, but it's going to be a long time.'"

According to Levon's memoir, on the way back to his room, Richard stopped in to smoke a joint and talk about the evening's performance. It is unknown what they talked about, but Arlie remembers Richard returning to the room agitated. Arlie and Elizabeth Danko hadn't attended the show that night. They got loaded and tag-teamed the Band's laundry, which had built up after a week on the road.

Chapter 12 | Sleeping (1976–1986)

Levon said in his memoir that Richard was in decent spirits, and that they talked about the shitty conditions of the road and decided to pick up their conversation again the next day. Richard returned to his room between 2:30 and 3:30 a.m. and crawled into bed with Arlie. They lay together for a bit before Arlie fell asleep. Not long after, Richard got out of bed.

Earlier in the 1980s, when visiting friends in Toronto with Arlie, Richard had said if he fell off the wagon again, he would kill himself. He had almost died when he quit cold turkey before; there was no way he could handle that again. In the witching hours of March 4, 1986, Richard drank again to euthanize the pain in his heart that had resurfaced during the Band's hard winter tour.

Robbie said to *Rolling Stone* in 1986, "The indication that I've got was that he started to drink again . . . if so, it probably just fogged up his mind and made him really just very unhappy with himself, really disappointed in himself."

Richard was fucked either way and refused to be trapped. If he drank, he was dead; if he quit, he was dead. He drove his life harder than any vehicle he'd ever had, and in Levon's words, "Richard wasn't afraid to go early or come late."

Richard was burdened by guilt. He was without hope, and it was too late. There's not much worse than being too late.

He went to the dresser, grabbed his bottle, and raised the last sweet sips of his beloved Grand Marnier to his lips. He was drunk. He tapped out and sniffed up the last bit of cocaine he had on the tabletop. He took a hard drag on his cigarette and walked into the sickly tiled bathroom of the hotel and sat down on the edge of the tub. He swung around and put his feet in. The music was over, the only accompaniment being the insect buzz of fluorescent lights and the residual ringing in his ears from years of music making.

The best rock 'n' roll singer around. Richard Manuel, piano player, drummer, songwriter, musician. Revol and Hawk, Beak. Sweet Richard.

The film reel of his life flickered in his mind's eye and spun off the spool.

Richard went blank. He didn't think about Kiddo, Pierre, Paula, Josh, Arlie, his brothers, or his bandmates. He didn't look forward to new music, nor did he care. He couldn't feel anything. He sat like Rodin's *Thinker* and took the deepest breath he had taken since the birth of his first child. He pulled the belt he had bought on his recent trip to Portugal from his pants and looped it around his neck. He fastened the ends around the shower rod end closest to the wall. Richard Manuel never walked out of the bathroom. He was forty-two years old.

Richard in performance at the Stratford Theatre, November 2, 1985. *Courtesy of the Jane Edmonds estate and the Stratford Festival archives*

Chapter 12 | Sleeping (1976–1986)

POSTSCRIPT

For the entire time that they had been friends, Richard would call his former Hawks manager Bill Avis on his birthday. March 4, 1986, was the first time Avis didn't get that call.

John Till said to the *Stratford Beacon Herald* in 2015, "The legacy he left us was his body of work. You just must listen to the music he made to be proud of Richard. . . . He could always see the bright side of things and he never lost that incredible smile; he knew how to smile."

After Richard's death, both Eric Clapton and Robbie Robertson released musical tributes to their friend, Clapton with 1986's "Holy Mother" and Robbie with "Fallen Angel," on his 1987 self-titled solo record.

The repercussions of Richard's death rippled far and wide.

Clapton said in 2023, "As a friend, he was available, he listened, he was keen to be in a dialogue, and honest, just honest and true. These are all the things you aspire to being. Very hard to be, and very painful to be. I think Richard suffered a great deal with knowing too much about everything, really. It was a huge burden for him to be so humble and so knowledgeable at the same time."

Robbie told Paula Cocozza of the *Guardian* in 2019 that his decision to get the Band off the road was "because of my deep concerns for Richard's well-being. It was shattering to me when Richard died. I was afraid of this for many years. The idea was to be protective. Because although we were all riding in the caravan, some people were much more vulnerable to the disease of addiction than others."

Richard's passing effectively ended the Band . . . until it didn't. The Band stopped working for a moment, entering a period of reassessment and realization. Then in 1993 they reconvened without Richard and Robbie and recorded the fine record *Jericho*. That iteration paid their respect to Richard's memory by including the Richard-sung "Country Boy" on *Jericho* and later "She Knows" on 1996's *High on the Hog*.

Unfortunately, a nasty public feud took place in the '90s after Levon Helm's biography ignited various accusations against Robbie Robertson. Shots had been fired, and Band fans chose their sides. Because of the angry divisiveness, the Band and its admirers became fractured.

Richard's legacy was consumed by the animosity, his voice again quieted by voices louder than his. As time moved on, his contributions to the Band and to rock 'n' roll music were increasingly in danger of being lost.

Richard left behind something that will endure. In addition to his children, Richard's music is his testament and his truth. His humor and genuine concern for others will define him. Richard's legacy is in his songs, and in the memories of every single person who shared a smile with him. Richard was inducted into the Rock and roll Hall of Fame in 1994 as a member of the Band.

In 2004, Richard was honored with a bronze plaque and remembrance bench in his hometown. In 2022 his home on 138 Well Street was recognized with a blue plaque from Heritage Stratford.

In 2015, Richard's son, Josh, helped establish the Richard G. Manuel Music Award at Western University in London, Ontario, awarded annually to a performance music student at the Don Wright Faculty of Music.

"I just want to **break even.**"
– Richard Manuel

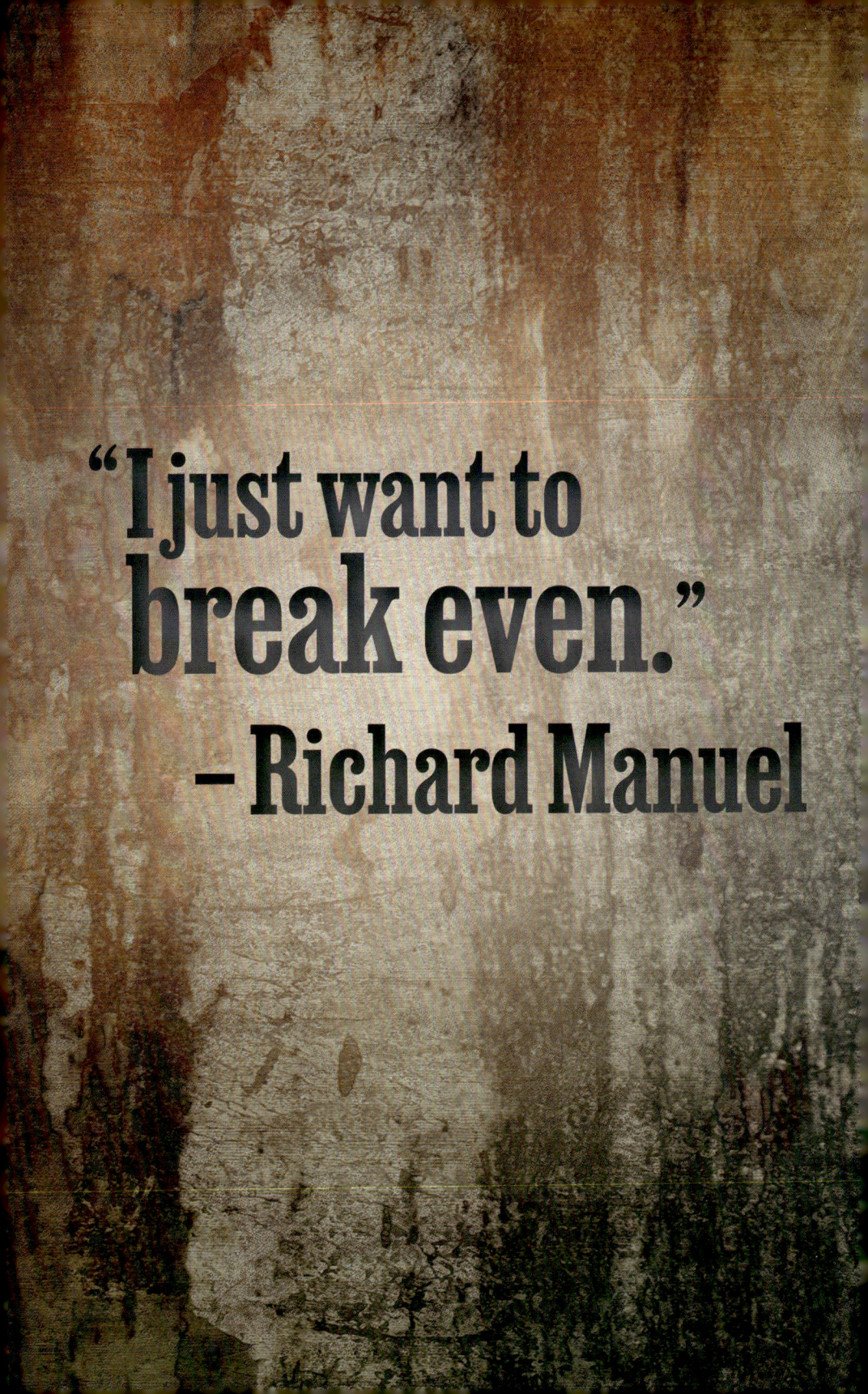

BIBLIOGRAPHY

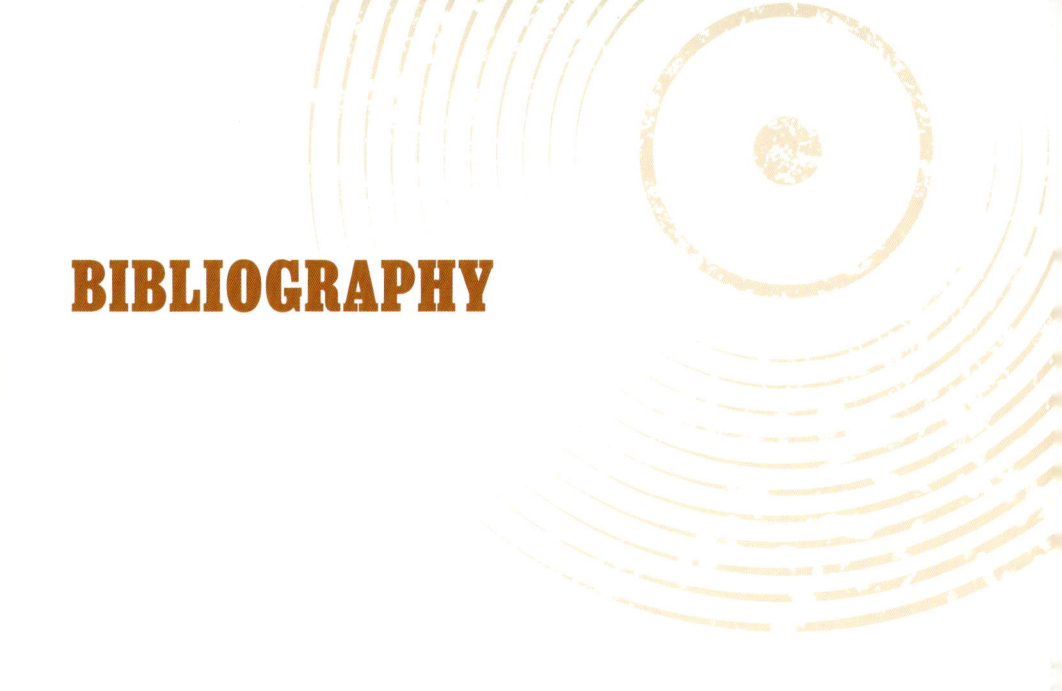

Books

Bukowski, Charles, and Brice Matthieussent. *Women*. Paris: B. Grasset, 2011.

Forno, Joe. *Levon's Man: Woodstock, the Death of Richard Manuel, and My Decade Managing the Band*. Self-published, Bearsville Publishing, 2021.

Graham, Bill, and Robert Greenfield. *Bill Graham Presents: My Life Inside Rock and Out*. Cambridge, MA: Da Capo, 2004.

Gray, Michael. *Song & Dance Man III*. London: Burns & Oates, 2000.

Griffin, Sid. *Million Dollar Bash: Bob Dylan, the Band, and the Basement Tapes*. London: Jawbone, 2007.

Hawkins, Ronnie, and Peter Goddard. *Ronnie Hawkins: Last of the Good Ol' Boys*. Toronto: Stoddart, 1989.

Helm, Levon, and Stephen Davis. *This Wheel's on Fire: Levon Helm and the Story of the Band*. Chicago: Chicago Review Press, 2000.

Heylin, Clinton. *Judas! From Forest Hills to the Free Trade Hall: A Historical View of the Big Boo*. Pontefract, UK: Route, 2016.

Hoskyns, Barney. *Across the Great Divide: The Band and America*. Milwaukee, WI: Hal Leonard, 2006.

Hoskyns, Barney. *Small Town Talk: Bob Dylan, the Band, Van Morrison, Janis Joplin, Jimi Hendrix & Friends in the Wild Years of Woodstock*. London: Faber & Faber, 2017.

Kelly, William E., and Laura Musmanno Albert. *300 Years at the Point*. Somers Point, NJ: Somers Point City Clerk, 1994.

Kubernik, Harvey, and Ken Kubernik. *The Story of the Band: From Big Pink to the Last Waltz*. New York: Sterling, 2018.

Landy, Elliott. *The Band Photographs, 1968–1969*. Milwaukee, WI: Backbeat Books, 2015.

Nin, Anaïs. *Nearer the Moon: From "A Journal of Love"; The Unexpurgated Diary of Anaïs Nin, 1937–1939*. Boston: Houghton Mifflin, 1996.

Pickering, Stephen. *Bob Dylan Approximately*. Philadelphia: David McKay, 1975.

Robertson, Robbie. *Testimony: A Memoir*. New York: Crown, 2016.

Robinson, Dean. *Not the Last Waltz, and Other Stratford Stories*. Self-published, Stratford Printing and Graphics, 2019.

Romano, Sally Mann. *The Band's with Me*. San Francisco: Blurb, 2018.

Sanders, Daryl. *That Thin, Wild Mercury Sound: Dylan, Nashville, and the Making of Blonde on Blonde*. Chicago: Chicago Review Press, 2019.

Schneider, Jason. *Whispering Pines: The Northern Roots of American Music from Hank Snow to the Band*. Toronto: ECW Press, 2009.

Simon, John. *Truth, Lies & Hearsay: A Memoir of a Musical Life in and out of Rock and Roll*. Self-published, 2018.

Smith, Cathy. *Chasing the Dragon*. Toronto: Key Porter Books, 1984.

Taplin, Jonathan. *The Magic Years: Scenes from a Rock-and-Roll Life*. Berkeley, CA: Heyday Books, 2022.

Wallis, Ian. *The Hawk: Ronnie Hawkins & the Hawks*. Kingston, ON: Quarry, 1996.

Young, Geoffrey. *The Riot Act*. Lowell, MA: Bootstrap Productions, 2008.

Zollo, Paul. *Conversations with Tom Petty*. London: Omnibus, 2012.

Articles

"11 Arrested, Stratford Address Given." *Toronto Daily Star*, February 1, 1965.

Aronowitz, Alfred. "Music Scene. The Band: An Outsider's Insights." *New York Sunday News*, December 1973.

Aronowitz, Alfred. "Friends and Neighbors Call Us the Band." *Rolling Stone*, August 24, 1968.

Associated Press. "The Band to Waltz Again." *London Free Press* (Toronto), September 17, 1985.

"Band's Manuel Stars in New Movie Drama." *Ottawa Journal*, October 30, 1970.

"The Band: The Shape They're In." *Rolling Stone*, December 8, 1983.

Batten, Jack. "The Band Comes Home." *Toronto Daily Star*, January 17, 1970.

Beeb, Michael. "The Band Plays On: Danko and Manuel Are Back on the Road Again." *Baltimore Sun*, April 21, 1980.

Bender, William. "Down to Old Dixie and Back." *Time*, January 12, 1970.

Bliss, Karen. "Robbie Robertson Explains How the Band Doc 'Once Were Brothers' Came Together." *Billboard*, September 5, 2019.

Boucher, Caroline. "The Band—or When the Booing Ended." *Disc and Music Echo*, May 29, 1971.

Bourret, Susan. "Join Dylan—See the World." *Stratford (ON) Beacon Herald*, n.d.

Bowman, Rob. "Life Is a Carnival." *Goldmine*, July 26, 1991.

Cannon, Geoffrey. "The Band: A Report from Paris." *Melody Maker*, May 5, 1971.

Cocozza, Paula. "Robbie Robertson: 'I Didn't Know Anybody Who Didn't Do Drugs.'" *The Guardian*, October 8, 2019.

Cohen, Eliot Stephen. "The Philosophy of Ronnie Hawkins." *Goldmine*, January 10, 2023.

Crouse, Timothy. "The Band Opens Schaefer Festival." *Boston Herald Traveler*, June 24, 1970.

Cudworth, Laura. "Rock and Roll and Love Was in the Air." *Stratford (ON) Beacon Herald*, July 28, 2008.

Dadic, Zac. "Australia 1966 Approximately." *Isis*, April 2016.

Dadic, Zac. "Australia 1966 Approximately Part 2." *Isis*, June 2016.

Dadic, Zac. "Australia 1966 Approximately Part 3." *Isis*, August 2016.

Damsker, Matt. "The Band Kicks Off Its West Coast Tour." *Los Angeles Times*, March 2, 1984.

DeRiso, Nick. "Garth Hudson: Why the Band's 'Basement Tapes' Are Still 'Special and Treasured.'" *Something Else!*, November 5, 2014.

DeRiso, Nick. "Garth Hudson on the Band's Influences, 'Basement Tapes' and Tragic Losses" *Something Else!*, August 2, 2015.

DeRiso, Nick. "The Band's Overlooked 'Cahoots' Held a Few Musical Treasures." *Something Else!*, September 15, 2015.

Dougherty, Steve. "A Haunting Suicide Silences the Sweet, Soulful Voice of the Band's Richard Manuel." *People*, March 24, 1986.

Easton, Shelley. "Manuel Could Not Resist Offer to Play in Hometown." *Stratford (ON) Beacon Herald*, September 17, 1985.

Ellis, Tom, III. "Paul Butterfield: The Final Note." *Blues Access* 31 (Fall 1997).

Ferry, Antony. "Let's Face an Awful Truth: Dylan's Gone Commercial." *Toronto Daily Star*, November 15, 1965.

"For the Smartest Sport Shirts in Town the Revols Suggest That You Visit Hudson's Men's Wear Department." *Stratford (ON) Beacon Herald*, September 22, 1961.

Fulford, Robert. "Dylan: Youth's Hair-Raising Sensation." *Toronto Daily Star*, September 18, 1965.

"Garth Hudson." *Clash*, April 30, 2008.

Gill, Andy. "Back to the Land." *Mojo*, November 2000.

Glover, Tony. "A Wonderful New Group." *Eye Magazine*, November 7, 1968.

Goddard, John. "When Dylan Got Rocked." *Toronto Star*, November 18, 2000.

Goddard, Peter. "Remembering Manuel." *Montreal Gazette*, March 6, 1986.

Goebel, Ron. "Local Boys Make Grade: Revols Head for US Tour." *Stratford (ON) Beacon Herald*, September 28, 1961.

Goldberg, Dan. "Van Morrison Interview." *Jazz and Pop*, December 1970.

Goldman, Stuart. "Band Will Waltz Again." *Los Angeles Times*, February 27, 1983.

Goldstein, Richard. "Big Pink Is Just a Home in Saugerties." *New York Times*, August 4, 1968.

Harris, John. "Mixing up the Medicine." *Mojo*, December 2003.

Helm, Levon. "The Music." *Razor*, February 2004.

Hentoff, Nat. "Dylan: The Times Are A-Changin' Again." *New York Times*, February 10, 1974.

Hilburn, Robert. "The Band Comes Back to California." *Los Angeles Times*, November 30, 1971.

Hilburn, Robert. "Uneven Entry by the Band." *Los Angeles Times*, March 19, 1977.

Himes, Geoffrey. "The Band: Rockin' On." *Washington Post*, October 18, 1983.

Holland, William. "The Band Loose and Easy on a Clear Summer Night." *Evening Star* (Washington, DC), June 15, 1970.

J. P. ". . . They ARE the Band." *Record Mirror*, September 5, 1968.

Kelly, William. "Jersey Shore Nightbeat: Levon & the Hawks—Summer of '65." *Jersey Shore Nightbeat*, April 26, 2012.

Kelton, Jim. "Save the Last Waltz for Sonny Boy." *Blues Review*, November 2001.

Kubernik, Harvey. "Across the Great Divide with Robbie Robertson—a Portrait of the Artist as a Mystery Man." *Crawdaddy!*, March 1976.

Landau, Jon. "Cahoots." *Rolling Stone*, November 11, 1971.

Levenson, Bob. "Autopsy Turns up Drugs, Alcohol." *Orlando Sentinel*, March 12, 1986.

Levenson, Bob, and Prakash Gandhi. "Suicide Was about an Hour after Concert, Autopsy Finds." *Orlando Sentinel*, March 6, 1986.

Levin, Martin. "The Lonesome Death of Richard Manuel—the Day the Music Died." *Toronto Life*, March 1996.

Lewis, Matthew. "Music from Big Pink's Neighborhood." *BigO Magazine*, August 2000.

Logan, Nick. "There's Still Togetherness." *Hit Parader*, December 1971.

Lopate, Mitch. "He Shall Be Levon." *Gritz*, Fall 2002.

Marks, Ken. "Vibrant Music by the Band." *Berkshire Eagle* (Pittsfield, MA), July 19, 1976.

Marlowe, John. "Off the Record." *Miami News*, May 12, 1982.

McCollum, Charlie. "The Band Is Just the Same Old . . ." *Washington Star*, July 19, 1976.

Merrill, Sam. "Mason Hoffenberg Gets in a Few Licks." *Rolling Stone*, November 1973.

Montanini, Chris. "Stratford's John Till, Ken Kalmusky, Original Members of the Revols, Honored with Bronze Stars." *Stratford (ON) Beacon Herald*, November 26, 2020.

Morrison, Thelma. "Legendary Rockers to Play Benefit for Stratford Festival." *Kitchener-Waterloo (ON) Record*, September 17, 1985.

"Music Obituary: Richard Manuel, 1943–1986." *Rolling Stone*, April 24, 1986.

Ochs, Ed. "Tomorrow." *Billboard*, September 12, 1970.

Palmer, Robert. "A Portrait of the Band as Young Hawks: Rolling Stone's 1978 Feature on 'the Last Waltz.'" *Rolling Stone*, March 29, 2011.

Pinnock, Tom. "The Band, Bob Dylan and Music from Big Pink—the Full Story." *Uncut*, July 31, 2015.

Plowman, Bruce. "Bob Dylan Mixes Sentiment with Rock and Roll." *Chicago Tribune*, November 27, 1965.

Ransom, Kevin. "The Band." *Guitar Player Magazine*, May 1995.

Reaney, James Stewart. "Bandmates, Admirers Fund Scholarship in Richard Manuel's Name." *London Free Press* (Toronto), January 15, 2015.

Riedstra, Lutzen. "The Revols Remembered." *Stratford (ON) Beacon Herald*, July 28, 2008.

Robertson, Robbie. "We Were the Band." *Vanity Fair*, November 2016.

Schwachter, Jeff. "Somers Point 65." *Atlantic City Weekly*, November 3, 2005.

Scott, Jane. "Everybody Won with CSN&Y and Company in the World Series of Rock." *Cleveland Plain Dealer*, September 4, 1974.

Simmons, Galen. "Stratford Home of the Band's Keyboardist Recognized with Blue Plaque." *Stratford (ON) Beacon Herald*, May 19, 2022.

Simmons, Michael. "Robbie Robertson Interviewed." *Mojo*, January 2017.

Singer, Jonathan. "The Band—Where from Here?" *Hit Parader*, December 1972.

Snyder, Patrick. "The Band: Drifting toward the Last Waltz." *Rolling Stone*, December 16, 1976.

Spencer, Ruth Albert. "The Band—Interviews with a Woodstock Legend." *Woodstock (NY) Times*, March 21, 1985.

Spencer, Ruth Albert. "Conversations with the Band—Garth Hudson." *Woodstock (NY) Times*, March 28, 1985.

Stephen, Jim. "The Band Nassau Coliseum, Uniondale, NY." *Billboard*, September 14, 1974.

Sullivan, Ronald. "The Changing Shore: Old Timers Hold On in Some Places but for the Most Part the Changing Jersey Shore Belongs to the Young." *New York Times*, August 24, 1965.

Thompson, Bob. "Stratford Fundraiser—They're Striking up the Band." *Toronto Sun*, October 30, 1985.

"T.O. Music Notes: The Band Plays On." *Now Magazine*, October 31–November 6, 1985.

Toet, Barend. "On Tour with the Band: All Members Interviewed Exclusively." *Oor*, 1971.

Vandenberg, Paul. "Rock Musician's Contribution Remembered by Friends, Family." *Stratford (ON) Beacon Herald*, March 10, 1986.

Vaughn, Peter. "The Audience Agrees the Band Is Better Late than Never." *Minneapolis Star*, March 23, 1970.

Wenner, Jann. "Bob Dylan Talks: A Raw and Extensive First Rolling Stone Interview." *Rolling Stone*, November 29, 1969.

Wilonsky, Robert. "The Great Divide." *Dallas Observer*, February 4, 1999.

Wishart, Scott. "The Voice of the Band." *Stratford (ON) Beacon Herald*, February 21, 2015.

Yorke, Ritchie. "From Stud to Star: Ronnie Hawkins." *Rolling Stone*, September 20, 1969.

Online sources

Björner, Olof. "Skeleton Keys: Bob Dylan 1966." www.bjorner.com/66.htm. 2000. Accessed December 9, 2023.

Björner, Olaf. "Still on the Road." www.bjorner.com/still.htm. February 4, 2022. Accessed December 9, 2023.

"Bob Dylan, the 1966 Live Recordings: The Untold Story behind the Recordings." Official Bob Dylan YouTube Channel. November 11, 2016. https://www.youtube.com/watch?v=xLG0T2IeGBY.

Caffin, Carol. "Ronnie Hawkins Talks about 'The Boys'—Then and Now." BandBites (website). https://theband.hiof.no/articles/BandBites.html. Accessed November 26, 2023.

Dowson, Anne Lagace. "Words after Dark" interview with Robbie Robertson. *Montreal Gazette*, November 18, 2016. https://www.youtube.com/watch?v=wXtow6a4E-k.

"Frank Spinelli and the Sled Hill Cafe." Woodstock Arts website. January 12, 2012. woodstockarts.com/frank-spinelli-and-the-sled-hill-cafe/#more-2491. Accessed January 17, 2024.

Gardner, Fred. "Last Waltz Out-Takes." *Anderson Valley (CA) Advertiser*, April 26, 2012. theava.com/archives/15352. Accessed December 1, 2023.

Hoiberg, Jan. The Band website. theband.hiof.no (updates discontinued). Accessed April 3, 2023.

Bibliography 377

Hoskyns, Barney. Rejected liner notes for the Band 2000 Remaster series. https://theband.hiof.no/articles/hoskyns_ln_remasters.html. Accessed November 26, 2023.

Kelly, Jeremy, dir. *Tears of Rage: The Story of Richard Manuel*. Pilot film. Uploaded Sept. 3, 2018. https://www.youtube.com/watch?v=nBpKG0DH1w8.

LeBeau, Jennifer, dir. "Bob Dylan and the Band: the Basement Tapes—the Legendary Tales." The Official Bob Dylan YouTube Channel. December 5, 2014. https://www.youtube.com/watch?v=uHabUwIlzh8&t=582s.

"The Legacy of Tony Mart, Memory Lane, 1965: From Conway Twitty to Bob Dylan." Tony Mart's website. tonymart.com/memory-lane-tony-mart/Tony-Marts-memory-lane-1965.html. Accessed February 16, 2024.

Myers, Paul. "Wizard Wednesdays: Robbie Robertson and the "Polaroid Sound" of Todd Rundgren." *Pulmyears Music Blog*, October 27, 2010. pulmyears.wordpress.com/2010/10/27/wizard-wednesdays-robbie-robertson-and-the-polaroid-sound-of-todd-rundgren/. Accessed January 31, 2022.

Stavropoulos, Laura. "Robbie Robertson Reflects on 'Music from Big Pink.'" UDiscover Music, August 31, 2021. https://www.udiscovermusic.com/stories/robbie-robertson-music-from-big-pink-interview/. Accessed January 3, 2022.

Stumple, Bob. "Ray Charles Video Museum: Ray Charles—Quotes." Ray Charles Video Museum. https://raycharlesvideomuseum.blogspot.com/p/ray-charles-quotes.html. Accessed February 20, 2024.

Temperley, David, Iris Ren, and Zhiyau Duan. "Mediant Mixture and 'Blue Notes' in Rock: An Exploratory Study." *Music Theory Online* 23, no. 1 (March 1, 2017). mtosmt.org/issues/mto.17.23.1/mto.17.23.1.temperley.html#.

"Van Morrison Admits That He Is No Fan of Fame." Raidió Teilifís Éireann, August 29, 2015. www.rte.ie/entertainment/2015/0829/724337-van-morrison-admits-that-he-is-no-fan-of-fame/. Accessed January 22, 2024.

Other media

The Band: Made in Japan—Japan Tour 1983. Pioneer PILP-2016, 1983, Laserdisc.

Bowman, Rob. The Band Remaster series, liner notes. Capitol Records, 2000, CD.

Bowman, Rob. *A Musical History*, liner notes. Capitol Records 724357740906, 2005, CD.

Clapton, Eric. *Whispering Pines: Live at the Getaway 1985*, liner notes. Dreamsville Records, 4988927040827, 2002, CD.

Davidson, Martin, dir. *Eddie and the Cruisers*. Los Angeles: Embassy Pictures, 1983.

Dylan, Bob, and Don Alan Pennebaker, dir. *Eat the Document*. Burbank, CA: ABC Television, 1972.

Gladwin, Tim. "The Music of Richard Manuel." CIUT-FM, Toronto, Ontario, November 14, 1987.

Grebb, Marty. Letter to Richard Manuel estate, n.d. Private collection.

Hall, Mark, dir. *The Band: The Authorized Video Biography*. Stamford, CT: Capital Cities / ABC Video, 1995.

Loder, Kurt. Interview with Robbie Robertson. SiriusXM Radio, February 11, 2020.

McAndrew, Jack, dir. *The Band Is Back*. Pioneer Artist Video. 1983.

Paikin, Steve, and Paula Todd, hosts. Interview with Garth Hudson. *Studio 2*, TVO Ontario. May 22, 2003.

Rhodes, Doug. "Richard Manuel." Remarks presented at the dedication of the band shell in Upper Queens Park, Stratford, Ontario, August 4, 2008.

Roher, Daniel, dir. *Once Were Brothers*. Toronto: Bell Media Studios, 2019.

"Rock and Roll: Shakespeares in the Alley; Interview with Robbie Robertson [Part 1 of 4]." GBH Archives. Accessed February 3, 2024. http://openvault.wgbh.org/catalog/V_C253AF32055B421A9C0BCD3552E9328A.

Scorsese, Martin, dir. *The Last Waltz*. Los Angeles: United Artists, 1978.

Smeaton, Bob, dir. *Classic Albums the Band: The Band*. London: Eagle Rock Entertainment, 1997.

Smeaton, Bob, and Frank Svitanovich, dirs. *Festival Express*. Los Angeles: New Line Home Entertainment, 2004.

Solt, Andrew, dir. *Imagine John Lennon*. Los Angeles: Warner Bros., 1988.

White, Timothy. *Timothy White's Rock Stars—Eric Patrick Clapton*. *Westwood One Radio Show*, WO 89-L, December 23, 1989.

INTERVIEWS

All interviews were conducted by the author.

Ed Anderson: Zoom interview, October 23, 2022.

Bill Avis: in-person interview, April 29, 2023.

Graham Blackburn: phone interview, June 12, 2022.

Rob Bowman: phone interview, August 27, 2021.

Larry Campbell: phone interview, September 11, 2022.

Cindy Cashdollar: phone interview, September 2023.

Eric Clapton: phone interview, February 3, 2022.

Bryan Davies: phone interview, September 30, 2021.

Sharon DeFilippo: phone interview, September 2021.

Butch Dener: phone interview, August 2021.

Michael DeTemple: phone interview, March 5, 2023.

Rob Fraboni: in-person interview, July 28, 2023.

Joe Forno: in-person and phone interviews, August 2021 through December 2023.

John Gershen: phone interviews, August 2023.

John Hammond Jr.: phone interview, October 4, 2021.

Sandy Helm: phone interview, April 5, 2024.

Ian Kimmett: phone interview, September 2023.

Elliott Landy: phone interview, February 13, 2022.

Bob Kalmusky: several in-person and phone interviews, October 2021 through April 2023.

Chuck Kelly: in-person interview, April 28, 2022, and several phone conversations, September 2021 through November 2023.

Arlie Manuel: numerous phone and email interviews, July 2022 through December 2023.

Jane Manuel: numerous in-person interviews, May 2022 through November 2023.

Kathryn Manuel: numerous in-person and phone interviews, October 2021 through December 2023.

Paula Manuel: several email, in-person, and phone interviews, May 2023 through March 2024.

David Marsden: phone interview, August 6, 2021.

Carmen Mariotta: phone interview, August 28, 2021.

Mary Martin: phone interview, September 30, 2021.

Anthony Millington: phone interview, September 24, 2023.

Van Morrison: email interview, April 2024.

Mike Neel: phone interviews, July through September 2023.

Larry Packer: phone interview, October 24, 2023.

Brian Pawley: phone interview, February 2022.

Garth Picot: phone interview, May 8, 2022, followed by in-person interview, May 2022.

Sally Romano: email interview, August 2022.

Bill Scheele: phone interview, May 7, 2022.

John Sebastian: in-person and phone interviews, July 2023.

John Simon: email interview, June 2023.

Frank Smith: phone interview, September 18, 2022.

Jon Taplin: phone interview, January 20, 2022.

John Till: phone interview, August 14, 2021, followed by numerous emails.

Jim Weider: phone interview, July 30, 2021.

Sam Wyatt: in-person interview, April 2022.

Several of Richard's schoolmates, friends, and acquaintances from Stratford also contributed tidbits of vital information over the course of the author's research.

RICHARD MANUEL DISCOGRAPHY

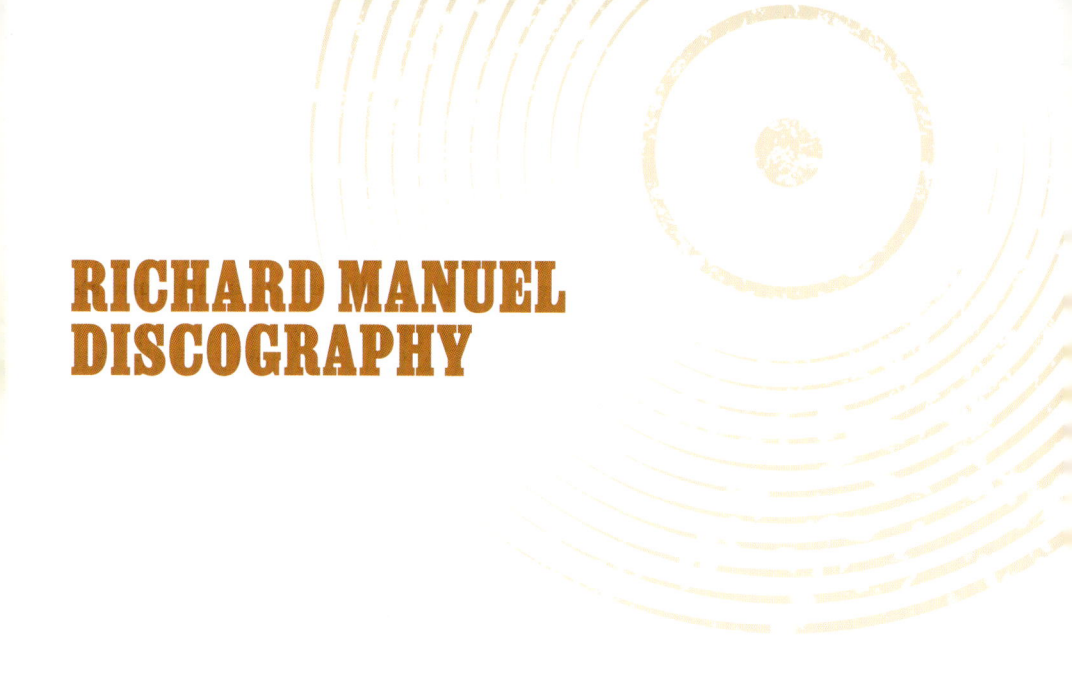

In chronological order, based on date of performance.

Ronnie Hawkins and the Hawks. "Who Do You Love"/"Bo Diddley." Roulette 4483, 1963, 45.

Ronnie Hawkins and the Hawks. "There's a Screw Loose"/"High Blood Pressure." Roulette 4502, 1963, 45.

Ronnie Hawkins and the Hawks. *The Best of Ronnie Hawkins*. Roulette 25255, 1964, LP.

The Canadian Squires. "Uh, Uh, Uh"/"Leave Me Alone." APEX 76964, 1965, 45.

Levon and the Hawks. "The Stones That I Throw"/"He Don't Love You." ATCO 6383, 1965, 45.

Levon and the Hawks. "Go, Go, Liza Jane"/"He Don't Love You." ATCO 6625, 1965, 45.

Dylan, Bob. "Can You Please Crawl Out Your Window"/"Highway 61 Revisited." Columbia 4-43477, 1965, 45.

Dylan, Bob. "I Want You"/"Just Like Tom Thumb's Blues." Columbia 443683, 1966, 45.

You Are What You Eat (original soundtrack recording). Columbia OS 3240, 1968, LP.

Woody Guthrie: The Tribute Concerts. Bear Family Records 5397102173295, 2017, CD.

The Band. *Music from Big Pink*. Capitol SKAO 2955, 1968, LP.

The Band. *The Band*. Capitol STAO-132, 1969, LP.

The Band. *Stage Fright*. Capitol SW-425, 1970, LP.

Simon, John. *John Simon's Album*. Warner Bros. S39658, 1970, LP.

The Band. *Cahoots*. Capitol SMAS-651, 1971, LP.

The Band. *Rock of Ages*. Capitol SABB-11045, 1972, LP.

Charles, Bobby. *Bobby Charles*. Bearsville BR2104, 1972, LP.

Borderline. *Sweet Dreams and Quiet Desires*. Avalanche AV-LA-016-F, 1973, LP.

The Band. *Moondog Matinee*. Capitol SW-11214, 1973, LP.

Dylan, Bob. *Planet Waves*. Asylum 7E-1003, 1973, LP.

The Band. *Northern Lights–Southern Cross*. Capitol ST-11440, 1975, LP.

Bob Dylan and the Band. *Before the Flood*. Asylum AB-201, 1975, LP.

Bob Dylan and the Band. *The Basement Tapes*. Columbia 33682, 1975, LP.

Clapton, Eric. *No Reason to Cry*. RSO 1-3004, 1976, LP.

The Band. *Best of the Band*. Capitol ST-11553, 1976, LP.

Danko, Rick. *Rick Danko*. Arista AB-4141, 1977, LP.

The Band. *The Last Waltz*. Warner Bros. 3WS-3146, 1978, LP.

Traum, Happy. *Bright Morning Stars*. Greenhays Recordings, GR-703, 1980, LP.

Raging Bull (soundtrack). Capitol Records. 72435-60322-2-4, 2005, CD.

Hudson, Garth. *Music for Our Lady Queen of the Angels*. Other People's Music, 623235660223, 2005, CD.

Kent State (soundtrack). RCA. ABL1-3928, 1981, LP.

Nelson, Willie. *In the Jailhouse Now*. Columbia 38095, 1982, LP.

Raitt, Bonnie. *Green Light*. Warner Bros. BSK-3060, 1982, LP.

The King of Comedy (soundtrack). Warner Bros. 92-3765-1, 1983, LP.

Groce, Larry. *Medicine Man*. Broadbeach Records Number Seven, 1983, LP.

Manuel, Richard. *Whispering Pines: Live at the Getaway 1985*. Dreamsville Records, 4988927040827, 2002, CD.

Petty, Tom. *Southern Accents*. MCA-5486, 1985, LP.

The Band. *Jericho*. Pyramid Records 081227156428, 1993, CD.

The Band. *High on the Hog*. Pyramid Records 081227240424, 1996, CD.

Archival collections

In chronological order, based on release date.

The Band. *Across the Great Divide*. Capitol D207193, 1994, CD.

Ronnie Hawkins and the Hawks. *The Roulette Years*. Sequel Records WED CD 266, 1995, CD.

The Band. *A Musical History*. Capitol 724357740906, 2005, CD.

Dylan, Bob. *Another Self Portrait, 1969–1971*. Columbia Legacy 888837348829, 2013. CD.

Dylan, Bob. *The Bootleg Series Vol. 11: The Basement Tapes Raw*. Columbia Legacy 0885750161314, 2014, CD.

Dylan, Bob. *The Bootleg Series Vol. 12: The Cutting Edge 1965–1966*. Columbia Legacy 888751244122, 2015, CD.

Dylan, Bob. *The 1966 Live Recordings*. Columbia/Sony Legacy LC00162, 2016, CD.

Richard Manuel

Songs Composed by or with Richard Manuel

In chronological order:

"Eternal Love"

"Promise Yourself"

"Beautiful Thing"

"Words and Numbers"

"Ruben Remus" (J. R. Robertson and Richard Manuel)

"Katie's Been Gone" (J. R. Robertson and Richard Manuel)

"Tears of Rage" (Bob Dylan and Richard Manuel)

"Orange Juice Blues (Blues for Breakfast)"

"In a Station"

"Lonesome Suzie"

"When You Awake" (J. R. Robertson and Richard Manuel)

"Whispering Pines" (J. R. Robertson and Richard Manuel)

"Jawbone" (J. R. Robertson and Richard Manuel)

"Sleeping" (J. R. Robertson and Richard Manuel)

"Just Another Whistle Stop" (J. R. Robertson and Richard Manuel)

"Breaking New Ground" (Gerry Goffin, Carole King, Richard Manuel)

INDEX

4% Pantomime, 256

A

Allman Brothers, 283

Academy of Music, 226, 262–267, 271–272, 277, 291

Arkansas, 20, 42–44, 46, 52–53, 57–58, 61, 67–68, 71, 81, 99, 106, 122, 137, 140, 188, 215, 359

B

"Baby, Let Me Follow You Down," 143, 323

"Ballad of Hollis Brown," 292

The Band (album), 222, 224, 226–228, 233, 237, 248

The Basement Tapes, 152, 157, 166, 175

Bearsville, 154, 234, 254–257, 279, 281, 329–330, 332, 349, 353, 355

Bearsville Studio, 254, 256, 258, 275, 278–281, 334–335

"Beautiful Thing," 149–150, 167, 190, 309, 388

"The Best of Everything," 337

Bland, Bobby "Blue," 20–22, 27, 37, 44, 45, 58, 61, 66–67, 74, 89, 97–98, 112, 120, 256, 281, 308

Blonde on Blonde, 126, 131, 143

Borderline, 277–279, 334

C

Cahoots, 254–260, 262, 300, 305

Campbell, Larry, 179, 222, 224, 334

Charles, Ray, 20–22, 33, 37, 45, 52, 58, 61, 65, 67–68, 73–74, 76, 80, 88, 97–98, 101, 112–113, 150, 256, 261, 308, 321, 335, 340, 353, 360

Clapton, Eric, 188, 195, 199, 244, 274, 299, 308, 323, 325, 344, 348, 360, 363, 369

Cream, 188

D

Danko, Rick, 44, 63, 65, 75, 77, 86, 90, 107, 112, 144–145, 149, 162, 198, 200, 234, 236, 261–262, 279, 283, 306, 324, 328, 341, 352–353, 361

Deanie's, 185, 257

Dylan, Bob, 79, 85–86, 94–95, 101–102, 110, 116, 119, 123, 132, 137, 142, 145, 148, 150, 152, 154, 167, 177, 180, 215, 222, 262, 267, 271, 285, 287, 308, 351

E

Elliot, Cass, 165, 198, 274

F

Fillmore East, 212, 225

Forno, Joe Jr., 345, 348–349, 355, 358

Fraboni, Rob, 286, 304, 336

G

Gahr, David, 178, 226

"Georgia On My Mind," 39, 51, 75, 89–90, 98, 112, 150, 317, 321–323, 327, 343, 359

Gershen, Jon, 277–279

Getaway Club, 348, 352, 359

Grateful Dead, 247–248, 283–285, 339, 341

Grossman, Albert, 79, 101–102, 110, 116, 148–149, 151, 184–185, 226, 239, 254, 273, 330, 361

H

Hammond, John Jr., 85–86, 98, 101–102

Hawkins, Ronnie, 12, 14, 42–43, 45, 47–52, 57, 59, 62, 65, 74, 76–77, 80, 92, 95, 110, 127, 137, 157, 183, 187, 268, 323, 344, 350

"He Don't Love You (And He'll Break Your Heart)," 120, 225

Helm, Levon, 13, 21, 43–44, 58, 65, 68, 75, 85, 116, 119, 131, 153, 161, 222, 224, 238, 253, 273, 282, 348

Hudson, Garth, 64–65, 74, 77, 88, 112, 122, 127, 145, 278

I

Illjes, Bob, 345, 352

"In a Station," 173–174, 180, 182–183, 190, 209, 222–223, 250, 263, 274, 310

"I Shall Be Released," 159, 169, 180, 183, 201, 217–218, 247, 249, 261–262, 264, 291, 293, 303, 310, 323, 334, 353

Islands, 327

Isle of Wight, 215, 217, 219, 228, 267

J

"Jawbone," 222, 224, 388

"Just Another Whistle Stop," 241, 251, 253, 300, 303, 353, 361, 388

"(Just Like) Tom Thumb's Blues," 121, 133, 143, 292–293, 296

K

"King Harvest (Has Surely Come)," 225–226, 262, 264, 266, 291, 293, 312, 322–323, 349, 353

Kalmusky, Ken, 27, 37, 40, 51, 122, 356

"Katie's Been Gone," 161, 166, 173, 190, 304, 388

Kelly, Chuck, 13, 16–17, 20, 22, 73, 150, 162, 363

Index 393

L

Landy, Elliott, 184, 187

Levon and the Hawks, 85, 87, 90–91, 95–97, 100–103, 106, 110–111, 115–116, 120–121, 123–124, 183, 219

"Like a Rolling Stone," 144–145, 267, 271, 296

"Lonesome Suzie," 166, 174, 180, 344, 388

"Long Distance Operator," 130, 169, 183

M

Malibu, 11, 285–286, 288, 297–301, 304, 310, 313, 325, 328–329, 336–337, 353

Manuel, Arlie (Litvak), 325–332

Manuel, Donald, 12, 14, 18, 20, 26, 169, 196, 334, 349, 364

Manuel, James "Pierre," 14, 18, 20, 30–31, 62, 187, 196, 310, 339, 366

Manuel, Jane (Kristiansen), 92–93, 104, 139, 153, 180, 195, 196, 228, 234, 324

Manuel, Joshua, 300, 330

Manuel, Kathryn, 62, 196, 334

Manuel, Gladys "Kiddo," 14, 18–21, 27, 62, 187, 196, 339, 366

Manuel, Paula, 228, 246, 301, 366

Marsden, David (Mickie), 31, 35, 40, 45, 49, 52, 59

Martin, Mary, 79, 101, 116, 124, 256

Moondog Matinee, 282–284, 327

Morrison, Van, 101, 193, 227, 244, 256, 277, 322–323

Music from Big Pink, 115, 159, 161–162, 164–165, 169, 173, 175, 180, 183, 186–188, 190, 193, 195, 198–200, 203, 208, 215, 219, 225, 227, 310, 333, 337

N

Northern Lights-Southern Cross, 288, 304–305, 307

O

"Orange Juice Blues (Blues for Breakfast)," 147, 164–165, 169, 183, 198, 206, 274, 304, 388

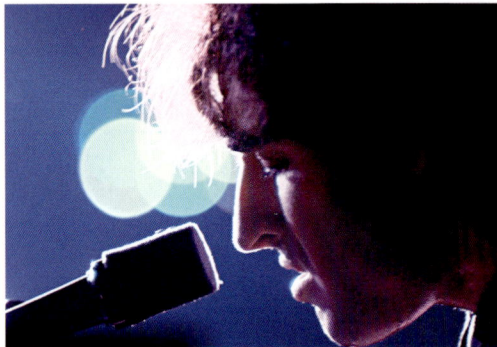

P

Petty, Tom, 337

Picot, Garth, 12, 40, 46, 51, 53, 57, 60, 62, 122, 150, 356

Port Dover, 14, 38, 45, 87, 89, 120

Priest, David, 19, 39, 65

R

Raitt, Bonnie, 336, 338

Rhodes, Doug, 26–27, 36, 40, 48, 58, 61, 122, 356

Robertson, Dominique (Bourgeois), 153, 154, 184–185, 361

Robertson, Robbie, 26, 44, 46, 50, 58, 61, 65, 83, 86, 101, 111–112, 115, 119–120, 145, 162, 166, 172, 186, 224, 245, 251–252, 291, 306, 339, 351, 369

Rock-A-Rama, 50, 318

Rockwood Club, 52–53, 56–59, 61, 71, 76, 143, 162, 173, 352

Romano, Sally (Mann), 297–298

S

Saturday Night Live, 317–318

Saugerties, 152, 163, 166, 173, 178, 182, 194, 198, 267

Scheele, Bill, 212, 228, 275, 281, 283, 286

Scheele, John, 248

Scorsese, Martin, 321

Sebastian, John, 333, 362

Shangri-La Studios, 304–305, 307–310, 324–327, 338, 344

"The Shape I'm In," 7, 249, 251, 264, 284–285, 291, 322–323, 328, 340–341, 348, 353, 365

"Share Your Love," 12, 39, 80, 84, 89, 97, 256, 281, 285, 291, 335, 348, 359

Simon, John, 152, 165, 174–175, 203, 206, 209, 222, 236, 250, 252, 272–273, 279, 365

Sled Hill Café, 193

"Sleeping," 241, 250

Index   395

Smith, Cathy, 79, 180, 292, 310, 315, 317, 338

Somers Point, New Jersey, 103–104, 106–107, 109, 111, 116, 120, 185

"Something There Is About You," 287, 292–293

Stage Fright (album), 188, 238, 241, 245–248, 250, 252–255, 260, 271

The Staple Singers, 73, 163, 168, 225, 324, 333

Stoll Road, 152, 163, 173, 267

Stratford, Ontario, 11–12, 14–18, 22–23, 25–27, 29–33, 35–39, 44, 46–47, 49–53, 57–58, 61, 63, 73, 76, 95, 98–99, 130, 136, 150, 155, 162, 167–168, 180, 182, 187, 188, 196, 216, 225, 247, 268, 275, 310, 316, 318, 328, 333–335, 339, 350–351, 355–356, 358–359, 370

Stratford Beacon-Herald, 27, 53, 351, 369

Stratford Festival, 11, 18, 38, 350

Summer Jam, 283–285

T

Taplin, Jonathan, 124, 178, 184, 195, 206, 212, 215, 234, 239, 246, 261, 271

"Tears of Rage," 159, 167–169, 171–175, 182, 200, 209, 216, 219, 227, 256, 263, 274, 310, 312–313, 360

Till, John, 8, 21, 26, 33, 37–38, 40, 42, 46, 51, 216, 247, 356, 369

Tony Mart, 103–106, 110, 116, 138

Toronto, 17, 20, 44–45, 50, 52, 57, 67, 71, 73, 79, 85, 89, 91, 93, 99, 101, 104, 116, 120–121, 128, 139, 196, 215, 237, 247–248, 262, 291–293, 314, 333, 351, 366

"Tough Mama," 287

Traum, Happy, 198, 201, 334

Transcontinental Pop Festival, 247

Turtle Creek, 275, 277, 306, 327

U

"Up On Cripple Creek," 203, 206, 222, 226, 228, 253, 258, 262, 264, 284–285, 303, 322

W

Watkins Glen, 283, 285

"The Weight," 168, 171–172, 199, 217–218, 225, 247, 253, 285, 328, 360

Well Street, 14, 19, 25–26, 31, 40, 46, 73, 99, 150, 196, 334, 370

"When You Awake," 222, 250, 291, 388

"Whispering Pines," 203, 222–224, 241, 344, 354–355, 388

"Who Do You Love," 75, 77, 83, 144, 323

Winkler, Jim, 16, 20, 26–27, 40, 60, 62, 122, 356

Winterland, 206, 209, 314, 316–317, 321–322

"Words and Numbers," 165, 167, 169, 388

Woodstock, 11, 22, 148, 151–155, 157–158, 160, 163–164, 168–169, 172–173, 178, 182–188, 193–195, 198, 200–201, 212, 216–217, 219, 226–228, 234, 238–239, 242, 244, 252, 256–257, 262–263, 272–273, 276–278, 285–286, 288, 298, 304, 310, 317, 323, 327, 329, 333–334, 339–341, 345, 348–349, 354, 361

Woodstock Festival, 216

Woodstock Playhouse, 239, 244

Williamson, Sonny Boy II, 98–100, 102, 106, 151, 164

Winter Park, Florida, 364

Y

Young, Neil, 303, 323–324

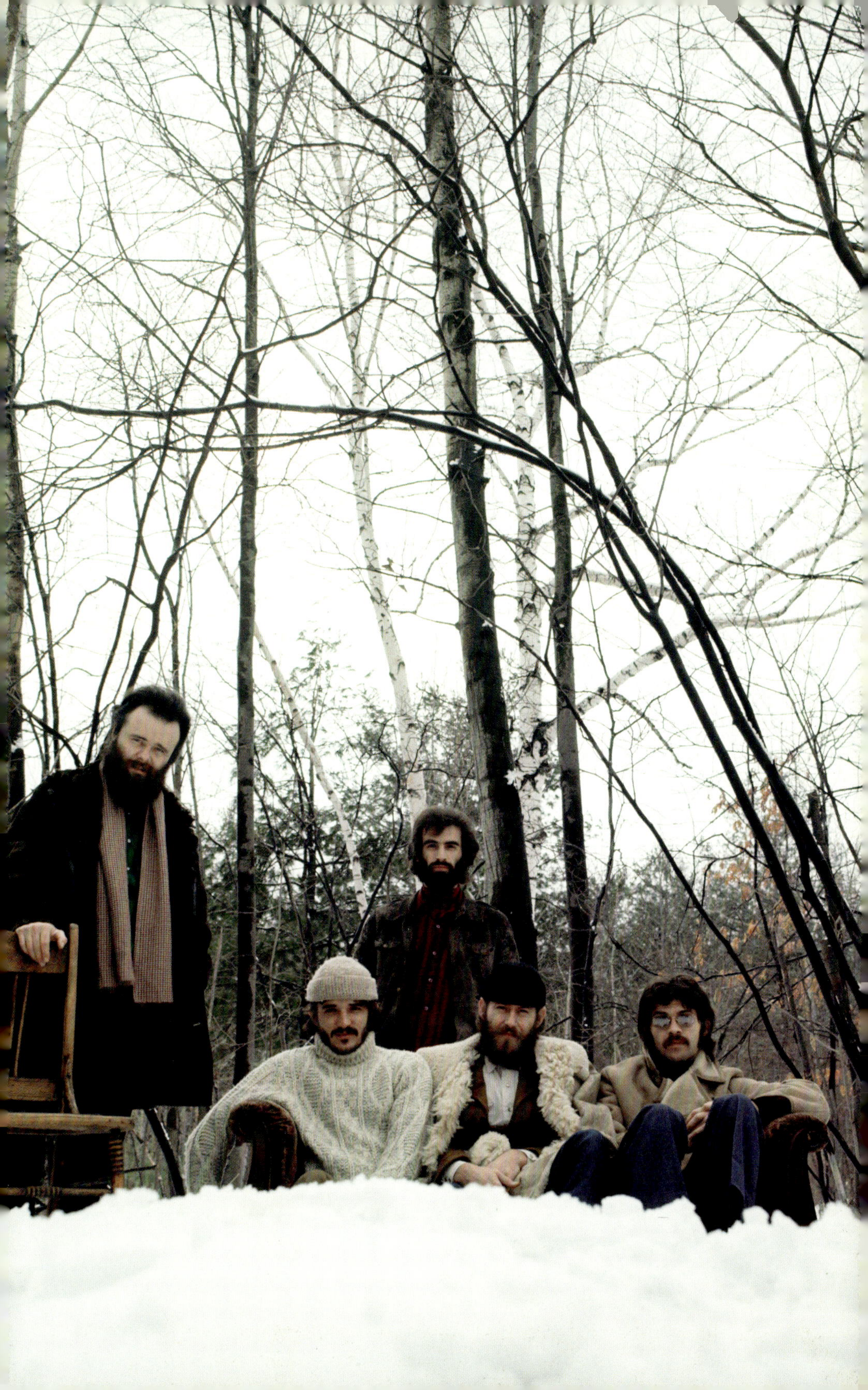